CALVINISM
& the Problem of Evil

CALVINISM
& the Problem of Evil

Edited by
David E. Alexander
and **Daniel M. Johnson**

PICKWICK *Publications* · Eugene, Oregon

CALVINISM AND THE PROBLEM OF EVIL

Copyright © 2016 Wipf and Stock Publishers. All rights reserved. Except for brief quotations in critical publications or reviews, no part of this book may be reproduced in any manner without prior written permission from the publisher. Write: Permissions, Wipf and Stock Publishers, 199 W. 8th Ave., Suite 3, Eugene, OR 97401.

Pickwick Publications
An Imprint of Wipf and Stock Publishers
199 W. 8th Ave., Suite 3
Eugene, OR 97401

www.wipfandstock.com

PAPERBACK ISBN 13: 978-1-62032-578-0
HARDCOVER ISBN 13: 978-1-4982-8476-9
EBOOK ISBN 13: 978-1-5326-0102-6

Cataloguing-in-Publication data:

Names: Alexander, David E., editor | Johnson, Daniel M., editor.

Title: Calvinism and the problem of evil / edited by David E. Alexander and Daniel M. Johnson.

Description: Eugene, OR: Pickwick Publications, 2016 | Includes bibliographical references.

Identifiers: ISBN 978-1-62032-578-0 (paperback) | ISBN 978-1-4982-8476-9 (hardcover) | ISBN 978-1-5326-0102-6 (ebook)

Subjects: LCSH: Calvinism. | Theodicy.

Classification: BX9422.3 .C3515 2016 (print) | BX9422.3 .C3515 (ebook)

Manufactured in the U.S.A.   07/12/16

Contents

Acknowledgments | vii
Contributors | ix
Introduction | 1
—David E. Alexander and Daniel M. Johnson

1. Calvinism and the Problem of Evil: A Map of the Territory | 19
   —Daniel M. Johnson

2. Molinist Gunslingers: God and the Authorship of Sin | 56
   —Greg Welty

3. Theological Determinism and the "Authoring Sin" Objection | 78
   —Heath White

4. Not the Author of Evil: A Question of Providence, Not a Problem for Calvinism | 96
   —James E. Bruce

5. Orthodoxy, Theological Determinism, and the Problem of Evil | 123
   —David E. Alexander

6. Discrimination: Aspects of God's Causal Activity | 145
   —Paul Helm

7. On Grace and Free Will | 168
   —Hugh J. McCann

8. The First Sin: A Dilemma for Christian Determinists | 187
   —Alexander R. Pruss

9. Calvinism and the First Sin | 200
   —James N. Anderson

10. A Compatibicalvinist Demonstrative-Goods Defense | 233
    —Christopher R. Green

11 Calvinism and the Problem of Hell | 248
  —Matthew J. Hart

12 Calvinism, Self-Attestation, and Apathy toward Arguments From Evil | 273
  —Anthony Bryson

Acknowledgments

WHILE MANY PEOPLE HAVE helped us in different ways with this project, none has helped us more than Alex Hoffman, a graduate student in philosophy at Baylor University and former student of David E. Alexander. Alex's willingness, timeliness, and overall attitude as he worked on anything and everything we needed was exemplary. Thank you, Alex, for your hard work, humor, and patience while working with technophobes.

Contributors

David E. Alexander, Associate Professor of Philosophy, Huntington University, Huntington, Indiana.

James N. Anderson, Associate Professor of Theology and Philosophy, Reformed Theological Seminary, Charlotte, North Carolina.

James E. Bruce, Associate Professor of Philosophy, John Brown University, Siloam Springs, Arkansas.

Anthony Bryson, Instructor of Philosophy, South Central College, North Mankato, Minnesota.

Christopher R. Green, Associate Professor of Law and H. L. A. Hart Scholar in Law and Philosophy, University of Mississippi School of Law, Oxford, Mississippi.

Matthew J. Hart, PhD candidate, University of Liverpool, Liverpool, United Kingdom.

Paul Helm, formerly Professor of the History and Philosophy of Religion, King's College, London.

Daniel M. Johnson, Associate Professor of Philosophy, Shawnee State University, Portsmouth, Ohio.

Hugh J. McCann, Professor of Philosophy Emeritus, Texas A & M University, College Station, Texas.

Alexander R. Pruss, Professor of Philosophy, Baylor University, Waco, Texas.

Greg Welty, Associate Professor of Philosophy, Southeastern Baptist Theological Seminary, Wake Forest, North Carolina.

Heath White, Associate Professor of Philosophy, University of North Carolina at Wilmington, Wilmington, North Carolina.

Introduction

—David E. Alexander
and Daniel M. Johnson

In recent years there has been a popular evangelical resurgence of Calvinism, led by a prominent group of pastors, theologians, and hip hop artists such as John Piper, Tim Keller, Al Mohler, R. C. Sproul, Mark Dever, and Lecrae.[1] In fact, in 2009, *Time* magazine listed what they called the "New Calvinism" as one of ten factors currently changing the world. This resurgence, however, does not seem to have been reflected in the academic world of Christian philosophy. If anything, there has been movement in the opposite direction, toward open theism. This is illustrated by Michael Rea's recent two-volume collection of representative work by professional philosophers on philosophical theology over the last three decades or so.[2] In those topic areas of philosophical theology where one might expect to see Calvinism represented—the topics of providence and of the inspiration of Scripture—the collection contains not a single essay defending a Calvinist (or even a Thomist-compatibilist) perspective, though it contains many essays defending Molinist, simple foreknowledge, and open theist views. Rea is not to be faulted; this distribution accurately captures the recent tendencies of Christian academic philosophy. Calvinism simply is not a live option for most Christian philosophers.

Why is this so? It is not because there is overwhelming evidence or knock-down arguments available in favor of libertarian accounts of free will and against compatibilist accounts. The free will literature remains as deeply divided as ever between compatibilism and libertarianism. Neither

---

1. For something of a chronicle of this surge, see Hansen, *Young, Restless, and Reformed*, and Piper, "The New Calvinism and the New Community."
2. Rea, *Oxford Readings in Philosophical Theology*.

is it because new evidence has been discovered in Scripture. The exegetical arguments for and against Calvinism remain much the same as they were hundreds of years ago, and in any case that wouldn't explain why the opposition to Calvinism is so much more noticeable among Christian philosophers than theologians. Finally, it is not because Calvinism is a philosophically bankrupt or useless position. In point of fact, Calvinism (as it has always done) provides powerful solutions to some of the most pressing problems in philosophical theology—the question of the compatibility of divine foreknowledge and providence with human free will and the question of the relationship between divine inspiration and human authorship in Scripture, to name just two.

No, the reason that Calvinism has not been a live option for most academic philosophers is the central role that libertarian accounts of free will have played in the philosophical responses to the problem of evil over the last half-century. Many Christian philosophers feel that they need a libertarian view of free will in order to handle the problem of evil, and philosophers have perhaps felt that need more keenly than theologians because they are more often engaged with non-Christian and anti-theistic philosophers and their arguments. At the very least, the most developed of the defenses against the problem of evil have often employed a libertarian conception of free will as an essential part,[3] and so Christians seeking a well worked out reply to the problem of evil will be guided away from Calvinism. It isn't as if Calvinist responses to the problem of evil have been thoroughly worked out and decisively refuted, though; for the most part, they haven't been tried, at least in the contemporary literature.[4]

This volume is intended to help fill that void. Every one of the essays is an exploration of one or more of the ways in which evil might be thought to pose a special problem for Calvinistic strains of Christianity, and most of them (though not all of them) develop and defend Calvinistic responses to those arguments. The result is a relatively thorough investigation of the charge that evil poses more of a problem for Calvinism than it does for non-Calvinistic strains of Christianity, along with a multifaceted Calvinistic response to that charge.

3. Or at least it appears to many to play an essential part. Others have suggested that some of the responses to the problem of evil that appeal explicitly to libertarian free will could jettison that commitment without loss. See, for example, Turner, "Compatibilism and the Free Will Defense," 125–37.

4. This qualification is important. As James Bruce's contribution aims to show, Francis Turretin spilled plenty of ink attempting to show that Calvinism has no special problem with respect to evil, and many of the other papers in this volume appeal to various elements of Aquinas's metaphysics to show that even the strongest versions of divine providence are defensible in the face of evil.

In this introduction, instead of summarizing each article in turn, we will try to show how the various articles fit together and move the discussion forward. We will follow the category system introduced in Daniel Johnson's essay (chapter 1), beginning with a series of preparatory issues and then moving on to three distinct problems that evil poses for Calvinism: the objection that Calvinism makes God the author of sin, the problem of the first sin, and the ordinary axiological problem of evil.

PREPARATORY ISSUES

The focus of the volume is the problems that evil poses for Calvinism. However, there are a number of other, related issues that pop up repeatedly in the essays and that are important for the central discussion. The first is the question: what exactly is Calvinism? A number of essays—notably, those by Daniel Johnson (chapter 1) and Heath White (chapter 3)—distinguish between two strands of Calvinist thought: the Calvinist doctrines regarding salvation (especially sin and grace) and the Calvinist doctrine of providence. They note that while the two strands fit together in a variety of ways they are in principle separable. Many of the authors in the volume focus on Calvinist views of providence, but Calvinist soteriology comes up in some discussions, and it is important to distinguish between the two and understand their relationship.

A second, related issue is the precise sort of determinism that is required by traditional Calvinist understandings of providence. The authors generally concur that God decides everything that is going to happen and it happens because of God's decision, and so God has exhaustive control over the world. But many authors make the point that this does not imply that everything which happens is determined by some other event in the natural world. If Calvinism implies a kind of determinism, then, it is not any sort of natural determinism (where events are thought to be determined by created causes and the laws of nature) but a kind of theological determinism (where events are determined by the will of God, which operates in quite a different way than creaturely powers do). We may ordinarily think of determination in terms of the sort of causal powers that creatures exert, and so our judgments about determination may be unreliable when applied to the sort of determining power exerted by God. Hugh McCann (chapter 7) even resists calling this determination at all, because he regards that language as having the misleading connotation that God's activity is an external determining factor of human actions; he thinks it is better to think of human actions as partly constitutive of God's willing, something like the content of God's intention, rather than as the result of his willing. So it is important to be careful about precisely what sort of determinism is entailed by Calvinist views of providence, and to be aware of the possibly misleading connotations of the language of determination.

The third issue that repeatedly pops up is the view of free will that is required by Calvinism. This point follows from the last. Calvinists are committed to saying that moral responsibility and any sort of free will that is necessary for moral responsibility are compatible with whatever sort of determinism is entailed by Calvinist views of providence.[5] But because there is a variety of kinds of determinism that a Calvinist might accept (even to the point of regarding the label "determinism" as too misleading to be useful), there is a corresponding variety of kinds of compatibilism about free will that a Calvinist may accept. There are two particularly significant varieties of compatibilism. One view, in the spirit of Jonathan Edwards, says that free will is compatible with one's decision being determined by one's own mental states, which may be determined by prior causes within the realm of creation; this sort of view most resembles the typical compatibilist views on offer in the philosophical literature on free will. Another view, perhaps in the spirit of Thomas Aquinas, denies that free will is compatible with determination by any created causes and asserts that free decisions can only be fully determined by the sovereign power of God. Hugh McCann arguably holds a species of the latter view, but he regards it as so unlike the standard, Edwards-style compatibilism that he insists his view is in fact a libertarian view of free will. So there are a variety of views of free will that may be thought compatible with Calvinism, and it is controversial even to say that Calvinism requires compatibilism about free will.

The fourth issue is the question of evidence in favor of Calvinism. Though none of the essays in the volume have as their primary purpose the presentation of evidence in favor of Calvinist views of salvation and providence—since they are instead focused on a particular set of objections to Calvinism—a few of the authors felt it important to at least sketch some of the arguments that might be given in favor of Calvinism. They did so in order to show that the burden of proof does not automatically lie with the Calvinists; just as Calvinists have to face significant challenges posed by evil, so too must their opponents face a variety of significant challenges. A survey of arguments in favor of Calvinism can be found in section 1 of David

---

5. And if free will is not needed for moral responsibility, then it may be that Calvinists can accept incompatibilism about free will and determinism and simply embrace compatibilism about moral responsibility and determinism, which is what John Martin Fischer calls semi-compatibilism. See, for example, Fisher, "My Compatibilism," 296–320.

Alexander's essay (chapter 5), section 5 of Daniel Johnson's essay (chapter 1), section 4 of James Anderson's essay (chapter 9), and section 5 of James Bruce's essay (chapter 4), which develops Francis Turretin's case for Calvinist views of divine providence.

THE "AUTHOR OF SIN" PROBLEM

One important fact that emerges from these essays is that there isn't just one problem that evil might be thought to pose for Calvinism. There are a variety of problems. The most familiar is the ordinary problem of evil, which we call the axiological problem of evil because it is often put in terms of the relative value of the evil in the world and the good that comes of it: if God is all-good, all-knowing, and all-powerful, how could there be evil and suffering in the world? The standard response is to argue that, as far as we know, there could be a great good that outweighs the bad of the world's evil and suffering, and which God couldn't bring about without allowing that evil and suffering. Thus God is morally justified in allowing evil—preserving his perfect goodness—even though he knew that our world would contain evil—preserving his omniscience—precisely because the great good cannot be had without the allowance of evil—preserving his omnipotence. The most commonly identified candidate for this outweighing good is free will, and therein lies the problem for Calvinism: it doesn't appear that Calvinists (given their belief in a kind of theological determinism) can appeal to the free will defense.[6] That is why the ordinary axiological problem of evil is often thought to cut more keenly when wielded against the Calvinist.

There are at least two other problems that evil might be thought to pose for Calvinism, though. One is a special problem posed by the Christian doctrine of the Fall, which we will discuss in the next section. Another is the charge that Calvinism entails that God is the author of sin in some objectionable sense. Even if the Calvinist can identify some outweighing good that requires evil for its existence and therefore solve the axiological problem of evil, the thought goes, it would still be true that Calvinism entails that God is too intimately involved in the bringing about of evil, involved in a way that is incompatible with the perfect goodness of God. So Calvinism entails that God is the author of sin in some objectionable way even if God has an excellent reason for bringing sin and evil about.

Johnson (chapter 1) points out that the "author of sin" charge is actually a family of arguments rather than a single argument. The general form

---

6. But, see Turner, "Compatibilism and the Free Will Defense," 125–37, for a challenge to this common assumption.

of the argument claims that the increased power over every aspect of the creation that Calvinism ascribes to God entails that God is involved with evil in some objectionable way. But in what objectionable way, exactly, is God involved with evil, if Calvinism is true? There are as many versions of this argument as there are objectionable properties that might be thought to attach to God on a Calvinistic view. There are at least four different features of God's relationship to evil that have been discussed under the heading of the "author of sin" charge: God's causation of evil, God's intentions with respect to evil, God's desires with respect to evil, and God's love of those who do and suffer evil.

Because there are at least four (and possibly more) different arguments that go under the heading of the "author of sin" charge—four different ways in which Calvinism might be accused of making God the author of sin—there cannot just be one kind of reply to the "author of sin" objection. Each version of the argument calls out for its own kind of reply. Adding to the complexity, there are at least three different kinds of replies that might be given in response to each of the arguments in the "author of sin" family. The first is to deny altogether that Calvinism entails that God has the objectionable property in question—deny that Calvinism entails that God causes sin, or deny that Calvinism entails that God intends sin, and so on. The second is to deny that it is objectionable for the property to attach to God—claim that it wouldn't be contrary to God's goodness if God did cause sin, for instance. The third is a *tu quoque* strategy, which is to argue that God's bearing the objectionable property is entailed by the views of non-Calvinist Christians if it is entailed by Calvinism, so if there is a problem for Calvinism, there is one for non-Calvinist Christian views as well. This would imply that it isn't Calvinism that generates the problem but doctrines shared in common between Calvinists and other sorts of Christians. These three kinds of replies are compatible; you can consistently give all three to each version of the "author of sin" problem. Also, it is possible to rely on one sort of reply to one of the versions of the argument and a different sort of reply to another. Each of these three sorts of replies can be found somewhere in the essays in this volume. In the remainder of this section we will briefly summarize those replies.

God's causation and God's intentions. Two of the versions of the "author of sin" objection are closely related, though not identical: the charge that Calvinism entails that God *causes* sin and evil, and the charge that it entails that God *intends* that sin and evil occur. Some of the authors treat these two together and give replies that apply to both arguments at once, while others strictly separate the two. Greg Welty (chapter 2) focuses exclusively on the argument that Calvinism entails that God *causes* sin and evil, and he pursues the *tu quoque* strategy in response.[7] He argues that if Calvinism entails this, then so does Molinism (a prominent alternative to Calvinist views of providence). According to Molinism, God uses his knowledge of what free beings will do if put in various situations (God's "middle knowledge" of the "counterfactuals of creaturely freedom") in order to decide what situations to create. Welty develops a thought-experiment involving a gun firing a sentient bullet (the Bullet Bill character from the Mario line of video games) to argue that God's use of this knowledge to arrange what sin and evil will happen is relevantly analogous to the responsibility for sin and evil that God bears if a Calvinist view of providence is true.

Heath White (chapter 3) carefully separates the charge that theological determinism entails that God causes sin from the charge that theological determinism entails that God intends for sin and evil to occur. He denies that theological determinism implies either objectionable property: even if theological determinism is true, God neither intends nor causes evil. Each argument rests on a distinct mistake, he says. The argument regarding God's causation of evil rests on a mistake about the nature of evil. Because evil is an absence of a certain sort of good (a "due good")—the famous privation theory of evil—it is a mistake to say that God causes evil. The argument regarding God's intentions toward evil, on the other hand, rests on a mistake about creation. On the correct view of creation, he argues, it turns out that God intends all of the good things in the world he chooses to create without intending any of the bad things in that world, not even as a means to the good in the world.

David Alexander (chapter 5) and Daniel Johnson (chapter 1) give responses that apply to both versions of the "author of sin" charge at once, addressing a combined argument that Calvinism entails that God intentionally causes sin and evil. Both grant for the sake of argument that Calvinism entails that God has both properties, but try to undercut the claim that those properties would be incompatible with God's perfection. Alexander argues that two influential ideas undercut the argument that it would be morally objectionable for God to intentionally cause sin. The doctrine of analogy (the idea that descriptions apply to God only analogously to the way the same descriptions apply to creatures) undercuts the claim that God causes or intends evil in the same sense that humans cause or intend evil, which undercuts the argument that it would be wrong for God to cause or intend evil. Since God's causing and intending evil is only analogous to humans' causing and intending evil, the fact that it would be wrong for humans to

---

7. Though it should be noted that it may be possible to adapt the argument in Welty's paper to serve as a reply to other versions of the "author of sin" objection as well.

do so does not imply that it would be wrong for God (or incompatible with his perfection) to do so. Alexander, like White, also appeals to the privation theory of evil but in a somewhat different way. Alexander argues that the privation theory of evil coupled with the corresponding philosophical thesis that being and goodness are convertible (i.e. identical) also undercuts the moral judgment that God ought to bring about nothing but good.

Johnson argues that the judgment that it would be wrong (or incompatible with God's perfection) for God to intentionally cause sin and evil is dependent on an analogy between human action and God's action that transfers a judgment of blame from one to the other. To attack this argument by analogy, he points out a series of morally relevant disanalogies between God and creatures. One set of disanalogies is moral. One such disanalogy (among others) is that God is the king and ruler of the world, the source of all being and goodness and the fount of all wisdom, and so may well have the right and responsibility to direct the destinies of other beings, a right that no human has toward another human. Another set of disanalogies is metaphysical. There is a tremendous difference in the basic nature of God's exercise of his causal powers and humans' exercise of their causal powers, so that we should hesitate to transfer moral judgments about one sort of causation to the other (this is basically the same point that Alexander makes in his treatment of analogy). Johnson adds an argument that the traditional Reformed distinction between God's "doing" something and God's merely "permitting" or "allowing" it is an attempt to highlight this metaphysical difference between divine and human action, and he explores a variety of ways to draw that distinction.

James Bruce (chapter 4) explores Francis Turretin's treatment of the problem. First, he admits that God intentionally causes sin, but insists that God's bringing sin about is an action that belongs in a distinct metaphysical category from the action of a human in choosing to sin. God's action in upholding and directing the world is so disanalogous to creaturely causes (Turretin calls it "hyperphysical" as opposed to this-worldly "physical" causes) that it is proper to say that the human will determines itself (undetermined by any ordinary physical cause) even while it is also true to say that God meticulously directs the soul to act as it does (hyperphysically). The principle that the agent is responsible for the evil it brings about, though true when applied to creaturely, physical causes, does not extend to the categorically different, hyperphysical actions of God in providence. He adds that God concurs with sin differently than with goodness, such that God deserves credit for the good that happens but no blame for the bad, and explores a variety of ways in which God might direct the human will to evil without actively bringing it about in the same way that he actively brings about good. One crucial distinction is that between the action itself and the wickedness of the action: Bruce (following Turretin) argues that it is possible for God to intend and cause the action without intending and causing the wickedness of the action, because the wickedness of the action is not an intrinsic property of the action but a relation between the action and the divine law, and because this wickedness is a kind of privation rather than a positively existent thing. Second, he employs the *tu quoque* strategy: he argues that even non-Calvinist Christians must assert that God intentionally sustains evil actions in existence, and so they have functionally the same problem that Calvinists do in terms of God's intimate involvement in the process of bringing sin about.

James Anderson (chapter 9) and Paul Helm (chapter 6), while focusing primarily on other subjects, add their voices to the chorus arguing that God's action in bringing about or "ensuring" (in Helm's language) that evil occurs is radically different than human actions that bring about evil, and that we should be humble, and therefore skeptical, about our ability to understand and assess that action. Both add that this skepticism should extend to our intuitions about whether God's actions in determining human free decisions are coercive in a way that undermines human freedom or dignity.

Hugh McCann is well-known for developing a view of providence and freedom that emphasizes the difference between divine and human action, a crucial element to which White, Alexander, Johnson, Anderson, Helm, and Bruce (expositing Turretin) all appeal. In his essay (chapter 7) he develops an account of grace that fits with that view of providence and freedom.

God's desires. A third version of the "author of sin" charge is the argument that Calvinism entails that God desires that sin and evil occur, which is directly contradicted by specific passages in Scripture. The standard Reformed response has always been to draw a distinction between two senses in which God might desire something—between his descriptive or sovereign will and his prescriptive or preceptive will—and charge the argument with equivocation between those two sense of "desire" or "will." Many have said that this idea that "there are two wills in God" is incoherent. Johnson (chapter 1) argues that this distinction between two senses of "desire" or "will" is not only not incoherent but perfectly ordinary and commonsensical. Further, he argues that any solution at all to the ordinary axiological problem of evil, from any theistic perspective, will require endorsing precisely this distinction and so every version of Christianity will need to accept it.

God's love. The final version of the "author of sin" charge that is treated in this volume is the charge that Calvinism entails that God fails to love some of his creatures, or at least that he fails to love his creatures in the way that a perfect being would love them. This argument sometimes focuses on God's allowance of any sin and evil to occur, but it often focuses specifically on those who are condemned to hell. Paul Helm (chapter 6) explores what sort of love a perfect being would have, specifically focusing on the divine attribute of omnibenevolence. He argues that the common assumption that a perfect being would love everyone to the same extent is false because such a being could not in fact love everyone maximally or equally. He grants that a perfect being would love everyone to some degree, but adds that we should be skeptical about our ability to discern precisely to what degree a perfect being would love everyone.

David Alexander (chapter 5) uses the privation theory of evil to argue that God does in fact love those in hell by willing their good, simply by virtue of the fact that he sustains them in existence. He does not will their good to exactly the same degree that he wills the good of others, but it is not obvious (Alexander argues) that this is a requirement of perfect love.

Daniel Johnson (chapter 1) gives an illustration of a human general who loves his son but sends him to die defending a city. This shows, he argues, that while love does require that one desire the good of the beloved, that desire for the beloved's good may appropriately be overridden by other concerns, such as a greater good that can only be achieved to the detriment of the beloved. It follows, he argues, that Calvinism entails that God fails to love those who are lost only if there is no greater good brought about by their loss. In other words, this argument only succeeds against Calvinism if Calvinism has no solution to the ordinary, axiological problem of evil. If that problem can be solved, this one is solved along with it. So the problem of God's love for the lost depends on and reduces to the ordinary axiological problem of evil.

THE PROBLEM OF THE FIRST SIN

It is a central feature of the Christian story that sin entered the world through the sinful decisions of a being (angels first, and human beings afterward) who was not sinful or blameworthy before that first sinful decision. That doctrine might be thought to present a puzzle for Calvinist views of providence. What could be the cause of that first sin? If you believe, as a libertarian about free will does, that human free will involves the ability to generate a decision that is not simply a function of the human's prior character or environment, then perhaps the performance of a sinful action by a previously sinless person would be more explicable—it is just in the nature of free will to generate new actions not entirely explicable in terms of previous events or states of affairs. But if some version of determinism is true, where is the first sin coming from? This problem is different than either the "author of sin" problem or the ordinary axiological problem of evil; even if both of those problems are solved, this one may well remain. However, it is important that both of the authors in this volume who focus their discussions primarily on this problem regard it as caught up with the "author of sin" problem—what you say about the "author of sin" problem, they think, directly impacts what you can and must say about the problem of the first sin. So it is perhaps best to think of the problem of the first sin as introducing a new complication into the discussion of the "author of sin" problem.

Alexander Pruss (chapter 8) draws a distinction between two views of providence and free will, a Thomist view (like McCann's) and an Edwardsean Calvinist view, and argues that theological determinists (including Calvinists) must choose one or the other. He then argues that the theological determinist faces a dilemma. The Thomist view handles the problem of the first sin well because it allows that one's actions are not completely determined by one's character and one's environment, but does not handle the "author of sin" objection well (specifically, the version of the argument that focuses on God's intentions) because it has God failing the moral requirement that no one should intend that evil occur even for the sake of a greater good. The Edwardsean view may handle the "author of sin" problem more effectively, but does not handle the problem of the first sin well. That is because, he argues, if one's decision is completely determined by one's character and one's environment, then it must be the case that either one's character is already vicious in some way or one isn't responsible for the decision at all. So the Christian claim that there was in fact a first sin committed by someone who before that sin was not vicious proves incompatible with Edwards-style compatibilism.

James Anderson (chapter 9), in addition to discussing the "author of sin" objection, philosophical challenges to compatibilist views of freedom, and the weaknesses of non-Calvinist views of providence, pursues two lines of reply to the problem of the first sin. First, he offers a suggestion as to what Adam's first sin might have been like, inspired by the work of Alfred Mele on the phenomenon of *weakness of will* (akrasia). A weak-willed decision, Mele argues, results from a kind of mismatch between our evaluations of the objects of our desires and the motivational strength of those desires. Such a decision, interestingly, need not flow from a generally weak-willed character. Anderson concludes that Adam's decision may have been a weak-willed action that did not flow from a prior vicious character trait but was still determined (by Adam's character and his environment) in the way compatibilists think is compatible with free will. He adds that saying that the (non-vicious) mismatch between evaluations and motivations (which causes the sinful, weak-willed action) might arise in the ordinary course of events "is no more problematic than the standard Christian claim that Adam was created sinless but not impeccable, uncorrupted but not incorruptible."[8] Second, Anderson pursues a *tu quoque* reply against Christian views who advocate a libertarian view of free will. Even if Calvinists must retreat to an appeal to mystery, he argues, the libertarian view that free actions are genuinely undetermined by any previous event introduces a kind of mystery or randomness into the first human sin (and, indeed, any human free action) that is no more respectable than the Calvinist's appeal to mystery.

THE ORDINARY (AXIOLOGICAL) PROBLEM OF EVIL

Solutions to the ordinary, axiological problem of evil usually proceed either by identifying possible reasons God might have for allowing evil (the free will defense, the soul-making defense) or by defending the more modest claim that even if we can't identify any such reasons, our evidence still does not support the conclusion that there is no such reason (skeptical theism, the Moore switch). The most popular defenses are probably the free will defense and skeptical theism, and many have thought the free will defense indispensable, or close to it, for an adequate solution to the ordinary problem of evil. The problem is that it appears, at least initially, that Calvinists cannot employ the free will defense. They are free to think that free will is tremendously valuable, perhaps valuable enough to outweigh the badness of the world's evil and suffering. But it seems that they are not able to think that free will is connected to evil in the right way. Since they regard free will to be compatible with divine determination of human actions, it seems they must admit that God could allow human beings to act freely while at the same time determining that they act rightly. Most theological determinists (including Calvinists) have agreed that the free will defense is unavailable to them.[9]

The question, then, is whether the free will defense is really as indispensable as some have thought. Daniel Johnson (chapter 1) mentions that other well-known defenses may be available to the Calvinist, such as the soul-making defense and the Leibnizian appeal to the value of having a

---

8. James Anderson, chapter 9 of this volume.

9. We say "most" because at least some theological determinists have advocated modified versions of the free will defense. See, for example, McCann, "Author of Sin," 144–59.

law-governed world. However, the kind of defense or theodicy that is perhaps most visible in the Reformed tradition, an appeal to the value of divine glory, has also been significantly neglected in the recent philosophical discussion of the problem of evil. Johnson, Christopher Green (chapter 10), and Matthew Hart (chapter 11) each set out to develop and defend importantly different versions of the divine glory defense. Green (without mentioning the notion of glory specifically) and Hart focus on the epistemic or "demonstrative" goods associated with divine glory. The thought is that God may allow evil in order to demonstrate his character by his response to evil, for the sake of the deeper appreciation this causes in the humans who are aware of this demonstration. Green argues that these epistemic goods—the good of human appreciation and knowledge of God—are, as far as we know, good enough to outweigh the badness of the evils that make them possible, in part because for all we know those epistemic goods may be infinite in their extent (extending infinitely forward in time). The biggest objection he faces is the question of whether evil is strictly necessary for these goods: couldn't God just directly implant appreciation and knowledge of him in our heads, or perhaps make a really good movie where he tells us about himself? In response, Green appeals to the notion of a *mode of presentation*—he argues that even if God could do such a thing, there is still an added value to that same information being presented in another way (say, by God's responses to actual evil). So even if human beings could gain the information without evil, there is an additional value to their also apprehending it through God's demonstration of his character by his response to actual evil.

Hart (chapter 11) develops the divine glory defense specifically with reference to perhaps the most difficult of evils for the Christian theist to explain: the eternal suffering of the inhabitants of hell. He argues that there is a whole series of important truths about God—he lists, by our count, thirteen—which human beings would fail to fully appreciate were it not for the existence of hell. Like Green, and anyone else developing a defense against the problem of evil, Hart must answer two questions in the affirmative: are these epistemic goods worth all the evil they are supposed to justify, and are these goods impossible for God to achieve without allowing evil? He makes distinctive arguments in each case. First, he argues that even if the knowledge of God gained by those who are saved doesn't exceed the pain and suffering of those who suffer in hell, still God may be justified in weighing the good of the elect over the suffering of the damned. That is because, generally speaking, human beings are justified in preferring the good of their own family (those closest to them) over those who are not family. And it is a permissible view, he thinks, that only those who are saved are rightly called the "children" of God, his adoptive family; or at least that the sense in which all humans are to be called "children" of God by virtue of being created by him is a less important or central sense as the way in which those who are saved are to be called "children" by virtue of their adoption by God. Second, Hart argues that there is at least one epistemic good that cannot be had without the actual existence of hell, even if mere propositional knowledge could be had another way (say, through God telling us about himself): direct, accurate perceptions of God's attributes. Such perceptions cannot be had without actual demonstrations of those attributes that we perceive. And this direct perception, Hart argues, is valuable over and above mere knowledge of God's attributes.

Johnson (chapter 1) argues that the epistemic goods that Green and Hart focus on are just one aspect of the notion of glory. Another aspect of the notion of glory—another aspect of the idea of God "manifesting" himself—is the notion of the exercise or expression of a power. In other words, when God demonstrates his love in forgiving sin, there are two distinct aspects of the glory that God accrues: there is the loving action itself (which is properly thought of as "glory," an action manifesting God's attribute of love) and the knowledge and appreciation of God that creatures gain by beholding this loving action (which is also properly thought of as "glory," for it is a sort of manifestation of God to the understanding of his creatures). Green's and Hart's versions of the divine glory defense features the second element in glory. Johnson's features the first. Johnson argues that this version of the divine glory defense has several advantages. First, there are certain of God's attributes that he cannot manifest in this sense—he cannot act in such a way that he expresses these attributes—without evil. God cannot forgive without sin that needs forgiveness, he cannot have mercy without someone who deserves judgment, and he cannot express his justice without wrongdoers to righteously judge.[10] Second, this aspect of glory is closely related to something else that philosophers have widely recognized as intrinsically good—Aristotle's notion of the actualization of potential. The exercise of a power, Aristotle thought, is intrinsically good. It is arguable, in fact, that the intrinsic good of a being's exercise of its powers is proportional to the greatness of those powers and that being—a human being thinking is a more magnificent and intrinsically better event than a frog jumping. So if anything plausibly can be thought to be good enough to outweigh the badness

---

10. Johnson argues that Alvin Plantinga's "Supralapsarianism, or O Felix Culpa" is in fact a version of the divine glory defense despite never using the word, because this is basically the good that Plantinga identifies in that essay. That shouldn't come as a surprise; a major motivation for the historic position of supralapsarianism was to preserve the idea that God ordains sin for his own glory.

of the evil in the world, it may well be the self-expression of the infinitely good God.

Aside from the free will defense, probably the most popular defense against the problem of evil is skeptical theism, which is a kind of appeal to mystery: perhaps we cannot identify a reason that would justify God in allowing evil, but why would we expect to be able to identify such a reason even were it there? Unlike the free will defense, skeptical theism is not even apparently incompatible with Calvinism.[11] Skeptical theism has been extensively developed and defended by philosophers over the past thirty years. Because of the way the debate unfolded historically, however, some have the idea that skeptical theism is only effective against a particular version of the problem of evil, namely, the evidential problem of evil, while the free will defense remains necessary to reply to the logical problem of evil. Johnson (chapter 1) argues that this idea is mistaken, and that skeptical theism is just as effective a reply against the logical problem of evil as it is against the evidential problem of evil, because the logical problem involves an appeal to evidence (to support its premises) just as much as the evidential problem does. He also argues that the same point applies to the Moore Switch.

Many treatments of the problem of evil fail to recognize the Moore Switch as a distinct sort of reply. One way of explaining the Moore Switch is to point out that even if evil, considered on its own, constitutes evidence against the existence of God, it may be that the contrary evidence in favor of the existence of God is so good that it outweighs the evidence provided by evil, such that God's reasons for allowing evil simply becomes a puzzle to be solved instead of a serious reason to reject the existence of God. Anthony Bryson (chapter 12) argues that this point (that the total evidence may support the existence of God even if evil, isolated from the rest of our evidence, counts against it) is not the Moore Switch proper. The Moore Switch, he says, appeals more specifically to *perceptual* evidence: we can see clearly that we have hands, and so any skeptical arguments for the conclusion that we don't know whether we have hands just become interesting puzzles to solve rather than real reasons to doubt whether we have hands. The fact that we have hands is more obvious to us than the premises of the supposed skeptical arguments, so those skeptical arguments just end up being *reductio ad absurdum* arguments against the assumptions that lie behind the arguments. Some have thought that belief in God is like this: at least some people can simply perceive that God exists or that certain Christian doctrines are

---

11. While neither are traditional Calvinists (as far as we can tell) it is noteworthy that perhaps the two names most often associated with skeptical theism, Alvin Plantinga and Stephen Wykstra, hail from Reformed traditions and have taught for all or a large portion of their careers at Calvin College.

true, and so the argument from evil against the existence of God simply becomes a *reductio ad absurdum* refutation of at least one of the premises of the argument.

One way of arguing that some people can perceive the existence of God is the Reformed epistemology movement associated with Alvin Plantinga, which argues that belief in God and in the truth of certain doctrines can be properly basic or foundational, generated by a sense of deity or by an internal testimony from the Holy Spirit.[12] One way some in the Reformed tradition have expressed an idea similar to this one is to say that the Scriptures are *self-attesting* in some sense. Bryson argues that the idea that Scripture is self-attesting fails. One of his arguments is that it fails to account for the process of canonization, the procedures by which the various books of the Bible were recognized as the word of God. He also argues that the appeal to the self-attestation of Scripture incoherently appeals both to intuitions that support a kind of epistemic internalism and to intuitions that support the contradictory view, epistemic externalism. He concludes that an appeal to the self-attestation of Scripture does not support a viable version of the Moore Switch defense against the problem of evil.

CONTRIBUTIONS AND CONCLUSIONS

We will conclude by drawing some broad conclusions about the ways in which this collection of essays advances the discussion of the relationship between Calvinism and the problem of evil.

Perhaps the most important contribution of the volume as a whole is this: the essays in this volume collectively constitute a forceful and multifaceted challenge to anyone who would argue that Calvinism entails that God is the author of sin in some objectionable sense. Anyone who desires to make that argument in light of this volume will need first to specify *in what sense* Calvinism entails that God is the author of sin (that he intends sin, causes sin, desires sin, fails to love those who are lost, or some other objectionable property) and second to answer the variety of arguments intended to show either that Calvinism does not entail that God is the author of sin in that sense, or that it is not objectionable for God to be the author of sin in that sense, or that other sorts of Christianity make God the author of sin in that sense, if Calvinism does.

---

12. The presuppositionalist movement in Christian apologetics, associated especially with Cornelius Van Til, also relies heavily on this idea. As a result, the Moore Switch (though not identified by that name) features prominently in presuppositionalist replies to the problem of evil.

A second important contribution is the re-introduction of the divine glory defense into the mainstream philosophical discussion and the further development of that defense.[13] This defense cries out for more philosophical development and discussion, especially given the Biblical emphasis on God's pursuit of his own glory. This volume offers two significantly different ways to pursue that defense (by Green and Hart on the one hand and Johnson on the other), each of which focuses on a different element of the phenomenon of divine glory.

A third important contribution is a re-examination of the Moore Switch. Bryson's investigation shows, at the least, that the influential Reformed epistemology movement provides a unique approach to the problem of evil, one that may possibly succeed even if every other defense against the problem fails. The Moore Switch therefore is a distinctive and distinctively Reformed approach to the problem of evil. It deserves to be mentioned in the same breath as the other major approaches to the problem of evil, and that means that the debate over the problem of evil is directly impacted by and should encompass the debate over religious epistemology.

The volume makes contributions to a number of other debates that call out for further discussion: the nature of divine love, the nature and cause of the first sin, and the precise relationship between Calvinist soteriology and philosophical views about free will and providence, just to name a few. The relationship between Calvinism and the philosophical problem of evil is a complex topic, and warrants the careful and clear treatment that characterizes the best contemporary analytic philosophy. This volume, we believe, makes a significant stride in that direction.

---

13. Because Alvin Plantinga's "Supralapsarianism, or O Felix Culpa" is arguably a version of the divine glory defense, though Plantinga never uses the word, he probably deserves the credit for reintroducing the defense into the contemporary philosophical discussion.

BIBLIOGRAPHY

Fisher, John Martin. "My Compatibilism." In *The Philosophy of Free Will: Essential Readings from the Contemporary Debates*, edited by Paul Russell and Oisin Deery, 296–320. New York: Oxford University Press, 2013.

Hansen, Collin. *Young, Restless, and Reformed: A Journalist's Journey with the New Calvinists*. Wheaton, IL: Crossway, 2008.

McCann, Hugh J. "The Author of Sin?" *Faith and Philosophy* 22, no. 2 (2005) 144–59.

Piper, John. "The New Calvinism and the New Community: The Doctrines of Grace and the Meaning of Race." desiringGod.org, March 19, 2014. http://www.desiringgod.org/articles/the-new-calvinism-and-the-new-community.

Rea, Michael, ed. *Oxford Readings in Philosophical Theology*. 2 vols. Oxford: Oxford University Press, 2009.

Turner, Jason. "Compatibilism and the Free Will Defense." *Faith and Philosophy* 30, no. 2 (2013) 125–37.

1

Calvinism and the Problem of Evil
A Map of the Territory

—Daniel M. Johnson

THE MAIN SOURCE OF the resistance of Christian academic philosophers to Calvinism is the problem of evil. Despite the many philosophical and theological advantages of Calvinism, and the lack of philosophical consensus in favor of libertarian accounts of the will, the mainstream of Christian philosophy has resisted Calvinism because of a general sense that Calvinism makes the problem of evil—far and away the most serious philosophical challenge to theism—harder to solve. At least some of the reason for this general sense is that Calvinistic treatments of the problem of evil are comparatively underdeveloped in the contemporary literature. However, there is a long history of reflection on evil in the Reformed tradition that remains largely untapped in the contemporary discussion.

My aim in this essay is to argue that there are enough resources in the Reformed tradition to mount quite a convincing reply to the argument that Calvinism is worse off with respect to the problem of evil than are other Christian traditions. In order to make that case, I will give a careful map of the various difficulties that evil might be thought to pose for Calvinism. There are a host of concepts and distinctions to be found in the Reformed tradition that are relevant for thinking about evil, but it is often not obvious how exactly they are relevant. My goal is to develop and explore each concept in a thorough way, and show how they coalesce into a convincing reply to the various problems posed by evil. The result will be a conceptual map of the territory covered by the relation of Calvinism to evil.

1. SETTING THE STAGE: WHAT IS CALVINISM?

There are at least two importantly distinct strands of thought that go under the heading of Calvinism, and each involves a number of subclaims. I'll call the two Calvinist soteriology and Calvinist determinism.

Calvinist soteriology. The Calvinist picture of salvation goes basically like this: fallen man is unable to turn to God with saving faith, because fallen man is *unwilling* to turn to God (and is therefore responsible for his rebellion). Every believer is infallibly brought to faith, sustained in faith, and sanctified by the omnipotent power of the Holy Spirit. Those who are brought to life are not chosen because of their worthiness, for they are as undeserving as any; what reason God has for choosing those he does remains a mystery.

The famous acronym TULIP captures this fairly well. Total Depravity (better: Total Inability) is the claim that fallen humans are fundamentally opposed to God and unable (because unwilling) to turn to God. Note that Calvinists will not deny that humans are able to avoid sin in whatever sense of "ability" is necessary for responsible action; they simply deny that this "ability" is metaphysically ultimate or absolute, so there is also an important sense in which humans are, ultimately speaking, unable to turn to God. Unconditional Election says that God chooses whom he will regenerate and save (his decree of election) independent of any good or bad thing they might have done, since they are as blameworthy as those he chooses not to regenerate and save (his decree of reprobation). Limited Atonement (better: Definite Atonement) says that Jesus died in order to actually save the elect and only the elect.[1] Irresistible Grace (better: Efficacious Grace) says that the regenerating and saving power of the Spirit is not resistible by human

---

1. This one hangs people up. It seems to me that the Calvinist can say everything that the Arminian does, plus more. The Arminian thinks that there is a sense in which God died for everybody. But even the Arminian doesn't quite think this; in fact, the Arminian thinks that God died in order to *offer* salvation to everybody, such that *if* they repent and have faith they will be saved. Even on the Arminian view, after all, God has the power to override free will, but he chooses not to because free will is so valuable. The Calvinist can say all of this: Jesus certainly died in order to *offer* salvation to everyone, such that *if* they repent and have faith they will be saved. The Calvinist just says something more: Jesus also died in order to *actually accomplish* the salvation of the elect, not merely to offer them salvation. So the Calvinist gets everything the Arminian does with regard to the purpose of the atonement, plus something extra. This has not been well understood by many parties to the debate.

beings precisely because it *changes* what those human beings want and will. Perseverance of the Saints says that, because the Spirit's grace is irresistible, the Spirit's power shepherds the elect infallibly all the way to glory.

Calvinist determinism: Calvinist soteriology is really just a series of claims about fallen humanity. Calvinists usually accompany this soteriology with a complementary picture of the entire course of history: God is in control of everything, and has from eternity ordained all that has come to pass and will come to pass. At the same time, human beings are genuine agents and are responsible for their actions.

The strands are distinct, but they are tied by this: each entails a denial of libertarian views of moral responsibility (with a qualification forthcoming in a moment). Calvinist soteriology claims that humans are responsible though unable (in the absolute metaphysical sense of "ability" that libertarians think essential to responsible action) to avoid sin; Calvinist determinism says humans are responsible even though how they act is decreed by God. Both strands are pastorally important. Realization of Calvinist soteriology is important for generating gratitude, humility, and freedom from anxiety; Calvinist determinism is important for generating proper reverence and also for freedom from fear and anxiety.

Though the two do go together, there may be important positions that accept the first strand and deny the second. For instance, you might think that Adam had the sort of absolute metaphysical power to act otherwise that was outside God's control, but fallen humanity no longer has the ability to avoid sin (though it is still responsible for that sin). This would require an unusual position on the connection between free will and moral responsibility, but it is an example of a position which accepts the first strand and not the second.[2] On some readings, Augustine may take this view. This may qualify as a Calvinist position, and it is the sort of position that many Calvinists would be friendly to. Calvinist soteriology is more important to many of them than Calvinist determinism, which is to say that they are more committed to their position about fallen humanity than to their position about Adam and Eve.

I said that each strand of Calvinism entails the denial of libertarian views of moral responsibility. It is important, though, to clarify exactly what

2. Matthew Hart and Daniel Hill described to me the following view of free will and moral responsibility that would fit nicely with this Augustinian position: Libertarians are correct about free will and responsibility, and Adam had libertarian free will when he fell. All of us were quite literally "in Adam" and made his choice along with him—this cries out for a lot of metaphysical refinement—which is why we are responsible for the fall. Since that fall, we are all in a state analogous to that of a drunk person: we are not currently free, but are responsible for what we do because we are responsible for getting ourselves into this state.

consequences that accepting both strands of Calvinism has for accounts of free will. The Calvinist has two basic sorts of options. First, the Calvinist can accept that free will is a necessary condition of moral responsibility, and claim that free will is compatible with Calvinist determinism and Calvinist soteriology. Second, the Calvinist can deny that free will is a necessary condition on moral responsibility. The first is by far the more common today, but the second has important examples. I'll treat each in turn. Calvinism is not compatible, in my opinion, with Derk Pereboom's outright denial of moral responsibility, since I don't see how the central theses of Christianity (and therefore Calvinism) that human beings are guilty before God, deserving of punishment, and forgiven because of Christ can be preserved on his view.[3]

First, Calvinist compatibilism about free will: Calvinists can accept many of the compatibilist theories of free will on offer in the literature today. Jonathan Edwards' *Freedom of the Will*, according to which an action is free just in case it is the result of the *motives* of the agent, is a classic statement of this sort of compatibilist theory of free will, and many Calvinists follow Edwards here. However, there is an importantly different sort of view of free will available to the Calvinist. The contemporary literature on free will categorizes views on free will in a fairly strange manner. The current literature defines compatibilism as the thesis that free will (along with moral responsibility) is compatible with determinism. So far, so good. But then much of the contemporary literature defines determinism as the thesis that the state of the world at any given instant, plus the laws of nature, entails the state of the world at any other instant. Notice that this is a sort of natural or this-worldly determinism, since it does not take into account the possibility of determination that flows only from a God whose decisions lie outside of time. Calvinists who think that free will is necessary for moral responsibility are not committed to the thesis that free will is compatible with this sort of determinism; they are only committed to the thesis that free will is compatible with *divine* determinism—the thesis that everything that happens is determined by God's decree. The contemporary terminology has the curious consequence, then, that some Calvinist views actually count as libertarian views, since they claim that free will is incompatible with natural determinism but compatible with divine determinism.

Examples of Calvinist views which count as libertarian in the contemporary terminology are the views of Hugh McCann and Jack Crabtree (perhaps following Aquinas), according to which human free actions cannot be

---

3. His heroic efforts to do so notwithstanding—see Pereboom, "Theism and Libertarian Free Will."

fully determined by this-worldly causation but only by God's different, transcendent causation.[4] According to McCann, what is different about God's transcendent, creative causation is that it doesn't operate as an external determining condition of the resultant creation. Instead, the creation (including creaturely actions) just is the content of God's intention, which means that we in fact have our being in God and are not "acted upon" or "undergo or suffer anything"[5] when we act, even though we act according to God's decree. McCann (and Crabtree) therefore claim that the "ability to do otherwise" that is essential to human freedom is much stronger than the kind of ability admitted by Edwards-style compatibilists.[6] However, they still deny that this ability is an absolute metaphysical ability that evades God's control, and so their view entails Calvinist determinism and is compatible with Calvinist soteriology.[7] It is hard to know how to classify this sort of view of free will. It counts as libertarian on the contemporary category system, and it certainly shares some of the traditional libertarian opposition to Edwards-style compatibilism. McCann, in fact, embraces the contemporary terminology and claims to be a libertarian.[8] However, the view also asserts that free will is compatible with complete divine determination of human free actions, and so seems to warrant the label "compatibilism." For the purposes of this essay, I will count the McCann/Crabtree view as a sort of compatibilism because it shares with compatibilism the characteristic I am interested in—compatibility with Calvinism.

Second, Calvinists have the option of denying free will so long as they deny that free will is necessary for moral responsibility. There are a couple of possible versions of this view. On one view, the Calvinist may claim that "free will" means the absolute metaphysical ability to do good and turn to God, in which case pre-Fall and glorified humanity has free will

---

4. See McCann, "Divine Sovereignty," 582–98; McCann, "Author of Sin," 144–59; and Crabtree, *Most Real Being*. Both Crabtree and McCann lay significant weight on the analogy between God's sovereign activity and the activity of an author in telling a story, though Crabtree probably relies on the analogy more heavily than does McCann.

5. McCann, "Author of Sin," 157.

6. For their respective critiques of Edwards, see McCann, "Edwards on Free Will," 27–43; and Crabtree, *Most Real Being*, 213. Crabtree's reason for rejecting Edwards-style compatibilism is a version of the brainwashing argument, often classed in the contemporary literature as a "manipulability argument."

7. McCann says "if we thought controlling our destiny meant limiting God's options in any way, we ought to have known better" ("Author of Sin," 156).

8. And even though Crabtree's book is subtitled "A Biblical and Philosophical Defense of Divine Determinism," a recent review of it in *Faith and Philosophy* categorized Crabtree's view as a sort of agent-causal libertarianism. Johnson, "Review of The Most Real Being," 109–12.

but post-Fall humanity does not, while Christians have it in some degree. This is probably Calvin's position; he thinks that "free will" is too exalted a thing to ascribe to sinful humanity. On another view, the Calvinist may agree with the agent-causal libertarians that "free will" is the power to be a mini-creator-from-nothing, and assert that human beings never had and never will have such a power.[9] This may be Luther's view and would look something like John Martin Fischer's semi-compatibilism, the claim that moral responsibility is compatible with determinism while free will is not. This means that free will is not necessary for moral responsibility. These sorts of views will turn on what exactly "free will" means. Calvin and Luther may be using the term in a different way than we do, such that they are not really disagreeing with Edwards when they deny free will and he affirms it. On the other hand, it may be that the term "free will" gets used in a variety of ways, such that the Calvinist may want to deny its reality in some senses and accept it in others. In any case, the Calvinist is committed to accepting the sort of free will that is necessary for moral responsibility, if there is any such thing.

My point so far is that the Calvinist has a number of options in taking a position on free will. First, the Calvinist can affirm free will and give a compatibilist story about it. There are a number of importantly different compatibilist views available, some of which won't even count as compatibilist on the contemporary category system. Second, Calvinism can deny free will so long as it also denies that free will is necessary for moral responsibility. There are a number of different positions that might motivate such a denial. Finally, it is possible to accept only Calvinist soteriology while rejecting Calvinist determinism, ascribing the God-independent sort of free will to Adam and Eve but denying it to post-Fall humanity. This position would preserve the core of Calvinism, its soteriology, though it would require an odd view as to the relationship between moral responsibility and free will.

---

9. The Calvinist could ascribe our belief that we have such a power to the sinful human desire for autonomy. This doesn't require saying that everyone who believes in this sort of free will does so because of their own sin. It simply means saying that human sinfulness in general is what led to this conception. For a similar sentiment, see McCann, "Author of Sin," 149.

2. THE FIRST DISTINCTIVE CALVINIST PROBLEM WITH EVIL: CALVINISM MAKES GOD THE AUTHOR OF SIN

In addition to needing to take a different tack than libertarians do toward the ordinary axiological problem of evil, Calvinism faces difficulties with evil that alternative views do not. There are at least two. The first is the famous objection that Calvinism makes God the author of sin in some objectionable sense. My thesis in this section will be that there are many different versions of this objection and that there are plausible responses on the part of Calvinism to every version of the problem.

According to Calvinist determinism, God works out everything according to His will. God is in control of the course of history, and nothing falls outside his plan. In fact, there is a sense in which God brings about or causes everything that happens—including sin and evil. This poses a problem. Doesn't this make God the "author" of sin in an objectionable sense? To be precise, the argument is this: the charge that if Calvinism were true, then God must stand in some objectionable relation to the evil which occurs even if God were to have a good reason for allowing it (the "no good reason" charge is the common problem of evil and will be treated separately). There can be as many versions of this charge as there are purportedly objectionable relations that Calvinism has God standing in to evil. What that means is that the "author of sin" objection is actually a family of different objections. Each member of the family must have to have something to do with the extra power over evil that Calvinism ascribes to God. The three versions of the argument I will treat are the charges that Calvinism has God doing wrong by intentionally causing evil, that it has God desiring that evil occur, and that it has God failing to love those who are lost. These cover importantly different sets of issues; alternative charges (of which I am aware, anyway) generally retrace the same ground. It is enormously important that these different arguments not be conflated. The Reformed tradition gives very different replies to each, and it will not do to confuse them.

It can be difficult to distinguish the "author of sin" problem from out-and-out rejections of Calvinist views of free will. In order to discover whether *evil* poses a special problem for Calvinism, we must *grant* the Calvinist claim that when God determines people to do evil, he brings it about that they do so freely and responsibly, and so does them no injustice by blaming them for it. Rejecting this assumption moves the discussion from the topic of evil to the topic of free will, because praiseworthy actions of humans then pose just as much a problem as evil actions do. My goal here is to find and address any special problem posed for Calvinism by evil, and in this context the Calvinist picture of free will must be granted lest the whole question be begged from the outset.

2.1 The First Charge: Calvinism Entails that God Intentionally Causes Evil

The first member of the "author of sin" family of arguments focuses on the following feature of the Calvinist story: God's intentional action in bringing about evil. The argument would go like this: according to Calvinism, God intentionally causes others (his creatures) to do moral evil; but it is always wrong to intentionally cause others to do moral evil; therefore, according to Calvinism, God does wrong, which is impossible, and so Calvinism must be false. In fact, this version of the argument runs two distinct properties together: God's *intentions* with respect to evil, and God's *causation* of evil. Some kinds of replies may require us to distinguish those two properties.[10] I will treat them together, however, because I will grant for the sake of argument that Calvinism implies that God intentionally causes evil.

The premise I question is the second: why think that it is always wrong to intentionally cause others to do moral evil? We're assuming, after all, that God has some great good that he accomplishes by doing so and cannot accomplish otherwise (the search for such a good is the common problem of evil, treated separately). The critic of Calvinism generally defends the premise by extending our moral judgments about human actions to God's actions: in most (perhaps all) of the cases of human beings intentionally causing others to do moral evil, even with some greater good in mind, those human beings do wrong. Human beings shouldn't play with fire in that way, by bringing about an evil as a means to a good. Why isn't it the same for God?

The first thing to ask is whether non-Calvinist, libertarian views fare any better than Calvinism does, either philosophically or with respect to Scripture. Some libertarian views could say this: God intends to bring about beings with free will because of the great goods to be had from free will, but does not intend that they sin; he doesn't even know whether they will sin until he makes the decision to create them, and then does his best to bring about a further set of great goods from the sin when it turns out that they do sin. In this case, God does not intend sin at all, even as a means to the great goods that sin can lead to. It is less obvious whether libertarian views with a stronger doctrine of divine providence, like Molinist views,

---

10. Heath White's contribution to this volume crucially relies on distinguishing them.

fare better than Calvinism does on this point.[11] The normal Molinist story is that God actualizes a possible world with sin in it because only possible worlds with sin in them achieve the greatest goods. This language implies that God intended that the sin and evil happen because of the great goods for which it is necessary. At the least, Molinists will need to do some work to get out of this objection.

It is another question whether the libertarian position is consistent with Scripture. It seems that Scripture does portray God as intending particular sinful actions by humans in order to bring about good from them. Consider, as one example, the case of Joseph and his brothers. His brothers act evilly in selling him into slavery, but Joseph tells them later that "you meant evil against me, but God meant it for good" (Gen 50:20); earlier Joseph says, "Do not be distressed or angry with yourselves because you sold me here, for God sent me before you to preserve life. . . . So it was not you who sent me here, but God" (Gen 45:5, 8). This is a clear case where an evil action is ascribed to God (though under a different description—God's action in bringing it about is not evil), and it sure looks like God intended that action (God "meant it for good") for the good that would come of it.

Regardless of how libertarians fare with respect to this problem, though, it remains a problem for Calvinists. Suppose we grant for the sake of argument that human beings always do wrong when they intentionally bring it about that another does a moral evil. The argument for the second premise of the argument against Calvinism is based on an analogy between human beings and God, and so is vulnerable to the pointing out of relevant disanalogies between the activity of humans and the activity of God in bringing it about that humans do evil. A major Calvinist reply to this charge, then, is this: God's mode of activity in bring it about that humans do evil does not render him complicit in the evil, and his activity in sovereignly directing the world is relevantly disanalogous to the activity of human beings when they intentionally bring about evil.

How is God's sovereign activity relevantly different from the activity of humans? One difference that has been much emphasized by Calvinists is a moral one: God is the ruler of the cosmos, the source of all existence and all goodness, and self-existent; human beings are not. One consequence of this difference is that God is subject to no external law and so by definition incapable of acting in rebellion against any such law; human beings, by contrast, are subject to the law of God. Some Calvinists have identified *rebellion* as the essence of sin. McCann, for instance, argues that intentionally bringing

---

11. See Greg Welty's contribution to this volume for an argument that Molinism is no better off than Calvinism with respect to this problem. Jonathan Edwards makes the same point; it is his first argument in *Freedom of the Will*, part IV, section IX.

about evil is neither necessary nor sufficient for wrongdoing; wrongdoing requires knowing disobedience of a divine command. It follows that God does no wrong in bringing about evil since he has no law to answer to and so does not act rebelliously in doing so.[12] Another closely related difference between God and man, referred to by Paul in Romans 9, is that human beings are created by God and in a certain sense belong to God, while no human being is the creation of or belongs to another human being in that sense. Therefore, as Paul insists, God has rights with respect to directing the destinies of human beings than no human being has with respect to another human being. Yet another possible related difference between God's position and ours is that God can employ means-ends reasoning that would be dangerous for us (because of our limited knowledge) and which God may have categorically forbidden us as a result. There may be other moral disanalogies between God and man attending to God's role as ruler of the universe (his rulership or sovereignty), a role not shared by any human being.

Some Calvinists have thought these moral disanalogies between God and man sufficient to answer this version of the "author of sin" problem.[13] Many, however, have wanted more: a metaphysical disanalogy between the sovereign activity of God in directing the world (even to evil) and ordinary human action in bringing about evil. In much Reformed thought, this has given rise to a further distinction between two types of *divine* action, one type that is more like human action and one type distinctively divine and sovereign. Only human action and the kind of divine action that is relevantly like it would be subject to blame for the intentional causation of evil. The Reformed have often used the term "allowing"—obviously in a merely analogical sense of the word—to describe God's sovereign mode of activity so as to communicate God's lack of blameworthy complicity in the sin he sovereignly determines. The term "doing" describes his other mode of activity, the sort more like human activity. Calvinists have often used this doing/allowing distinction in order to distinguish between the way in which God acts in bringing people to faith and the way in which he acts in leaving them to their sin, to claim that there is a difference between the way God executes the decree of election and the way he executes the decree of reprobation—God actively brings the elect out of their sin when he regenerates and saves them, but merely allows the reprobate to remain in their sin.[14]

---

12. McCann, "Author of Sin," 149–52; an earlier version of precisely this argument is made by Gordon Clark, *Religion, Reason, and Revelation*, chapter 5.

13. Clark thinks it sufficient to answer the problem of evil *simpliciter* (*Religion, Reason, and Revelation*, chapter 5).

14. Many critics of Calvinism have ignored this disanalogy that many Calvinists have insisted on between the decrees of election and reprobation, and so have

One metaphysical strategy for explaining a doing/allowing distinction is broadly Thomist, and it is probably Jonathan Edwards' view.[15] Suppose that the privation theory of evil is true, and evil is the absence of good. More precisely, evil is the absence in a substance of a good that should be there—a good that characterizes the proper functioning of that substance. All being is good *qua* being, and so evil is merely the absence of a certain sort of being (a being that should be there). All beings would cease to exist were God not to continue to sustain them in being. If all this is true, then we have the materials for a sort of doing/allowing distinction. God causes only good, since his activity in sustaining beings sustains only good. God can determine that evil happens simply by ceasing to sustain in being some good and allowing it to fade from existence. So God only does good and merely allows evil by ceasing his sustaining activity with respect to the corresponding good.[16] This would help to reply to the argument by allowing one to simply deny altogether that Calvinism implies that God causes evil, because evil is not a substance that can be caused, but it doesn't imply much about God's intentions and so doesn't help much with that part of the argument.

A different strategy among the Reformed doesn't deny that God causes evil, but instead focuses on the radical difference between God's power and the power exerted by creatures. God's activity in allowing human evil is relevantly different than the human's doing of the evil because God's allowing something is an instance of the sort of causation he exerts in creation *ex nihilo* and conservation from annihilation—a form of causation human beings have little understanding of and have never exerted themselves. The central idea is that God's creative and conservative causation is radically different from creaturely causation, merely analogous to it, and so not subject to all of the same moral evaluations as it is. There may be a variety of ways to try to understand this difference—if McCann is right, God's causation is not an external determining condition of our action but constitutive of our action—but surely it is true, whether we understand it or not, that God's creative and conservative causation is radically different than our own, and so we should hesitate to transfer moral judgments about human modes of activity to God's mode of activity. God's creative and conservative causation, according to this strategy, is perhaps more closely analogous to the causation of an author when writing a story: the author causes everything that happens, but the author is not blameworthy for the actions of his characters,

---

consistently caricatured the doctrine of double predestination.

15. For Edwards' discussion of the view, see his analogy with the sun in his *Freedom of the Will*, part IV, section IX.

16. This is a slightly different use of the privation theory of evil for theodical purposes than that outlined in Newlands, "Problem of Evil."

though he is responsible for the worthiness of the story as a whole. George Lucas did not kill the children in the Jedi Temple and so is not blameworthy for that; Anakin Skywalker did and is.

This can give rise to a doing/allowing distinction in a number of ways. One friendly to Edwards-style compatibilism is to invoke a distinction between remote and proximate causation. The remote/proximate distinction for creatures is something like this: I am the proximate cause of an event just in case there are no intermediate causes (or perhaps intermediate agential causes) between my action and the event, while I am the remote cause of something just in case there are such intermediate (agential) causes.[17] The remote/proximate distinction for God is not quite the same distinction, because God is always upholding everything that happens and so is always in some sense a proximate cause of it. The divine remote/proximate distinction would instead have to be something like this, merely analogous to the creaturely distinction: God is the remote cause of an event just in case there is a causal explanation of the event involving created agency; God is the proximate cause of an event just in case there is no causal explanation of the event involving created agency. The doing/allowing distinction would map on thus: God does an event just in case he is the proximate cause of it, while he allows the event just in case he is the remote cause of it.

A slightly modified version of this strategy is friendlier to the Crabtree/McCann view of free will. On their view, every human free decision has no full causal explanation in terms of created things, and so on the previous strategy God counts as directly doing every human free action, including the sinful ones. We could supplement the story like this. Perhaps God can exert two very different kinds of causation: the transcendent causation by which he upholds the world and directs all of its activities, and immanent causation relevantly like that which creatures exert. He exerts the second sort of causation when he is incarnate or comes in theophany—when he is "present" in a particular part of the world in a special way. If this is true, then a different remote/proximate distinction can be made. God merely allows something just in case he causes it only by virtue of his transcendent mode of causation (whether or not the event has a causal explanation in terms of created things). God does something just in case he causes it by virtue of his immanent mode of causation—when he is "present" in that special way. God must "write himself into" the story of creation in order to be ascribed actions directly.[18]

---

17. Actually, it may be that there must be intermediate intelligent or agential causes for me to be the remote cause.

18. Guillaume Bignon uses counterfactuals to give a helpful semantics for the term "allows" which, so far as I can tell, would be compatible with any of the foregoing ways

All these ways of drawing a doing/allowing distinction are subject to counterexamples, however, and some of those counterexamples are Scriptural. All of these accounts exclude too much from counting as a divine doing (rather than allowing). Matthew 6:26–32 says that God feeds the birds and clothes the flowers, but at least the McCann-friendly doing/allowing distinction outlined in the last paragraph rules that God merely allowed the birds to be fed and the flowers to be clothed. More forcefully, the point of this passage is to teach that God provides for human beings—and surely God provides for us through the actions of others. This refutes the McCann-friendly account rules that all human free actions are merely allowed by God. The Edwards-friendly account (along with the Thomistic account) seems to fare better, but it seems true that God can provide for us even through the evil actions of others (the story of Joseph is full of this)—and since all the accounts rule that God merely allows the evil actions of others, they cannot say that God *provides* through the evil actions of others. Also, every account falls to passages like Genesis 50:20 and Exodus 4:21 where God is positively ascribed the action of bringing it about that a human does an evil (that Joseph's brothers sell him into slavery, or that Pharoah's heart is hardened and he does not let the Israelites go).[19] In short, the fact that all the strategies rigorously rule that human evil actions are always merely allowed by God actually causes them to run afoul of Scripture, which seems to at least some of the time describe the bringing about of human evil actions as something that God *does*, not merely allows.

That may seem to spell the doom of the whole doing-allowing distinction altogether. However, if it does, it also spells the doom of this whole line of argument against Calvinism, since it would force us to admit that God does actively bring it about that humans do evil. Calvin himself rejected any distinction between God's acting and his permitting (especially permitting evil) on the basis of Scripture, but he intended it as a sweeping argument for Calvinist determinism.[20]

I prefer a different strategy altogether. The key is to remember that the whole point of the doing/allowing distinction in the first place is simply to highlight the metaphysical difference between God's actions and human actions. We can do that while discarding the doing/allowing language altogether, but I think there is a useful way to save that language. Instead of drawing a rigorous distinction between divine doing and divine allowing,

---

of drawing the metaphysical distinction between God's doing and God's allowing. See his "Excusing Sinners and Blaming God," chapter 10, section 2, part 8.

19. See also Deut 2:30 and Josh 11:19–20.
20. Calvin, *Institutes*, 1.18.

suppose we treat these terms differently. Start with the basic idea that God's action is radically different than human action, whether human doing *or* human allowing. Then notice that, though God's action is disanalogous in important ways to both human doing and human allowing, it is at the same time *analogous* to both human doing (in some ways) and human allowing (in other ways). If that is so, it can be appropriate to use the term "doing" when describing God's actions when we want to highlight the analogies between human doing and divine action (namely, that the agent is the source of the event) and appropriate to use the term "allowing" when we want to highlight the analogies between human allowing and divine action (namely, the possibility of a lack of blameworthy complicity in the event). "Doing" and "allowing" become context-sensitive ways of highlighting analogies rather than rigorous ways of picking out a metaphysically real distinction between two types of divine action.[21] This seems to me to be the best way to understand the doing/allowing distinction, and it supports the Reformed attempt to highlight a metaphysical disanalogy between God's mode of action and human modes of action in bringing it about that others do evil.

There almost certainly are other options for the Calvinist at this point.[22] I have said enough to show, though, that the Calvinist can point to disanalogies between divine sovereign action and human action which are relevant to the moral evaluation of acting so as to intentionally bring it about that another does evil. I haven't succeeded in refuting all possible ways of spelling out this charge, however. Whether the disanalogies I have pointed out count as morally relevant will depend on the moral assumptions involved in the argument, and I haven't considered all possible moral assumptions. However, I have outlined the raw material—moral disanalogies between God and man tied to divine rulership or sovereignty (and other divine attributes) and metaphysical disanalogies tied to divine power—that can be used to construct replies to a wide variety of versions of this charge.

There is at least one more Calvinist option for responding to this version of the "author of sin" argument, and that is to take the Augustinian

---

21. Anyone friendly to the Thomistic ideas of simplicity and analogy should find much to like about this strategy, though it can appeal even to those who don't like the Thomistic ideas.

22. A different metaphysical strategy that some Reformed thinkers have tried to develop is to use the notion of final causation rather than efficient causation to explain divine sovereignty. I'm unsure how to work this out, and so I won't try here. Yet another metaphysical strategy is Leibniz's, according to which each being has a complete concept which includes all of their actions, sinful or not. God only chooses which complete concepts to create—he couldn't prevent someone's sin except by choosing not to create that person. This strategy carries the very high metaphysical cost of saying that all of a person's actions and relations are essential to that person.

position described above. The Calvinist can claim that Adam and Eve had the sort of God-independent power of choice that libertarians think free will is, while still denying it of post-Fall humanity. This involves a denial of Calvinist determinism but retains Calvinist soteriology. This sort of Calvinist could accept the libertarian story described above about God's intentions with respect to sin.

2.2 The Second Charge: Calvinism Entails that God Desires that Evil Occur

A second version of the "author of sin" objection focuses on a different feature of the Calvinist story: God's *desires* with respect to evil. The argument goes like this: If Calvinism is true, then God desires that evil occur; but God does not desire that evil occur; therefore, Calvinism is not true. The second premise is supported by Scriptural evidence. The longstanding Calvinist response is to charge the argument with equivocation by drawing a distinction between two senses of "desire." There is a sense in which God desires that evil occur, in that he has ordained it to occur (God's will of decree, or decretive will), but there is another sense in which God does not desire that evil occur (his will of command or precept, or preceptive will), which means that Calvinism handles the Scriptural evidence. There are other names for the distinction: God's decretive will is sometimes called his sovereign will, his descriptive will, or (less felicitously, in my opinion) his hidden will, while his preceptive will is sometimes called his moral will, his prescriptive will, or (again, not felicitously) his revealed will.

This Calvinist claim that "there are two wills in God" is often accused of obscurity or outright contradiction. I will argue that this accusation is mistaken. In fact, the distinction between multiple senses of "desire" is a perfectly familiar phenomenon from ordinary life and makes perfectly good sense when applied to God.

Before I show this, though, I should note that there is good Biblical evidence that there are states of affairs which God desires in one sense and does not desire in another.[23] There are verses which make clear that God does not desire evil actions of any sort,[24] and yet there are particular examples of evil actions which God is said to have desired, intended, or willed.[25] Even with respect to the eternal loss of some human beings, there are verses which make clear that God does not desire that any be lost, oft-cited by critics of

23. Much of this evidence is collected in Piper, "Two Wills in God," 107–32.
24. Matt 7:21; Matt 12:50; 1 John 2:17.
25. Acts 4:27–28; Acts 2:23; Gen 50:20; Isa 53:4, 10; Rev 17:17.

Calvinism,[26] but at the same time there are verses which seem to ascribe to God precisely the desire denied him by those verses.[27] The most natural conclusion is that there is some important sense in which God does not desire these things and at the same time a sense in which he does desire them. Critics of Calvinism have sometimes focused only on the Biblical evidence about God's desires with respect to the lost and ignored the evidence about God's desires with respect to evil actions more generally, though the latter evidence supports the distinction between God's decretive and perceptive wills just as much as the former.

There really isn't anything particularly mysterious about these various senses of "desire"—we make precisely this distinction with ease in all sorts of ordinary situations. Here's one: suppose that Jeff and Georgia are the parents of five children. They love having children, and want to have another child. However, they don't believe that it would be responsible of them to have another child, because that would limit their ability to discharge their responsibilities (with respect to their time, their energy, or their money) to all of their children. They therefore decide not to have a sixth child. There is certainly a sense in which they do want to have another child. There is also a sense in which they do not want another child—because they see many of the negative consequences of having a child. Situations like this abound. There are perfectly ordinary senses of "desire" in which I can desire X (in one sense) and not desire X (in another sense) at the very same time.

What is really going on here? The example is enough to show that it is possible to desire something and not desire it at the same time, but it would be helpful to have a philosophical account of that. Here is one such account. Any rational being (including God) can have a constellation of goals, a whole host of states of affairs which are recognized as valuable and desired. Not every goal in that constellation need be compatible with every other goal, however. Human beings have many limitations which restrict which groups of goals are mutually achievable. God has very many fewer limitations, but he is still limited (if it is even right to describe it that way) by metaphysical possibility. When these limitations are recognized, the rational being must choose which of the goals to realize and which to leave unrealized. Suppose that Y is a goal of God's, something he desires, but that Y is incompatible with some other goal Z which God determines to be worth giving up Y in order to achieve. God can still truly be said to desire Y, but he can also truly be said to not desire Y in light of his desire for Z and

---

26. 1 Tim 2:4; 2 Pet 3:9; Ezek 18:23, 32.

27. 1 Sam 2:22–25; Deut 28:63. For an extended version of this argument, see Piper, "Two Wills in God," 107–32.

the incompatibility (which he recognizes) between Y and Z. God's decretive will is just the set of actions he ultimately decides on, all things considered. He (as any rational being) still retains many unsatisfied desires (in the non-decretive sense), and must choose to bring about (and therefore desire in the decretive sense) certain things he might truly be said *not* to desire (in the non-decretive sense), because they are necessary means to something he does desire (in the non-decretive sense).[28] God's preceptive will is some subset of his overall desires, including some desires which he chooses to satisfy and some which he does not. Presumably, conversational context can determine what sense of "desire" is being used. For instance, when a dictator is asked, "What do you want to do with the prisoner?" by his subordinates, he is being asked for his all-things-considered desire (his decretive will, as it were) because he is being asked for a decision; other contexts may make it clear that the expressed desire is not one the speaker ultimately would choose to satisfy.

The existence of a preceptive will in God which is not identical to his decretive will presupposes some limitation on God's part, but only the limitation that is necessary to solve the ordinary problem of evil—the limitations imposed by metaphysical possibility. It does not presuppose any distinctively human limitations like ignorance or weakness of will. In the above example, Jeff and Georgia may know perfectly well all of the negative consequences of having another child and not be sinfully tempted to have a child in the face of those consequences, but they may nevertheless still retain their desire to have another child. Similarly, God may know perfectly well all of the good things that come from allowing evil into the world and remain resolute in his decision to allow that evil while nevertheless retaining his desire that no evil ever come into his world.

It is a further question *which* subset of God's desires constitutes his preceptive will. It is not the entire set of God's desires, because not all of those are mutually compatible. Nor is it the subset of desires that ultimately gets satisfied, for that is his decretive will. How do we specify the relevant subset of desires that counts as the prescriptive will? My initial inclination is to resist the need to do so at all. Why think there is a unique subset of desires that makes up God's prescriptive will? For most purposes, it is sufficient to say that there is an important sense in which God does not desire the existence of any evil or the eternal death of any human being, and we can say this without committing to the existence of a unique prescriptive

28. This allows for the existence of certain emotions in God like sadness—which Calvin at least would be happy to admit and which Scripture strongly supports. Calvinism is certainly not committed to an impassive God, as some of the stereotypes of Calvinism would suggest.

will. The only reason I can think of to want a unique prescriptive will is if you think that God's prescriptive will is what determines human moral obligations—if, in other words, you espouse a divine will theory of moral obligation. A divine command theory has no such requirement but needs only the commands that God actually issues.[29] A divine will theorist, then, will need some way to identify a unique, consistent set of desires which determine moral obligation. Perhaps there is some way to do so; for my part, I take that to be a reason to prefer a divine command theory of moral obligation to a divine will theory.

The classical Reformed distinction between God's preceptive will and his decretive will is quite familiar from our ordinary course of experience. Moreover, it appears that libertarians need precisely this distinction in order to handle the ordinary problem of evil. Surely, from a libertarian perspective, God desires to ensure that no evil come into the world, a desire that conflicts with his desire to actualize beings who make free choices. He decides not to ensure that no evil come in—and so in a sense does *not* desire to ensure that no evil come in to his world.[30] The libertarian needs precisely the distinction that defuses this argument against Calvinism. This version of the "author of sin" charge therefore fails as an objection against Calvinism.

2.3 The Third Charge: Calvinism Entails that God Fails to Love the Lost

The third version of the "author of sin" problem focuses on yet another feature of the Calvinist story: God's love for the lost. It claims that Calvinism has God acting against the requirements of love. The argument has three premises:

(L1) God loves all people.

(L2) If God loves someone, then he will always seek that person's good.

---

29. This is why I said that it is not felicitous to call the decretive/prescriptive distinction a distinction between God's hidden will and his revealed will. The only way the latter terms capture the former distinction is if the term "revealed will" connotes divine commands rather than divine willings, and that is less than ideally precise. The decretive will of God is not obviously less accessible to us epistemically than is his preceptive will, given that there are many difficult moral questions and that everything that we know about what actually has happened, is happening, or will happen is knowledge of God's decretive will.

30. Notice that this is not the familiar distinction between antecedent and consequent will made by libertarians. This is a further distinction within the antecedent will of God. Edwards makes precisely this argument (that even non-Calvinist Christians need this distinction) in *Freedom of the Will*, part IV, section 9.

(L3) If Calvinism is true, then there are some whose good God does not seek.

It follows that Calvinism is false. This is the strongest, most emotionally and Scripturally powerful version of the "author of sin" problem. Divine love features at the very heart of the story of redemption, and the first premise at least initially seems powerfully supported by a number of passages in Scripture. Some Calvinists have tried to restrict many of those passages to the elect, and with respect to some of them they are surely correct; but it hard to deny that God bears at least some sort of love for all human beings.[31] I will therefore grant the first premise for the sake of argument, though it is important to be on our guard against equivocation—if the argument is to succeed against Calvinism, it must be that the sort of love that God bears toward all is the sort that Calvinism must deny that God bears toward all.

The argument therefore turns on the second and third premises. These premises might be formulated in a number of ways in order to get precisely that requirement of love that Calvinism has God violating, and I don't want to get hung up on that task. The burden of the objector is to get a requirement of love that is strong enough that premise 3 is true (that Calvinism has God failing that requirement) but still weak enough to be plausible. The most plausible requirements of love—for example, that love for a person requires one to desire that person's good—are too weak for premise 3 to be true, because the Calvinist can say that God does desire the good of those who are lost but some other great good outweighs that desire.

Now that we understand the burden of the objector, I will sketch the Calvinist response to the argument. First, there may be a kind of love which does carry with it strong requirements, requirements of the sort that would render the second and third premises true (Romans 8:28 suggests that there is). However, God may not bear *that* sort of love for everyone but may bear it only for his people (the elect), which is all Romans 8:28 says. In other words, the objector must argue that it is God's *general* love, his love for everyone, that carries with it requirements strong enough to render both the second and third premises true. Second, with this in mind, why should we think that God's general love carries such strong requirements? Perhaps all that is required by that general love is a very strong desire for the good of the beloved, but a desire that can be overridden when some other sufficiently great good can be achieved. Imagine a general of an army, whose son (whom he loves dearly) is a captain in the army. Suppose the general finds himself in a situation where he must sacrifice his son's company to save a large city with a civilian population. Could he do so and be consistent with the demands of

---

31. See Carson, *Difficult Doctrine*.

his love for his son? Clearly, he can, even though his actions are not in his son's best interest. Why not the same for God? He loves humans, but given some great good that can only be achieved by allowing some to be lost, why would his general love prevent him from doing so?

In order to argue that God's love would preclude him from allowing any to be lost, the critic would have to argue that there is no sufficiently great good that God could accomplish only by allowing some to be lost. But now this argument has collapsed into the ordinary problem of evil, and the problem of the lost is just one evil among many to be explained. The argument from love, therefore, collapses into the ordinary problem of evil, and Calvinists cannot reply to the argument from love only if they cannot reply to the ordinary argument from evil. I will argue in section 4 that the Calvinist has many plausible options to reply to the ordinary problem of evil.

I conclude that the "author of sin" problem, in all three of its forms, does not constitute a good objection to Calvinism. There are plausible responses to all three arguments. The first version, focusing on intentional action, requires a more powerful anti-Calvinist case regarding the morally relevant characteristics of divine action; the second version, focusing on desire, is simply refuted by the Reformed distinction between the divine preceptive and descriptive wills; and the third version, focusing on divine love, ultimately collapses into the ordinary problem of evil.

3. THE SECOND DISTINCTIVE CALVINIST PROBLEM WITH EVIL: THE PROBLEM OF THE FIRST SIN

The second distinctive problem posed by evil for Calvinism is the Problem of the First Sin, or the Problem of Sin in the Garden. The Calvinist view of responsibility and freedom is built for post-Fall humanity: human beings are born sinful, and their sinful actions follow from their sinful nature. It is not surprising that human beings are causally necessitated to sin, because they are born with a sinful nature. Pre-fall humanity—Adam and Eve—is a different story. Creation was good, and therefore so were Adam and Eve. Why did they sin? Were they necessitated to sin by their natures? If so, it looks like they must have been distorted in some way, which would seem to contradict the goodness of creation. If they were not necessitated to sin by their natures, though, then must it not be true that they were not necessitated to sin at all? Would it not then be true that they had something like what libertarians think is necessary for free will, the absolute metaphysical ability to act in alternative ways, independently of the control of God?

This problem is a bit difficult to make precise, and an argument against Calvinism derived from it may take a number of different paths. The first thing to note about the problem, though, is that it is mirrored by two problems for libertarians. First, libertarians have a hard time explaining the fact that all post-Fall humanity is and must be sinful. If responsible action requires the ability with respect to each action to avoid wrongdoing, then it must be that each person must be able to avoid wrongdoing with respect to each action they take, at least if they are responsible for those actions. If each person is able to avoid wrongdoing with respect to each of the actions for which they are responsible, then it must be that each person is able to avoid wrongdoing with respect to all of those actions together. But that is just to say that all of us are able to lead perfect lives, which seems blatantly contradicted by Scripture and the history of Christian theology.[32] Call this the Problem of Sin in a Fallen World. Second, libertarians have a hard time explaining the fact that glorified humanity is not and cannot be sinful. Surely the Christian hope involves inhabiting a place (we call it heaven) in which all sin is eliminated for eternity. But if free will is such a great good, we must have it there; and if it involves the ability to sin outside the control of God, then Christians must have the ability to sin in heaven. If heaven lasts for eternity, moreover, then sin must actually happen in heaven. Call this the Problem of Sin in Heaven.[33]

In short, Calvinists have a problem with explaining the *contingency* of Adam and Eve's sin, while libertarians have a problem with explaining the *necessity* of fallen humanity's sin and the *impossibility* of glorified humanity's sin. Nevertheless, the Problem of Sin in the Garden is still a problem for Calvinists, and one they should not shy away from. I'll suggest a few directions toward possible solutions to the problem.

One way to solve the problem, a way compatible with Edwards-style compatibilism, is simply to insist that a good (non-vicious) nature may, when combined with a specific circumstance, causally necessitate a sin. Causally necessitated blameworthy action need not reveal a blameworthy defect of character. The Calvinist who takes this strategy may still allow there to be much truth in the principle that undergirds the criticism—the principle that responsible, causally necessitated action reveals a defect of character. The Calvinist can agree that blameworthy, causally necessitated action reveals at least an immature, not fully developed character (as

32. For an extended version of this argument, see Johnson, "Libertarianism Entails Pelagianism."

33. Obviously, there have been many attempts to solve these problems from a libertarian perspective. My point is just that there are problems which parallel the Problem of the First Sin that faces Calvinists.

distinct from a blameworthy or vicious character)—Adam and Eve were not the fully mature saints that believers will be when glorified. The Calvinist may even agree that if one's nature necessitates one to sin in a wide range of circumstances, then one's nature must be blameworthy or vicious in some way—but still may insist that some specific circumstances may trigger a sin without requiring that one's nature be blameworthy or vicious. This strikes me as the most plausible solution to the problem of the first sin.

A second way to solve the problem, also compatible with Edwards-style compatibilism, is to deny that the goodness of creation means that Adam and Eve couldn't have developed distorted character traits before their first actual active sin. Perhaps Adam and Eve slowly developed a distortion in their character, a distortion they didn't have at the time of their creation, which explains their sinful action.

A third way to solve the problem is to embrace the Crabtree/McCann view and claim that Adam and Eve were not necessitated to sin by their natures and circumstances. Instead, they were determined to sin only by the transcendent causation of God, which is not responsibility-cancelling. This solves the problem rather nicely, which means that the Problem of Sin in the Garden seems to apply most powerfully against Edwards-style compatibilism.

A fourth way to solve the problem is to go with the Augustinian view and claim that Adam and Eve actually had the sort of power libertarians identify with free will, while fallen humanity and glorified humanity do not—they are necessitated, respectively, to sin and to act righteously. This Augustinian view therefore helps to solve both of the distinctive problems with evil that afflict Calvinism, and in fact it seems designed to solve the Problems of Sin in the Garden, in the Fallen World, and in Heaven (which may have been a big part of its motivation in the first place). In light of its usefulness, it may be worthwhile to revisit accounts of the relationship of moral responsibility to free will that fit with this view.

4. CALVINIST RESPONSES TO THE COMMON PROBLEM OF EVIL

The common problem of evil can be formulated thus: if God is all-good and all-powerful, whence evil? If God is all-good, it seems that he would do all within his power to prevent evil; and if he is all-powerful, he would succeed in his efforts to prevent evil. The normal response is to deny the first horn of the dilemma: it is true only that if God is all-good, then he would do all within his power to prevent evil, *unless* there is some greater good the achievement of which requires the existence of evil. Contemporary debate over the problem of evil is primarily an attempt to answer this question: are there such greater goods which necessitate the existence of evil?

Two interrelated distinctions have shaped the current debate, between *logical* and *evidential* forms of the problem of evil and between *theodicy* and *defense*. The logical problem of (or argument from) evil claims that God's nature (his goodness and his power) are metaphysically incompatible with evil, such that it is metaphysically *impossible* for God to coexist with evil. The evidential problem of (or argument from) evil claims merely that it is very *unlikely* that God would allow the evil that actually exists, such that our observation of such evil constitutes good evidence that God does not exist. The second distinction, between a theodicy and a defense, is a bit harder to pin down. A theodicy claims to show God's actual reason for allowing evil—the greater good which actually justifies God in allowing evil. A defense claims merely to show that God *could have* allowed evil, often by identifying a greater good that *could be* God's reason for allowing evil. The trouble with this distinction is that ambiguity of the modal claim in the characterization of a defense. The words "could have" are ambiguous between metaphysical possibility and epistemic possibility. There are actually four strategies for replying to the argument from evil, two each for the logical and evidential arguments:

1. Show that it is metaphysically possible for God to have a good reason for allowing evil. (First reply to the logical problem of evil.)

2. Show that *the evidence is not against* the view that it is metaphysically possible for God to have a good reason for allowing evil. (Second reply to the logical problem of evil.)

3. Show that God *actually* has a good reason for allowing evil. (First reply to the evidential problem of evil.)

4. Show that *the evidence is not against* the claim that God actually has a good reason for allowing evil. (Second reply to the evidential problem of evil.)

(3) is theodicy. It is harder to tell which of the other three options count as a defense. (2) and (4) are structurally parallel. Neither purports to show that God actually or possibly (in the metaphysical sense) has a good reason to allow evil. Instead, they claim to show that the objector *has insufficient reason* to think that God *doesn't* actually or possibly have a good reason to allow evil. This is enough to defeat either the logical or the evidential argument from evil, because it denies that there is evidence to support the premises

of the arguments. In other words, even the logical problem of evil is really about evidence, and the strategies laid out in (2) and (4) are attempts to deny the force of the evidence. Both (2) and (4) seem to count as defenses, then.

(1) is the strange one. It seems to be what Plantinga meant to accomplish with his Free Will Defense—he meant to decisively show that it is metaphysically possible that God coexist with evil, not merely that there is no reason to think that it is impossible that God coexist with evil. However, (1) is dialectically superfluous when it comes to defusing arguments from evil. (1) is insufficient to defuse the evidential argument from evil, and whatever strategy *is* sufficient for defusing the evidential argument (strategies (3) and (4)) renders (1) unnecessary for defusing the logical argument from evil. Here's why: suppose we identify a metaphysically possible good which necessitates evil. We may know beyond a shadow of a doubt that this metaphysically possible good is *not actual*, or that it does not justify allowing all the evils that we know to exist in the actual world. In that case, identifying the possible good hasn't done much to defuse the argument from evil, since there is a very natural switch to the evidential argument, and the original defense is useless against the evidential problem since we know that the identified good is not actual. What is more, (2) is weaker than (1) and still defuses the logical problem of evil, and accomplishing strategy (4), which is the weakest way to defuse the evidential problem of evil, entails accomplishing (2) but not (1). So achieving (4) is both necessary and sufficient for defusing the argument from evil, and (1) is superfluous.

I conclude that it is really (4) that is the desirable defense strategy, since it is the weakest claim which still defuses both arguments from evil. This is important for at least two reasons. First, we can follow van Inwagen in claiming that a *defense* is really all that is needed even for the evidential problem of evil.[34] The common belief that defenses are built only for the logical problem of evil is false. Second, this shows that even the logical problem of evil is about evidence—evidence for the claim that it is impossible that God coexist with evil. We can deny that there is good evidence for a claim without proving the claim false. This means that skeptical theism (and Rowe's Moore Switch) can be applied to the logical problem of evil as well as to the evidential problem of evil. Occasionally someone will claim that the Free Will Defense is needed for the logical problem of evil while skeptical theism (or the Moore Switch) is sufficient to meet only the evidential problem; this claim is false (I'll develop this more in a bit).

---

34. Inwagen, *Problem of Evil*.

With these distinctions in hand, we can move on to the main question. What handicaps does Calvinism face when attempting to answer the common problem of evil, and how might it overcome these handicaps? The only tool that Calvinism is missing is the ability to appeal to libertarian views of free will. Libertarian accounts of free will are only of use for explaining moral evil done by agents (and those natural evils which are results of moral evil). We should therefore focus on the subject of moral evil. I'll discuss three defenses that seem in the spirit of Calvinism, each of which may be individually sufficient to defuse arguments from evil and which complement one another: the Divine Glory Defense, the Mystery Defense (skeptical theism), and the Moore Switch. I'll conclude by mentioning a few other defenses that are compatible with Calvinism.

4.1 The Divine Glory Defense

If we are attempting to discern the reasons that God might have for allowing evil, it stands to reason that we should start by looking at the main reasons God has for doing any of the things he does. Over and over again, Scripture portrays God as seeking his own *glory*. It identifies divine glory as the motivating force behind all sorts of God's actions.[35] If this is God's primary motivation, or one of his primary motivations, for many of his actions, then we might expect it to be a primary motivation for his allowance of evil. We have some confirmation of that in the ninth chapter of Romans, a traditional focal point for biblical arguments for Calvinism, in which Paul also suggests that divine glory might provide an explanation for God's allowance of evil. Paul is discussing the very difficult problem (for him) of those Israelites who have not accepted the gospel of Christ, and makes this suggestion:

> What if God, choosing to show his wrath and make his power known, bore with great patience the objects of his wrath—prepared for destruction? What if he did this to make the riches of his glory known to the objects of his mercy, whom he prepared in advance for glory—even us, whom he also called, not only from the Jews but also from the Gentiles? (Rom 9:22–24 NIV)

The notion of glory is present in this passage not only when the word is explicitly used but also when it says that God chose to "show" and "make known" his wrath, power, and mercy.

---

35. For the best compilation and treatment of this evidence, see Edwards, *Dissertation*; especially part 2.

A development of the divine glory defense needs to show that divine glory has two features: first, that it is tremendously good, good enough to be worth allowing the moral evil in our world for its sake, and second, that it cannot exist without the evil that exists, or at least that certain kinds or amounts of glory cannot exist without the evil that exists. Showing that divine glory has these two features requires at least a basic understanding of the nature of glory. What is divine glory? As it turns out, this isn't an easy question to answer. Thomas Aquinas says that glory is a "manifestation of someone's goodness"[36] and so we might conclude that the glory of God is a manifestation of the goodness of God. This seems like a good start; glory seems to have something to do with the *display* or *manifestation* or *making known* of an excellence. The basic divine glory defense argues that there are certain excellences of God (justice and mercy, for example) that cannot be displayed or manifested in the creation unless there are evils to be punished or forgiven. God is *good*, and so the ways that he relates to evil reflect deep truths about his character. The existence of his character does not require the existence of evil (as in Manichaeism), but the *display* of that character in creation may very well require the existence of evil.

The details of this defense depend crucially on a clearer account of glory. What exactly is it for God's goodness to be "manifested" or "displayed"? Aquinas mainly regards the "manifestation" of goodness involved in glory as a kind of epistemic good, a mental state had by those who are appreciating and knowing the good thing. Jonathan Edwards, however, thinks that the response of appreciation is just one "moment," as he puts it, of the larger complex thing that is glory. Another "moment" of glory, another kind of "manifestation" of goodness, is the spectacular deed that constitutes a realization or expression of God's nature and character. A third "moment" of glory, a third thing to which the term glory can refer, is the excellence itself that is (and deserves to be) manifested in action and appreciated.[37] Edwards, in short, thinks that the term glory can represent a number of different perspectives on a complex phenomenon: the phenomenon of a spectacularly excellent being manifesting his excellence in spectacular actions and eliciting a (deserved) response of appreciation from observers. It

---

36. Aquinas, *On Evil*, 342.

37. Aquinas comes close to recognizing this as a distinct sort of glory; he says that "we also speak of glory in a third way insofar as one's goodness consists of reflecting on it, namely, insofar as one considers one's own goodness under the aspect of its clarity, as something to be manifested to, and admired by, many people" (Ibid, 342). So it seems that the excellence itself is properly called "glory" when regarded under the description "worthy of being manifested." This comes very close to Edwards' view, though Aquinas still leaves out the second sort of glory—the manifestation of goodness in the form of a deed expressing that goodness.

seems to me that Edwards' conception of glory makes the most sense of the Biblical evidence and of our ordinary conceptions of glory, but I'll leave the defense of his claim to him[38] and focus on one limitation: he never really says what logical relation each of the "moments" of glory have to the whole. Are they necessary but insufficient conditions, where you don't have glory until you have all of them? I prefer a different account, one which seems closer to how Edwards talks. It is right to identify each "moment" on its own as a kind of glory: an excellent being (even if that excellence is not manifest in action or widely known) is in a sense "glorious" and therefore has glory; spectacularly good actions expressing excellence constitute glory even if unknown; and appreciation is a sort of glory even if misplaced. But each moment calls out for the others: misplaced appreciation is a sort of glory, but a false sort, and appreciation is rightly directed only to genuinely spectacular beings and actions; spectacular excellence calls out for actions that express it; and spectacular beings and spectacular deeds deserve to be recognized and appreciated.

If something like this is right, then there are really two aspects to the divine glory that God seeks (since the sort of "glory" that simply refers to God's excellence itself cannot be increased or decreased by his actions): the excellent deeds that express excellences of God on the one hand, and the epistemic goods (knowledge, appreciation, understanding, acquaintance, and so on) associated with apprehending those excellent deeds on the other. It follows that there are two different (though possibly complementary) directions that a divine glory defense against the problem of evil might take, focusing on one or the other of these two aspects of glory.

The first direction for the divine glory defense focuses on the epistemic goods of knowing, appreciating, and becoming acquainted with the excellence of God. It seems obvious that knowledge of God and appreciation of God is tremendously good and valuable, if God really does exist. It may even be that such appreciation of and communion with God is in fact the chief end of human beings and the central component of what it is for a human being to flourish. The challenge for this version of the divine glory defense is the second feature that is needed to make the defense work: is evil, especially the amount and variety of evil that actually exists, necessary for these epistemic goods? Couldn't God have simply imparted the knowledge of himself to each creature, or just told them about himself, or perhaps sent them dreams that vividly show how he would respond to evil were there any? I think that the key to meeting this objection is to identify a variety of epistemic goods and argue that some of them—or some amount of some

---

38. Edwards, *Dissertation*.

of them—cannot be had without evil. It may be that bare propositional knowledge of God's various attributes might be had from God's testimony about himself, without any actual evil, but it may also be that there are other epistemic goods than propositional knowledge that cannot be had in such a way. Perhaps there is a kind of *acquaintance* with God's character that cannot be had without God actually expressing that character in response to real evil, and perhaps there is a kind of deep *understanding* of God that cannot be had without this sort of acquaintance. Something like this, I take it, is Christopher Green's strategy in his essay in this volume, when he argues that God's actual expressions of mercy and justice and so on in response to various kinds of evils furnish his creatures with *modes of presentation* of facts about God that are themselves epistemic goods, even if those very facts about God can be presented in other ways, ways not requiring the existence of evil.

The second direction for the divine glory defense—in my view, the more promising direction—focuses on the excellent deeds that express the excellences of God instead of on the epistemic goods of appreciating and knowing God's excellences.[39] These excellent deeds seem to have both of the features that make them good candidates to serve in a defense against the problem of evil. First, they are tremendously good—an activity expressing an excellence is itself excellent. In fact, this good (activity expressing excellence) has long been recognized as an important intrinsic good; Aristotle, and Aquinas following him, made it the centerpiece of his account of human flourishing. Of course, the good that humans realize when they act expressing an excellence is not exactly the same as the good that God realizes when he acts expressing an excellence; for example, if God is pure act (as Aquinas thinks) then it is not correct to say that his activity in his creation involves the actualization of potential, which is one of the ways in which Aristotle describes the human good of activity expressing excellence. However, God's activity expressing an excellence seems relevantly analogous to human activity expressing excellence, at least enough for us to be confident that it is in fact intrinsically good. Moreover, the goodness of an action expressing an excellence seems to be proportional to the greatness of the being whose excellence is being expressed. A human being's exercise of a rational power, for instance, is far greater than a grasshopper's exercise of its jumping ability. By extension, because God is unimaginably greater than human beings are, so too is the expression of his excellence unimaginably greater than the

---

39. This second form of the divine glory defense turns out to be a version of what Daniel Howard-Snyder calls the "higher-order goods defense," but focuses on the expression of divine characteristics rather than human characteristics. Howard-Snyder, "Theodicy," 324–39.

expression of human excellences. In fact, if God is far and away the best thing in existence, far greater even than the sum total of everything else that exists, it doesn't seem like much of a stretch to say that actions by God that express his character may well be the very best states of affairs that could exist other than the existence of God himself. So this aspect of divine glory does seem to be tremendously good, the sort of thing that could outweigh the badness of evil.[40]

Second, certain of these actions expressing divine excellences do in fact require evil. To give examples inspired by the above Romans passage: God cannot express his mercy and forgiveness without sin to forgive and undeserving sinners to whom mercy can be shown, and God cannot express his justice by punishing wrongdoers without wrongdoing to punish. There are a number of aspects of God's character that cannot be expressed by God's actions in creation unless there are various kinds of evil present in creation. Alvin Plantinga's "O Felix Culpa" defense points out the most important of God's self-expressive actions that couldn't happen without evil: the unimaginably great goods of incarnation and atonement, which express God's mercy and love and many other excellent character traits.[41] Plantinga's defense, then, is a version of the divine glory defense (though he never mentions glory explicitly), which shouldn't come as a surprise, given the fact that he identifies his defense as a version of supralapsarianism and the fact that, historically, the major motive for supralapsarianism was to preserve the claim that God ordained sin and evil for his own glory. The astonishingly great goods of incarnation and atonement, however, don't exhaust the self-expressive actions of God that might explain evil; the Romans passage mentions the expression of God's justice and wrath through his punishment of evildoers. This is less comfortable, but it may well be an important part of the explanation of why God allows the specific kinds and amounts of evil that he does. And though it may be uncomfortable, it doesn't seem implausible: human acts expressing justice are intrinsically good, and so divine acts expressing perfect justice are also intrinsically good, and unimaginably greater than any human action. If they are that good, then it is plausible that they would make the evil that enables them to happen worth the cost.

---

40. I will confess that the good of divine glory often does not seem good enough to me to outweigh the evils in this world. But the fact that the good of glory is proportional to the greatness of the being whose glory it is makes me think that I fail to appreciate the good of God's glory because I fail to appreciate *God*. So the problem is with me rather than with the defense itself. I am unable to properly appreciate the greatness of God and therefore also the deeds of God.

41. Incarnation could happen without evil, but atonement could not, and so incarnation in a world without evil would have a very different character.

Many of the objections to this sort of defense amount to version of the "author of sin" objection, to which I will not return.[42] One objection is worth mentioning, though, because the reply illuminates an important feature of divine glory. The objection is that this defense seems to portray God as using human beings as mere means to his own ends rather than as ends in themselves. Let us suppose that God does love at least the elect (his people) with the sort of love that requires him to treat them as ends in themselves rather than as mere means to his own ends.[43] Is this incompatible with the claim that he ultimately seeks his own glory with all his actions? I don't believe so. Treating someone as an end requires seeking what is good for them. The greatest good for human beings is surely communion with God—presence with and knowledge of God. So if God seeks as an end to bring human beings to presence with and knowledge of himself, then he seeks their good as an end. But consider again the nature of glory—divine glory is a *display* of God. What is a human's communion with God but a display of God to that human? Therefore, when God seeks the greatest good for human beings, he thereby seeks his glory. They aren't really different things at all. The greatest human good (communion with God) is not a means to God's glory but is partially *constitutive* of God's glory. Therefore, it is possible for God to seek his glory in all things and still treat the elect as ends in themselves. Edwards is strikingly insistent on this point: he forcefully denies that God uses his people as a means to his glory, because the flourishing of his people partially constitutes his glory.[44]

I conclude that the divine glory defense is quite promising, and it explains many of the same classes of evil that the free will defense is thought to explain. The divine glory defense is of course also available at least to the Molinist (as Plantinga's use of it makes clear) and perhaps also to those with other views, but its presence helps significantly to mitigate the loss of the free will defense by the Calvinist.

---

42. For instance, the "Munchausen-by-proxy" objection that Plantinga discusses seems to me a combination of the first and third versions of the "author of sin" objection—which helps to show that both objections apply to Molinism as much as to Calvinism, because Plantinga is writing from a Molinist perspective.

43. Clearly, God does allow some to come to grief in order to achieve a greater good, and so treats the lost as a means to a further end. The question is whether love requires that God not do that—the love objection again. I have argued that love does not require that we never treat someone as a means to an end.

44. This insistence is found all over the place in Edwards, *Dissertation*.

4.2 The Mystery Defense—Skeptical Theism

Suppose we creatures cannot discern any reason that seems to us adequate to justify God in allowing the evils we in fact do see. Does it follow that the existence of such evils constitutes evidence against the existence of God? Not necessarily, for why would we *expect* to be able to discern God's reasons for allowing evil? God is transcendent and incomprehensible, the source of all being and goodness, the foundation of the cosmos, and his mind encompasses all truth and all possibility. We are small, inadequate, finite minds, and our comprehension of the world is laughable compared to God's. It should not surprise us if we cannot understand God's reasons for acting as he does, and in particular, his reasons for allowing the evils that exist. Our role as creatures is to worship, not to demand explanations.

This observation forms the heart of the Mystery Defense, which in the contemporary conversation has come to be known as "skeptical theism." This defense has received the attention of the very best Christian philosophers and has benefitted by a great amount of sophisticated epistemological development, which I cannot hope to canvass here.[45] The sentiment behind skeptical theism resonates strongly with Reformed theology, with its emphasis on the Creator/creature distinction (which has played a significant role already in discussion of the "author of sin" problem and the Divine Glory Defense). Also, the Reformed have generally been quick to note that mystery is a major theme of some of the Bible's most sustained discussions of evil—Job and Ecclesiastes, in particular, are saturated with it. So the Mystery Defense is precisely the kind of defense the Calvinist would be attracted to, and many Calvinists have been attracted to it over the centuries.

Some in the contemporary discussion think of skeptical theism as a reply to the evidential problem of evil but not to the logical problem of evil, for which the Free Will Defense is thought to be necessary. My reflections earlier, as to the nature of a defense, have shown this to be a mistake. If the Mystery Defense succeeds as a defense against the evidential argument from evil (by showing that, for all our evidence shows, God actually has a good reason for allowing the evil that exists), then it also succeeds as a defense against the logical argument from evil (by showing that, for all our evidence shows, it is metaphysically possible for God to have a good reason for allowing evil). If anything, our grasp of *what could be* probably falls even farther short of God's than does our grasp of *what actually is*. Suppose I cannot even perceive any *metaphysically possible* reason for God to allow evil. I still should not conclude that there is no such reason, because it is not

---

45. For a summary of the discussion, see Dougherty, "Skeptical Theism."

the case that I should expect to see such a reason if there is one. The Mystery Defense is therefore at least as effective against the logical argument from evil as it is against the evidential argument.

The Mystery Defense, therefore, if it is effective, renders the Free Will Defense unnecessary. This is particularly important for the dialectic between Calvinists and libertarians, since many libertarian theists themselves think that the Mystery Defense is necessary to reply to the evidential argument from evil. Though they are willing to say that libertarian free will is a metaphysically possible reason for God to allow evil, many are unwilling to say that such free will is actually the reason God has allowed the evils we see in our world—perhaps because it does not seem good enough to justify allowing the really horrific moral evils we have seen, or because it is of no use in explaining some of the natural evils that have occurred. Whatever their reason for thinking the Free Will Defense inadequate to meet the evidential argument from evil, many libertarians have thought the Mystery Defense necessary.[46] The Calvinist can agree with them—and point out that this renders the Free Will Defense unnecessary. This situation undercuts in a powerful way the argument that Calvinism does not have adequate resources for meeting the common problem of evil because of its rejection of libertarian accounts of free will.

4.3 The Moore Switch

Suppose that the Divine Glory Defense is completely unconvincing and that the Mystery Defense proves hard to swallow. Suppose that it really seems to you that it *is* surprising that you can't figure out why God would allow the evil he does, so that the fact that you can't tell the reason that God would have for doing so does constitute evidence against his existence. That is, suppose you decide that, in the absence of all other information, the existence of evil would lead you to think that there is no God.

It doesn't follow that you should give up believing in God. After all, the evidence you get from the fact that you can't tell what reason God would have for allowing evil is just one small part of your total evidence, and it can be overwhelmed by other kinds of evidence. Suppose you also think that there wouldn't be any such thing as good *or* evil if there were no God; in that case, the existence of evil also gives you evidence that there is a God. In fact, your evidence for the existence of God may be strong enough that the right way to react to your inability to figure out God's reasons for allowing

---

46. For an example, see Howard-Snyder, "Theodicy," 324–39.

evil isn't disbelief in God at all, but belief that God *must* have a good reason and just hasn't seen fit to share it with you.

This move is what William Rowe called the "Moore Switch" in his original paper on the evidential problem of evil.[47] Even if, abstracted away from everything else you know, the existence of evil would count against belief in God, it may *not* count against belief in God when it is combined with everything else you know. In other words, the evidence provided by your inability to discern God's reasons for allowing evil can be outweighed by other evidence, and can support many different conclusions depending on what evidence it is combined with. Now, Rowe applied this observation only to the evidential problem of evil, but my earlier reflections as to the nature of the logical problem of evil shows that it can be applied to the logical problem as well—because the strength of the logical problem depends on the *evidence* for its premises, particularly the premise that it there is no metaphysically possible reason for God to allow evil. Suppose you cannot discern a metaphysically possible reason for God to allow evil, and it really seems to you that this would be surprising if God existed. That is, you decide that even the possible existence of evil constitutes evidence against the existence of God. Other evidence may yet overwhelm this evidence, and lead you instead to think that God does exist and that there *must* be a metaphysically possible reason for God to allow evil, even though you can't figure out what it is. The Moore Switch, then, can be performed on the logical problem of evil as well as on the evidential problem of evil.

What all this shows is that a good offense is a good defense—that is, even in the absence of a way to undercut the argument from evil, the conclusion of the argument can still be rejected if enough evidence is amassed for the existence of God to outweigh the evidence advanced against the existence of God. Reformed epistemologists can insist that everyone knows God (by the sense of deity) and that Christians know Christ and Scripture by the internal testimony of the Holy Spirit, and argue that this massively overwhelms any evidence to the contrary provided by our inability to discern God's reasons for allowing evil. This evidence for the existence of God may even be so strong that it would be misleading to say that our inability to discern God's reasons gives evidence against his existence, since that is the case only if that evidence is isolated from all our other evidence—it would be less misleading to say that our inability to discern God's reasons just gives us evidence for thinking that he has a reason that he hasn't decided to share with us. Reformed epistemology, therefore, should count as an important

---

47. Rowe, "Varieties of Atheism," 335–41.

distinct Reformed reply to the problem of evil by virtue of strengthening the Moore Switch.

This strategy can be combined with the previous two defenses, and in fact the Mystery Defense can be taken in degrees. It may be that you don't want to go all the way with the Mystery Defense and say that it isn't surprising at all that we can't discern God's reasons for allowing evil, but you may still want to acknowledge much of the force of that defense and say that it is only a little bit surprising that we can't. If it is only a little bit surprising, then the evidence we get against the existence of God is easily overcome by contrary evidence.

4.4 Other Defenses

The defenses I have outlined really are just featured parts of larger defenses, since there are many other goods which can and probably do enter into the explanation of God's allowance of evil. For instance, one important good that almost certainly features in the correct explanation is the good of a universe with regularity and predictability, with law-governed processes. This great good is a precondition of morally significant lives, of rationality, of beauty, and of many other good things, and if this is one of God's goals, it significantly restricts his options with respect to preventing evil.[48] There are probably many other preconditions of morally significant lives which could enter into explanations of God's allowance of evil. The libertarian version of the free will defense is the most famous of these kinds of defenses, but there are others that are friendlier to Calvinism. One example is Hugh McCann's recent Calvinist-friendly free will defense, according to which the presence of real evil in life is necessary if genuine choices are to be made between good and evil.[49] Another, more famous example is the soul-making defense, traceable to Irenaeus and popularized by John Hick.[50] The key claim of the soul-making defense, that character traits which are developed through hard choices made during trial and tribulation are intrinsically better than comparable character traits created directly by God, is available to the compatibilist just as much as it is to the libertarian.

All this goes to show that it is far from obvious that libertarian free will is essential to a satisfying response to the common problem of evil. The

---

48. This sort of defense is usually identified with Leibniz; Peter van Inwagen incorporates it into his defense in "Problem of Silence," 135–65.

49. McCann, "Author of Sin," 144–59.

50. Hick, *God of Love*.

Calvinist's resources for replying to that problem are not decisively reduced by the loss of the traditional free will defense.

5. WHY CARE? THE ADVANTAGES OF CALVINISM

It may be helpful to outline some of the advantages of Calvinism, as a reminder of why we should care about whether Calvinism can meet the problems of evil we have been discussing.

The first and foremost advantage of Calvinism is its conformity with Biblical evidence. Romans 9 remains a powerful source for arguments in favor of Calvinism, and many other passages and themes in Scripture lend themselves to Calvinistic interpretations. There is a formidable body of work making this point done by Reformed theologians and biblical exegetes since the Reformation (including Calvin, Turretin, Owen, and Bavinck, to mention just a few).

A second advantage of Calvinism, which is really an extension of the first, is its ability to cope with the Problem of Sin in a Fallen World and the Problem of Sin in Heaven. As I said earlier, just as Calvinists have trouble explaining the contingency of Adam's sin, libertarians have trouble explaining the inevitability of sin after the Fall and the impossibility of sin in heaven. The more inevitable sin seems to fallen human beings—and there are Scriptural passages which seem to teach nearly straightforwardly a Calvinist degree of inevitability—the harder it is for libertarians to explain. Likewise, the impossibility of sin in heaven has caused much concern among advocates of the Free Will Defense.

A third advantage of Calvinism, one that early and mid-20th century Calvinists made much of (Warfield, Van Til, Packer), is its ability to explain the compatibility of divine inspiration and human authorship in Scripture. There is a tension between the two only if God's total control over human action is incompatible with genuine human free agency. If, as the Calvinist asserts, divine control and human free agency are perfectly compatible, then the apparent tension more or less dissolves.

A fourth advantage of Calvinism is its ability to explain the compatibility of freedom with divine foreknowledge. Freedom is compatible with divine foreknowledge, says the Calvinist, because freedom is compatible with divine foreordination. The apparent incompatibility between divine foreknowledge and human freedom has driven many libertarians to open theism over the last century. Calvinism is far more in the mainstream of traditional orthodox Christianity and traditional theism in general than is open theism, and so whatever force the foreknowledge argument has should support Calvinism.

A fifth advantage of Calvinism, even if the foreknowledge argument does not succeed, is its powerful and streamlined account of divine providence. Open theism is a very weak account of providence, but simple foreknowledge views really aren't any stronger as an account of providence, because according to simple foreknowledge views God cannot *use* any of his foreknowledge in deciding what to do on pain of explanatory circularity. The best (perhaps only) candidate for a strong libertarian account of providence is Molinism, but Molinism is afflicted with problems attaching to its key notion of a counterfactual of creaturely freedom. Moreover, Molinism may very well make God the "author of sin" in the same sense that Calvinism does, and so may be missing some of the features that libertarian opponents of Calvinism might find essential in a view of providence. Given Molinism's problems and the weakness of the doctrines of providence that are supported by simple foreknowledge and open theist views, Calvinist determinism looks quite attractive by comparison.

Finally, those who are convinced by philosophical arguments for compatibilism about free will may find Calvinist determinism quite attractive, or at least the rejection of competing libertarian accounts of free will. This is only an advantage for some, of course; others will find arguments for compatibilism severely lacking. There are other advantages of Calvinism, but I have canvassed some of the most significant. In light of Calvinism's advantages, the discussion of its most serious difficulty—the relationship it posits between God and evil—becomes all the more significant.

BIBLIOGRAPHY

Aquinas, Thomas. *On Evil*. Edited by Brian Davies, translated by Richard Regan. Oxford: Oxford University Press, 2003.

Bignon, Guillaume. "Excusing Sinners and Blaming God: A Calvinist Assessment of Determinism, Moral Responsibility, and Divine Involvement in Evil." PhD diss., Middlesex University and London School of Theology, 2015.

Carson, D. A. *The Difficult Doctrine of the Love of God*. Wheaton, IL: Crossway, 2000.

Clark, Gordon. *Religion, Reason, and Revelation*. 2nd ed. Hobbs, NM: Trinity Foundation, 1995.

Crabtree, J. A. *The Most Real Being: A Biblical and Philosophical Defense of Divine Determinism*. Eugene, OR: Gutenberg College Press, 2004.

Dougherty, Trent. "Skeptical Theism." In *Stanford Encyclopedia of Philosophy*, edited by Edward N. Zalta. Last modified January 29, 2014. http://plato.stanford.edu/entries/skeptical-theism/.

Edwards, Jonathan. *A Dissertation Concerning the End for Which God Created the World*. In *Works of Jonathan Edwards*, vol. 1, edited by Paul Ramsey. New Haven, CT: Yale University Press, 2009.

———. *Freedom of the Will*. In *Works of Jonathan Edwards*, vol. 1, edited by Paul Ramsey. New Haven, CT: Yale University Press, 2009.

Hick, John. *Evil and the God of Love*. 2nd ed. New York: HarperCollins, 1977.

Howard-Snyder, Daniel. "Theodicy." In *Readings in the Philosophy of Religion*, edited by Kelly James Clark, 324–39. 2nd ed. Buffalo, NY: Broadview, 2008.

Johnson, Daniel M. "Libertarianism Entails Pelagianism." Unpublished manuscript.

Johnson, Robert Aaron. "Review of The Most Real Being: A Biblical and Philosophical Defense of Divine Determinism." *Faith and Philosophy* 25, no. 1 (2008) 109–12.

McCann, Hugh J. "The Author of Sin?" *Faith and Philosophy* 22, no. 2 (2005) 144–59.

———. "Divine Sovereignty and the Freedom of the Will." *Faith and Philosophy* 12 (1995) 582–98.

———. "Edwards on Free Will." In *Jonathan Edwards: Philosophical Theologian*, edited by Paul Helm and Oliver Crisp, 27–43. Burlington, VT: Ashgate, 2003.

Newlands, Samuel. "The Problem of Evil." In *Routledge Companion to Seventeenth Century Philosophy*, edited by Dan Kaufman. Abingdon, UK: Routledge, forthcoming.

Pereboom, Derk. "Theism and Libertarian Free Will." Paper presented at the Annual Meeting of the Central American Philosophical Association, Chicago, IL, February 17–20, 2010.

Piper, John. "Are There Two Wills in God?" In *Still Sovereign: Contemporary Perspectives on Election, Foreknowledge, and Grace*, edited by Thomas Schreiner and Bruce Ware, 107–32. Grand Rapids, MI: Baker, 2000.

Rowe, William. "The Problem of Evil and Some Varieties of Atheism." *American Philosophical Quarterly* 16, no. 4 (1979) 335–41.

Van Inwagen, Peter. *The Problem of Evil*. Oxford: Oxford University Press, 2008.

———. "The Problem of Evil, the Problem of Air, and the Problem of Silence." *Philosophical Perspectives* 5 (1991) 135–65.

2

Molinist Gunslingers
God and the Authorship of Sin

—Greg Welty

Molinists often claim that their view of divine providence is preferable to a classical Calvinist view, because Calvinism makes God the author of sin whereas Molinism does not. For instance, in his recent book, *Salvation and Sovereignty: A Molinist Approach*, Ken Keathley asserts that Calvinism is subject to a dilemma to which Molinism is not subject, namely, "adhering to a deterministic view of sovereignty without blaming God for the fall of Adam."[1] On Molinism, God "is perfectly free from the sin and evil of this world,"[2] and "God is not the author of sin,"[3] but on Calvinism God is not perfectly free from sin and evil, and he is the author of sin.

To these charges, Calvinists have standard replies ready at hand. For instance, in part IV, section 9 of *The Freedom of the Will*, Jonathan Edwards distinguishes between two different senses of the phrase "author of sin," such that God is the author of sin in one sense, but not in the other. According to Edwards, God is not the author of sin in the sense that God himself is—with respect to any specific sin—"the Sinner, the Agent, or Actor of Sin, or the Doer of a wicked thing." So if by "author of sin" we mean that God is the *doer* of evil, the agent who actually performs the sinful act and with

---

1. Keathley, *Salvation and Sovereignty*, 4.
2. Ibid., 19.
3. Ibid., 25.

wicked intentions, then no, God is not the author of sin. Edwards says "it would be a reproach and blasphemy, to suppose God to be the Author of Sin" in that sense. It "is infinitely to be abhorred." But according to Edwards, God is the author of sin in the sense that he ordained the existence of sin. He is "the Disposer and Orderer of Sin." He is "a disposer of the state of events, in such a manner, for wise, holy, and most excellent ends and purposes, that Sin . . . will most certainly and infallibly follow." So if by "author of sin" we mean "one who ordains that moral evil shall in fact occur," then yes (says Edwards), that appears to be the repeated teaching of Scripture. But since God is not the author of sin in the first sense, he has no moral culpability or blame in the matter.[4]

Unfortunately, this distinction is not going to do it for the Molinist critic of Calvinism. The Molinist already believes that God ordains whatsoever comes to pass, and this includes ordaining that acts of moral evil come to pass. As Keathley puts it, "Of course, God is the ultimate cause of all that exists."[5] What bothers the Molinist is that, on Calvinism, God seems to be the *sufficient* cause for various acts of sin that occur in his universe, and this means that God is *responsible*—morally responsible—for every sin that occurs. In addition, given this sufficient causation in Calvinism it's hard to deny that God is *culpable* for the sin that occurs; he is not only responsible but blameworthy. In short, the Molinist will insist that the *way* that God ordains sin on Calvinism is by way of causal determinism, which implies that God is the sufficient cause of sin, which implies that God is a sinner, with all the responsibility and culpability that that entails. Whereas on Molinism, all of this is avoided.

What I intend to argue is that Molinists may be making two mistakes when they adjudicate this particular dispute in favor of Molinism. First, by imputing to Calvinists the thesis that God governs his universe by way of strict causal determinism, many Molinists may be overlooking the apophatic character of Reformed definitions of divine providence, as these are enshrined in historically Reformed confessions of faith. For Calvinists, these negative formulations are not a defect but a feature; they are there by design. Second, even if Molinists are correct in thinking that Calvinism must make God the sufficient cause of sin, such that he is its author and blameworthy for it, Molinists' own model of divine causation is *sufficiently analogous* to sufficient causation, such that Molinism inherits all of the alleged Calvinist liabilities anyway, with respect to divine authorship of sin, responsibility, and blame. You might say that the first mistake is finding in

4. Edwards, *Works of Jonathan Edwards*, 399.
5. Keathley, *Salvation and Sovereignty*, 139.

Calvinism something that may not be there; the other mistake is failing to find in Molinism something that may in fact be there.

CALVINISM AND CAUSAL DETERMINISM: APOPHATIC DEFINITIONS OF THE DECREE

Concerning this first point, in his essay "Of God's Eternal Decree," Paul Helm provides extended commentary on the following definition of divine foreordination, found in the *Westminster Confession of Faith* III.1 (also found, near verbatim, in the parallel paragraph in the 1689 London Baptist Confession of Faith):

> God from all eternity, did, by the most wise and holy counsel of His own will, freely, and unchangeably ordain whatsoever comes to pass; yet so, as thereby neither is God the author of sin, nor is violence offered to the will of the creatures; nor is the liberty or contingency of second causes taken away, but rather established.

Helm points out that this definition consists of a positive claim ("God from all eternity, did, by the most wise and holy counsel of His own will, freely, and unchangeably ordain whatsoever comes to pass") that is followed by a series of negative claims, "three significant denials," or what B. B. Warfield called "protecting clauses": (i) "neither is God the author of sin," (ii) "nor is violence offered to the will of the creatures," (iii) "nor is the liberty or contingency of second causes taken away . . ."[6] On Helm's view, "there is no attempt to explain why there is the decree, nor (in particular) to explain how it is that although God decrees all that comes to pass, yet no violence is done to the will of the creature, nor are liberty and contingency taken away, but are rather established."[7] There is no explanation of how the positive claim can be true in light of the negative claims; no detailed model or mechanism is provided that would illuminate for us their interrelations. This seems exactly right. The attempt to construct such a detailed model is not forbidden, but the authors, signers, and adopters of this confession do not grant such models the status of Reformed confessional consensus.

Helm continues: "In this sense, the structure of the wording of the decree is a piece of negative theology. The logical structure of this part of the chapter, the prominence of 'yet so . . . neither . . . nor . . . nor' is similar

---

6. Helm, "Of God's Eternal Decree," 147.
7. Ibid., 143–44.

to that of the Chalcedon definition's 'withouts.'"[8] Again, this seems exactly right. Chalcedon does not attempt to penetrate into the mystery of the hypostatic union, such that we can see *how it is* that Christ is one Person with two natures. It simply states this, and then protects the positive claim by a series of protecting clauses: "without division, without separation, without conversion, without confusion." So the Westminster definition of the decree is a cop-out, I suppose, only if the Chalcedonian definition is.

Given this apophatic definition of the decree, the confessional authors leave it a mystery why (for instance) if God ordains everything that comes to pass, and if human sin comes to pass, God is not responsible or culpable for those sins. It doesn't explain how, in light of God's comprehensive decree, the liberty or contingency of second causes are not taken away. How does God as primary cause of what occurs relate to all of the created, responsible secondary causes? My only point here is that the thesis of universal causal determinism, or divine sufficient causality of sin, is not in play here; it is simply not to be found. (As Helm points out, "it is crude and misleading to assimilate the working of the divine decree to intramundane models of causation, and particularly to general physical determinism.")[9] But *without* the notion of causal determinism or divine sufficient causality, this definition of the decree does not make God the author of sin in the first, objectionable sense ("the Sinner, the Agent, or Actor of Sin, or the Doer of a wicked thing"), though it allows for God being the author of sin in the second, unobjectionable sense (God ordains that moral evil shall in fact occur).

It is important not to lump all Calvinists into the same category. There are the "mysterian" Calvinists who rest content with apophatic formulations, in the grand historical tradition of Chalcedon. It's not clear *they* make God the author of sin in any objectionable sense. And then there are the "creative" Calvinists (the "industrious" Calvinists?) who supplement or "fill out" the confession's teaching on the decree with the thesis of universal causal determinism, and perhaps even occasionalism. If they are subject to critique, so be it, but we need to be clear just who is saying what, rather than claiming that Calvinists—as a group—eschew mystery and apophasis in favor of causal determinism, divine causal sufficiency, and so on.[10]

---

8. Ibid., 144.

9. Ibid., 154.

10. I return to these themes of paradox, inscrutability, *sui generis* divine causation, and apophasis in my conclusion at the end of this chapter.

MOLINISM SUFFICIENTLY ANALOGOUS TO SUFFICIENT CAUSATION, FOR ALL MORAL INTENTS AND PURPOSES

Secondly—and here I embark on a much longer point—let's assume that everything I just said is wrong, or at least inadequate to deflect the concern. Let's assume for the sake of argument that Molinists are right in their views of what Calvinists must believe if their characteristic claims about divine providence (both positive and negative) are to "make sense." Let's say that Calvinism *must* make God the sufficient cause of sin, such that his decree just is a divine activity that guarantees that sin comes to pass, and so he is its author in an objectionable sense. What I want to argue is a simple case of modus ponens:

1. If divine causation in Molinist providence is *sufficiently analogous* to sufficient causation, then Molinism inherits all of the Calvinist liabilities anyway, with respect to divine authorship of sin, responsibility, and blame.

2. Molinist providence *is* sufficiently analogous to sufficient causation.

And so it follows that:

3. Molinism *does* inherit any Calvinist liabilities with respect to divine authorship of sin, responsibility, and blame.

Thus, given our ordinary intuitions about cases involving sufficient causation and moral responsibility, Molinism makes God the author of sin (in the objectionable sense) if Calvinism does. My strategy will be to elicit our ordinary moral intuitions in a range of relevant cases, such that my minor premise is adequately supported: Molinist providence is sufficiently analogous to sufficient causation for all moral intents and purposes. I start with the "ordinary gun" case.

THE "ORDINARY GUN" CASE

What I call the "ordinary gun" case is described as follows: I pull a gun out of my pocket, aim it at a person at point-blank range, and pull the trigger. I have in fact murdered him, and I bear moral responsibility for murdering him. I am the author of this sin, because it was 'up to me' how I used my libertarian free will in this case. I could have refrained from pulling the trigger. No one coerced me into pulling the trigger. I pulled the trigger knowing that this gun was in good working order, and knowing what ordinarily happens when you pull triggers on working guns at point-blank range. Knowing all this, I am responsible not just for the fact that I pulled the trigger, but that the man died as a result. And it doesn't matter if my intention in killing him was to bring about a further effect (such as my winning the New York City Marathon). I'm still responsible for killing him.

Our metaphysical and moral intuitions here seem clear: I am the author of this sin, and I bear moral responsibility for bringing about the man's death. Let's review six aspects of the "ordinary gun" case. *First, I actualize a set of circumstances* in which something else happens. That is, *I pull the trigger.* Pulling the trigger brings about a real effect in the world: it releases a spring-loaded hammer in the gun, which hits the explosive cap (the primer) at the rear of the bullet, which explodes, igniting the gunpowder (the propellant) in the bullet, which creates gas pressure that sends the bullet down the barrel of the gun at high speed towards its target.

Second, my action of actualizing a set of circumstances *is not (by itself) sufficient for the outcome*: the death of the person I'm aiming at. Imagine that I pull the trigger in an environment where laws of nature pertaining to momentum, or friction, or inertia, or explosions, or gas pressure, or conservation of mass-energy, or even gravity, do not obtain. It's pretty clear that in the absence of these laws of nature, not much of anything will occur beyond my actualizing the initial set of circumstances. You might say that my actualization of circumstances would be impotent, apart from the laws of nature. To give another illustration: if I release a pen in this room, it will fall to the ground, but if I release the same pen in zero-gravity, it will float. What makes the difference here is not what I do, but the environment in which I actualize the circumstances. Merely releasing the pen is not (by itself) sufficient for the intended outcome.

Third, in order to kill the man with my gun, *I am relying upon laws of nature which are only contingently the case.* None of our well-confirmed physical theories give us any indication that the laws of nature are logically necessary. We can certainly imagine the force of gravity being stronger or weaker than it actually is, either because the gravitational constant is different, or the exponent in the denominator of the law is different (e.g., rather than $F = G\ m_1 m_2 / r^2$, we have $F = G\ m_1 m_2 / r^3$ or $F = G\ m_1 m_2 / r^{1.5}$). Additionally, as theists it seems quite plausible that *God* could have made different laws of nature obtain; they are contingent in virtue of being (quite literally) contingent on the will of God. Advocates of the argument for God from the fine-tuning of the laws of nature have produced plausible defenses of the contingency of these laws.

Of course, there are various philosophical accounts of laws of nature on offer. Perhaps the laws are separate from the objects they govern, being a contingent tie between universals that then get instantiated in particulars (i.e., David Armstrong or Michael Tooley). Or perhaps the laws are constitutive of objects, such that the law of gravity is understood in terms of substances having particular powers and having liabilities to exercise those powers, which is the view of laws of nature presupposed by Richard Swinburne throughout his book *The Existence of God*, a view which "was the way familiar to the ancient and medieval world, before talk of 'laws of nature' became common in the sixteenth century. It was revived by Rom Harré and E. H. Madden in *Causal Powers*."[11] But neither view of the laws of nature—as separate from objects or constitutive of objects—requires us to regard these laws as anything other than *contingent* realities. In firing the gun, then, I am relying on further realities being the case, and these realities didn't *have* to be the case. Laws governing momentum, friction, inertia, explosions, gas pressure, conservation of mass-energy, and gravity only contingently hold. In other possible worlds, different laws of nature (or different specifications of these laws) hold. Nevertheless, knowing that various laws of nature are *in fact* the case, I fire the gun, and I am responsible for the outcome.[12]

Fourth, the contingent *laws of nature* on which I rely to get the job done are useful to me precisely because they *ground the truth of counterfactuals about what would occur in various circumstances*. Laws of nature are not mere accidental generalizations which describe what in fact happens. They ground counterfactuals about what *would* occur if such-and-such takes place, and these counterfactuals are true even if the circumstances specified in their antecedents are never actualized. The law of gravity tells me that this pen would fall to the ground if I were to release it. Even if I don't release the pen (and put it back in my pocket), nevertheless there is a truth about what *would* have happened if I *had* released the pen. Likewise, if I don't pull the trigger on the gun, all the laws of nature pertaining to momentum, friction, inertia, etc. still obtain, and tell me what *would* have

---

11. Swinburne, *Existence of God*, 32–33.

12. There are some who subscribe to an "essentialist" account of the laws of nature as metaphysically necessary (in the same way that "water is H2O" is metaphysically necessary). I think the conceivability considerations mooted in the previous paragraph cast doubt on this view. For two critiques of the essentialist picture, see Lange, "Scientific Essentialism," 227–41; and Sidelle, "Metaphysical Contingency of Laws of Nature," 309–36. I should stress that, as far as I can tell, conceding an essentialist account of the laws of nature would not undermine my argument in this section. It's not as if the *necessity* of the laws (if they are necessary) would absolve me of culpability in the ordinary gun case. The point is that I am relying on such laws being in place, in order to get the job done.

happened if I had pulled the trigger. Indeed, this knowledge of true counterfactuals vouchsafed to me by my knowledge of laws of nature is precisely why these laws are useful to me in intelligently and intentionally bringing about effects. In firing the gun, I act on this knowledge, and my expectation of the outcome is well-grounded. The counterfactuals assure me ahead of time what to expect, and in this knowledge lies (at least in part) my responsibility for the outcome. The act of pulling the trigger is not analogous to pulling the lever on a slot machine, or flipping a coin.

Fifth, the laws of nature are not up to me; they are (from my perspective) "prevolitional" truths on which I rely to get the job done. It is not up to me that laws pertaining to explosions, inertia, mass-energy conservation, and so on actually obtain. I can neither repeal nor establish the law of gravity; it is only open to me to act in accordance with it. Consequently, in killing the man by firing the gun, I am relying on truths over which I have no control. They are (again, from my perspective, as the agent who chooses to fire the gun) brute facts that help me bring about the outcome. Both my choice to pull the trigger and the obtaining of the laws of nature are contingent matters. But one is up to me (my choice to pull the trigger), and the other is not (the laws). (Notice how the consequence argument for incompatibilism stresses this truth: neither prior states of the universe nor the laws of nature are up to me.)

Sixth, I bear responsibility for killing the person in "the ordinary gun case." I bear responsibility because I actualize circumstances in which I rely on contingent prevolitional truths about what would occur if I were to actualize those circumstances. Knowing that that would occur, I pull the trigger. The contingency of these truths does not absolve me of responsibility. The fact that I don't control these truths does not absolve me of responsibility. The fact that my action of pulling the trigger, strictly speaking, is not sufficient for the outcome, does not absolve me of responsibility.

THE "BULLET BILL GUN"

Parallels to the "Ordinary Gun" Case

What I call the "Bullet Bill gun" case is described as follows: I pull a gun out of my pocket, aim it at a person at point-blank range, and pull the trigger, thus killing the person. However, this gun is different from an ordinary gun. When I pull the trigger, it creates *ex nihilo* a Bullet Bill in the chamber. "Bullet Bill" is a character in Nintendo video games (*Super Mario Brothers, Mario Kart Wii, Super Mario Galaxy 1 & 2*, etc.), typically represented as a black metal bullet with eyes and an evil grin, who chases Mario as soon as Bullet Bill is shot out of a cannon, gun, etc. For my purposes, I assume that Bullet Bill is sentient, a homunculus encased in steel, possessing libertarian free will. I further assume that the one who fires the Bullet Bill gun knows the relevant counterfactuals of creaturely freedom (CCFs) about each Bullet Bill that gets created, and that he uses that knowledge to kill people with the gun. For instance, he may know that the next trigger pull would create Bullet Bill A, who (if created) would freely fly out of the barrel and kill Angie, that the next trigger pull would create Bullet Bill B, who (if created) would freely fly out of the barrel and kill Beth, that the next trigger pull would create Bullet Bill C and kill Caroline, and so on.

I maintain that if I had such a gun and used it in this way, then I would bear moral responsibility for every death I brought about through my use of it, the same as any murderer would. Analogously to the "ordinary gun" case, I am the author of this sin, because it was "up to me" how I used my libertarian free will in this case. I could have refrained from pulling the trigger. No one coerced me into pulling the trigger. I pulled the trigger knowing that this Bullet Bill gun was in good working order, and knowing what ordinarily happens when you pull triggers on Bullet Bill guns at point-blank range. In fact, by knowing the relevant CCFs I know what would specifically happen after the next three trigger pulls on the gun. Knowing all this, I am responsible not just for the fact that I pulled the trigger, but that Angie, Beth, and Caroline died as a result. And it doesn't matter if my intention in killing them was to bring about a further effect (such as my winning the New York City Marathon). I'm still responsible for killing them.

I submit that our metaphysical and moral intuitions in the Bullet Bill case are at least as clear as in the "ordinary gun" case, such that I am the author of this sin, and I bear moral responsibility for bringing about these deaths. Like the "ordinary gun" case, I actualize circumstances (pulling the trigger), circumstances that are not (strictly speaking) sufficient for the outcome. Rather, I rely on contingent CCFs about Bullet Bill, even as in the "ordinary gun" case I rely on contingent laws of nature. Like laws of nature, the CCFs are counterfactuals about what would occur in various circumstances, and like laws of nature, what these CCFs are is not up to me. They are "prevolitional" truths in either case. By analogy to the "ordinary gun" case, then, I bear responsibility for killing the various persons by way of my "Bullet Bill gun."

There are of course *differences* between the "ordinary gun" case and the "Bullet Bill gun" case, chief of which is the existence of Bullet Bill. But the question is whether these differences are *relevant* for the purpose of assessing *my* moral responsibility in each case.

Ordinary Bullet Vs. Bullet Bill: A Relevant Difference?

For instance, in the "ordinary gun" case the bullet is not morally responsible for much of anything, being an ordinary bullet lacking mental states, consciousness, intentions, a will, and so on. Ordinary bullets are not agents, whereas in the "Bullet Bill gun" case, Bullet Bill is an agent, who is himself morally responsible for killing the people he kills. Despite the fact that there are true counterfactuals that passively record what Bullet Bill would do in a particular set of circumstances, it is nevertheless up to Bullet Bill to fly out of the chamber and go this way or that. In another possible world Bullet Bill (in the same exact circumstances) flies beside Angie and strikes up a friendly conversation, rather than blowing her up.

So there *is* a clear difference here in the two cases because of a difference in the bullets. But does Bullet Bill's individual responsibility somehow lessen *my* responsibility, the one who aims and shoots the Bullet Bill gun and thereby kills three people in rapid succession? I don't see how. It just doesn't strike me as plausible that the man who wields the Bullet Bill gun is any less responsible simply because he didn't directly *cause* Bullet Bill to do what he did. Indeed, in the "ordinary gun" case I don't directly cause the killing; I do so indirectly by way of contingent, prevolitional realities pertaining to gun and bullet, realities over which I have no control. In each case the fact that I *capitalize on and exploit* such prevolitional contingent realities is what *grounds* my responsibility (far from lessening it).

To be clear, with the "ordinary gun" I do not make it the case that, given initial circumstances, the bullet *would* fly out of the chamber and kill someone. What the bullet would do, and subjunctive truths about what the bullet would do, is up to the laws of nature, the properties of the bullet, etc. None of that is up to me. But I do make it the case that the bullet *will in fact* fly out of the chamber and kill someone. What the ordinary bullet in fact does is up to me. Likewise, with the Bullet Bill gun I do not make it the case that, given initial circumstances, Bullet Bill *would* fly out of the chamber and kill someone. What Bullet Bill would do, and subjunctive truths about what Bullet Bill would do, is up to brute facts about Bullet Bill. None of that is up to me. But I do make it the case that Bullet Bill *will in fact* fly out of the chamber and kill someone. What Bullet Bill in fact does is up to me. So the cases seem perfectly parallel precisely where they need to be parallel for the purposes of assessing the moral responsibility of the shooter. I am responsible for there being a bullet which does what it in fact does (kill a man), even as I am responsible for there being a Bullet Bill who does what he in fact does (kill a man).

Sufficient Vs. Insufficient Cause: A Relevant Difference?

What about the fact that, apparently, in the "ordinary gun" case I am the sufficient cause of the bullet's speeding down the chamber and killing the person, but in the "Bullet Bill gun" case I am, apparently, *not* the sufficient cause of Bullet Bill speeding down the chamber and killing the person? If Bullet Bill but not the ordinary bullet has libertarian free will, than how can I be the sufficient cause in both cases? The problem (as I see it) is that any disambiguation of "sufficient cause" will be contextually dependent. Depending on which factors we hold fixed, I am (alternately) an insufficient cause in both cases and a sufficient cause in both cases. I think this continued parallel supports my overall case. Let's examine this further.

I certainly don't give the (ordinary) bullet the propensity it has to behave a certain way under particular circumstances. So in that respect I am not the sufficient cause of its traveling down the chamber. But my actualization of initial circumstances is sufficient for the outcome *given other things* (such as laws of nature), things which are not up to me but which I exploit to bring about the outcome. So (speaking *very* strictly), I am not the sufficient cause of the bullet's speeding down the chamber. Why then do we naturally say, in most conversational contexts, that I am? Because in assessing whether I am the sufficient cause, we do not ordinarily take into account those realities over which I have no control (such as the laws of nature); rather, we stipulate that those are in place and then ask whether, *given those realities*, my action is sufficient for the outcome. And, of course, it is.

The Bullet Bill case seems exactly parallel in the same respects. I certainly don't give Bullet Bill the propensity he has to behave a certain way under particular circumstances. So in that respect I am not the sufficient cause of Bullet Bill traveling down the chamber. Nevertheless, my actualization of initial circumstances is sufficient for the outcome *given other things* (such as the relevant CCFs), things which are not up to me but which I exploit to bring about the outcome. So (speaking *very* strictly), I am not the sufficient cause of Bullet Bill's speeding down the chamber. Why then is it natural—even here—to say that I am? Because in assessing whether I am the sufficient cause, we do not ordinarily take into account those realities over which I have no control (the CCFs); rather, we stipulate that those are in place and ask whether, *given those realities*, my action is sufficient for the outcome. And, of course, it is.

I conclude that I bear responsibility in the ordinary gun case, and cause the bullet to do what it does, even though I don't cause the laws of nature to be what they are. Likewise, I bear responsibility in the Bullet Bill case, and cause Bullet Bill to do what he does, even though I don't cause the

CCFs to be what they are. In neither situation do I cause what *would* be the case. But in both situations I do cause what *will* be the case. So we can take our pick. If we wish to speak very strictly, and say that the "Bullet Bill gun" is a case of insufficient causation at best, then we can say the same about the "ordinary gun" case. On the other hand, if the "ordinary gun" case is a case of sufficient causation (ignoring the relevant counterfactuals which must also be in place), then so is the "Bullet Bill gun" case. At the very least, the parallels are such that my causal involvement when I wield the "Bullet Bill gun" seems *sufficiently analogous to cases of causal sufficiency*, that the ascription of moral responsibility goes through.

MOLINISM

Given the preceding, the application to a Molinist doctrine of providence can be brief. On Molinism *God actualizes circumstances* in which he knows (say) that an assassin will take out a number of targets. God's act of placing the assassin in those circumstances *is not (by itself) sufficient* for the murderous outcome. In addition to the actualization of circumstances, *there need to be true CCFs* about how the assassin would behave in those circumstances, and God is provident on Molinism because *he relies on these contingent truths about the assassin*, truths over which God has no control. These brute facts about the assassin are accurately described by *prevolitional truths that are not up to God in any way* (for instance, they are not grounded in God's nature or his will). As in the Bullet Bill case, on Molinism God is not responsible for what the assassin *would* do if placed in a particular set of circumstances. But if I've described the Bullet Bill case correctly, *he is responsible for what the assassin will in fact do*. After all, it is up to God to create an assassin with the liability to kill in a particular circumstance *and it is up to God to actualize that circumstance*. Since *this dual divine action ensures the outcome*, how can God not be said to have caused the outcome, and to be responsible for it?

In effect, I am assimilating the case of Molinist divine providence *over* an assassin shooting a gun, to the case of an assassin shooting a gun. From this perspective, created agents are God's gun (or at least his bullets). If the bullets are sentient, then sure, the bullets deserve blame. But that is a separate matter once we step back and look at the larger picture, and reflect on these analogies. God's firing of the gun is sufficient (given other things) to bring about the effect. Is that not also the case with the "ordinary gun" and the "Bullet Bill gun" cases? In each case the action is "sufficient (given other things)." So I conclude that on Molinism, God is the author of sin if, when I fire my ordinary gun, I am the author of sin. I don't directly put the bullet into the victim's heart; I do so by way of reliance on objects behaving according to the laws of nature. God doesn't directly put the assassin's bullet in the victim's heart. He does so indirectly by reliance on agents behaving according to CCFs. In the end, I am looking for a relevant moral difference between these cases. What is the difference between someone who brings about an effect by way of actualizing a circumstance and relying on a law of nature, and someone who brings about an effect by way of actualizing a circumstance and relying on a CCF? Any moral difference? In fact, in the Molinist case things are even worse when it comes to responsibility, since the first agent (God) has *infallible* knowledge of the outcome of his choice, something not had by the ordinary assassin (who has probabilistic knowledge only). The infallible knowledge on the part of God affords him a degree of exact control over the outcome not had by ordinary assassins.

In his "Introduction to Luis de Molina," Alfred Freddoso states in a particularly explicit way the doctrine of divine providence that Molina wishes to uphold:

> God, the divine artisan, freely and knowingly plans, orders, and provides for all the effects that constitute His artifact, the created universe with its entire history, and executes His chosen plan by playing an active causal role sufficient to ensure its exact realization.[13]

So on this view of providence, which Molina is said to share with his detractors (such as Bañez), God "plays an active causal role sufficient to ensure [the] exact realization" of "all the effects" in his creation. Molinists' giving God such a role has consequences that are often overlooked for the 'author of sin' issue. It seems to me that Molinists have studiously focused on articulating a model in which the human agent remains responsible in a strong libertarian sense. But they have not sufficiently attended to the fact that, if Calvinism makes God the author of sin and responsible for the fact that sin comes to pass, then the Molinist model of providence does as well. These latter questions do not go away for Molinists simply in virtue of preserving human libertarian free will.

We can summarize the parallels between the ordinary gun, the Bullet Bill gun, and Molinism, in the following way:

1	2	3
Ordinary Gun	**Bullet Bill Gun***	**Molinism**

13. Freddoso, introduction to *On Divine Foreknowledge*, 3.

I pull the trigger	I pull the trigger	God actualizes circumstances (in which an assassin operates)
My action is not sufficient for the outcome	My action is not sufficient for the outcome	God's action is not sufficient for the outcome
I rely on contingent laws of nature	I rely on contingent CCFs about Bullet Bill	God relies on contingent CCFs about humans
The laws ground true counterfactuals about what would occur in various circumstances	The CCFs are counterfactuals about what would occur in various circumstances	The CCFs are counterfactuals about what would occur in various circumstances
What the laws are is not up to me; they are "prevolitional" truths.	What the CCFs are is not up to me; they are "prevolitional" truths.	What the CCFs are is not up to God; they are "prevolitional" truths.
I bear responsibility for killing the person	I bear responsibility for killing the person (by analogy to the ordinary gun case)	God bears responsibility for killing the person (by analogy to the Bullet Bill case)

(CCFs = "counterfactuals of creaturely freedom")

We can then ask: What is the moral difference, if any, between the agent in column 1 and the agent in column 2? Likewise, we can ask: What is the moral difference, if any, between the agent in column 2 and the agent in column 3?

ANSWERS TO OBJECTIONS

I turn to consider six different objections to the preceding parity argument.

Objection 1: "You fail to acknowledge relevant differences between the cases. It is simply not up to God what the assassin would do. The assassin has libertarian free will, and (ordinary) bullets don't." Answer: But in the "ordinary gun" case, am I off the hook because it's not up to me that guns and bullets have the properties they do? Because it's not up to me that bullets have powers and the liability to exercise those powers in particular circumstances? Do I fail to be responsible for killing a man with a gun, simply because laws about momentum and mass-energy conservation and explosions aren't up to me? I think the answer to all these questions is "no." So why would appeal to the prevolitional status of contingent brute facts about the assassin be relevant in the Molinist case?

Objection 2: "In the 'ordinary gun' case, given the circumstances and the laws of nature, the bullet could not do otherwise than what it does. But on Molinism, agents can do otherwise in the same exact circumstances." Answer: Yes, but how does this help? After all, God creates the agents he actually creates, not other agents he could have created, and these agents that God creates are such that they would do what is described in the relevant CCF. The choice to go ahead and create these kinds of agents was up to him.

In addition, strictly speaking, given the circumstances *and the truth of the relevant CCF*, the agent cannot do otherwise than what he in fact does in those circumstances. Yes, there is a possible world in which the agent does otherwise in the same circumstances, but *that* is a world in which the relevant CCF is *false*. Likewise, there is a world in which the bullet behaves differently despite the same trigger pull, but that is a world in which the laws of nature are different.

Here is where the facts stand, on Molinism: (1) God creates an agent who has the following property: he would do X if placed in circumstances C; (2) God didn't have to create an agent who has that property, but he did so anyway; (3) God actualizes circumstances C; (4) God didn't have to actualize circumstances C. In virtue of (1) and (3), God's twofold activity *ensures* that the agent's sin will come about. In virtue of (2) and (4), it is up to God to act as he does in these two respects. Therefore, God both makes it the case that the sinful events will come about, and he is responsible for making it the case. This is *in addition to* any responsibility we want to assign to the sinful agent.

Objection 3: "Causation requires the laws of nature. These are appealed to in the first case, but not in the second or third. That's why the first is a case of causation, but not the others." Answer: But causation does not require the laws of nature. If it did, then God couldn't cause the world to exist, since *he* didn't make use of laws of nature in creating the world. But surely God caused the world to exist (including its laws). So causal relations can obtain even apart from laws of nature. In addition, given libertarian free will I cause my volitions, and that doesn't involve laws of nature. So both creation and libertarian free will argue against the assumption that causation *per se* requires the laws of nature. Any causation—in the absence of laws of nature—would need at least true counterfactuals stating what would happen if certain events came to pass. For instance, if it's not a fact that "If God were to will there to be an apple, there would be an apple," then God can't cause there to be an apple.

Objection 4: "You commit a fatal equivocation in your comparison between the counterfactuals associated with laws of nature, and the CCFs associated with libertarian free will. Yes, they both disclose to us prevolitional, contingent realities. But laws of nature are deterministic in their consequences; not so for CCFs." Answer: It's not clear that this claim is true, or even relevant. It may not be true, because fundamental laws in quantum physics seem to be probabilistic and even indeterministic, but clearly I can be morally responsible if I construct and use a gun whose operation depends on the truth of these laws of quantum physics. It's not relevant, because we can well imagine that only probabilistic laws of nature hold. Clearly, we would still regard someone as culpable for his use of a gun (whether an "ordinary gun" or a "Bullet Bill gun"), even if he only made use of prevolitional, contingent truths about what would be *highly likely* to occur. (And, in the ordinary case, no gun operates with 100 percent efficiency; this does not lessen culpability.) In fact, it looks as if Molinism would only increase the culpability, since God has infallible knowledge of how the agent *would* behave (not merely knowledge of how the agent would *likely* or *probably* behave), and then he creates agents who *would* so behave.

Objection 5: "At best, all you've shown is that God is responsible for the *outcome* of the assassin's sin: the death the assassin brings about. You haven't shown that God is responsible for the assassin's sin itself. And it is this latter claim that is needed, to show that God is the author of sin in the objectionable sense." Answer: Strictly speaking, this isn't the case. In the "ordinary gun" case, I not only bring about the end result (the death of the person); I bring about the intermediate state—the bullet speeding down the barrel of the gun. As far as I can tell, I can make the same argument with respect to the intermediate state that I made with respect to the end state: *both* states involve my actualizing circumstances in which a substance with powers, and liabilities to exercise those powers in those circumstances, would in fact exercise those powers. And again, as far as I can tell, the "Bullet Bill gun" case is parallel in these respects.

Objection 6: "On Molinism, God's actualization of circumstances doesn't *cause* agents to do what they do. But pulling a trigger *does* cause the bullet to do what it does. You've missed an elementary feature of Molinism." Answer: My point is that what happens in Molinist providence is *sufficiently analogous* to what happens in sufficient causation, such that claims about authorship, moral responsibility, and culpability go through. So even if the actualization of circumstances is not (strictly speaking) a sufficient cause, this won't affect the larger argument. Thus, we need to get some clarity on *why* Molinist providence isn't a sufficient cause of what occurs. If the factors cited are also present in the "ordinary gun" case, then—unless we wish to reject our clear intuitions about that ordinary case—it looks like those intuitions transfer to the "Bullet Bill gun" and Molinist cases. For instance, one reason to think Molinist providence isn't a sufficient cause is that (strictly speaking) God's actualization of circumstances isn't sufficient for a particular outcome. But in the "ordinary gun" case, my actualization of circumstances isn't sufficient for a particular outcome either. Or again, maybe Molinist providence isn't a sufficient cause because what agents would do in various circumstances isn't up to God. But in the "ordinary gun" case, what the bullet would do in various circumstances isn't up to me. So what, exactly, is the *relevant* difference between the two cases that makes a *moral* difference?

Objection 7: "Yes, in the Bullet Bill case, both Bullet Bill *and* the wielder of the Bullet Bill gun intend to hit their target—they have the same intentions, and so are culpable in that respect. But Molinists deny that *God* intends all the sinful actions intended by human agents. His intentions and purposes are different from the evil intentions and purposes of the wicked through whom he works. So Molinists don't have to accept that their theory of providence makes God the author of sin."[14] Answer: notice that this objection doesn't dispute the underlying causal metaphysic that I argue is common to all three cases (ordinary gun, Bullet Bill gun, and Molinism). Indeed, the objection concedes that the wielder of the Bullet Bill gun *is* culpable, even though Bullet Bill caused his own intentions. Instead, the objection attempts to deflect divine culpability, not by disputing any metaphysical parallels between Molinism and efficient causation, but by insisting that God doesn't *intend* the sins that he ordains. Human agents intend their sins for evil ends, whereas God intends to work such sins for very good purposes, and it is those good purposes which he intends, not the sins. I say, "Amen! This is a fine piece of reasoning." But it is equally available to Calvinists, and has in fact been employed by Calvinists for centuries. Paul Helm summarizes: "In the case of evil, whatever the difficulties may be of accounting for the fact, God ordains evil but he does not intend evil as evil, as the human agent intends it. In God's case there is some other description of the morally evil action which he intends the evil action to fill. There are other ends or purposes which God has in view."[15]

The reason why this is a fine piece of reasoning has little to do with Molinism and everything to do with the basic moral fact that intentions are not closed under known entailment. If S intends that p, and S knows that p implies q, it does not follow that S thereby intends q. So let's say that God intends the world he creates in virtue of some property p that applies to the whole: its overall intrinsic value, or the fact that it tends to promote his glory, or manifests the full range of his attributes. God intends the world in virtue of this property p, even though he knows that his creation of the world implies sinful human intentions q. Since intentions are not closed under known entailment, it does not follow that God thereby intends q. As

---

14. This objection was inspired by Ken Keathley in conversation.
15. Helm, *Providence of God*, 190.

Aquinas puts it when talking about killing in self-defense, "Nothing hinders one act from having two effects, only one of which is intended, while the other is beside the intention . . . Accordingly the act of self-defense may have two effects, one is the saving of one's life, the other is the slaying of the aggressor."[16] So if Molinists get the doctrine of double effect, so do Calvinists.

Since this final objection appeals to a strategy already available to Calvinists, it seems that the argument ("sufficient cause therefore culpable author of sin") does nothing to distinguish Calvinism from Molinism. It should therefore be dropped from the Molinist repertoire of objections to Calvinism. The objection then confirms the overall thesis of this paper: there are no resources *distinctive to Molinism* that can help deflect the "author of sin" charge.

CONCLUSION

Authorship of Sin, Responsibility, and Culpability

Molinism is often said to combine the best of both worlds: a meticulous doctrine of providence typically associated with the determinism of Calvinism, and a libertarian view of free will typically associated with the indeterminism of Arminianism. As I read it, Molinists want God to have all of the *benefits* of sufficient causality in providence, but none of the *responsibilities* (literally!), at least if that responsibility involves culpability. They want a providence in which it is *as if* God is the sufficient cause of events (for the purpose of meticulous control over the outcome), even though he isn't *really* the sufficient cause. In the "authorship of sin" objection, what bothers Molinists is not so much the *sufficient causality* involved in Calvinism, but what that sufficient causality seems to *entail* for the Calvinist: God's authorship of sin, and his subsequent moral responsibility for it, and his culpability. My main point has been that these latter consequences seem to be involved in the Molinist view anyway, once we attend to requisite analogies that elicit clear moral intuitions.

Of course, there are various strategies available to the Molinist, in order to defend the claim that—in spite of the cases we've considered—God can be responsible for the fact that evil occurs without being *culpable* for that evil. First, they can *appeal to paradox*, by adapting the Plantinga-inspired epistemology advocated in James Anderson's recent *Paradox in Christian*

---

16. Aquinas, *Summa Theologica* II–II, q. 64, a. 7 *respondeo* (Baumgarth and Regan, *On Law, Morality, and Politics*, 226–27).

Theology: An Analysis of Its Presence, Character, and Epistemic Status. Second, they can *appeal to inscrutability*, an approach inspired by either Austin Farrer's agnosticism about the modality of the divine action, or some adaptation of Alston's/Wykstra's inscrutability thesis with respect to the problem of evil.[17] Third, they can *appeal to the Creator/creature distinction*, and the consequent *sui generis character of divine causation* (both pursued by Paul Helm in various venues).[18] As earlier argued, the relation between God and evil can be defined apophatically,[19] even as the union of Christ's natures in one person is defined apophatically in Chalcedonian Christology.

Perhaps these and several other strategies are available to help Molinists avoid the "author of sin" problem, by grounding a distinction between responsibility and culpability. But clearly none of these strategies rely on any distinctive *Molinist* themes. They are strategies Calvinists have been using for centuries. They are available to Molinist and non-Molinist alike. But if there are no conceptual resources *distinctive to Molinism* to block the notion that God is the author of sin, if Molinists must fall back on typical Calvinist strategies in this regard, then is Molinism really preferable to Calvinism in avoiding the conclusion that God is the author of sin? Or should Molinists simply drop this claim from their repertoire of alleged advantages of Molinism over Calvinism?

I agree with Keathley when he says,

> We are brethren, not adversaries, working in a mutual effort. Until we cross the veil, none of us has arrived on the journey of faith. So I look forward to this cooperative effort, convinced that the end result will be that we are better and more faithful witnesses of our common salvation. Calvinism and Molinism are much more similar than they are dissimilar, so I endeavor to avoid what might be called the narcissism of trivial differences.[20]

I too want to avoid the narcissism of trivial differences. In fact, what I have argued here is in that spirit: that when it comes to the "author of sin" issue, "Calvinism and Molinism are much more similar" than Molinists let on![21]

---

17. Cf. Farrer, *Faith and Speculation*, 66; Alston, "Inductive Argument," 29–67; Wykstra, "Humean Obstacle to Evidential Arguments from Suffering," 73–94.

18. Helm, "Augustinian-Calvinist View," 167–69 (also alluded to in the first section of this chapter).

19. *Westminster Confession of Faith* 3.1, 5.4

20. Keathley, *Salvation and Sovereignty*, 14.

21. Immediately preceding the earlier cited passage in part IV, section 9 of Edwards, *The Freedom of the Will* (cf. no. 4 above), Edwards notes that "But if this be so, this is

Scriptural Testimony to Double-Agency or Double-Causation

On my view, Molinists should just bite this bullet anyway, because of the fairly substantial range of Scriptural texts that testify to the phenomenon of "double-agency" or "double-causation." For instance, consider the case of King Saul's suicide. "Therefore Saul took his own sword and fell upon it . . . Thus Saul died . . ." (1 Chr 10:4, 6). Who killed Saul? Saul killed Saul, by committing suicide. "Therefore the LORD put him to death . . ." (1 Chr 10:14). Who killed Saul? God killed Saul. God put him to death. We might want to say that God killed Saul by way of Saul killing Saul, but saying that doesn't magically convert two causal claims into one. If God killed Saul—that is, "put him to death"—then God caused his death. (After all, if you don't *cause* someone's death, you can scarcely be said to have *killed* him.) And here I think that Molinists have a problem in accounting for the fullness of what the text is saying. If all you say is that God merely permitted Saul to die, that he permitted Saul to kill himself, that's not the same thing as killing Saul. So if God killed Saul, and the way Saul got killed was by his own suicide, then God caused Saul's death-by-suicide. There may be a mystery here as to *how* these causal claims (primary and secondary) can be both true and consistent with other things we confess to be true, but there's no mystery as to whether *there are* two causal claims to be accounted for. Yet what many Molinists want to say is that there is only one cause of Saul's sin, not two.

Or consider the case of Job's losses. Clearly the responsible human agents who took away Job's servants were the Sabeans and the Chaldeans; these individuals killed Job's servants, they "struck down the servants with the edge of the sword" (Job 1:15, 17). But on Job's account of the matter, it was the Lord who took them away (Job 1:21), and his brothers and sisters agreed with this assessment (Job 42:11). So the Sabeans and Chaldeans took them away (by murdering them) and the Lord took them away—not merely

---

a difficulty which equally attends the doctrine of Arminians themselves; at least, of those of them who allow God's certain foreknowledge of all events. For on the supposition of such a foreknowledge, this is the case with respect to every sin that is committed: God knew, that if he ordered and brought to pass such and such events, such sins would infallibly follow . . . Therefore this supposed difficulty ought not to be brought as an objection against the [Calvinist] scheme which has been maintained, as *disagreeing* with the Arminian scheme, seeing 'tis no difficulty owing to such a *disagreement*; but a difficulty wherein the Arminians share with us. That must be unreasonably made an objection against our differing from them, which we should not escape or avoid at all by agreeing with them" (398–99). In the elided material Edwards describes the case of Judas's betrayal according to a kind of Molinist Arminianism. If so, then it seems that Edwards anticipated my main point in this chapter, although I believe I have provided a distinct way of supporting this parity claim. (Thanks to Dan Johnson for bringing this to my attention).

allowed them to be taken away. God brought about the taking away, but the taking away is constituted by the sinful actions of the Sabeans and the Chaldeans (how *else* did the servants die?). So there are two causal claims to be accounted for, but many Molinists seem to want to reduce these to one claim, because of the fact that human sin is involved.

In none of these texts is God described as a *merely* passive permitter. Nor is he described as someone who *merely* brings about circumstances. Rather, he brings about the events themselves; he brings about what occurs in the circumstances. He brings about the death of Saul (not just its circumstances). He brings about the losses of Job (not just their circumstances). It seems to me that we cannot have it both ways. We cannot say that God brings about these sinful episodes, but that he does not have any authorship in any sense. To bring about *is* authorship. This doesn't mean "authorship" in the sense denied by many Christian confessions. It doesn't mean that God is the actor or agent or doer on the historical stage, performing these events in real time.[22] But it has to mean at the very least that he brought these events about. Given these and other texts,[23] and given the analogies I've described, I don't see what is gained by a Molinist approach to this issue, either exegetically or morally.

---

22. This, I take it, is the sense of "authorship" denied in the *Westminster Confession of Faith*, the *Second London Baptist Confession of Faith*, and the *Abstract of Principles*, for instance.

23. Gen 45:4, 50:20; Exod 4:21; Judg 14:3–4; 1 Sam 2:25; 1 Kgs 12:15; 2 Chr 25:20; Ps 105:25; Amos 3:6; Acts 4:28; Rom 11:36.

BIBLIOGRAPHY

Alston, William. "The Inductive Argument from Evil and the Human Cognitive Condition." *Philosophical Perspectives* 5 (1991) 29–67.

Anderson, James. *Paradox in Christian Theology: An Analysis of Its Presence, Character, and Epistemic Status*. Waynesboro, GA: Paternoster, 2007.

Baumgarth, William P., and Richard J. Regan, eds. *On Law, Morality, and Politics*. Indianapolis: Hackett, 1988.

Edwards, Jonathan. *Freedom of the Will*. Vol. 1 of *Works of Jonathan Edwards*, edited by Paul Ramsey. New Haven, CT: Yale University Press, 1957.

Farrer, Austin. *Faith and Speculation*. London: Black, 1967.

Freddoso, Alfred J. Introduction to *On Divine Foreknowledge (Part IV of the Concordia)*, by Luis de Molina, 3. Translated by Alfred J. Freddoso. Ithaca, NY: Cornell University Press, 1988.

Helm, Paul. "The Augustinian-Calvinist View." In *Divine Foreknowledge: Four Views*, edited by James Beilby and Paul Eddy, 161–206. Downers Grove, IL: InterVarsity, 2001.

———. *Perspective: Westminster, Yesterday, Today, and Tomorrow?*, edited by Lynn Quigley, 143–161. Edinburgh Conference in Christian Dogmatics. Rutherford House, 2006.

———. *The Providence of God*. Downers Grove, IL: InterVarsity, 1994.

Keathley, Ken. *Salvation and Sovereignty: A Molinist Approach*. Nashville: B & H Academic, 2010.

Lange, Marc. "A Note on Scientific Essentialism, Laws of Nature, and Counterfactual Conditionals." *Australasian Journal of Philosophy* 82 (2004) 227–41.

Sidelle, Alan. "On the Metaphysical Contingency of Laws of Nature." In *Conceivability and Possibility*, edited by T. Szabó Gendler and J. Hawthorne, 309–36. Oxford: Clarendon, 2002.

Swinburne, Richard. *The Existence of God*. 2nd ed. New York: Oxford University Press, 2004.

Wykstra, Stephen. "The Humean Obstacle to Evidential Arguments from Suffering: On Avoiding the Evils of 'Appearance.'" *International Journal for Philosophy of Religion* 16 (1984) 73–94.

3

Theological Determinism and the "Authoring Sin" Objection

—Heath White

This essay defends theological determinism (hereafter, TD) from the charge that it makes God "the author of sin." The verdict is Not Guilty.

THE THESIS

Theological determinism is of course a form of determinism. Determinism is a form of conditional necessity: given these facts or events over here, some other fact or event over there *must be the case* or *must occur*. The "must" can come in different flavors, depending on the type of determinism in view, but for our purposes, it is a "must" of metaphysical necessity. It is a further requirement on determinism that the determining facts explain the determined facts and not vice versa.

Obviously this could get complicated, but fortunately, theological determinism is a rather simple kind of determinism. The determining factor is God's will, and the determined facts are every (other) contingent state of affairs.[1] So, for precision,

---

1. A *contingent* state of affairs is one which is actual but not necessary, i.e. which could be other than it is. I am six feet tall and speak English as my first language, but (had my early nutrition and upbringing been different) I might have been taller or shorter, and had Swahili or Uzbek as my first language. On the other hand, that 2+2=4,

Theological determinism: (i) the facts about God's will wholly determine every other contingent fact, and (ii) the facts about God's will explain every other contingent fact.

The two clauses together say, roughly, that God's will determines, settles, or fixes every other fact about the world that could have been other than it is. This means that there is no detail of the universe that is undetermined by God's will. In particular, contingent facts about human wills, or about what humans would freely choose in such-and-such circumstances, or about other events in the creation like coin flips or gamma rays, are not ultimately or brutely contingent, in that they can be explained, completely, as the results of what God willed. Thus, according to the proponent of TD, while there may be events undetermined by physical causes there are no earthly events undetermined by *any* causes. In particular, there may be human actions which are not determined by any antecedent physical or psychological states, but there are no human actions which are undetermined by anything whatsoever.

For this reason, theological determinism rules out *libertarian free will*. Libertarian free will is an alleged power of human beings to choose between alternatives in a way that is undetermined by anything whatsoever. Since, according to TD, God's will determines everything, including human choices, it does not take a logician to see that TD and libertarian free will are incompatible.

Another consequence of TD is that God's will is maximally specific. He does not will to create *a* man (some man, any man) but *this particular* man, in all his manly individuality. He does not intend to bless an individual somehow, or to have him wind up blessed sometime, but he wills to bless an individual in some very specific way and time. Nothing is left to chance; nothing lies outside his providence. This "meticulous providence" is of course one of the primary attractions of TD; without TD or something close to it, it becomes difficult to maintain that God is in full control of history.

TD does *not* say that God is the sole agent in the universe, or that other agents do not act. There are other agents, and they do act, which is to say, their wills are effective. But TD says that their willings, and the efficacy of those willings, are events which are brought about and explained by God's will.

I want to elaborate on this basic position in several ways. TD comes in a number of possible versions, and I want to identify one which I think is most promising. To explain it, I want to exercise the imagination a little bit, as I think that will aid understanding as much as any formal definition.

---

and that I am not a bacterium, are necessary truths. Two and two could not be anything but four, and no bacterium would be *me*.

THE "PICTURE"

One way of thinking about God's relationship to his creation goes like this. God created seven billion or so other agents, all with libertarian free will, and turned them loose. These seven billion and one agents tend to get in each other's way. We are all quite familiar with our projects being frustrated by our recalcitrant fellow human beings. God is in much the same situation, except that he is vastly more powerful, intelligent, and long-lived than the seven billion others that he must outwit, outplay, and outlast. This is more or less the vision of creation entertained by Open Theism.[2]

According to the theological determinist, this view is completely wrongheaded. On TD, God is complete and utter master of what goes on in creation, because he simply decides on it all and then executes his decisions. God is not one agent acting in the universe, on a par with various other agents, differing only in his degree of power and insight. No—God is the ultimate agent, the one that makes it all happen, including the other agents and their exercises of agency. What they do, they do because of God's will, and there is no looseness in the causal relations between his will and theirs. His position vis-à-vis other agents is not that of a grandmaster playing a 90-dimensional chess match against seven billion opponents, not even if we add that he somehow has advance knowledge of what moves they will or would make.

Another way of thinking about God's relationship to his creation is like the former except that, instead of granting agents libertarian free will, God has created a deterministic world and turned it loose. In the Newtonian image, the universe is a giant piece of clockwork. People act, but their actions are completely governed by the initial conditions created by God, and the ironclad natural laws governing the universe. This is more or less the vision of the 18th-century deists, and it is a form of TD. However, it is not the form of TD I prefer.

The deist God is completely sovereign, but he is not eternal, or at least his eternity plays no role in the explanation of his sovereignty. (That is, nothing about the deist God's control of the universe would be lessened if we said that he created the initial conditions and natural laws of the universe, and then died off.) Also, on standard lines the deist God does not interact with his creation, or if he does it is by ad hoc tweaks to the clockwork mechanism. If he does interact with the creation, it is necessarily a matter of suspending natural laws, and his action takes place in time. The version

---

2. For details on this theological perspective, begin with Pinnock et al., *The Openness of God*.

of TD I will defend has a rather different picture of God's relationship to creation. Let me give an analogy for what his position is like.

We can think of the theological determinists' God like an author in relation to his characters. This analogy gets right that God does not exist in the same time sequence as the creation, just as the events in a character's life do not exist on the same timeline with events in the author's life. It also gets right that while, in a good book, there are causes and explanations for the actions of the characters, there is no need for deterministic causes and explanations. God can exercise deterministic control over a creation which contains indeterministic causes. Where the analogy goes most wrong is that while an author's characters are simply representations, God does not create representations of agents but the real thing. That is, what an author literally creates are proper names and descriptions which do not refer to anything. What God literally creates, on the other hand, are real people.

Let us leave off analogies in favor of the marginally more rigorous method of "pictures." My preferred theologically determinist picture gets very clear, I believe, when we combine the ideas of divine eternity and creation ex nihilo. God creates the universe out of nothing, but an eternal God (unlike the deist one or the Open Theist one) does not create the first instant of creation, so to speak, and then step back to watch it unfold. Since God is eternal, he does not have to wait for history to unfold; the entire historical sequence of the universe is what God creates, all at once. This is not too hard to visualize if you imagine the universe as a four-dimensional block of spacetime, and God just zapping the whole block into existence.[3]

The block of spacetime has a time dimension, and slices taken across this dimension will differ from one another, so there is alteration *in the creation* over time. Yet there is no alteration *in the creator* over time, as time is simply a dimension of the creation and not something that the creator participates in. What is immediately obvious is that, on this model, every time-slice (that is, every event of the creation) is wholly caused by God, who zapped it into being, down to the smallest detail. As a consequence, there is no question of a being within the block of created spacetime opposing or resisting God's will.

The sense in which God (or an act of God's will) is the cause of some event in the world differs from the sense in which, say, a prior event in the creation is its cause. Borrowing some standard terminology, the kind of causation God exercises is *primary causation*, while intramundane causes are instances of *secondary causation*. On the deist picture, the distinction

---

3. If "blocks of spacetime" sounds too abstract, substitute a very long filmstrip. Then each moment of time in the creation is a single frame of the filmstrip.

between primary and secondary causes is basically the same as the distinction between remote and proximate causes: God gets the first ball rolling, as it were, with his primary causation, and then that ball subsequently impacts another and another and another, and we call these secondary causes. On my eternalist view, the picture is quite different. I like to use this image: the balls rolling into one another can be represented by horizontal arrows, which are secondary causes, while underneath the whole structure is a large vertical arrow, representing God's primary causation of the entire system of created events and secondary causes.

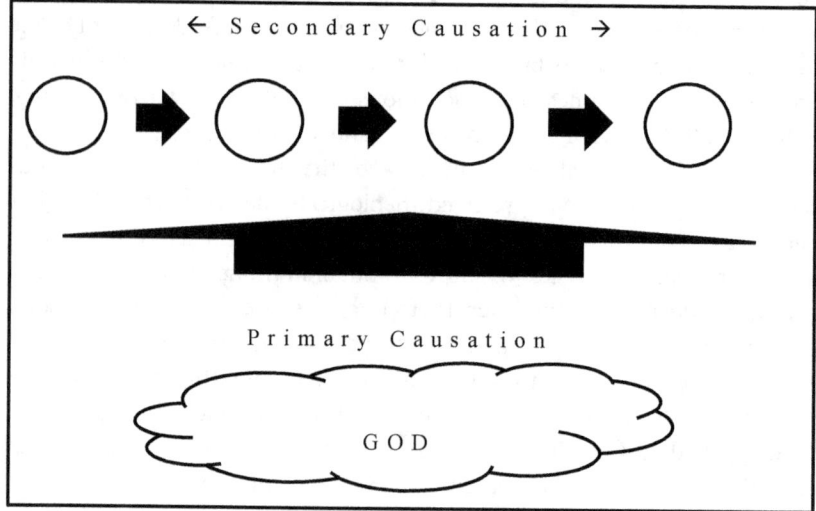

God's primary causal activity brings things into existence; he makes something rather than nothing. Intra-worldly secondary causes make one thing happen rather than another. It follows that the determinism in this model is exclusively theological, and there need be no causal determinism in the created order. God can create as random a universe as you like, in the sense that he can create a universe where, for example, there is no set of simple natural laws that describe all or nearly all of the events in the universe. On the other hand, it will not be random at all in the sense that it will be exactly the universe God intended to create. We might mark this distinction by saying that TD is committed to *primary determinism*, determinism in the order of primary causation, but not *secondary determinism*, that is, determinism in any order of secondary causation.

THE DEPRAVITY ARGUMENT

The distinction between primary and secondary determinism is relevant to a common theological argument against libertarian free will. Versions of it are popular in Calvinist and some Thomist and Lutheran circles, and a philosophical version has been advanced by Lynne Rudder Baker.[4] I shall call it the *Depravity Argument*. The essence of the argument is that, on a biblical and Christian understanding, human beings without the grace of God are completely "dead in sin." That is, they are attracted to evil, and this attraction runs so deep that there is nothing they can do about it. Consequently, they are unable to act in ways that please God, unable to desire God, unable perhaps even to desire to desire God. Only divine grace can alter this wretched state of affairs and change an individual into someone who desires the true good, God, and desires to act so as to please him. It follows that such sinful human beings lack libertarian free will, at least of the interesting sort that would allow them to choose between good and evil, because the good choices are not genuine possibilities for them.

Calvinist versions of the argument continue by claiming that divine grace is necessarily efficacious: God, being omnipotent, cannot try and fail to change a sinner's heart. It follows that for a recipient of this sort of grace, certain kinds of evil choices are no longer genuine possibilities, as God simply will not allow backsliding beyond a certain degree. In this way, too, libertarian free will is curtailed.

I am not going to be using the Depravity Argument. (I am not going to argue that there is anything wrong with it, though for the record I think there are more and less plausible versions of it.) I am going to leave it aside because the sort of determinism it postulates is psychological, and therefore secondary, determinism. In the claims that unregenerate human beings are determined to evil, and that regenerate human beings are determined to seek God, the immediate determining factors are facts about the orientation of human souls rather than facts about God's will. My version of TD does not turn on such factors.

Here is a perspective on what is going on with the Depravity Argument. The philosophical heritage from Augustine includes two threads. The first thread views God as First Cause and ultimate ground of all Being, and this idea gets sharpened into theological determinism as I have defined it. Its theological root is the doctrine of creation. This kind of determinism applies to humans, animals, cabbages, and everything else; it would apply even if humans had never sinned or, given that they have, if there were no

---

4. Baker, "Why Christians Should Not Be Libertarians," 460–78.

possibility of their salvation. It applies to the afterlife and to angels just as much as to human life on this earth.

The second thread views fallen human nature as irremediably weak and corrupt without divine assistance, and this idea gets sharpened, especially under pressure of the Pelagian controversy, into the claim that grace is necessary for salvation. Its theological roots lie in the doctrines of the Fall and original sin. The second thread does entail a kind of determinism, in that certain actions or dispositions are impossible for fallen human beings. However it is important not to confuse this form of secondary theological determinism with the primary theological determinism deriving from the first, creation-oriented Augustinian thread. My aim in this essay is to follow out that first thread and leave the second aside.

"AUTHORING SIN"

TD faces a number of objections, most of which I have no space to address. I want to concentrate on one historically resonant objection, namely that TD makes God "the author of sin." Sin is simply moral evil, the most salient instance of evil in the world, so the real problem is that TD makes God the author of evil.

This objection is not the same as the more general problem of evil. The problem is not that God is supposedly all-good and all-powerful, and yet there is evil in the world. The "authoring evil" problem, rather, is that God appears to be intimately bound up with the production of this evil. Therefore, it appears, God is responsible for the evil in the world, and maybe this means he is even evil himself.

We can see what is at stake in this problem by noting how one popular reply to it fares, given TD. Often it is said that God "does" good but "allows" us fallen human beings to do evil. In the context of TD, unfortunately, there is precious little room for this doing/allowing distinction. God brings about whatever exists; all events are settled by his will. There is no such thing as God merely allowing some other fallen agent to do evil, on their own account, since whatever such an agent does is determined by God's will.

The accusation that TD has God "authoring evil," then, amounts to the accusation that TD has God doing and not merely allowing evil. Such a view, not unnaturally, is held to be theologically untenable, and therefore TD is held to be theologically untenable.

What, however, does it mean to say that God "does" evil, rather than merely allows it? There are two different ways to understand the claim. First, it could be the claim that God *causes* evil. Second, it could be that God *intends* evil.

These two versions of the "authoring evil" objection are importantly different. Not everything I cause, even knowingly cause, I intend. For example, I am constantly *causing* my shoe soles to wear down by walking around in them, but even though I know this is happening I do not, properly speaking, *intend* it. I would be perfectly happy if my shoe soles lasted forever. On the other hand, not everything that I intend, even successfully intend, I cause. I may intend my children to get a good education, without educating them myself, and I may intend to throw a party that does not include (say) the president of the United States, without doing anything to prevent him from coming.

Since the two versions of the objection are different, their solutions are different also. I will begin by addressing the first version of the objection, that TD makes God cause evil, and then move on to the second version of the objection, that TD makes God intend evil. Both versions have satisfactory replies, I believe. TD does not imply that God is the author of evil.

DOES GOD CAUSE EVIL?

Does God cause evil? The general tenor of theistic reflection on this question is that no, God does not cause evil, and especially that he does not cause the particular moral evil that is sin. Yet if, as TD holds, God has caused the entire world down to the last detail, then (apparently) he has created all the aspects of it, both good and evil. There seems to be no room for holding that God does *not* cause evil. Nevertheless, the history of Christian reflection contains a classical way of threading this needle, which TD can take advantage of.

Consider a syllogism drawn from the works of Thomas Aquinas. Aquinas is committed to both of the following claims:

> God's knowledge is the cause of what it knows.
> God knows everything, both good and bad.[5]

It certainly seems to follow that

> God's knowledge is the cause of everything, both good and bad.

Yet Aquinas does not wish to say that God causes anything bad. He avoids saying it by appeal to the Augustinian principle that all evil is a privation.

---

5. Aquinas, *Summa Theologica* 1.14.8 and 1.14.9.

Only good is *real*; bad is simply an absence of something good.[6] Thus Aquinas can say that God's knowledge causes only the good, because only the good is, so to speak, there to be caused. God knows propositions about the bad aspects of things simply as a consequence of knowing about the absence of good things.

Here is an analogy. Suppose God creates a piece of Swiss cheese. There is something to the intuition that, properly speaking, God causes the cheese, but he does not cause the holes in the cheese. The holes are just areas without cheese; they are not, properly speaking, real things themselves. God knows the boundaries of the cheese are delimited in certain strategically spherical ways, and thus he knows the cheese has holes. But his knowledge that the cheese has holes does not cause the cheese to have holes, since strictly speaking the holes are not things to be caused.

The Augustinian idea is that this basic strategy can be applied to all kinds of evil. So for example, God does not cause death per se. Rather, he causes individuals to exist with a limited span of earthly life. At the end of their span they cease to be alive, but God does not cause the absence of life, since it is genuinely an absence.

The story can be applied to moral evil, also. God causes in Ebenezer Scrooge a desire for material resources, which in and of itself is not bad. However he fails to cause in Scrooge any compassionate impulses toward the poor. Scrooge then proceeds to act on his desires, which involve him in hoarding wealth while failing to act compassionately. The diagnosis of his moral failures is an absence of good motivation, but speaking strictly God does not cause absences. When God does cause the presence of compassionate impulses, Scrooge becomes a better man, and God is the cause of that.

One difficulty with the Augustinian view is that it threatens to prove too much. If evil is a privation, God does not cause it, because it is a mere absence, a non-entity. By the same token, however, one might think, no one else causes evil either! On the other hand, intuitively there must be something wrong with this objection. If a mouse came along and nibbled another

---

6. This doctrine is presented a number of places by Augustine and elsewhere in the Christian tradition. For one classic reference, see Augustine, *Enchiridion on Faith, Hope, and Love*, chapter 3.

Strictly speaking, a privation is an absence of a good that is "due," i.e. that ought to be there. Some goods are due by nature: for example, the inability to fly is a privation of good (and hence an evil) in a sparrow, but not in a human being. Other goods are due by convention or contract. For example, if I promised to give you $1000 for your used car, but have not paid up, you don't have the $1000 that is currently in my possession. Since the money is due you, the absence of it is a privation in your case, but its absence from anyone else's pocket is not a privation, since it is not due them.

hole in our cheese, we would say the mouse did cause the new hole in the cheese. Here is another case: when a chromosomal disease causes a child to develop a deformity, we say the disease caused the deformity.[7]

In the case of the mouse nibbling the hole, it seems right to say that the mouse alters the boundaries of the cheese, and these new boundaries entail the existence of a hole where there wasn't one before. This kind of "causation of privation" requires change over time: first one set of cheese-boundaries, then another set later. God's primary causation, however, doesn't operate over time, so God will not be a cause of privations in this way.

In the case of the disease causing deformity, it seems right to say that the disease acts by preventing or altering the normal development of the child. There is one pattern of causation—normal development—which results in a non-deformed child, and then there is the disease, which causes alterations in that pattern of causation. The disease cannot cause anything in the absence of some independent causal pattern or structure. God's primary causation does not operate in the context of any other causal pattern, though. So his will does not alter or affect any causal pattern that would have gone on in some independent way without it. Thus God does not cause privations in this manner either.

Human beings, however, might cause moral evil in either manner. Return to the case of Scrooge. In the story, as a young man Scrooge certainly desired some level of wealth, but he also desired love. He later abandons this second desire. One might think of such an abandonment as nibbling a hole in one's soul, as it were. As his life continues, a series of choices instills in him the habit of miserliness, and this habit proceeds to pervert his decisions and distort his relationships as his life goes on. One might think of his miserliness as a disease working moral deformity over time.

The Augustinian view that all evil is a privation has an impressive pedigree and it survives initial inspection. It also gives content to the classic position that God does everything that is good, and merely permits or allows everything that is evil: God "allows" holes in cheese, disasters in the world, and sinful souls, not in the sense that he shares his sovereign control with other agents, or leaves things up to chance, but in the sense that he does not create everything as a perfect instance of its kind, leaving "absences" which amount to evils. Finally, the Augustinian view has the dialectical advantage that many Christians who are not theological determinists are friendly to it.

---

7. In the deformity case, what is "absent" is not anything physical, because the deformity could be an extra thumb, for example. Rather, the absence or privation is of the correct order or normal state of the child.

CAUSATION AND RESPONSIBILITY

The Augustinian strategy, I believe, can answer the charge that God causes evil. However, there is a legitimate sense in which this strategy might be seen as mere sophistry in the face of the real problem indicated by the accusation that, according to TD, God is the author of evil. For the main motivation for insisting that God causes no evil is undoubtedly to absolve God from responsibility for evil. But then a *non sequitur* threatens. If God creates a piece of Swiss cheese, it may be strictly correct to say that he does not cause the holes in the cheese, but it would defy credulity to say that God is not responsible for the holes in the cheese. Likewise, if the world contains miserliness and death, we do not allow God to avoid responsibility for these evils merely by describing them as absences.

The fallacy is so obvious that one might wonder how intelligent people could fall into it. I think the explanation becomes clear if we consider the following analogy: one car is stationary, and another car drives into it. Which car caused the crash?

If all we care about is the physics of the situation, I have already given the answer: the path of a moving car intersected with a stationary car, and there is nothing else to say. However, when asking about the cause of a car wreck, we are not ordinarily asking a question to which physics alone will provide us an answer. For example, if I add that the stationary car was stopped at a red light, then the intuitive thing to say is that the moving car caused the accident, since that driver should have been paying attention to the traffic signals. On the other hand, if I add instead that the accident took place in the middle of a highway, one is likely to think that the stationary car caused the accident, since it had no business sitting at a dead stop in the middle of a highway.

In these enriched cases, we come up with different answers to the question of which car caused the accident, because the notion of causation in play is not the bare (meta)physical one. It is, rather, an implicitly normative, responsibility-laden concept. The real question behind, "Which car caused the accident?" is "Which car is blameworthy for the accident?" and part of what explains the answer is the normative background of rights and duties. Now we can see more clearly the motivation for the Augustinian solution. That God is not responsible (i.e., blameworthy) for evil follows from the claim that evils are mere privations of goods, *together with* the assumption that God has no duties or responsibilities to cause goods in his creatures.

Consider this passage by Garrigou-Lagrange, a conservative Thomist friendly to TD, which illustrates the pattern of argument nicely:

> [The objection runs:] If, in fact, the bestowal of efficacious grace is the cause of one's not resisting [sufficient grace], which is a good, then its non-bestowal is the cause of one's resisting, which is an evil.... [In reply:] The Thomists say... the fact that grace is not bestowed is not the cause of the omission of the salutary act. The omission is a defect that proceeds solely from our defectibility and by no means from God. *It would proceed from Him only if He were bound, if He owed it to Himself, to keep us always in the performance of good* [which he does not] ... Thus ... it is not true to say that man resists or sins because he is deprived of efficacious grace. He resists by reason of his own defectibility, *which God is not bound to remedy*.[8]

One lesson is that the Augustinian metaphysics—that evil is a privation of good—cannot be presented as any kind of a solution to the problem of evil in the absence of the associated moral claim that God does not owe us any goods. The morals are at least as controversial as the metaphysics.

At this point we might want to step back and reconstrue the nature of the "authoring evil" objection. The deep problem, we might think, is not answered by the Augustinian strategy, the claim that God does not *cause* evil. For we can imagine various scenarios in which this was true but in which God was, in objectionable ways, "authoring evil." Suppose, for instance, that God created Judas with the intention that he would be damned forever; or suppose that God created Scrooge with the intention that he would inflict misery on those around him. It does not matter whether God has some further purposes for these actions, whether to display his glory in the redemption of Scrooge or to redeem the world through the sacrifice of Christ. The objection is that God has intentionally brought about (we will not say "caused") various evils. This version of the "authoring evil" objection is not helped by the Augustinian strategy, and requires a different response.

DIVINE INTENTION, DIVINE FORESIGHT

Morally speaking, there is a vast gulf between intending to do an evil, and having some evil be a merely foreseen consequence of something else one does. To take standard examples, inflicting civilian casualties as a foreseen side-effect of bombing a military target in wartime is permissible under the laws of war, while intentionally killing civilians as a means of terrorizing a country into submission is not. Giving a terminally ill patient a painkiller, in order to relieve suffering, knowing that it may hasten their demise is

---

8. Garrigou-Lagrange, *Predestination*, 332–33 (emphasis added).

compassionate medicine, while giving a patient a painkiller with the intention of hastening their demise is medical murder.

One traditional way of understanding these moral claims is by way of the Principle of Double Effect (PDE). There are various versions of this principle, but the generally agreed outline contains four clauses an action must meet to be morally permissible:

i. The action is not intrinsically wrong (it is good or at least indifferent)

ii. At least one good effect is intended

iii. No evil is intended, as an end or a means

iv. The good done provides a good enough reason to produce the evil.

The version of the "authoring sin" objection we are considering can be construed as the assertion that, if TD is true, God violates the third clause of the PDE. He is in the position of well-intentioned but murderous doctors, or generals who seek a quick peace through terrorizing civilian populations.

TD holds, indeed, that God's will determines every other contingent fact. It does not follow that God *intends* every other contingent fact. All of what happens is a consequence, indeed a deterministic consequence, of God's action of primary causation, but not all of what happens need be an intended consequence. Some of what God brings about may be foreseen but not intended.

Recall for a moment the picture I drew earlier of God's eternal creation of the universe as a four-dimensional block. How might he choose which block to create, from among the infinity of possible blocks of spacetime? We can imagine God contemplating a large number of schematic blueprints of such blocks. He takes note of the good aspects and the bad aspects of each block. Any good aspect he would see as a reason to create the block (i.e., that universe); any bad aspect he would see as a reason not to create the block. (Good and bad just are reasons for action, and why would God ignore a reason for or against some action?) God weighs his various reasons for creating, along whatever the proper scheme of values is. He then creates the right world, or picks one of a set of eligible candidates. His reasons for creating the world he does are simply that world's good aspects, and all these aspects are intended. The bad aspects he foresees but does not intend.[9] On this picture of God's creative activity, no evil is intended.

This solution might be thought too quick. As a possible counterexample, consider that the existence of compassion in the world is a good

---

9. For a considerably more thorough treatment of this view of God's reasons for acting, see Pruss, "Omnirationality," 1–21.

aspect of it. However, a world with the virtue of compassion in it needs instances of suffering to be compassionate about. If God intends a world in which compassion arises, and suffering is a necessary means for that end, does not God intend the suffering? The objection only needs the claim that one who intends an end intends any necessary means to that end.

The reply to this objection turns on the claim that, from God's point of view, suffering, though a necessary *condition* of compassion, is not a *means* to the end of compassion. And the "from God's point of view" part makes reference to the distinction between the secondary causes that operate as part of the created order, versus the primary causation which characterizes the relationship between God and the creation as a whole.

First a simple point. If I intend to do an action A, not just any necessary condition of A is an intended means. Not even every action of mine required for the performance of A is an intended means to A. To shoot a basketball through a hoop, I must disturb the air, but disturbing the air is not a means to shooting a basket. On the other hand, tossing the ball is a necessary means. Since intending the end involves intending any necessary means, anyone who intends to shoot a ball through a hoop intends to toss the ball as a means to that end. The reason why tossing the ball is a means to making a basket, while disturbing the air is not, is that tossing the ball causes the ball to go through the hoop, while disturbing the air does not. So if God intends instances of suffering as a means to the end of developing compassion in his creatures, it will only be because the suffering causes the compassion.

In the realm of secondary causes, it does. If you or I were (unwisely) to try to engineer compassion in our children by subjecting their siblings to suffering, we would thereby be intending the suffering as a means to the end of engineering compassion, because the point of our activity would be to cause compassion by means of causing suffering. And if God were like a deist God, so that he had to operate through the order of secondary causes (even though he creates this causal order), the same result would follow: God would have to intend evil, albeit for good ends.

However, an eternal God exercises primary causation, and the question is whether the suffering is a means in that order. We do not answer this question by looking at the order of secondary causes. The authorial analogy may be helpful: an author writes a story about an avalanche, and then in the story the avalanche causes the destruction of a village. The author didn't have to write it that way, however. From his point of view, both the avalanche and the destruction of the village are simply, and independently, caused by his fingers on the word processor. Now, there may be elements of means-end reasoning within the author's mind: he may write the part about the village being wiped out because he wants a tragic plot device, and he may have the hero get the girl because he wants the story to have a happy ending. But we don't discover what the author intends as a means to what, by appeal to the causal forces at work in the story.

So even if, in the created world, the experience of suffering is a necessary condition (or cause) of the development of compassion, it does not follow that the suffering is God's means to bring the compassion about. We can simply allow that whatever good aspects to suffering there are ("being a [secondary] cause of the development of compassion" would be one) are intended by God, while whatever negative aspects there are ("being painful" presumably being one) are merely foreseen.

Thus it is perfectly possible for the theological determinist to hold that God *intends* the good aspects of the world but merely *foresees* the evil aspects. There is no need to hold that God ever intends evil, although his will determines every detail of creation.

Returning to the PDE specifically, so long as (i) creating the world is not intrinsically wrong, (ii) there is at least some good in the creation, and (iv) the good aspects of creation, weighed against the bad aspects, are a good enough reason to create the world—all these conditions strike me as very plausible—there is no fear that God has, in his creative activity, failed to conform to the moral requirements of the PDE.

Let me apply this result to a chestnut of Reformed theology, which is also the most important test case for the worry that TD has God intending evil. Supralapsarians and infralapsarians disagree about the order of the Fall (or more broadly, the occurrence of sin) and the various elements of redemption (Incarnation, Atonement) in God's plan. (The order in question is their logical order, not their temporal order; both decrees are eternal.) Supralapsarians believe that God's ultimate end in the creation is the display of his glory in the redemption of some and the judgment of sin in everyone else. This requires sin in the world, so God ordains the Fall as a step in his ultimate plan. This certainly sounds like God intending that humans sin in order to have something to redeem and punish, and insofar as that is in fact what the supralapsarian holds, they fall afoul of the objection that a perfectly good God should never intend evil. Infralapsarians, wishing to avoid this consequence, believe that God decrees the Fall (perhaps as a merely foreseen side effect of granting human beings freedom) and then institutes his plan of redemption as a way of mitigating the disaster. This sounds to supralapsarians like the sovereign God of the universe having to resort to Plan B shortly after he starts his plan for creation. My argument will be that both these views are mistaken.

An analogy might go like this. Suppose that one month I stop going out to eat for lunch, to the tune of about $50, and at the same time increase my spending on philosophy books by the same amount. Assume that ceasing to go out to lunch is broadly "bad"—I *liked* eating out—and more philosophy books is broadly "good." The "supraluncharians" will analyze my motives this way: I decided to buy $50 more of philosophy books each month, cast around for a way to pay for it, and chose to stop going out for lunch. The "infraluncharians" will say, instead, that I stopped going out to lunch, found myself with an extra $50, and chose to spend it on philosophy books.

But there is another alternative. It might be that I contemplated a series of budgetary-cum-lifestyle alternatives: the one where I stop going out to lunch; the one where I maintain my present patterns of spending and lunching; the one where I buy $50 more of philosophy books; and the one where I both buy more books and stop going out to lunch. And it might be that I rank them in that order, from least desirable to most desirable. Then I choose the most desirable alternative, which happens to be buying books and not buying lunch. There does not need to be a logical order to the two decisions; neither is a means to the other.

That is how all goods and evils are in the eyes of God, I suggest. In the lapsarian case, God contemplates a universe with a Fall but no redemption, one with no morally significant activity, an Incarnation but no Fall, and an Incarnation and Atonement in a Fallen universe. He ranks them in that order,[10] and creates an instance of the best alternative. The Fall need not be a means to redemption, and the redemption need not be a response to the Fall. Rather, what appeals to God about this world, and what he intends, is the redemption of creation, and the Fall makes that possible but is not part of what God intends.

SUMMARY AND CONCLUSION

On my preferred version of theological determinism, an eternal God creates the entire spacetime universe from nothing. As such, he is utterly sovereign over every aspect of it.

One worry about this view is that it makes God "the author of sin." This worry can be fleshed out in at least two ways. One charge is that it makes God the *cause* of sin. This charge can be answered with Augustine's doctrine that evil is a privation, a mere absence, and hence God does not, properly speaking, cause it.

---

10. The important part of this ordering is the last (most desirable) item in the sequence.

That reply, however, does not exhaust the force of the "authoring sin" worry. For what we might really worry about is the purity of God's will. That is, what we might really worry about is whether God *intends* evil, including the moral evil of sin, even if only for ultimately good purposes. Any intention to bring about evil would impugn the goodness of God. The Principle of Double Effect is one way to clarify this accusation.

If we understand the distinction between primary and secondary causation, however, we will see that the defender of TD ought to hold that God *intends* only good while he merely *foresees* various evils. For example, the defender of TD ought to hold that God intends the towering goods of Incarnation and Atonement while merely foreseeing the Fall that gives them point. This means that God does not, after all, violate the PDE.

So on either version, the "authoring sin" objection to theological determinism falls flat. One can believe and trust in a completely sovereign God, without worrying that he either causes or intends evil.

BIBLIOGRAPHY

Aquinas, Thomas. *The Summa Theologica of St. Thomas Aquinas.* 2nd rev. ed. Translated by Fathers of the English Dominican Province. London: Burns, Oates & Washburne, 1920–25.

Baker, Lynn Rudder. "Why Christians Should Not Be Libertarians: An Augustinian Challenge." *Faith and Philosophy* 20 (2003) 460–78.

Garrigou-Lagrange, Réginald. *Predestination.* Charlotte, NC: TAN, 1998.

Pinnock, Clark, et al. *The Openness of God: A Challenge to the Traditional Understanding of God.* Downers Grove, IL: InterVarsity, 1994.

Pruss, Alexander R. "Omnirationality." *Res Philosophica* 90 (2013) 1–21.

4

Not the Author of Evil
A Question of Providence, Not a Problem for Calvinism

—James E. Bruce

If God determines that an evil action occurs, God is the author of that evil action. This conditional seems obvious to many people, but Calvinists deny it. Calvinists believe that God determines particular evil acts without being responsible for their evil. Even trickier still, Calvinists want God to receive the glory for all the good actions that he determines, but no blame for the bad ones.

Let's call the overall belief that Calvinism makes God responsible for evil the author of sin objection. For reasons that will become obvious, let's call the belief that *if God determines an evil action, then he's responsible for that evil action* an application of the *common axiom* to divine and human agency. Let's call the tricky business of giving God praise for all good actions but no blame for any bad ones the *asymmetry claim*.

Calvinists refute the author of sin objection by denying that the common axiom applies to divine and human interaction and by defending an asymmetry claim. Their opponents endorse the author of sin objection against Calvinism by affirming the application of the common axiom. They may also deny the asymmetry claim.

Our guide through these issues is Francis Turretin (1623–1687).[1] Turretin considers the author of sin objection in the context of a broader discussion of divine providence, showing that widely held Christian doctrine requires a Calvinist conclusion to the question of meticulous providence. Turretin offers an account of human freedom in order to show how God controls all things and how God, though not morally responsible for any evil, gets credit for what is good. Turretin makes his approach all the more credible by criticizing alternative accounts of God's providential government.

This chapter has five main sections. The first connects Christian providence with Calvinist meticulous providence. The second responds to two objections to Calvinist providence; the first is from the common axiom and the second is from a non-Calvinist conception of human freedom. The third major section develops an account of human freedom compatible with Calvinist providence, answering both metaphysical and moral objections along the way. The fourth section defends the asymmetry claim by exploring God's permission, desertion, and operation as well as man's deficiency. The fifth and final section offers arguments against rival accounts of providence in order to show that they do not offer a credible explanation for how God is not the author of sin; how they embrace a non-Christian account of providence, or how they are metaphysically implausible.

I. FROM CHRISTIAN PROVIDENCE TO CALVINIST PROVIDENCE

§1

For Turretin, God's relationship to sin falls under the providence of God. But what exactly *is* providence? It consists of two things: (1) divine conservation and (2) divine governance.[2] To justify this position, Turretin appeals to God's intimate care for his creation, and, unsurprisingly, to those scriptural

---

1. Turretin, *Institutes*. References to the *Institutes* follow my approach taken in Bruce, *Rights in the Law*: x.y.z (a:b) in parenthesis indicates x, the topic; y, the question; and z, the paragraph, in any edition. When I quote directly from the English version, I will include the volume, *a*, and the page number, *b*. Three numbers by themselves refer to a topic, question, and paragraph; a zero in the third position indicates that the text is part of the question of the section, rather than part of the paragraphs constituting the answer. Two numbers by themselves, separated by a colon, indicate a volume and page(s) in the English translation.

2. Turretin, *Institutes*, 6.4.1.

passages that show God's care for the smallest things, like the number of hairs on our head (Luke 12:7), etc.[3]

He also connects our belief in (1) with our belief in (2): God conserves creation only if he providentially governs it. Calvinism's detractors affirm the premises but not the conclusion of the following argument:

1. God is loving. (premise)

2. If God does not control and direct particular evils, then God is not loving.(premise)

3. If God is loving, then God controls and directs particular evils. (contrapositive, 2)

So, 4. God controls and directs particular evils.(modus ponens, 1,3)

The argument is valid. It involves contraposition and one instance of modus ponens.[4] Christians universally affirm (1). As (3) follows from (2) and the conclusion from (1) and (3), (2) is the disputed premise. How can a non-Calvinist Christian deny premise (2)? Let's try to do just that while still affirming the first premise that God is loving. Consider for the sake of argument that God does not control and direct particular evils but that God is loving. Either God permits particular sins from inactivity or inattention or he permits them by attentive activity, i.e., a conscious choice. If he permits sin from inactivity or inattention, he's not loving, because surely a lover is active in his care and support of his beloved, and attentive to her joys and sorrows. So it cannot be the case that God doesn't control and direct particular evils from a lack of interest. The only other option is that he must permit evil by a conscious choice. Now if God permits sin by a conscious choice, then he either permits things to happen generally, or he allows only particular things to happen. If he allows things to happen generally, then God is not loving, because he does not seek the good of his beloved: he has chosen to have no control over the particular evils that strike his beloved. If, however, he allows only particular things to happen, then God does, in fact, control and direct particular evil—which is what the non-Calvinist is trying to deny. So a non-Calvinist must be committed to the position that God permits evil things to happen generally, not evil things in particular. If God is loving, then God controls and directs evil. Because God is loving, God controls and directs evil.

---

3. Ibid. 6.3.2–4 (1:498).

4. Remember that *if not q, then not p* is logically equivalent to *if p, then q* (each being the contrapositive of the other).

This argument can be reworked in a number of ways, using God's justice, his goodness, etc., but the basic point is that Calvinists follow the logic of God's attributes to their logical conclusion. Because God is loving, he controls and directs particular evils.

II. TWO OBJECTIONS TO CALVINIST PROVIDENCE

§2

One obvious reply to this conclusion is that God cannot control and direct particular evils, because, if he does, then he is morally responsible for those evils. Turretin recognizes that there is a *common axiom* that supports this objection. It says that action and effect belong to the principal rather than the instrumental cause: we hold, e.g., that a man is responsible for a murder, not his handgun. If God determines that *A* kill *B*, then God is responsible for the murder, not *A*—but only if the common axiom applies.

Turretin offers two arguments to persuade us that it does not. First, though the common axiom holds good in homogeneous causes, it does not hold in heterogeneous ones.[5] Divine and human causes are "not of collateral and equal causes, but of unequal and subordinate."[6] God acts through "a concourse of the first, universal and hyperphysical cause," whereas human agency is "of the second, particular and physical cause."[7] God sustains the free agency of humanity by his awesome power, but he does not do so by physically forcing humans to be free—a contradiction in terms. Instead, God upholds and directs their free choices by a hyperphysical, previous concourse. More obviously needs to be said. Accordingly, we will deal with Turretin's arguments about human freedom generally in §4; about God's interaction with sinful human decisions in §§6–8, and, finally, about Turretin's specifically Calvinist approach to the interaction of divine causation and human causation in §11.

If Turretin is right in his analysis of heterogeneity and can show that divine and human causes are heterogeneous, then he has obviated the problem that the common axiom causes for Calvinism. God can determine something without being the author of sin, because the causes are different and so God, the primary cause, is not responsible for the evil action. That's the first argument against the common axiom, which Calvinism's

---

5. Turretin, *Institutes*, 6.7.24.
6. Ibid., 6.6.5 (1:512).
7. Ibid., 6.6.5 (1:513).

antagonists uses to support their claim that Calvinism makes God the author of sin.

Turretin offers a second argument against the common axiom. God acts on and in a man *as a man*, an agent with free, rational choice. God does not use a man as a man uses a sword; otherwise, God would be responsible for the sin that the man does. Though the common axiom holds when irrational instruments are used by a principal, rational agent, it does *not* hold when "metaphorical and mixed instruments which have something of their own mixed (by which they work) . . . do not borrow from the principal cause."[8] Writing about the human will, Turretin writes, "Although it determines itself, this nevertheless does not hinder it from being determined by God because the determination of God does not exclude the determination of man."[9] The point: God can determine that man will freely determine something. God can freely choose that a man choose to do something freely and not under compulsion. Naturally, Turretin will need to say something more to make these claims plausible; he does so, by defending a particular conception of human freedom. We will consider his defense in §§4–5.

§3

For now, let's consider a second objection to a Calvinist understanding of providence.[10] The first is that the common axiom makes God the author of sin, if God controls and directs particular evils. The second objection is that God cannot control and direct particular evils because "God is unwilling to do violence to the free will granted to the creature by himself."[11] Turretin offers a trenchant critique of this claim. If God in principle never violates freedom of the will as non-Calvinists understand freedom, then God can never hinder sin—but that's absurd. So the non-Calvinist must say that God can hinder sin, by violating freedom of the will. But that creates a new worry: God prevents some evil and not others. Why? If the answer is the intrinsic value of human freedom, then that's small comfort to someone faced with a

---

8. Ibid., 6.7.25 (1:524).

9. Ibid., 6.4.16 (1:505). My corrected translation of the Latin: *Quamvis verò seipsam determinet, non obstat tamen quominus determinetur etiam à Deo, quia determinatio Dei non excludit determinationem hominis.*

10. Ibid., 6.7.9. Turretin names the Arminians as theological opponents on this issue.

11. Ibid. 6.7.9 (1:517). My corrected translation of the Latin: *Arminiani causam, vel unam, vel praecipuam esse putant, quod nolit Deus vim inferre libero arbitrio creaturis à se concesso.*

deep sorrow; God allows a horrific, particular evil to occur for the sake of a metaphysical feature of the world (namely, human freedom).

The non-Calvinist can surely bolster this appeal with appeals to a greater good, e.g., John Hick's soul-making.[12] But there are two problems with this appeal to soul-making: first, these replies are open to the Calvinist. Turretin himself appeals to the greater good that can result from allowing evil; he quotes Augustine on this point and then adds, "For if he had not permitted evil, his punitive justice would not have appeared, nor his pardoning mercy, nor the wisdom by which he turns evil into good, nor that wonderful love manifested in sending his Son into the world for the salvation of the church."[13] And the Calvinist can say something more: God was right there when the evil happened; he was still in charge.

Second, if the justification for God *not* acting is the foreseen benefits to others, then non-Calvinists must confront the following sober state of affairs: the so-called "beneficiaries" of an evil may not be the recipients of the evil. For example, *A* kills *B* but in so doing gives an opportunity for *C* to display courage. Evil overall is justified by *C*'s soul-making, but *B* suffered. *B* died. This choice of *C* over *B* strikes the non-Calvinist as unworthy of God's goodness. So what can the non-Calvinist say? One option is that God had no other choice: to create creatures like us, he had to leave open the possibility of evil. But, again, that's small comfort to *B*'s parents, or his children. So non-Calvinists generally go shopping for an answer more in keeping with their moral outlook. Proposed solutions include universalism and a post-death opportunity for conversion.[14] But notice that these maneuvers narrow the non-Calvinist position considerably and come with their own set of problems. Universalism is not a solution for libertarian freedom of the will but a denial of it; people have no choice about the most important choice of their lives. A post-death opportunity for conversion for those who have never heard the gospel undermines Christian evangelization; after all, regardless of whether or not we make a sacrifice to send missionaries, etc., people will have an opportunity to hear the gospel.[15]

---

12. See Hick, *Philosophy of Religion*.

13. Turretin, *Institutes*, 6.7.9 (1:518).

14. See, e.g., Swinburne, *Is There a God*, for flirtation with the former, and Evans, *Historical Christ*, for advocacy of the latter.

15. It's even worse than that: people who have never heard the gospel will presumably hear the gospel in their own language, not through the broken stammering of a missionary trying to speak their language, and they will hear it for the first time after they die—so any physicalist who has never heard the gospel will be presented with the gospel after having realized that his metaphysical outlook is altogether mistaken, given that he's still alive.

An even more satisfying view is one that says that God, though not the author of evil, providentially arranges and controls it, so that we can receive even great hardship—even the death of *B*!—from the Lord God Almighty. That's indeed more comforting; it's called Calvinism.

III. CALVINIST FREEDOM

§4

We must now deliver on something that we promised in §2. Remember that Turretin claims that the common axiom cannot make God the author of sin because humans are rational creatures who make free choices. One obvious objection is that divine determination robs people of their genuine freedom, so that, if Calvinism is true, then God is the author of sin, because he's using people as nonrational instruments. To respond, Turretin distinguishes between two kinds of necessity. There is a kind of necessity that is destructive of liberty, but that's not the only kind of necessity there is: there is a necessity that is hypothetical. Consider the following distinction: though it's true that, necessarily, whatever God wills, happens; it's not the case that, whatever God wills, happens necessarily. That's because God wills some things to happen contingently. So "necessary things take place necessarily, free and contingent things, however, freely and contingently."[16] Even as God decrees what people will do, "they also determine themselves by the proper judgment of reason and the free disposition of the will." By predetermining acts, "God does not compel rational creatures or make them act by a physical or brute necessity." That's because "they act both consistently with themselves and in accordance with their own nature."

What then is human freedom? A liberty in keeping with human nature requires (1) election/choice (*ek proaireseōs*) and (2) spontaneity (self-determination). The free human will determines itself "as the proximate cause of its own actions by the proper judgment of reason and the spontaneous election of the will."[17] Consequently, people can spontaneously choose to do something even though they are determined by God to do so. As Turretin puts it, "they are so determined by God that they also determine themselves."[18]

Notice that there are actually *two* efficient causes of a human action, not just one. Nevertheless, there's only *one* efficient cause—the human

---

16. Turretin, *Institutes*, 6.6.6 (1:513).
17. Ibid., 6.6.7 (1:513).
18. Ibid., 6.5.11 (1:508).

agent—that is also the proximate or formal cause. God chooses that we do things, and we cannot do them without him. Yet when we do them, we really and truly do them.[19] Isn't it ridiculous to think that two causes can effect one, single action?[20] Turretin's answer is that it's not "a new thing for one and the same action to be considered in different ways, either physically or morally."[21] To show it isn't new, Turretin appeals to Aquinas, Cajetan, and Alvarez as fellow believers in the claim that God can be the cause of an action qua x but not the cause of an action qua y.[22] Additionally, as we shall see in §11, Turretin thinks that this simultaneous cause of one event is the only way to understand the providential interaction of God with free human choices.

Turretin's opponents could accuse him of misrepresenting the nature of human freedom in order to avoid the force of the common axiom against divine determination. They can claim that there's an equilibrium (*isorropia*) understood as counterbalancing forces (*amphirrepes*) that is essential to freedom of the will.[23] Turretin replies by distinguishing between two kinds of indifference.[24] The *faculty* of the will considered by itself is indifferent: a man choosing can choose otherwise at another time through the exercise of his will. Yet the will *in operation* is not indifferent: a man choosing cannot choose otherwise. *He cannot do otherwise* must be accepted by the staunchest libertarians when talking about the moment of an agent's choice at a specific point in time. A libertarian may say that the agent is free to stop doing whatever he happens to do, but Turretin surely can say the same thing. All agree that an agent cannot choose to do something in choosing not to do something.[25]

We make these distinctions when we speak about our actions, too. The metaphysical distinctions are reflected in our language.[26] Taken in the

---

19. Ibid., 6.4.17–18.
20. Ibid., 6.5.15.
21. Ibid., 6.5.16 (1:509).
22. Ibid.
23. Ibid., 6.5.11 (1:508). *Amphirrepes* could be taken as the equilibrium that is achieved on a balance by mutually counterbalancing weights.
24. Ibid.
25. Cf. Rota, "The Eternity Solution," 165–86.
26. My analysis is greatly indebted to Knuuttila, "Medieval Theories of Modality." Knuuttila writes:

> One example of the prevalence of the traditional use of modal notions can be found in the early medieval *de dicto/de re* analysis of examples such as "A standing man can sit." It was commonly stated that the composite (*de dicto*) sense is 'It is possible that a man sits and stands at the

composite (*de dicto*) sense, *a man choosing can choose otherwise* means that a man can choose and not choose the same thing—which is impossible. I cannot eat and not eat the hamburger. However, taken in the divided (*de re*) sense, *a man choosing can choose otherwise* is true, because *a man choosing can choose otherwise at another time*. I can eat the hamburger today and not eat it tomorrow. For Turretin, the will is indifferent in this divided sense only.[27] Taken in this divided sense, the will can do otherwise at the moment of free choice. Nevertheless, in the composite sense, it cannot, because a man determined by God to do something will, in fact, do it. This other kind of indifference is not, however, essential to freedom. Remember that, for Turretin, freedom requires (1) choice and (2) spontaneity. Indifference is a feature of a faculty that can spontaneously choose, but it is not a necessary feature of the choice itself. Consequently, we can be determined by God to choose something freely.[28]

So the common axiom cannot be used against a Calvinist view of providence. Man is a rational agent who freely and spontaneously chooses to do and not to do things as the result of his own deliberations. He is thus responsible for his own wrongdoing, not God. We will say more about how God interacts with our deliberations in order to determine what we do without violating our freedom in §§6–8. For now we will consider a second objection to a conception of human freedom consistent with Calvinist providence.

§5

The first objection was metaphysical. The second objection is moral. We can frame this objection by quoting Roderick Chisholm, a prominent twentieth-century defender of libertarian freedom. He writes, "If we are responsible, and if what I have been trying to say is true, then we have a prerogative which some would attribute only to God: each of us, when we act, is a prime

---

same time' and that on this reading the sentence is false. The divided (*de re*) sense is "A man who is now standing can sit" and on this reading the sentence is true. Many authors formulated the divided possibility as follows: "A standing man can sit at another time" (§3).

27. William Lane Craig defends the Molinist position in a similar way in his reply to William Hasker. Craig, "On Hasker's Defense of Anti-Molinism," 236–39.

28. Notice how, for Turretin and his interlocutors, the key question is what we mean by *indifference*. Nowadays we are more likely to focus on the word *can* or *could*. For those familiar with recent debates in metaphysics, I am reminded at this point of Kadri Vihvelin's use of a dispositional account of free will to critique Frankfurt cases. See Vihvelin, "Free Will Demystified," 427–50; and also Frankfurt, "Alternate Possibilities and Moral Responsibility," 823–39.

mover unmoved. In doing what we do, we cause certain events to happen, and nothing—or no one—causes us to cause those events to happen."[29] Chisholm says that a person has moral responsibility only if he has an intrinsic power we normally attribute to God alone.

How can a Calvinist respond? First, note that Turretin's not denying that a person has intrinsic power. His point isn't that "second causes do nothing." It is, instead, that they "do nothing independently."[30] Remember that Turretin's central claim is that "whoever does spontaneously what he wills from a judgment of reason and a full consent of will cannot help doing that freely even if he does it necessarily."[31] Second, a non-Calvinist Christian must wrestle with the following: God still responds to evil action by sustaining and upholding it. So an explanation of how God relates to evil acts is still required for the non-Calvinist Christian, because God sustains acts, even if he does not govern them. Third, Chisholm rejects what Turretin takes to be obvious, namely, that God alone is the unmoved mover. Human freedom is not "absolute and independent," Turretin writes, "but limited and dependent upon God."[32] Turretin's claim here is not, I think, exclusive to Calvinism, but part of broader Christianity. Finally, a non-Calvinist Christian following Chisholm will still have to confront the metaphysical problem of how a man can choose and how God can spring into action to undergird and support that choice. We will consider this problem—more difficult to solve than the non-Calvinist will think—in §11.

Perhaps libertarian freedom only makes sense in a mechanistic universe created by the God of Deism, with God, like an artist, "invisible, refined out of existence, indifferent, paring his fingernails."[33] Of course, the Bible speaks too forcefully for Christians to take this position. Turretin offers the "remarkable instance of . . . Nebuchadnezzar drawing out an army against Judea rather than against Egypt [Ezek 21:21–24]." Given the severe language of Scripture, "it is not without reason that their actions are ascribed to the efficacious power of God."[34] Think about it: either the exile is something that God did, and so we have to explain how God can oversee and direct evil without being responsible for the evil, or the exile is not something that God did, and he's wrong to take credit for it!

---

29. Chisholm, "Human Freedom and the Self," 485.
30. Turretin, *Institutes*, 6.5.13 (1:509).
31. Ibid., 6.6.7 (1:513).
32. Ibid., 6.4.15 (1:504–505). See also ibid., 6.6.9.
33. Stephen Dedalus in Joyce, *A Portrait of the Artist*, 217.
34. Turretin, *Institutes*, 6.7.18 (1:521).

IV. DEFENDING THE ASYMMETRY CLAIM

§6

Thoughts of Nebuchadnezzar serve as a convenient segue to Calvinism's asymmetry claim. We have talked about God's interaction with free human choices generally, but more needs to be said about God's interaction with wicked choices in particular. In 6.7.21, Turretin quotes Augustine—who notes that Judas hands over Christ, and it is an evil, but the Father hands over the willing Son, and it is a good—to emphasize how there must be compatible, but rival, accounts of actions based on causation, a moral framework, or something else. Christ died for our sins, and was appropriately punished as a sin-bearing substitute. God did this work, and he deserves thanksgiving and praise for it. At the same time, Christ was inappropriately punished by the Romans, after Pilate declared him innocent.[35] In doing so, they did a great moral evil, an evil determined by God beforehand but one for which he is by no means culpable.

To explain this asymmetry, Turretin says that God concurs with the human will differently in good and evil actions, and he defends a distinction between the being of an act and the morality of it. About good choices, "God so previously moves the will as to be the author of them . . . by determining the will not only as to the thing (i.e., the good) . . . but also as to the mode so that what is done should be well done."[36] About evil actions, Turretin says that God "so concurs as neither to effect, assist, nor approve of them, but to permit and efficaciously direct." He does so "not by infusing wickedness, but by so determining rational creatures physically to the substance of the act in the genus of being, that they (when left to themselves failing from the law) move and determine themselves to bad actions in the genus of morals, performing them freely and voluntarily (*hekousiōs*)." Permission with regards to evil does not, Turretin believes, prevent God's decree "from being effectively occupied about the physical entity of the action itself."[37] God wills the matter but not the privation.[38] The result: "the guilt rests upon them alone, from which God is therefore free."[39]

---

35. Ibid., 6.7.21. Even if one disagrees with this account of the cross, surely Christians must believe that Christ did *some good* by dying; I know of no Christian account of the cross that sees it as altogether tragic and unredeemable.

36. Ibid., 6.6.8 (1:514).

37. Ibid., 6.5.10 (1:508).

38. I take this line—verbatim—from David Alexander, in a note on a draft of this chapter.

39. Turretin, *Institutes*, 6.6.8 (1:514).

Divine permission can't be a result of inactivity on God's part. It isn't negative, "a mere keeping back (*anergia*) or cessation of his will."[40] It's "not simply that God does not will to hinder sin." Instead, God "wills not to hinder" it.[41] Turretin labels a permission from inactivity an "otiose permission," which he rejects and attributes to the Pelagians; by contrast, a permission from choice is called an "efficacious affirmation."[42] Though some may think the distinction too fine, Turretin's point here is fascinating. It's not that God wills nothing at all in the presence of sin. There are actually "three degrees of providence about sin." "As to its beginning," Turretin writes, "he freely permits it; as to its progress, he wisely directs it; as to its end, he powerfully terminates and brings it to a good end."[43] Following Theodore Beza, Turretin says that if *permission* means not being complicit in evil, then he agrees with the language entirely. If *permission* means not caring, then it's "false and absurd," and no different from Epicureanism.[44] When we say that God allows evil to exist, we are saying something about God's active choice, not something about his passivity. Choosing to permit a particular evil is still a *choice*. This analysis helps bolster our argument for meticulous providence at the start of this chapter, in §1.

All in all, Turretin cautions Christians to avoid two extremes: one extreme says that God permits anything to happen; the other says that God is the cause of sin. "The former clashes with the providence of God, but the latter with his justice and holiness."[45] The providence of God must efficaciously order and direct evil; it cannot idly permit it, nor can it efficiently produce it.[46]

§7

So how does God permit sin without being the author of it? First, God permits sin by desertion. He does so "by withdrawing the grace opposed to sin or by not giving it so efficaciously as to enable him to overcome the assailing temptation."[47] God does not desert someone from pettiness; his reason for

---

40. Ibid., 6.7.7 (1:516).
41. Ibid.
42. Ibid.
43. Ibid., 6.7.4 (1:516).
44. Ibid., 6.7.7 (1:517).
45. Ibid., 6.7.1 (1:515).
46. Ibid., 6.7.2.
47. Ibid., 6.7.11 (1:518).

desertion is always just and holy.[48] There are three kinds of desertion: exploration (e.g., permitting Adam's temptation); correction (e.g., his people), and penal (e.g., God judges sinners by removing himself from them).[49] God "has a thousand ways (to us incomprehensible) of concurring with our will, insinuating himself into us and turning our hearts, so that by acting freely as we will, we still do nothing besides the will and determination of God."[50]

Yet God's involvement with sin cannot be desertion alone, given the biblical witness. Though some passages of Scripture can be explained passively (e.g., 2 Samuel 8:2; Genesis 6:19), "Scripture . . . speaks too emphatically (*emphatikōteron*) to allow us to rest in permission alone . . ."[51] He continues,

> "God told Shimei to curse David" [2 Sam 16:10]; "Evil spirits were sent by God being commanded to injure" [1 Kgs 22:23]; "He sends a spirit of error" [Isa 19:14]; "fills with drunkenness" [Jer 13:12–13]; "sends strong delusion that they should believe a lie" [2 Thess 2:11]; and innumerable other passages which are too strong to be explained of bare permission.[52]

So, at least occasionally, God does more than merely permit the sinner to act. Turretin offers three kinds of operations of God to make this claim plausible: "(1) the offering of occasions; (2) the delivering over to Satan; (3) the immediate operation of God in the heart."[53] Let's take each in turn.

First, God offers occasions for sin. Take "the commandments of God, the Egyptian plagues and the miracles wrought before Pharaoh" or the miracles of Jesus: "the former ought to have turned the heart of Pharaoh, the latter the hearts of the Jews, yet they hardened them the more."[54] We do not assign guilt to an authority who commands one thing, knowing that another thing will take place. Even in human affairs, we accept that sometimes authorities must act in a way that will most likely increase the guilt of the transgressor, without incurring guilt themselves—as when, for example, a police officer tells a thief to stop, knowing that, in doing so, the thief may run, and incur greater guilt, i.e., theft and fleeing arrest, not just theft.

---

48. Ibid., 6.7.13.
49. Ibid., 6.7.12.
50. Ibid., 6.6.1 (1:511).
51. Ibid., 6.7.14 (1:519).
52. Ibid.
53. Ibid., 6.7.15 (1:520).
54. Ibid.

Second, God delivers people over to Satan as a tempter, an accuser, and as an executioner and tormenter.⁵⁵ God is *not* responsible for the sin, though he is responsible for the handing over. But here God does not hand over innocent people for their torture, but guilty people for their punishment.

Finally, there *is* the internal and immediate operation of God. Turretin's goal here is faithfulness to the language of Scripture, e.g., Proverbs 21:11 speaks of the Lord turning a king's heart wherever he wills. How can God possibly do this work, without being the author of the action? In a brilliant passage, Turretin observes that God can give good ideas to people knowing that they will not use them in good ways. So, for example, "Pharaoh after the death of Joseph thinks he should see to it that the empire suffers no harm." It's "a good thought undoubtedly sent from God." However, "falling into an evil mind," the good thought "was perverted to the destruction of the people."⁵⁶ One may object that God cannot make these suggestions, because God cannot tempt people. This accusation misses the mark on what temptation is: temptation encourages transgression. God never does that.

§8

God doesn't will someone to do something sinful, nor does he encourage sin. "God," Turretin writes, "does not will sin to be done, but only wills to permit it."⁵⁷ In actively permitting sin to happen, God does not have "sin as an object precisely of itself."⁵⁸ Though God causes the human will, the human will alone is the cause of sin. Turretin can make this claim because of what the human will is. The free will of man comes in between the decree of God and the particular evil act, and, though God is the cause of the will in "the genus of being," he is not the cause of "the will failing as to the law in the genus of morals."⁵⁹ The "premotion of God," Turretin writes, "only pertains to . . . the substance of the act, but not to its wickedness."⁶⁰ The key here is that wickedness is a privation, caused by the fallen human will alone, and not God.⁶¹

Let's think about these claims some more. To show that God can direct evil without being the author of it, Turretin divides sin into three

55. Ibid., 6.7.16.
56. Ibid., 6.7.18 (1:521).
57. Ibid., 6.7.8 (1:517).
58. Ibid.
59. Ibid., 6.7.27 (1:525).
60. Ibid., 6.5.16 (1:509).
61. Ibid., 6.5.16 (1:510).

components: first, there is the entity of the act itself; second, the disorder or wickedness, and, finally, the consequent judgment.[62] Next, he considers how each thing relates to God. Concerning the entity of the act itself, we must affirm, as Acts 17:28 does, that we live and move and having our being in God, even when, sadly, we do evil. Concerning the wickedness itself, however, God has no relation at all. Concerning "lawlessness (*anomia*) itself, God can be called neither its physical cause (because he neither inspires nor infuses nor does it) nor its ethical cause (because he neither commands nor approves and persuades, but more severely forbids and punishes it)."[63] Finally, concerning the consequent judgment, God permits it, ordains it to a good end, and punishes it.[64]

A non-Calvinist Christian could object that "the wickedness is necessarily and inseparably annexed to such action,"[65] i.e., one could say that Turretin is mistaken to distinguish the wickedness from the action. It's true that Turretin makes a distinction between the morality of the act and the physical act itself, but we need to be careful about what he's saying—and what's not saying. Turretin's *not* saying that there aren't specific moral act-types that are universally proscribed: he has read the Ten Commandments! Turretin's point is that a physical action and our moral judgment of it are conceptually distinct. So, e.g., he left the store with her bag could be an instance of theft, or the conclusion of a business arrangement. Again, he pushed the knife into his chest could be a description of murder, manslaughter, or heart surgery. To the physical description of an act we must offer an account of its wickedness. It's not just any act but an act against the law that is wicked. Let's be clear: murder is always wrong; adultery is always immoral. Nevertheless, not every killing is a murder, and not every sexual act is an adulterous one. Incidentally, these claims are not ad hoc: Turretin appeals to similar distinctions in order to explain how God can command a killing but not a murder, in the case of Abraham and Isaac, and, in the case of the Egyptians, a taking but not a theft.[66]

"Therefore," he continues, "the reason why wickedness may be imputed to the human will is not simply because it produces the act in the genus of being (as a physical agent), but because it is man subject to the law who performs a forbidden act (as a moral agent)." An act is wicked because

---

62. Ibid., 6.7.3.
63. Ibid., 6.7.4 (1:516).
64. Ibid., 6.7.3.
65. Ibid., 6.5.16 (1:509).
66. See Bruce, *Rights in the Law*, chapter 6.

"it proceeds from a deficient created will."[67] Because the wickedness comes from this deficient will alone, it takes the blame for the sinfulness of the act, not God.[68] God is not the author of sin. We are.

V. AGAINST RIVAL ACCOUNTS OF PROVIDENCE

§9

Turretin's position becomes all the more plausible if he can delegitimize its rivals, and he tries to do just that. He lists "the three principal modes of reconciliation brought forward by our opponents" in 6.6.3: (1) prescience; (2) permission, and (3) indifferent flux.[69] Let's consider each in turn.[70]

First, prescience says that God's providence just is his knowing in advance what will happen. Turretin offers two objections. The first is moral: prescience doesn't solve the question of God's providence, because God still chooses to make the world that he foreknows. What happens must bear some relation to his free choices, not just to his foreknowledge—that is, to his will, not just to his mind.[71] If the Calvinist God is morally responsible for what happens in his world because he providentially governs it, then the God of simple foreknowledge is likewise responsible because he makes it and not another world. This objection is mitigated in the Molinist case by appealing to transworld depravity, but one can, legitimately I think, doubt transworld depravity (because of the Christian commitment to heaven) and also because, if transworld depravity is true, then it may have been better for God not to have created anything at all.[72]

The second objection to prescience is metaphysical. If God foreknows something, then it cannot not happen. That's not to say that if God knows that S will do A at t, then S must *necessarily* do A at t. God can know, infallibly, that someone in the future will *contingently* choose to do something (see our discussion, above, in §4). Nevertheless, God knows S will do A at

---

67. Ibid., 6.5.16 (1:510).

68. Ibid. Cf. David Alexander's chapter in this volume for discussion of the relationship between God and the deficient human will.

69. Ibid., 1:512.

70. Ibid., 1:511.

71. Ibid., 6.6.3.

72. On transworld depravity, see Plantinga, *God, Freedom, and Evil.* David Alexander calls the objection that simple foreknowledge is providentially useless the *crystal ball* problem. See, e.g., Hasker, "Why Simple Foreknowledge is Still Useless," 537–44, and, in the same volume, Hunt, "Contra Hasker," 545–50.

t, so *S* must do *A* at *t*. To those that would deny this claim,[73] consider the following: God not only *knows* the future; he tells people about it. God gives people knowledge concerning a future contingent event. For God to give *them* knowledge, the event must happen in their future. Even if everything is present to an eternal God, everything is not simultaneously present to us. So prescience still requires for things to happen because of God's choice and for those things to happen without fail. Prescience works within Calvinism; it is hard to see how it works outside it.

Bare permission tries to solve the relationship between providence and human freedom in another way: God allows but does not cause things to happen. Though Turretin believes we must appeal to permission when talking about God's relationship to evil acts, he believes that permission by itself gives an inadequate account of divine providence. First, there's the question of faithfulness to Scripture: God does more than offer a bare permission in, e.g., Genesis 50 (Joseph's brothers intended evil, but God intended good) or Acts 2 (he determined in advance for his Son to die). Bare permission alone cannot explain the biblical record on God's providential governing of human affairs.

Second, bare permission doesn't deliver the promised goods: the hope is to offer a robust account of providence without meddling too much in human freedom. But here bare permission fails. It doesn't preserve libertarian freedom (for those who want it), nor can it be an adequate explanation of providence. Consider libertarian freedom: God cannot permit just anything to happen; otherwise, what he foreknows, and what he prophesies, could really and truly not come to pass, which is absurd.[74] God does not permit just anything to happen, but *particular things*. Given that he permits particular things to happen, they will happen. They won't all happen necessarily, of course, but they will unquestionably happen, nevertheless.

There's also the problem that bare permission poses for providence: if God offers a bare permission always and only, then he's merely watching the show. He'd be an interested spectator, perhaps, but not the Lord God Almighty. He would not, properly speaking, govern the world, and, just as troublingly, bare permission calls into question God's love (see our discussion above in §1). If God doesn't govern the world, then there's no such thing as providence. But there is such a thing as providence, so God must govern the world. His providence cannot be bare permission.

---

73. And the list is legion: for, e.g., Boethians, it's impossible to say that something is in the future for God. Ockhamists say that our free choices affect God's knowledge. My objection here hopes to overcome these moves by talking not about divine knowledge at all but instead about human knowledge based on a divine promise.

74. Turretin, *Institutes*, 6.6.4.

Perhaps this argument moves too quickly. There's a third option, namely that God could choose to let a certain class of things happen, e.g., the class of things that are compatible with God's ultimate ends.[75] Here God could offer a bare permission and yet do so within the context of a divine plan—a plan that preserves libertarian freedom. Consider the following scenario: imagine an alphabet of possibilities, A to Z. If God eliminates all but one of those things from happening, then God permits only one thing to happen, e.g., Q, without actually causing it to happen directly. Furthermore, he can foreknow that Q will in fact happen.

It sounds good, but, on closer examination, such a scenario cannot do the work it is supposed to do. To see why, let's first recognize that the alphabet of possibilities must involve at least one agent, A to Z; if it did not, then no question of freedom would arise. (For example, if A to Z were steps in a mathematical proof, then God would not need to permit one or the other step to happen.) Second, we should identify which letter involves an agent. If it's a letter that isn't Q, e.g., X, then we have to ask how God keeps the agent or agents who want to actualize X from doing so. The supposed alphabet of possibilities, far from explaining how God providentially governs the world, simply obscures the issue. What does God do to prevent X from happening? One option is that God violates the libertarian freedom of the agent or agents who want to actualize X, so that they don't do so. Alternatively, if X is itself part of another network of possibilities, and God permits X not to happen by another process of elimination, there will be the further question of how that happens, etc. We are left either with a violation of libertarian freedom—a violation of what the non-Calvinist position was supposed to protect—or a vicious infinite regress. Neither option is palatable.

Perhaps it's better for the non-Calvinist Christian to say that God carefully arranges all other possibilities *not* involving agents. To continue our alphabet of possibilities above, imagine that an agent is only involved in Q. If, that's the case, then the agent has no choice but to actualize Q, because, by hypothesis, all other possibilities have been eliminated. No violation of libertarian freedom occurs because an agent is only present in Q, not the rest of the letters. But this move doesn't solve the problem for the libertarian: if an agent can only choose Q, he cannot do otherwise than choose Q, or he could do otherwise, but he won't—i.e., Calvinist-style approaches to these questions (consider our discussion of indifference in §4). So perhaps it's better to say that God could make it so that the agent could or could not choose Q on his own. Unfortunately for the non-Calvinist, we've now come full circle: that kind of bare permission is the one we just considered

---

75. I owe this objection to David Alexander.

and found reason to reject. It would be an abandonment of the doctrine of providence, not an explication of it. This modified version of bare permission devolves to the original kind. Neither works.

There's a third way to resolve the question of God's providence and human free will without being a Calvinist. One can appeal to what Turretin calls an *indifferent flux*. Turretin takes an entire question to settle this matter.[76] We turn to it now.

§10

For many non-Calvinists, there's a point at which, in an agent's decision-making, God is a decided non-actor. God clearly sustains everything, but there is some point at which, according to non-Calvinists, God's activity stops, and the agent's alone begins. As Turretin says, "they hold the influx of the first cause to be indifferent to this action or the contrary."[77] For many non-Calvinist Christians, *I* decide to do something, and then God sustains that choice. That's what his opponents mean by an indifferent flux: God upholds whatever the agent happens to choose. For Turretin, God isn't ever inactive; there are no stops or gaps in his interaction with the world. God doesn't see how I'll act and then uphold that action; on the contrary, God's activity superintends my own free choices, and my thoughts before my choices, etc. But these Non-Calvinist Christians introduce an element of time into the discussion, believing that "the second cause determines itself before the first cause acts."[78]

Turretin resists the idea of an indifferent flux in several ways. Consider two preliminary observations: first, God does not use an intermediary in order to act in and through men. He is everywhere present; his power is everywhere available, and his power comes from himself alone.[79] Second, God sustains specific actions.[80] Taken together, these fairly uncontroversial observations suggest that God immediately supplies power to an agent doing a particular act. Consequently, a general influx of divine power is

---

76. We're considering the text out of order. Here's the rationale: we will better understand why Turretin's discussion of previous concourse is important (question 5) when we see that Turretin is deploying it in order to reject an indifferent flux (question 7).

77. Turretin, *Institutes*, 6.4.4 (1:502).

78. Ibid.

79. Ibid., 6.5.3.

80. Ibid., 6.5.4 (1:506).

incomprehensible. God cannot supply a general power to do something without supplying power to produce a particular action or event.

Imagine for the sake of argument that God could supply power to the world in a general way without supplying power for particular outcomes. Think about it like money in the bank: if I am given twenty dollars, then I can use the money wisely or foolishly—investing in a racehorse or buying bonbons, burying the money in my backyard or even eating it. Similarly, Turretin's opponents can claim that God gives us a general power as agents, not particular power for specific actions.

There are several problems with this rival account, the most obvious of which is that it offers a Deist's account of God's interaction with the world rather than a Christian one. In Deism, God establishes the mechanism of the world and lets it run. The work of providence is all in the past: God gave the power (at creation or at the creation of the particular human), but humans do the work. That's not quite fair, of course, because one could add a Christian spin to this Deist account. We can call it the Deist Plus account: God gives power to agents initially and lets them go (the Deist account), but God can interrupt the matrix of agent causation by miraculous divine activity (the Plus part). That may sound like a solution to the problem, but it's not. It simply illustrates it: on this account, God does not sustain creaturely activity; he only provided the past means that creatures now use on their own. I think that's indistinguishable from Deism. Second, on the Deist Plus view, God does not govern creaturely action; indeed, he only *governs* the world when he *interrupts* it. Providence is reduced to policing. Finally, God's providence is always in the past in Deism Plus. Think about it: if you give me twenty dollars, I cannot say a week later that you are *now* supporting my decision to buy food. I can only say that I'm using money that you *gave* me (notice the past tense) in order to buy the food now. If God created the conditions for human flourishing and charged our agent batteries sufficiently, then we can be grateful to him, but we cannot say that he's now sustaining our activity. But that's wrong: whatever Acts 17:28 means, living, moving, and being in God surely means more than being grateful to him for providing the possibilities of creaturely action.

At the heart of the matter is the question of whether or not God acts in and through people or whether he only acts to support what people have chosen to do *after* they have chosen by themselves a particular course of action. Turretin believes that God's action is both "previous and predetermining" and "simultaneous or concomitant."[81] That's his third observation.

---

81. Ibid., 6.5.5 (1:506).

Turretin's opponents don't believe it: they deny a "previous and predetermining" concourse and affirm a "simultaneous or concomitant" one only.

Turretin uses two words that may raise some questions. The first is *concourse*, and the second is *previous*. George Musgrave Giger translates Turretin's Latin *concursus* with the English word *concourse*, but, unfortunately, this nineteenth-century English equivalent is as outdated today as the Latin it is supposed to replace. Perhaps *concurrence*—a simultaneous occurrence—is more intelligible to us today, though our main strategy will be to explain in contemporary language what Turretin is claiming, rather than to hide behind the technical vocabulary familiar to his seventeenth-century readers but unknown to us.

Second, Turretin uses the word *praevius* (previous). Normally, we think of something being *temporally* prior (i.e., before) or *logically* prior (i.e., antecedent). There's a sense in which the distinction Turretin is making is logical: the previous and simultaneous concourse "do not differ really, but only in reason," though "they can be considered distinctly."[82] But there's also a sense in which the distinction is neither logical nor temporal, either: according to Turretin, "the simultaneous concourse is nothing else than [the] continued previous concourse which not only flows into the causes themselves, that it may work in them, but into the effect itself, so as to act with them."[83] Notice how Turretin distinguishes the two: it is only with a *previous* concourse that God acts *internally* in the creatures themselves. Let's put the difference in a sentence: Calvinism's detractors deny the internal operation of God on the person at the moment of choice. So, though we will use Turretin's language of *previous concourse*, the reader will do well to think in terms of God's *internal operation* in the agent at the moment of the agent's free choice.

§11

Turretin offers four arguments for the previous concourse—that God acts internally in the agent at the moment of the agent's own free choice.

First, in 6.5.7, Turretin notes that God is the first cause and, as such, is the prime mover. The second cause cannot move itself, so God must move so that the second cause moves. Prior to an agent's own decision to act, God is already acting in the agent himself.

In response, someone could try to offer a rival account of how God is the first mover. *Pace* Turretin, God doesn't need to do any particular work

---

82. Ibid., 6.5.4 (1:506).
83. Ibid., 6.5.5 (1:506).

before a person acts; God merely sustains his faculties so that he can act on his own.[84] Turretin rejects this analysis. God cannot merely sustain the faculties that act independently, for then he wouldn't be the prime mover. If someone says that an action is established by the creature alone, and not God, then "on that very account it will be independent in acting and God could not be considered as the first cause of that motion."[85] But surely that cannot be the case.

Someone could object at this point that the types of causation are analogous but not univocal. Perhaps Turretin is wrongly assuming that divine and human causes are the same kind of causes.[86] But that's false: Turretin recognizes that we are dealing with different types of causation, one human and the other divine. The secondary cause of an action is human efficient causation, whereas the primary cause is divine and so hyperphysical, i.e., not a part of the world but acting on it. To see why, consider Aristotle's four causes, a paradigmatic instance of four different kinds of causes seamlessly working together.[87] It's this kind of analogous but nonidentical causal matrix that offers the best hope, I think, for someone wanting to say that *I choose* and that then *God the primary cause upholds my choice*. God acts only after I act, but there's no coordination problem, because the causes are analogous, not univocal, just as, in the Aristotelian case, the material cause is not the same as the formal cause, yet there is no problem of coordination when an efficient cause, e.g., a sculptor, fashions clay into a statue. We do not think anything strange is occurring. Similarly, a divine cause and a human cause can act simultaneously, even if God merely upholds the free human choice of the agent, because they act together like two of Aristotle's four causes.

Far from offering a solution to Turretin's objections, however, this analysis actually illustrates the basic problem facing Turretin's opponents. Material, formal, and final causes are not agential; only the efficient cause is. Turretin thinks that divine and human causation are analogical but both agential; his opponents would need to make them *equivocal* in order to avoid the force of Turretin's first argument. Think about it: if God is a cause the way that the clay or the form of the statue is the cause, then the appeal to a distinction of kinds solves the non-Calvinist's coordination problem, but it does so at a great cost. If God is like clay or a statue's shape, then God is

---

84. Ibid., 6.5.7.
85. Ibid., 6.5.7 (1:507).
86. I owe this objection to David Alexander.
87. I'm not defending Aristotle at this point, simply using his four causes as an example.

not an agent. Surely that's not a position open to the non-Calvinist Christian. But, given that God *is* an agent, even an analogous one, there's either no coordination problem, because he's working in and through human agents, or there is a coordination problem, because he starts and stops with human activity. The former solution is the Calvinist one; the latter problem arises within the non-Calvinist framework of divine and human agency.

The question of coordination arises only within the context of *denying* that God acts internally in the agent—i.e., it's a problem for Turretin's opponents, not for Turretin. For Turretin, God acts in all things, at all times, and in all places. There's no coordination problem, because God is always acting. For Turretin's non-Calvinist opponents, though, there is one, because *they* want to say that there are gaps in God's activity within which libertarianly free creatures make choices.

That's the first argument for God always being active, even in our free choices. The second argument also appeals to metaphysics. Like the first argument, it uses standard language taken from an argument for God's existence. The first argument appeals to a first cause or a prime mover; this argument appeals to the distinction between act and potency. Turretin states his argument clearly: "What is of itself indifferent to many acts, to act or not act, must necessarily be determined to act by another because what is potential (*in potentia*) cannot be reduced to actuality except by something which is in act (*in actu*)." "But," he continues, "every second cause (especially the will of man) is such. Therefore it is necessary that it be determined to actuality by some other external principle (which can be no other than God himself).".[88]

One could object that, though not God, we nevertheless have within ourselves the power to bring the will from potency to act. Turretin responds to this reply by making a distinction. First, he recognizes that the will does in fact have the power to act. All second causes do, in a way appropriate to them. But, second, he emphasizes that having the power of self-determination is different from having the power to produce a particular effect. To do *that*, we need "the previous motion of God to obtain the certainty of the event."[89] Though my faculties have the power to act, they do not have the power to act apart from God's power. The universe does not sustain itself. God does.

Initially, Turretin's language may strike one as occasionalist, a theory floated by Turretin's contemporary Nicolas Malebranche (1638–1715), who believed that God alone is the only true cause and that all other agents merely provide the occasion for a demonstration of God's causal power. But

---

88. Turretin, *Institutes*, 6.5.8 (1:507).
89. Ibid.

Turretin isn't an occasionalist: he really does believe that second causes have sufficient power to act and to determine themselves to act. God isn't the only causal agent; second causes really are causes. Yet, according to Turretin, the non-Calvinist must believe in a curious nonprovidential state of affairs: God will either be more directly involved in the effects of my choices than the choices themselves, or he will not. If he's more involved in the effects, then we have the interaction problem. He was waiting (to speak loosely) for me to choose and then he jumps to action. If, however, God's not more directly involved in the effects, then we have the specter of Deism: God's not involved in my choosing nor in its consequences—or he is involved, but in a fairly minimal way. To avoid the interaction problem and Deism, a Christian should affirm, with Turretin, that God works in and through the agent, even at the moment of choice, and not simply in response to what the agent does.

The third argument also appeals to metaphysics. Here Turretin pursues his conclusion by a process of elimination. There are three ways that "two free wills may be joined together and agree to elicit the same common action at the same time and immediately": (1) they are conjoined by a superior cause; (2) they are determined by their own nature to the joint action (and cannot do otherwise), or (3) "one determines the operation of the other and consequently determines the other cause to act."[90] Only (3) can belong to the first cause. The relationship between God and the human will cannot be (1), because the first cause can't be subordinated to another. Nor can it be (2), because God is not determined by his nature, and, furthermore, neither are many second causes—humanity, for example, does not act from natural necessity but from a freedom appropriate to human nature. So it must be (3), namely, that one cause determines the other. Given that God is the first cause, God must determine the creature, and not the other way around. After all, the goal is not to explain how two causes can "fortuitously" act together but to explain how they can act together so "infallibly and so certainly as to imply a contradiction for one to elicit such an action without the other," i.e., if God *happens* to act along with creatures, then God is not the first cause.[91]

The fourth argument concerns whether or not God's eternal decree can be frustrated. Because it cannot be, God "ought also in time to predetermine the will to the same acts."[92] The metaphysical case is straightforward: God doesn't will for something to happen (from eternity) and not will for

---

90. Ibid., 6.5.9 (1:508).
91. Ibid.
92. Ibid., 6.5.10 (1:508).

something to happen (in the present). Again, that's not so say that everything happens of necessity; God wills for certain things to happen contingently, too. But, in willing something to happen, he wills it to happen. Note that this argument has nothing to do with God's knowledge; the question is not whether or not God's *knowledge* of future contingent actions will be infallible. It's whether or not God can coherently will and not will something at the same time. The answer is that he cannot.

The above analysis shows that an agent cannot make a free and contingent choice independent from God's activity in the agent at the moment of choice. In sum, a general influx is impossible because God is the prime mover; because a general influx wrongly assumes a God-like power for humanity; because a general influx generates a terrible interaction problem; and, finally, because it creates a contradictory will in God, which is impossible.

So a general influx cannot do the work of explaining God's providential interaction with the world. Similarly, prescience and permission cannot by themselves explain God's just government over his creation. More is needed. For Turretin, the more that is needed consists in an account of human freedom that can explain how someone can freely choose something determined by God for him to do and how, if that choice is evil, the man alone receives the blame. Turretin offers an account of how God can determine an act without determining the immorality of it; indeed, each man, when he does evil, freely chooses to do what God has prohibited. Nevertheless, God is in control, knowing exactly what every man will do when placed in an occasion for sin.

CONCLUSION

Calvinists can be mischaracterized as hard determinists, not caring at all about secondary causes, while non-Calvinist Christians can be mischaracterized as trusting too much in secondary causes. Calvinism properly understood goes right down the middle: God kindly calls on us to do freely and willingly all that he has decided that we should do, using even the evil that we do to achieve his purposes. God's not the author of sin, but he is sin's master.

We began this chapter with God's love, so it's only appropriate that we end with it. A pious Christian, Turretin writes, ought to "cherish the thought that the singular and special providence of God watches for his safety, whether his business is with men or with other creatures."[93] Interestingly,

---

93. Ibid., 6.9.6 (1:537).

John Calvin himself is an example not of personal triumph but of enormous personal suffering: he was an exile, he lost his wife at an early age, and none of his children survived to adulthood. His consolation in the face of it all was a biblical outlook that now routinely bears his name.[94]

"Finally," Turretin writes,

> from the belief in providence arises the greatest consolation and incredible tranquility of mind for the pious. It causes them, resting peacefully in the bosom of God and commending themselves entirely to his paternal care, always to hope well from him in the future, not doubting but that he will ever perform the office of a Father towards them in conferring good and turning away evils . . . Hence, neither supinely neglecting means, nor carefully trusting to them, but prudently using them according to his command, they cast all their care upon the Lord . . . and in all their perplexities always exclaim with the father of the faithful, "The Lord will provide."[95]

---

94. I owe this point to Garry Williams.
95. Turretin, *Institutes*, 6.9.8 (1:538).

BIBLIOGRAPHY

Bruce, James E. *Rights in the Law: The Importance of God's Free Choices in the Thought of Francis Turretin*. Göttingen: Vandenhoeck & Ruprecht, 2013.

Chisholm, Roderick M. "Human Freedom and the Self." In *The Elements of Philosophy: Readings from Past and Present*, edited by Tamar Szabó Gendler et al., 480–88. New York: Oxford University Press, 2008.

Craig, William Lane. "On Hasker's Defense of Anti-Molinism." *Faith and Philosophy* 15 (1998) 236–39.

Evans, C. Stephen. *The Historical Christ and the Jesus of Faith: The Incarnational Narrative as History*. New York: Oxford University Press, 1996.

Frankfurt, Harry. "Alternate Possibilities and Moral Responsibility." *Journal of Philosophy* 66 (1969) 823–39.

Hasker, William. "Why Simple Foreknowledge is Still Useless (in Spite of David Hunt and Alex Pruss)." *Journal of the Evangelical Theological Society* 52, no. 3 (September 2009) 537–44.

Hick, John. *Philosophy of Religion*. 3rd ed. Englewood Cliffs, NJ: Prentice-Hall, 1963.

Hunt, David P. "Contra Hasker: Why Simple Foreknowledge Is Still Useful." *Journal of the Evangelical Theological Society* 52, no. 3 (September 2009) 545–550.

Joyce, James. *A Portrait of the Artist as a Young Man*. New York: Signet Classic, 1991.

Knuuttila, Simo. "Medieval Theories of Modality." In *Stanford Encyclopedia of Philosophy*, edited by Edward N. Zalta. Last updated February 5, 2013. http://plato.stanford.edu/archives/fall2013/entries/modality-medieval/.

Plantinga, Alvin. *God, Freedom, and Evil*. Grand Rapids, MI: Eerdmans, 1977.

Rota, Michael. "The Eternity Solution to the Problem of Human Freedom and Divine Foreknowledge." *European Journal for Philosophy of Religion* 2, no. 1 (Spring 2010) 165–86.

Swinburne, Richard. *Is There a God?* New York: Oxford University Press, 1996.

Turretin, Francis. *Institutes of Elenctic Theology*. Edited by John T. Dennison, Jr., translated by George Musgrave Giger. 3 vols. Phillipsburg, NJ: Presbyterian and Reformed, 1992–1997.

Vihvelin, Kadri. "Free Will Demystified: A Dispositional Account." *Philosophical Topics* 32 (2004) 427–50.

5

Orthodoxy, Theological Determinism, and the Problem of Evil

—David E. Alexander

There are two main parts to the paper. In the first part, I argue that at least ten major doctrines that most Christians the world over accept are either incompatible with libertarian free will (LFW) or are extremely difficult to reconcile with it. If the first part is right, then, given that these doctrines are true (or even that some of them are true), LFW is in big trouble. However, one major obstacle remains, namely, that by jettisoning LFW, I have made the problem of evil worse than ever. For, without LFW it seems that God is just as guilty of moral evil as we are. So even if it is true that to save the 10 doctrines I highlight, LFW has to go, getting rid of LFW implies that God is not morally good,[1] an implication perhaps at least as bad as giving up the 10 doctrines. In the second part of the paper, I address this worry. Christians need not fear; we can get rid of LFW and hold on to God's goodness.[2]

> 1. Some Christian philosophers think it is a mistake to think of God as morally good. They hold that God is good, indeed goodness itself, but that the idea that God is morally good is to confuse God with creatures. I am sympathetic to such concerns, but I will not explore them here.
>
> 2. Some of the doctrines discussed below can be, it seems, handled adequately by Molinism. I will not be discussing Molinism in this paper for two reasons. First, some of the doctrines listed below cannot be handled by Molinism. Second, Molinism either collapses into a version of theological determinism and thus is not a genuine alternative to the theses defended here, or Molinism is simply false. Space does not allow me to pursue a defense of that disjunction, so I will simply assume it.

1.0 GENERAL STUFF

The main thesis to be defended is the following:

> *Main Thesis—Complete Sovereignty*: God ordains all things according to the counsel of His will. That is, nothing happens or exists apart from God's ordaining it to happen or exist.

The main thesis implies the following:

> *Sub-Thesis—Sovereignty over Human Action*: Every action of every human is, in some sense, ordained by God. That is, no action of any human occurs apart from God, in some sense, causing or ordaining it to occur.

The sub-thesis is a consequence of the main thesis. If the main thesis is true then the sub-thesis is true. Now many will regard the sub-thesis as crazy. But if the sub-thesis is false, then so is the main thesis. In this part of the paper I argue for the sub-thesis. My modest goal in this paper is to get you to say to yourself "it is not crazy to believe that God, in some sense, causes every action of every human." My ultimate, more ambitious goal is to get you to say to yourself "it is true that God, in some sense, causes every action of every human." But for the purposes of this paper I will settle for the modest goal.

If the sub-thesis is true and humans are sometimes morally responsible for their actions, then the following must be false:

> *Libertarianism about Free Will (LFW)*: S is morally responsible for action A only if A is ultimately up to S.[3]

To say that A is ultimately up to S is to say that S is able to act completely independently. If S has ultimate control over some of his actions, then S can act independently of his genes, environment, desires, beliefs, and even God.[4] Ultimate control may imply a version of the principle of alternative

---

3. Hey, where's the principle of alternative possibilities? It may be there; you'll see. If you are uncomfortable with the version of LFW under that name in the text, feel perfectly and really free to change it.

4. Writing on the ultimacy condition for freedom and moral responsibility, Robert Kane states:

> When we trace the causal or explanatory chains of action back to their sources in the purposes of free agents, these causal chains must come to an end or terminate in the willings (choices, decisions, or efforts) of the agents, which cause or bring about their purposes. If these willings were caused by something else, so that the explanatory chains could be traced back further to heredity or environment, to God, or fate, then the ultimacy would not lie with the agents but with something else." (*Significance*

possibilities. The version that might be implied states that moral responsibility requires the ability to act otherwise at some point in the agent's career (perhaps at all points).

To see that the sub-thesis entails the falsity of LFW, assume that the sub-thesis is true. If it is, God, in some sense, causes S's A-ing.[5] But if God causes S's A-ing, then A is not ultimately up to S. If God causes S's A-ing, then A is caused by something outside of S, something distinct from S. Hence if the sub-thesis is true, then LFW is false. But many of you might think that LFW must be true. That is, how can we be free and morally responsible for our actions if something other than the human agent is the ultimate cause? I am going to try to convince you that it is very plausible to think that, given the truth of Christianity, LFW is false. It is simply false that if Christianity is true, then we have the kind of control over our actions required by LFW.

Summing up: The main thesis about God's complete sovereignty implies the sub-thesis about God's complete sovereignty over human actions. The sub-thesis about God's complete sovereignty over human actions implies that libertarian accounts of free will and moral responsibility are false.

The idea that I will try to get you to agree with is that, as Christians, we should believe that we are both morally responsible for some of our actions and that God is in complete control of everything that happens in the sense that God has ordained everything that happens. So, if it is true that God is the ultimate cause of all things (other than himself), then LFW must be false. Since Christians affirm that humans are responsible for some of their actions, it must be possible for us to be responsible for our actions and for God to have ordained all of them. So, it looks like the sub-thesis together with the claim that we are responsible for some of our actions implies the following:

---

of Free Will, 4, quoted in Baker, "Why Christians Should Not Be Libertarians," 469)

The important point for my purposes is that the ultimacy condition requires that the agent be able to act independently of God. Here's Baker's way of putting it:

> Let us say that an account of free will is libertarian if and only if it entails that a condition of a person S's having free will with respect to an action (or choice) A is that A is not ultimately caused by factors outside of S's control. Let us say that an account of free will is compatibilist if and only if it entails that a person S's having free will with respect to an action (or choice) A is compatible with A's being caused ultimately by factors outside of S's control." Baker, "Why Christians Should not be Libertarians. ("Why Christians Should Not Be Libertarians," 460)

5. Talk of God's causing S's A-ing, or God causing S to A is misleading at best. Below I will attempt to get a bit clearer on what it is that God causes.

> *Compatibilism about Free Will (CFW):* It is possible that S is morally responsible for action A and A is not ultimately up to S. That is, S's doing A is a morally responsible action even though S's doing A is caused by or ordained by something outside of S.[6]

Since many think that CFW is false, I need to present reasons for thinking that it is not. (Note that showing that CFW is true does not by itself show that the sub-thesis is true. What it shows is that one of the main reasons for denying the sub-thesis is a bad reason). I will do so in an indirect manner. There are lots of doctrines that most Christians affirm that seem to imply that LFW is false and CFW is true. If you hold to these doctrines, or even to just a few of them, you have reasons to endorse CFW.

1.05 Caveat

The ten doctrines listed below present problems for various versions of LFW, especially the version stated in 1.0. It is true, of course, that lots of Christian theologians and philosophers have attempted to respond to some of these problems, but simply due to space limitations I have not attempted to list those responses (and since I do not list them I have not attempted to challenge them either). The main point in bringing these doctrines up is to show that CFW does seem to be able to handle them more easily than LFW.

1.1 Doctrinal evidence that LFW is false and CFW is true.

A compatibilist account of free will solves a number of philosophical puzzles related to Christian doctrines that are either ecumenical in a strong sense (affirmed by various ecumenical councils and creeds) or ecumenical in a weak sense (affirmed by major Christian thinkers of various branches of Christianity throughout the ages). In what follows, I will briefly state the relevant doctrine and briefly state the apparent conflict between the doctrine and LFW. Because a few of the conflicts are less obvious than others I will spend more time on those.

   a. *Creation and Sustenance*: There is a radical distinction between the kind of creation God engages in and the kind that creatures engage in. God creates and sustains all things in their very existence. Nothing exists apart from God's creating and sustaining it in existence. No creature is able to create and sustain anything in that way. If LFW is true, then creaturely agents

---

6. I agree that not any old something outside of S can cause or ordain S to A and S remain responsible for A-ing.

are able to bring into existence actions, intentions, choices, etc. all on their own. But such power is uniquely divine. Hence, creaturely agents can do no such thing. So, LFW is false.

b. *Divine Aseity* (a se = from self):[7] If God is *a se*, then God is completely independent of everything. God is completely independent—God does not depend on anything for anything. God knows various truths (e.g. God knows that Obama is freely eating dinner). Is this bit of knowledge dependent on something other than God? If God's knowledge of what Obama is doing right now depends in any way on Obama, then God's aseity seems to be compromised. LFW makes God's knowledge of what we will freely do depend on us. CFW does not.

In other words, if LFW is true, then a portion of God's knowledge is dependent on things other than God. If LFW is true, God does not know what you will freely do tomorrow because he ordained it. Rather, if LFW is true, God knows what you will freely do tomorrow—granting for the sake of argument that he does—because he somehow sees you doing it tomorrow. His knowledge depends on you, not on what he ordains. This threatens divine aseity. But if CFW is true, then God knows what you will freely do tomorrow, because he ordained what you will freely do tomorrow. His knowledge of what you will freely do tomorrow does not depend on you at all; it depends solely on Him.[8]

c. *Doctrine of Divine Providence*: Nothing happens independently of God's will. God is in complete control of His universe. God is not surprised by anything that happens. LFW makes this a mystery. CFW does not. If LFW is true, then it is hard to see how God could be in complete control of the universe. For if LFW is true, then some things happen in the universe that God did not bring about. But if CFW is true, nothing happens in the universe that God did not bring about.

d. *Moral Perfection*: God is morally perfect in the sense that God cannot sin (or perform any evil acts at all). LFW makes this a mystery. CFW does not.

God is both perfectly free and morally perfect. If LFW is true and God is free, then it should be the case that God can sin. But moral perfection implies that God cannot sin. So either God is not morally perfect, God is not perfectly free, or LFW is false (at least with respect to God). But God is morally perfect and hence perfectly free. Thus, LFW is false.

---

7. For a similar argument, see Brower, "Simplicity," 105–28.

8. See Craig, "Nominalism," 44–65, for more on the doctrine of aseity and historical evidence supporting the view that the fathers that crafted the Nicene Creed really did think that God is the creator of all things visible and invisible.

e. *Freedom and Foreknowledge*: God knows the future exhaustively. Persons are free. LFW makes this is a mystery. CFW does not.

If LFW is true, then I must be able, at some point, to act other than I do. But if God knows from all eternity every act I will perform, how is it possible for me to act other than I do? If God knows that I will play basketball tomorrow, then it is true that I will play basketball tomorrow. But if it is true that I will play basketball tomorrow and God knows this, then it is very hard to see how I am able to avoid playing basketball tomorrow. But if CFW is true, then there is no problem here at all. God knows that I will play basketball tomorrow because He ordains all things.

We can approach this directly from the idea of ultimate control. If LFW is true, then I have ultimate control over some of my actions. If I have ultimate control over some of my actions, then I can act independently of God. If I can act independently of God, then God cannot know what I will do before I do it (there seems to be nothing to know prior to my action). Hence, if LFW is true, then God cannot know what I will do before I do it. But if CFW is true there is no problem here at all.

f. *Inspiration of Scripture:* The Bible is infallible. The process of writing the Bible did not violate or circumvent the integrity or personality of the author. LFW makes this a mystery. CFW does not.

If LFW is true and the biblical authors performed free and morally responsible actions in their writing of scripture, then it must have been the case that they could have written down all sorts of other things. That is, if LFW is true and the biblical authors' personalities were not overridden or circumvented while composing the Bible, then they must have been able to write something else.

But the Bible is the word of God and contains everything God willed it to contain. There is nothing in the Bible that should not be there and nothing got left out of the Bible that should be there. But if that is true, then the biblical authors could not have written anything other than what they actually wrote. So, the writers, with their personalities intact and freely writing what they wanted to, were not able to write something else. But if LFW is true, then that is false. However, if CFW is true, then there is no problem. For according to CFW it is possible for the biblical authors to retain their freedom and moral responsibility even though God was in complete control of the writing process.

g. *Original Sin*: Christianity maintains that the fall of Adam and Eve resulted in something bad for the rest of humankind. Either sin is inevitable or it is not. If it is inevitable, then LFW makes it mysterious. If it is not inevitable, then Pelagianism seems to follow. Pelagianism is a heresy and thus

Christians should believe that it is false. So, sin is inevitable. LFW makes this a mystery. CFW does not.

In explaining the badness of the fall we might take one of two options (there are others but these are very broad). One option is to say that the fall made it likely that we would fall into sin. But this fails because it entails Pelagianism. If it is likely but not inevitable that we will fall into sin, then it is possible for us to avoid sin and hence earn our way into heaven. But that is Pelgianism. Another option is to say that the fall made it inevitable that we would fall into sin. If this option is the right one, then LFW seems false. How can it be inevitable that we will sin and yet we are still responsible for it? If LFW is true, then it is very hard to see how the doctrine of original sin is true as well. But if CFW is true, there is no mystery here.[9]

h. *Incarnation*: Jesus is fully God and fully human. Not only did Jesus not sin, Jesus could not have sinned. LFW makes this a mystery. CFW does not.

It is odd to say that while Jesus did not sin he could have. Why? Because saying that Jesus could have sinned seems to suggest that there are circumstances such that if Jesus were placed in them, he would have sinned. That is, to say that Jesus could have sinned commits one to saying that he would have sinned in some situations. But do we really want to say that? I do not think so.

Consider this analogy: Suppose I told you that this glass I am holding is fragile. You would take me to be saying that the glass will break if dropped, or something like that. But now suppose I tell you that there is no situation whatsoever such that if the glass were placed in it, it would break. No matter what anyone does to the glass it will not break. Wouldn't you think it is false to say that the glass is fragile if it will not break in any situation whatsoever?

---

9. One might respond by saying that the inevitability of sin does not imply the inevitability of a particular sin. In other words, there is a scope ambiguity that when cleared up is perfectly consistent with LFW. To see this, suppose Max is born after the fall and performs 5 actions over the course of his life. The doctrine of original sin implies that Max will sin. So, at least one of the 5 actions Max performs will be sinful. But original sin is compatible with it being within Max's power to avoid sinning for each of his 5 actions while it not being possible for Max to avoid sinning for the whole set of actions. Max can avoid sinning in performing act1, and Max can avoid sinning in performing act2 ... But from that it does not follow that Max can avoid sinning in performing act1, act2, act3, act4, and act5. For example, it may be that by avoiding sin when performing act1, Max thereby cannot avoid sin when performing act2, or by avoiding sin when performing act2, Max thereby cannot avoid sin when performing act3. The ability to avoid sin for each act when taken individually is possible, but ceases to be possible when the acts are taken collectively perhaps due to some of the relations between the acts. While this seems true, it does not help so long as it is possible for there to be someone suffering from original sin who performs only one action.

In the same way it is false to say that Jesus could have sinned but there is no situation in which he would.

If you are not yet convinced maybe this will convince you. Let me grant for the sake of argument that Jesus could have sinned. I think what people are doing when they say this is separating Jesus' human nature from his divine nature. Jesus considered only as a human could have sinned, but Jesus considered as both human and God could not have sinned because his divine nature would not have allowed him to sin. But notice that neither view—the view that he simply could not sin, nor the view that he could but the divine nature would not allow it—will make much sense if LFW is true.[10]

If LFW is true, then in order for Jesus to be morally praiseworthy it must be true that he could have failed to perform his duty or he could have failed to be virtuous. But both views mentioned above deny this. Either he could not have sinned or the divine nature would not allow it. Either way Jesus is morally praiseworthy and he could not have sinned (either considered just as a human or considered as both God and man). So, Jesus gives us a nice example of someone morally praiseworthy and yet unable to do other than what is right or virtuous.[11]

i. *Salvation:*[12] Either God's grace is both necessary and sufficient for salvation or it is not. If God's grace is not necessary and sufficient for salvation, then either Pelagianism is true—God's grace is not necessary for salvation—or saved humans must perform some action to be saved—God's grace is not sufficient for salvation. Pelagianism is false. Hence, if God's grace is

---

10. To say that Christ is unable to sin is not to say that he is in some way externally constrained. So perhaps the person who wants to say that Christ could have sinned but he never would is simply trying to make salient the fact that Christ's impeccability arises from his character. So long as we agree that there is no possible circumstance such that if Christ were placed in it, he would sin, then the disagreement appears to be merely verbal.

11. What about the temptation of Christ? Some think that if Christ is unable to sin, then the significance of the temptation of Christ is either eliminated or reduced. Genuine temptation, some might insist, requires the possibility of giving in to it. I don't think this line of criticism will work. Suppose I offer you some heroin. I am tempting you to sin. So there is a temptation. But, for most of you, there is no inclination whatsoever to partake. Given your character, freely taking the heroin is simply not possible for you. So we have temptation without the possibility of giving in to it. We should also be careful not to confuse fallen humans with humans. Christ was fully human. But being fully human does not imply being a fallen human. So, Christ's being tempted in every way that we are does not imply that he was tempted in every way that a fallen human is tempted. It entails that he was tempted in every way that a human can be.

12. See Baker, "Why Christians Should not be Libertarians," 460–78, for a somewhat detailed Augustinian approach to this doctrine.

not necessary and sufficient for salvation, then humans must perform some action to be saved. Every human action is a moral action.[13] Hence, if humans must perform some action to be saved, then humans must perform a moral action to be saved. Either the moral action that humans must perform to be saved is good or bad.[14] It is not bad. Hence, the moral action that humans must perform to be saved is a good moral action. Humans deserve praise for performing good moral actions. Hence, the moral action that humans must perform to be saved is an action deserving of praise. But that is contrary to the overwhelming testimony of Scripture and tradition. Hence, God's grace is both necessary and sufficient for salvation. Hence, libertarian free will is neither necessary nor sufficient for salvation.

j. *Saints in heaven*: When the redeemed are raised from the dead they will not be able to turn away from God in rebellion. The redeemed are morally good. LFW makes this a mystery. CFW does not.

In heaven we will not sin anymore. Even better, in heaven we will not be able to sin anymore. And yet in heaven, we are good. So it is possible to be morally responsible for what we do and not be able to sin.

We can consider this doctrine directly from the viewpoint of ultimate control. If freedom and moral responsibility require independence from everything, including God, then it is very hard to see how being in heaven could guarantee sinlessness. No doubt being in heaven, given ultimate control, would significantly lower the likelihood of one's sinning, but not being likely to sin and not being able to sin are not the same thing, and the traditional doctrine tells us that once in heaven we can't rebel.

1.2 Methodological Consideration

The above doctrinal evidence suggests, at least, that Christians have some powerful reasons to rethink their commitment to LFW. But, giving up LFW still may be difficult. CFW may still seem somewhat crazy.

While CFW in isolation may still seem crazy to some, it should not seem all that crazy when considered in conjunction with ten doctrines above. One way to take a claim that initially appears to be crazy and turn it into a claim that doesn't appear crazy is to consider the initial claim in conjunction with one's commitments. For example, I am committed to the

---

13. See McInerny, "Ethics," 196–216, for a nice defense of this.

14. What about morally neutral actions? With Aquinas and others, I think there are morally neutral action-types, but no morally neutral action tokens. So the type of action required for salvation may be morally neutral (though this seems implausible as well), but the action token will not be.

claim that 2+2=4. Indeed, my commitment to that claim is at least as strong as my commitment to any other claim. It is at the center of my set of commitments. Giving it up is simply not a live option for me. As such, claims that conflict with that belief will be scrutinized with vigor. Suppose I run across a claim, call it E, that appears to be in conflict with my belief that 2+2=4. Suppose further that E looks quite plausible.[15] Now suppose I run across a claim, call it F, that does not initially look as plausible as E, but F neutralizes E in some way (perhaps it implies the falsity of E or perhaps it shows that E and 2+2=4 are not, after all, incompatible), and F seems to be the only proposition that does this. Now given the level of my commitment to 2+2=4, it seems perfectly reasonable for me to adopt F. Indeed, given the level of my commitment to 2+2=4, the plausibility of F may increase (that is, F in isolation may be implausible, whereas F may be more plausible when conjoined with the claims that 2+2=4, E, that 2+2=4 and E appear incompatible, and that F implies either the falsity of E or that the appearance of incompatibility between 2+2=4 and E is illusory).

Suppose that I am committed to the above ten doctrines. Suppose that LFW's initial plausibility is quite high and suppose that CFW's initial plausibility is not very high. Suppose that I come to believe that if LFW is true, then the ten doctrines are false. It is perfectly reasonable, then, for those of us committed to those doctrines (or committed only to some of them) to reject LFW and embrace something like CFW. Indeed, CFW starts to look more and more plausible as one begins to see its amicable relationship with all of the doctrines listed above.

2.0 AUTHOR OF SIN

But, all of the above may be all for naught. LFW and the ten doctrines look like they are incompatible. At the very least it is hard to see how to reconcile them and easy to see how to reconcile CFW and each of the doctrines. So, if you are committed to those doctrines, as I am, then embrace CFW. However, CFW appears to conflict with other doctrines that are just as commonly held as those mentioned above. In particular, it is hard to see how to reconcile CFW, evil, and God's goodness. Christianity is just as committed to God's goodness and the reality of evil in the world as it is to the above

---

15. One of my philosophy professors used to give the following example. Take two cups of substance x and two cups of substance y. Mix those substances together. The result will shock you, he'd say. We don't get 4 cups. Instead we get something like 3.95 cups. So, he'd ask, should we not be prepared to abandon our belief that 2+2=4 in light of such evidence. Needless to say, I, at least, had no such inclination whatsoever.

mentioned doctrines. Hence, we are, at best, at a stalemate. So in this section I need to say something about how the sub-thesis does not impugn God's goodness or deny the reality of evil.

Before doing that, it is important to notice that the defender of the sub-thesis may, at this point in the dialectic, claim at least a partial victory. If it is true that LFW and the ten doctrines above are incompatible or that reconciling LFW with the ten doctrines is very complicated, then CFW has a significant upper hand. The LFW advocate can claim that LFW and the ten doctrines are true and that the incompatibility is merely apparent. That is, embrace mystery. I am comfortable with the mystery move, but even here the CFW advocate has an advantage. CFW gets rid of ten mysteries for the price of one. Now the one mystery it takes on board may seem to be a lot more important than the other ten, but I don't see why we should think that. Why, in other words, think that reconciling God's goodness, evil, and CFW is more important and more of a burden for the CFW advocate than reconciling the ten doctrines and LFW is for the LFW advocate?

I think we can do a bit more than end by merely weighing the doctrines on either side against each other (and, no doubt, those who deny the sub-thesis will think that as well). What I hope to do here is present a couple of different ways to handle the worry raised by the sub-thesis and God's relationship to evil. Nothing said here will end the discussion, but I hope it will (a) allow new or at least more nuanced discussions to take place, and (b) move the discussion away from crass caricatures that have appeared in the literature.[16]

2.1 Divine and Human Action[17]

What I hope to do in this section is simply point out that a common line of argument against the sub-thesis fails as it stands. The argument I have in mind goes something like this:

---

16. For example, Baggett and Walls, *Good God: The Theistic Foundations of Morality*, 31–48.

17. In what follows it is crucial that readers keep in mind that we are now operating under the assumption that LFW, as defined here, is false, and that CFW is true. So, readers need to assume that, at the very least, human agents can be morally responsible even though God is the ultimate cause of every human action. Our goal is to see if this assumption implies that God is guilty of wrongdoing.

In this section and the next the influence of Augustine, Aquinas, and Edwards is, I think, fairly clear. Recent works have also influenced me. They are: McCabe, *God and Evil*; Davies, *Problem of Evil*; Grant, "Can a Libertarian Hold," 22–44; McCann "Author of Sin," 144–59; and Koons "Dual Agency," 397–410.

1. God is the ultimate cause of every human action

2. Some human actions are evil

3. Hence, God is the ultimate cause of evil actions.

4. Causing evil actions is evil.

5. Hence, God is evil.

When attempting to discern whether God is morally at fault in ordaining all human actions we need to do at least two things. First, we need to figure out just what action God performs in being the ultimate cause of all human actions. We need to do that because it may be that the action God performs in causing human action is relevantly different than the action humans perform in causing their acts. Second, we need some way of evaluating divine actions.[18] I won't have much to say in this section about the second task.

Consider a ball that is red or a cup that is one pound. It does not follow that the creator of the ball and the cup is one pound and red. The properties of the ball and the cup belong to it. And this is true even though the creator causes the red ball and the one-pound cup. In the same way, from the fact that I freely perform some action A, and God creates me freely performing A, it does not follow that God freely performs A. The action is properly attributed to me not to God. To evaluate God's action we need to get the action he performs in our sights. To evaluate my action we need to get the action I perform in our sights. I perform A. God performs [me A-ing].[19] Those are different actions. So if my action is evil, it does not follow that God's is. For example, my action may be properly described as an instance of lying. It makes no sense to say that God's action is itself an instance of lying. That my action falls short of the moral law does not imply that God's action falls short of anything.

Here's another way to think about these issues. Consider the following argument:

1. Socrates is powerful

---

18. Some, especially those influenced by the Reformed tradition, will cringe at the idea of evaluating divine actions. They need not. What is really going on here is attempting to discern what to say about divine actions given such-and-such a theory of divine control. If it is clear and obvious that the theory implies that divine actions are evil or cannot be praised, then it's the theory that is the problem, not the divine actions. So, divine actions are not really being evaluated at all.

19. Brackets are used to indicate exactly what it is that God causes. So, brackets around "me A-ing" and brackets around merely "A-ing" indicate different events and hence different things caused.

2. God is powerful

3. Therefore, Socrates and God are powerful.

The conclusion follows only if the predicate is the same in both premises. On the doctrine of analogy it is not. Roughly and briefly, the doctrine of analogy says that terms or concepts applied to creatures cannot be applied to God with the exact same sense. It is not merely that creaturely power and divine power are different because creaturely power is finite and divine power is infinite. If the difference were only a matter of degree, then the conclusion would follow. The difference is more subtle and interesting. Creaturely power and divine power are related in the way that, say, traveling at 100mph is related to traveling at 0mph. No speed at all is not really a kind of speed. It is more like the place from which all speed begins, but which is not a speed itself.[20] Or think about an image and the object imaged. The image may be very much like the object, but they are not the same kind of thing. To think otherwise is to commit a serious (and in some cases perverse) category mistake. Now, I think it can be shown that the doctrine of analogy follows from some of the doctrines mentioned in part 1, but for now just assume it. So, given the doctrine of analogy, the conclusion does not follow. The argument is invalid.

Now consider this argument:

1*. Socrates causes A

2*. God causes A

3*. Socrates and God cause A

Again, the argument is invalid on analogy. It is mistake to think of intramundane causation as the same as divine causation. Doing so is what causes a lot of the confusion around how God can be the cause of all things, and how I can cause something as well.

Now, I think that 2* in the context of 1* is misleading. What we should have is the following:

1**. Socrates causes A

2**. God causes [Socrates' A-ing]

3**. ???

Nothing even appears to follow from those premises. The problem with 2* given 1* is that it has God apparently causing the very thing that Socrates is causing. Given the distinction between primary and secondary

[20]. See Miller, *Most Unlikely God*.

causation, which just about every advocate of the sub-thesis holds to, that cannot be right.[21] When God brings about something in the world, He does not change anything. Rather, God brings about the world from nothing, and nothing isn't a something that can be changed. God's causal activity makes no difference to anything because without God's causal activity there is nothing that can be different. It is a mistake to think that when S causes A God causes S to cause A.[22]

So from the fact that I do wrong in A-ing it does not follow that God does wrong in causing [me A-ing]. Those are different kinds of actions, and different kinds of actions require different evaluations. Is it wrong for God to cause [me A-ing] where my performance of A is morally wrong? Well, here we need to get clear on what makes it the case that my action is morally wrong. In general, an action is morally wrong only if it falls short of the demands of morality.

Sam wants others to think he is smart. Sam believes that getting others to think he is smart requires getting others to believe that he came up with some idea that he in fact did not come up with. So, Sam tells others that he came up with the idea. Sam has done something morally wrong.

God causes [Sam telling others that he (Sam) came up with the idea]. God has not told the others that he (God) came up with the idea. Sam did that. Sam had an intention and acted on it. God had a different intention. Sam saw some good that he wanted and ignored other, more important goods, to achieve it. Did God do that? I can't see why we should think so. In particular, I can't think of some good that God is supposed to aim at in this scenario that He fails to achieve, but I can think of some good that Sam is supposed to aim at that he fails to achieve. So, at the very least, the original argument that purported to show that God commits evil when He is the ultimate cause of every human action fails. It fails for the simple reason that what He does and what the sinning human does are not the same doing. If God is at fault, it is not because Sam does something morally wrong and God does the same thing Sam does.

The argument that started this section gets off the track at both the first premise—God is the ultimate cause of every human action—and the fourth premise—causing evil actions is evil—for related reasons. The sub-thesis claims that God is, in some sense, the ultimate cause or ordainer of every human action. We are now in a position to add some substance to the clause "in some sense." God's being the ultimate cause of every human action is to be understood as God's causing [me A-ing], which is not the

---

21. Occasionalists are one important exception.
22. See McCabe, *God and Evil*.

same as God's causing [A-ing]. So, the first premise needs to be restated. Once that is done, the bite of the fourth premise disappears. When we read the fourth premise as though God is causing the evil action in the same way that I am, then it is natural to think that God is as morally responsible as me. But as we have seen that is not the way to understand God's complete and total sovereignty over human actions. God can cause my causing of an evil action without himself performing that action. Thus, read one way the first and fourth premise may be true but irrelevant, and read a second, preferred way the first premise comes out true, but the fourth premise is false or in desperate need of defense.

2.2 Goodness, Being, and Privations

In the previous section I sought to show that it is a mistake to think that when I perform some action God is merely the ultimate cause of my performance. Rather, God's being the ultimate cause of all that exists and happens, including human actions, has wider scope than that. God causes me acting and not simply my acting. If the latter were true, then God would be a coercive cause. God would be changing or manipulating me in some way. But when we get clear on the scope of God's causal activity it becomes clear that God does not change me in any way when He causes. But there is still a worry. Grant that the action that God performs and the action that I perform are different types of action and thus require different evaluations. It may still follow that God does something wrong by not creating me performing only good actions, when He clearly could have. Since God can create me performing only good actions He ought to do so. Since He does not, then He is to blame even if I am to blame as well.[23]

Christians have long maintained that God deserves the glory and praise for all the good things that exist and occur, and God deserves none of the blame for any of the bad things that exist and occur. One way of explaining this asymmetry is by appealing to the privation theory of evil and the convertibility of being and goodness. According to the privation theory of evil (PTE), evil is neither a substance nor a property of any sort. Rather, evil is the absence of some feature that should be present.[24] The feature that should be present is determined by the nature of the substance. Given the nature of humans, sight should be present. Given the nature of chairs, it is false that sight should be present. Related to PTE is the idea that goodness and being are convertible or identical. The idea here is that goodness

---

23. See Grant, "How God Causes the Act," 455–96.
24. PTE is not the claim that evil is a mere absence.

and being are the same thing, although the terms 'goodness' and 'being' have different senses. In fact, PTE and the identity of being and goodness are a package deal. You can't have one without the other.[25] The doctrine of creation and sustenance mentioned in part 1 above is also relevant here. According to it, God is the ultimate cause of the existence and continued existence of everything other than Himself. Since being and goodness are identical, God is ultimately responsible for every good thing. Since evils are not existents of any sort, God is not ultimately responsible for them. Or so the story goes.[26]

We can state the worry that started this section more precisely. Even if it is true that God cannot cause evil as such, God can cause good by causing being. The evil that I perform is evil because of an absence or lack of some sort of something that should be present—for instance, a failing to conform to the moral law or right reason. God could have caused the absent being to be. Hence, God could have and should have prevented the evil I perform. So, God is blameworthy. The central complaint then is that God not only could have created the absent being, He should have.

Once the complaint is aired, the reply is simple; God is under no obligation to create anything at all. Creation is a perfectly free act of God. God chose to create, but He might not have, and had he not created He would not have failed to perform some action that He should have. But if God is under no obligation to create, then He is under no obligation to bring into being those things that are not in being. If He is under no obligation to bring into being those things that are not in being, then He is under no obligation to create the being that is lacking in my performance of a sinful or morally wrong action. Hence, God is under no obligation to prevent the evil I perform. To suggest otherwise is, according to PTE and the identity of being and goodness, to suggest that God is obligated to create.

One might worry that God's not having any obligation to create or sustain anything is true prior to creation, but is false subsequent to it. The idea is that once God brings a world into existence new obligations arise, obligations that were not present prior to creation. I have no obligations,

---

25. Both PTE and the identity of being and goodness are defended in Alexander, *Goodness, God, and Evil*.

26. One might worry that PTE implies that evil is illusory. One shouldn't. Holes are not illusory even though, plausibly, holes do not have some kind of positive existence. They are absences. Blindness is not illusory even though, plausibly, blindness does not have some sort of positive existence. It is an absence. In the same way, evil does not have positive existence. Nevertheless, statements such as, "Adolph is a really evil guy" can still be true. PTE addresses the issue of what it is that makes such statements true. It does not imply that such statements are all false or meaningless.

one might think, to bring into being a child. But, once my child comes into existence, I have all sorts of obligations.

This objection has force, I think, insofar as we confuse the distinctive roles of God and creature. But once those roles are untangled, the objection loses much, if not all, of its bite. Once I bring a child into existence, I am obligated to do all that is in my power and consistent with virtue to keep the child in existence. But, it is not at all obvious to me that God has any such obligation even after He has created. In other words, God is not obligated to keep his offspring existing. Part of the reason for this asymmetry comes from an idea we have already encountered. God's relation to creation is not one of manipulation or coercion or even real change. Divine sustenance is not a matter of God merely upholding stuff that already exists apart from his causal activity. Divine sustenance is God's upholding in existence stuff that He is creating in existence. After creation, God does not have a completely different job to perform. He does not create the universe and then proceed to bring about various changes within it. Creatures bring about change by operating on already existing materials. God does not. Rather, God brings about the conditions that allow for creatures to bring about change by operating on already existing materials. One of those conditions is the existence of stuff to be acted upon. It is "in him we live and move and have our being" (Acts 17:28). God preserves in existence things that already exist by bestowing existence upon them, rather than by bestowing existence at one point and then doing something else later. The exact details of how this all works are beyond me.[27] As Herbert McCabe put it, "To say that God created the world is in no way to eliminate the intellectual vertigo we feel when we try to think of the beginning of things. Recognition of God's action does not remove any mystery from the world."[28] So, if we grant, as we should, that God is not obligated to create, then it follows from this account of creation and sustenance that God is not obligated to sustain anything in creation, since sustenance is simply a different way of looking at creation.

One final worry may remain.[29] Let's grant that God is not obligated to bring anything into existence and that once brought into existence God is not obligated to sustain whatever exists. But perhaps God is obligated to do something once he has created and sustained something. For example, God creates and sustains me. But there are all sorts of features that I lack that I should have given the kind of creature that I am. I do not have the kind of vision I should, I do not perform the actions I should, etc. So while God is

---

27. See McCann, "Author of Sin," 144–59; McCabe, *God and Evil*.
28. McCabe, *God and Evil*, 102.
29. Thanks to Dan Johnson for bringing this objection to my attention.

under no obligation either to create me or sustain me he is, the worry goes, obligated to create me and sustain me in a certain way once he has decided to create me and sustain me at all. Put differently and in terms of the privation theory of evil mentioned above, God is obligated to bring into existence the goods that should be present in creatures once those creatures exist.

I think there are a number of ways to reply to this objection, but I'll briefly present two here.[30] First, it is not obvious to me that there really is the obligation in question. I should add that it is not obvious to me that there is no such obligation. I'm really not sure what to think about the idea that God is obligated to create things with all of the features they are supposed to have. Part of the reason for my uncertainty is given below with my second reply below. Part of the reason is because I think it may be true that if God is under no obligation to create and is under no obligation to sustain, then God is under no obligation to create and sustain in certain way. Part of the reason is because I am not sure that it even makes sense for God to be under obligations. But another reason I am not sure what to think of this alleged obligation is because I am not sure how to think about the manner in which God creates. Does God create me in one action, you in another, Fido in another, and so on . . . ? Or is creation really just one act on God's part? I think that the ten doctrines probably imply that there is simply one act of creation. If that it is right, then it is that act that needs evaluating and not the individual components or manifestations of that one act. In other words, here just as before, we need to get clear on what action is under evaluation in order to figure out if some alleged obligation is violated. Furthermore, if creation is one action on God's part and not many, I have no idea how to think about that one action in the terms of the present worry. Suppose that God's action of creation is the making of a world, where worlds are concrete maximal states of affairs in the way that Plantinga and others suggest.[31] Do worlds themselves have features that they are supposed to have in virtue of being worlds? Perhaps they do, but I can think of reasons for thinking that only parts of worlds have features that they are supposed to have, while whole worlds do not. And if worlds do not (and even if they do, but that story is a bit more involved) have features they are supposed to have in virtue of being worlds, and if God's one act of creation is the creation of a world, then the present worry cannot apply to God.

30. For a very different sort of reply, see Alexander, *Goodness, God, and Evil*. There I argue that given the convertibility of being and goodness together with some plausible principles regarding natures that it is not possible for God (a) to create some creature that is more bad than good and (b) to create a world that is more bad than good. I think that conclusion has bearing on this worry, but I won't pursue it.

31. See Plantinga, *Nature of Necessity*.

You may not be as baffled as I am by some of the presuppositions of the alleged obligation. In that case here's my second reply to the worry mentioned above. As many have pointed out in responding to the problem of evil, it may be that there are other goods that outweigh the various absences in me that should be present, and such goods cannot be present without such absences. Hence, God is under no obligation to provide the good things that I lack because greater goods result, and God is permitted to create and sustain something without features it should have so long as there are greater goods that result that are unobtainable without the missing features. In other words, the principle behind this worry—God is obligated to create all of the features that a creature is supposed to have—is false. At best it needs serious qualifying. Perhaps the following will work: God is obligated to create all of the features that a creature is supposed to have unless (a) it is not possible for God to do so because by creating creature x with all of the features x is supposed to have entails that God cannot create creature y with all of the features it is supposed to have, or (b) it is not possible for God to do so without thereby losing some other valuable aspect of the creation, or (c) it is not possible for God to do so without thereby violating one of God's aims in creating.

2.3 Hell

During the last few years or so, there has been an uptick in the number of Christian scholars embracing the idea that the traditional doctrine of hell is false. In this last section, I will show how the above considerations can be used to help save the traditional doctrine, though I can only sketch how such a defense would go.

Jonathan Kvanvig sets out the traditional doctrine of hell as follows:

> The Punishment Thesis: the purpose of hell is to punish those whose earthly lives and behavior warrant it;
>
> The No Escape Thesis: it is metaphysically impossible to get out of hell once one has been consigned there;
>
> The Anti-Universalism Thesis: some people will be consigned to hell; and
>
> The Eternal Existence Thesis: hell is a place of conscious existence.[32]

---

32. Kvanvig, "Hell," 413–26.

One of the major objections to the traditional doctrine of hell is that it is incompatible with the goodness and love of God. God, it is claimed, is so good and loving that it is simply not possible for Him to consign or even allow his beloved creatures to undergo an eternity of, well, hell. Since the lives of those in hell are so bad, a perfectly good and loving God would do whatever it takes to ensure that no one winds up there. Since a perfectly good and loving God is also perfectly powerful, God can ensure that no one winds up there. Since God can and would ensure such a thing He must have done so. Hence, the traditional doctrine of hell is false.

Before proceeding it is important to notice that the above concern has particular bite for the defender of CFW. The LFW advocate, it seems to me, will have a hard, if not impossible, time arguing that God can and should ensure that no one winds up in hell for the simple reason that the LFW advocate can't really defend the claim that God can and should ensure that we choose God without doing serious damage to LFW.

Let's look at two issues: God's goodness and God's love. As we have seen goodness is identical with being and badness or evil is the absence of some good/being that should be present. So the badness of hell consists in the absence of something that should be present, most importantly, a right relation to God. As we have also seen, God is under no obligation to create anything at all, even subsequent creation. If that's right, then God is under no obligation to bring about a right relation between creatures and Himself. Hence, hell does not place God's goodness in jeopardy.

What is love? To a first approximation love is willing goodness for another. God's love is displayed in at least the following way: by creating and sustaining all that exists. Because goodness and being are identical, God's very act of creation and sustenance is an act of love, since it is an act of willing goodness for another. As Brian Davies notes with respect to Aquinas's understanding of the relation between goodness and love, "Aquinas [thinks] of love not as an emotion but as a matter of willing goodness for something. And since he takes God to be the creative source of all that is good in creatures, he naturally concludes that God loves all creatures insofar as he freely produces all that is good in them." If that is true in general, it is true in hell. God's willing the existence of those in hell is, at the very least, loving in that sense. So, from the claim that there are creatures in hell it does not follow that God does not love them. What does seem to follow is that God does not love to the same degree or in the same way that He loves creatures in heaven. But that's a new complaint. The original worry was that the traditional doctrine of hell is incompatible with God's love. The new complaint is the traditional doctrine of hell is incompatible with God's loving all creatures to the same exact degree. Given the identity of being and goodness, what love is, and PTE, the new complaint can be handled in the same way the complaint about God's goodness was handled. God is not obligated to create, and thus He does nothing wrong or evil is loving some creatures more than others, even if the differences in love are between the same kind of creatures.

CONCLUSION

At least ten doctrines give at the very least some prima facie plausibility to CFW. CFW is, in light of those doctrines, not crazy. Furthermore, when creaturely goodness and God's goodness and love are understood in terms of the doctrine of analogy, the privation theory of evil, the convertibility of being and goodness, and the uniqueness of God's act (or actions) of creation, the major obstacle to Christians' embracing theological determinism is removed (or at least significantly reduced). Theological determinists can appeal to responses to the problem(s) of evil that are just as sophisticated and prima facie plausible as their theological indeterminist brothers and sisters.

BIBLIOGRAPHY

Alexander, David. *Goodness, God and Evil*. New York: Continuum International, 2012.

Baggett, David, and Jerry Walls. *Good God: The Theistic Foundations of Morality*. New York: Oxford University Press, 2011.

Baker, Lynn Rudder. "Why Christians Should Not Be Libertarians: An Augustinian Challenge." *Faith and Philosophy* 20, no. 4 (October 2003) 460–78.

Brower, Jeffrey. "Simplicity and Aseity." In *The Oxford Handbook of Philosophical Theology*, edited by Thomas P. Flint and Michael Rea, 105–28. New York: Oxford University Press, 2009.

Craig, William Lane. "Nominalism and Divine Aseity." In *Oxford Studies in Philosophy of Religion*, vol. 4, edited by Jonathan Kvanvig, 43–65. Oxford: Oxford University Press, 2011.

Davies, Brian. *The Reality of God and the Problem of Evil*. New York: Continuum, 2006.

Grant, W. Matthews. "Aquinas on How God Causes the Act of Sin Without Causing the Sin Itself." *The Thomist* 73 (2009) 455–96.

———. "Can a Libertarian Hold That Our Free Acts Are Caused by God?" *Faith and Philosophy* 27 (2010) 22–44.

Kane, Robert. *The Significance of Free Will*. New York: Oxford University Press, 1998.

Koons, Robert. "Dual Agency: A Thomistic Account of Divine Providence and Human Freedom." *Philosophia Christi* 4 (2002) 397–410.

Kvanvig, Jonathan L. "Hell." In *The Oxford Handbook of Eschatology*, edited by Jerry L. Walls, 413–26. New York: Oxford University Press, 2008.

McCabe, Herbert. *God and Evil in the Theology of St Thomas Aquinas*. New York: Continuum, 2010.

McCann, Hugh J. "The Author of Sin?" *Faith and Philosophy* 22, no. 2 (2005) 144–59.

Miller, Barry. *A Most Unlikely God: A Philosophical Enquiry into the Nature of God*. Notre Dame, IN: University of Notre Dame Press, 1996.

Plantinga, Alvin. *The Nature of Necessity*. New York: Clarendon, 1974.

6

Discrimination
Aspects of God's Causal Activity

—Paul Helm

ORIENTATION

THIS PAPER LOOKS AT the theme of God's varied causal activity, in creating, controlling, and converting, from a Calvinist or Augustinian perspective. The Calvinist sees these divine activities not simply as aspects of God's love or care for his creation *per se*—though the Calvinist has a place for this—but as discriminatory in intent and accomplishment, where others may affirm less or no discrimination.

Christian theology in its mainstream has held that the creation is logically contingent, that this universe might not have been, and has rejected emanation, the idea that the universe is a natural extension of the being of God. Even if it is conceded that some universe or other is necessary, it is not necessary that this universe is created. Whatever account is given of how God decided to will this universe there were other possible universes. As a consequence we may say (leaving aside the important question of the character of God's freedom), that God's act of creation is a discriminatory choice which includes and as a consequence excludes. The actual universe includes you and me, for by the creative choice of God you and I are rendered actual, and it excludes a sister of mine, because she is not actual and so remains forever a possibility, unactualized. But the use of a referring expression such as "my sister" should not mislead us into thinking that a person exists in the realm of the unactualized, that she has a shadowy existence, and that in not being actualized she is, unlike me, being discriminated against. Certainly not. There is no female human, my sister, who has been disadvantaged in not being actualized. The point is, the act of creation is an act of making certain possibilities actual, of choosing, and of leaving other possibilities for ever unactualised. Choice and therefore discrimination figures in creation, though no one not chosen is discriminated against. Why God should create a universe with you and me in it is not clear and exclude a sister for me is not clear.

Any reader of the Bible must be struck by how much of it is structured by God's choice of some people and his passing by of others. Here we think of choice not as ensuing in actualization but as the choosing of some of the actual (or the to-be-actual) to special privileges, and (by implication) such privileges are denied to others. He chooses Abram, Isaac, (but not Ishmael) and Jacob (but not Esau, whom he hates, or if you prefer, loves less). He chooses the nation of Israel, and through Israel the Messiah, Jesus "my chosen" and, following the widespread rejection of Jesus by the Jews, he "turns to the Gentiles." The same principle of choice may be applied to the ministry of Jesus, who met with and talked to and befriended and helped some, and not others. He went to certain towns, and not to others. And it extends to the international Church of Christ in the New Testament, who are described as being "chosen in Christ" (Eph 2:4). God, the perfect being, acts differentially. In some instance the differences are necessary, and in other cases they are contingent, the outcome of choices and of other actions of God. In Scripture the two are more than once linked together, as in Psalms 89 and 147, for example. They are also linked together conceptually, in that discrimination has to do with control or "ensurance" as I shall later call it, and control and calling with the character of the choice. There are problems galore with these concepts, not least because they have to do with causation, itself a problematic concept *par excellence*. We can only hope to scratch the surface here.

A PERFECT BEING'S CHOICE

Divine salvific choice is explicitly linked in the Bible with what later came to be called Perfect Being Theology. The roots of such a theology are visible in the following passage, for example:

> For when God made a promise to Abraham, since he had no one greater by whom to swear, he swore by himself, saying, Surely I will bless you and multiply you." And thus Abraham, having patiently waited, obtained the promise. For people swear by something greater than themselves, and in all their disputes an oath is final for confirmation. So when God desired to show more convincingly to the heirs of the promise the unchangeable character of his purpose, he guaranteed it with an oath, so that by two unchangeable things, in which it is impossible for God to lie, we who have strong encouragement to hold fast to the hope set before us. (Heb 6:13–16)

A number of things are of interest here. The argument underlying the teaching of the passage may go like this:

> Necessarily, anyone who swears an oath, swears by someone or something greater than themselves.
>
> Necessarily, had there been a greater than God, then God would have sworn by that greater.
>
> As a matter of fact, God swore by himself
>
> Therefore, there is none greater than God
>
> Therefore, God is the greatest being

But that may be thought to be a little too quick. Perhaps from the passage we ought only to conclude that God is the greatest in respect of veracity, or faithfulness, leaving it an open question as to whether he is the greatest in love, or mercy, or other great-making properties. So perhaps to catch the thought of the writer we ought to conclude the argument differently

> There is none greater than God in respect of veracity, or of faithfulness, or of some other great-making property.
>
> Therefore, God is the greatest being in respect of faithfulness, etc.

It is interesting, however, that the writer affirms the greatness of God in an unqualified way, referring to *the one* besides whom there is no greater, and not simply to some great attribute of the divine being. It seems an appropriate inference from what he is saying to suppose that he is talking about the being of God, and therefore saying, or implying, that he is a being than which there is no greater. Not simply that he has this or that feature which is an instance of something than which no other possible instance can be considered greater.

So God is faithful to someone, to Abram who he had chosen, granting him a covenant promise, confirming it by an oath of immutable strength, and so illustrating his greatness, the greatest of all possible beings. But how could God be a Perfect Being and discriminate in such ways, making a covenant with Abraham only? By the standards currently regarded as great-making, is there not an incongruity, nay, an inconsistency, in saying that the God who chooses Abraham to whom he makes a promise could be the Most Perfect Being? This is because omnibenevolence is regarded as a great-making property. This is the crux of what I wish to explore in the first part of what follows.

GOD'S PERFECT GOODNESS

I think it is fair to say that Perfect Being theology is currently employed in the philosophy of religion and philosophical theology as common ground to which folk coming from different religious and theological positions, and from none, may find a philosophical meeting place and a source for formulating and discussing arguments. What brings them together are common procedures, rather than a set of doctrines, processes rather than products. One such procedure is that of thinking of God maximally, as the one who alone is worthy of worship. Another is that of ascribing (in Anselmic fashion) properties or attributes to God on the basis of the following question: Is it better to possess property A rather than not?

It is in answering this Anselmic question that some chafing is seen in Perfect Being Theology; is it better to be timeless than in time, to change than not to change, to be impassible than to have periods of emotional fluctuation? What may be said to have started as an avowedly Christian practice, in which it was believed, for example, that it is better (inter alia) for God to be triune than to be uni-personal, has become something that is much more flexible and adaptable.

In what follows I wish to concentrate on the following piece of perfect being theology: it is better to be a Creator than not to be.[1] But to be a Creator clearly involves the Creator in making choices, and a fortiori to be a Creator involves such choices. Or in language made familiar by Alvin Plantinga, for God to have one Design Plan means that in implementing that Plan the Creator must exclude other Design Plans. By God creating in accordance with a Design Plan, certain possibilities for those who are created are forever excluded. In the following discussion I shall extend this

---

1. For Anselm, creating *ex nihilo* is included in the idea that God is one than whom nothing greater can be thought. See Anselm, *Proslogion*, chapter 5.

thought to divine benevolence. The Design Plan chosen will commit the Creator to certain benevolent choices, and mean that other choices are less benevolent than if another Design Plan had been chosen.[2]

Considering perfect being theology and a biblical passage such as the one we noted, one important difficulty at the present time has to do with the understanding of God's perfect goodness. "Perfect Goodness" has had different, or somewhat different, connotations over the years. Sometimes God's goodness has been concerned with God imparting being or existence to creatures. Things are "very good" because they are created by God. Here the Bible's account of the creation is no doubt in view.

In earlier treatments of perfect goodness, divine goodness is only considered as a corollary of more prominent perfections. So in Anselm's *Proslogion* it is not until chapter 5 and especially chapters 22–25 that he introduces God's goodness as a reflection on the character that God must have in virtue of the fact that he is the creator of all goods. He is the supreme good, through whom every contingent good exists and is good. Goodness therefore has a decided ontological ring to it. Something or someone is good only insofar as it or he is an expression of the creative goodness of God.[3] And something that exists is evil to the extent that it is deficient in that mode of existence. The moral or spiritual qualities that beings may possess, or ought to possess, are thus a consequence of the kind of beings they are, the goodness of their Creator being expressed in their kind of being.

But this "ontological" reading of goodness tends not to be in the foreground at the present time. What is to the fore is an understanding of God's goodness as essentially the power to provide and impart pleasurable and person-fulfilling states of affairs to his creatures.

So the love of God is nowadays taken to be an aspect of the goodness of God, and that love has been thought of as God's benevolence or beneficence (in the sense of having good will toward human beings, and no doubt to the non-human creation, and doing good to them as a consequence). Nowadays almost all attention is focused on benevolence as being what matters in God's love, indeed as what that love consists in. Such benevolence when thought of as being possessed by God, the Most Perfect Being, is often referred to as "omnibenevolence." But what is that?[4]

To try to answer that question it is necessary to explore the concept of omnibenevolence or all-goodness as this finds expression in modern

---

2. As Alvin Plantinga has pointed out, a Design Plan entails "trade-offs." See, for example, Plantinga, *Warrant*, 38–47.

3. For discussion of these themes, see MacDonald, *Being and Goodness*.

4. For a rather different discussion of maximal greatness and value, see Hill, *Divinity*, 192–227.

statements of God's perfect being. For instance "God is omnibenevolent" is an expression that has formed part of a triad of propositions that has been used to discomfit those who wish to hold that the existence of a perfect God is consistent with the existence of evil. Thus:

> God is omnibenevolent (or wholly good)
>
> God is omnipotent
>
> There is evil

This is how the logical problem of evil is generated. According to J.L. Mackie, God is wholly good, and this implies that he "eliminates evil as far as he can,"[5] and that a being who is good and omnipotent "eliminates evil completely." Or, as Alvin Plantinga presents matters for the purposes of argument, "If God is omniscient and omnipotent, then he can properly eliminate every evil state of affairs."[6] So why aren't we all as happy and fulfilled as can be? It turns out that God is maximally benevolent in his intent but in fact he must respect the indeterministic choices of human beings, his creatures. Indeed on some accounts, endowing his human creatures with the power to make indeterministic choices is a component of God's omnibenevolence.

Proponents of the empirical argument from evil, such as William Rowe, employ the "good parent analogy": "God, if he exists, is . . . to us as loving parents are to their children."[7] This analogy is not, as far as I can see, to be found in Anselmic versions of Perfect Being Theology, though it has a history of its own that goes back quite a long way.[8] In what follows we shall not be directly considering the role of omnibenevolence in empirical arguments from evil, but instead we shall reflect further on the concept of omnibenevolence.

There have been a number of attempts to analyse divine omnipotence, but despite its prominence in the literature, fewer have been concerned with omnibenevolence, or with all-goodness or perfect goodness, expressions I shall use equivalently and interchangeably. Nevertheless the idea is that God's omnibenevolence must ensure a universal and equal distribution to all human beings beyond a certain threshold, unless this is prevented in some way by freely chosen human perversity. In the logical problem of evil

---

5. Mackie, "Evil and Omnipotence," 93.
6. Plantinga, *God, Freedom, and Evil*, 22.
7. Rowe, "Friendly Atheism," 89.
8. For example, it forms part of Sebastian Castellio's caricature and critique of John Calvin's theology (c. 1557). See Castellio's remarks and Calvin's rejoinder in Calvin, *The Secret Providence of God*, 39–40, 65–68.

it is sufficient to maintain God's omnibenevolence to argue that he would so distribute good states of affairs if he could. The empirical argument argues that it is clear that if God is omnibenevolent gratuitous evil, evil that occurs without any compensating good, cannot exist.

But recently Jeff Jordan has called into question this universal and equal distribution understanding of omnibenevolence, the "wide and flat" reading of it (as he calls it) that is widespread, if not uniform, among philosophical theologians who currently write on the problem of evil, theodicy, and kindred matters.[9] That is, in Jordan's words, such writers accept or assume that "God's love must be as wide as possible by having every human being as its object, and as flat as possible, with every human an equal recipient."[10] Jordan argues that such an understanding of God's benevolence is impossible.

In working out objections to the "flat and wide" view of God's benevolence, Jordan appeals to the following plausible principle of Perfect Being Theology

> (TD) For all properties F, if F is a deficiency when had by a human, then F cannot be a great-making property when had by God.[11]

He applies this principle to the widespread assumption that we have already identified, that God's omnibenevolence must be as wide and as flat as possible. But Jordan notes that the deepest and most characteristic expressions of human love and friendship are necessarily partial. This is not only a matter of fact, but it is appropriate, to love one's wife and children more than others' wives and children. That's a good thing to do. A life with deep attachments to certain people, involving the making of choices, is a richer life than one without, and so on. And we might reflect on the fact that Jesus had friends. Further, a person who endeavoured to love everyone equally would suffer unrequited love, and his relations with the objects of such wide and flat love would be shallow. A most perfect being could not have such a characteristic, therefore.

---

9. Jordan, "Topography," 53–69.

10. Ibid., 53.

11. Ibid., 58. Jordan defends this principle and discusses certain other principles in the course of refining his account. See Ibid., 55–60. In particular, he plausibly argues for the falsity of the principle that if X is an entailment of Y, and Y is a great-making property, then X is itself a great-making property (60). In endorsing Jordan's line here I am chiefly interested in his assertion that no property that expresses a human deficiency can be an attribute of God.

Jordan identifies two features of God's love; "The first consists of God having a disinterested concern for the one loved, with the second as God taking as his own the interests of the one loved."[12] There are Christian theologians, such as Jonathan Edwards, who maintained that God's love of men and women is grounded in his concern for his own glory, and that the whole of creation is the "theatre" of that glory. In which case his concern for the one loved would not be disinterested, since God's own glory is the "last end" of the creation. But even in such theology, God could still take as his own the interests of the one loved.

An objection to this line of argument is that God, having the resources of omnipotence, has infinitely varied ways in which he can be a friend to each human being, the friendship in each case being tailored to the unique character and situation in life of each human person. So that the flatness requirement could be re-expressed as, God has an equal regard to each human being, but that each human person being unique, the friendship of God with A is necessarily different from his friendship with B insofar as A is relevantly different from B. But then the contours of friendship would be different in a Perfect Being's case and that of a human being.

We need to have another distinction in mind, that between the interests of people and their best or true interests. Could it be that a Perfect Being must have the true interests of every human being at heart? Suppose that God permits the suffering of Henry, or the thwarting of his plans, in order in some way to benefit Harriet, furthering or fulfilling her true interests thereby, and suppose further that her benefit could not be achieved any other way. Then God could not identify with the true interests of everyone, for the true interests of everyone could not in these circumstances be realized, for those of Henry could not be realized. So to have and express the fulfilment of everyone's true interests could not be a great-making property for God. And as we all have incompatible interests, their fulfillment often being at the expense of others' interests, it follows that no one, not even God, can love every person at once in the deepest or truest sense possible.[13]

Another objection is that failing God's equally flat love to everyone, he must, if he is omnibenevolent, love everyone to some degree. He must love all, even though he loves some more fully than others.[14] We might think of a sort of threshold of benevolence to all, and interpreting certain assertions of Scripture as implying such a threshold. Assertions such as "The Lord is good to all, and his mercy is over all that he has made" (Ps 145:9). Perhaps

---

12. Ibid., 64.
13. Ibid., 65.
14. Ibid., 67.

the threshold does not need to be spelled out in "[H]e did good by giving you rain from heaven and fruitful seasons, satisfying your hearts with food and gladness" (Acts 14:17). The matter is made more complex by the idea of the prosperity of the wicked, so that what might in other circumstances be an act of beneficence in accordance with the true interests of the recipient, is in these circumstances to be thought of as a curse.

If God's omnibenevolence means that he must love each person to some degree, then to what degree? I think we have reason to be skeptical about our ability to answer this and suchlike questions. God is transcendent and incomprehensible, whose ways we cannot fully grasp, and as we have noted, the source of all being and goodness, the foundation of the cosmos, knowing the end from the beginning. By comparison our minds are small, we have limited information and are subject to various obvious weaknesses in our efforts to figure out the importance of data that we are ignorant of. If God's benevolence cannot be flat and wide in character, and we must therefore reckon with God making choices as to how his benevolence is distributed, choices which differentiate between one person and another, we might further speculate on this, but it may be that we are not in a position to know on what basis or on what principles the benevolence of God is distributed. How could it be otherwise? The Bible frequently strikes that note of mystery—in Job, and Ecclesiastes, and the Pauline epistles, for example.

The issue of the flatness of God's omnibenevolence might be approached from another point of view, namely the question, Is human life as we understand it such that God could reasonably be said to be equally benevolently upholding all human beings? In asking this question I have in mind such hum-drum but basic facts as the following; that some people are male and some are female; that some are born at earlier periods of human history than others, and that the child of a pair of parents necessarily cannot be their parent. Some people live in warm climates, others in temperate, and so on. Some live near the sea, while others never see it. Some are intelligent, some stupid; some weak, some strong; some healthy, some diseased. Notice that these are what we might call natural facts about people in general, facts about the creation. In any created world that is recognizably similar to ours, these basic differences will manifest themselves. As we are concerned with God's benevolence in regard to people occupying these general life-situations, and not his omnibenevolence in the abstract, then such facts are relevant to omnibenevolence in such worlds.

Earlier[15] we thought of God's creation as a choice between possible worlds. Perhaps there are possible worlds in which there are people, though

15. Some of the paragraphs that follow are adapted from Helm, "Can God Love the

not presumably human beings, who have no parents, worlds in which everyone who lives does so for exactly the same length of time, and in which no one lives any earlier or later than any other, and no one becomes diseased. But our world is not such a world, nor could it be, in the sense that it could not contain a race of people who were not recognizably similar to ourselves in at least these respects. Perhaps there could be sentient and intelligent beings who are, strictly speaking, not members of a race but are created individually, each member similar to the others but not begotten by another member or members but, like Adam and Eve, motherless and fatherless. But our world is not like that; there is a human race, and it seems to be a necessary feature of being human that one has an inherited genetic structure.

Of course it is difficult to establish what are and are not essential facts about human nature; it is easy to confuse what is uniformly true of human beings with what is necessarily true. But if having the genetic inheritance that a person in fact has is not necessarily true of that person, or the genetic inheritance of any naturally-born human being, we may be reasonably confident that there are some other asymmetrical properties which are essential. Similarly, there are possible worlds in which there are no climatic differences, and where landmasses are symmetrical, where people enjoy precisely the same climate and where each individual is equidistant from the sea and the mountains; where people are equally strong, intelligent and wise. But our world is not such a world.

As with space, so with time. Our world has one history, certain people living, and events occurring, before others. So even if the world were radically different from the way it is in fact, there would still be respects in which human beings were differently placed from each other; literally so. For each of us occupies a unique spatial and temporal position. We may be able to imagine a population of individuals each indistinguishable from the other except in terms of their position, and each of which simply record their position in their consciousness. Then this might be a population of monad-like individuals each of whom is equally or indifferently the subject of divine benevolence. But such benighted beings could hardly constitute a human race, nor would the individuals in question resemble human beings in significant ways.

Matters go deeper even than this. Each human being is an individual, with an individual consciousness and memory and an individual set of intentions. This is so even if we allow that consciousness is socially conditioned, or even socially created. And it is so even if, for the moment, we abstract from considerations of moral freedom and evil choice. Because I live

---

World?," 168–85.

later than Napoleon, necessarily he cannot remember some of the things that I remember; because he lived earlier than me, he could make plans that necessarily I cannot make; and so on.

The situation becomes decidedly more complex as considerations of an individual's character development over time are introduced. And it may be that once temporal development is introduced, flatness will have to be replaced by more diachronic considerations, such as "profile building." For it may be that the course of God's benevolence to a person at time t_1 will be less flat in order that at a later time t_2 it will be higher than it would otherwise be. Or, "flatness" might be construed not as a topographic but an aggregative feature. If God may benevolently bring about optimum moral growth in the character of every individual the result, though wide, will not be flat.

In discussing these questions I am suggesting that even aside from the usually-discussed questions of evil brought about by human choice, questions which currently tend to dominate the issue of the extension and intensity of God's benevolence, there is reason to think that in any world relevantly similar to our own God could not treat all people equally, and therefore he could not distribute his benevolence with undeviating uniformity to all human creatures. And if he logically could not do this, then clearly there could be no requirement that he do so. So we must conclude, I think, that a benevolence that is wide enough, embracing all, must nonetheless have a shape, a shape brought about by what God wills or permits for these different people differently placed from each of the others in the set.

So I am arguing that the biblical example of God's covenant with Abram considered earlier turns out to be consistent with the fact that emerges from this discussion, that God, considered as the Most Perfect Being, in creating must make choices. And further, that the Bible's portrayal of God as the one than which there cannot be a greater, who selects one man and makes a covenant with him, is feasible.

In the remainder of the paper I shall be concerned with the controlling or constitutive aspects of some divine discriminations. First, with God's ensuring all that comes to pass, his ensuring relation to all human choices, whatever their moral stripe may be. And then we shall consider the actions by which he ensures that those he destines for salvation actually receive and enjoy it, God's effective discriminations.

ENSURANCE[16]

Here I shall say only a little about the idea of God as an omni-decreer or omni-controller, an idea intrinsic to a Calvinist's version of theism. In *Eternal God* I argued *ad hominem* against secular determinists such as Antony Flew, that if such determinism is compatibible with human freedom then so may theistic determinism be.[17] Current discussion of controller arguments tend to move in the other direction, in that such arguments are introduced to strengthen our intuitions *against* secular compatibilism.[18] On the basis of controller arguments it is argued that determinism is inconsistent with the ascription of responsibility to the one determined. I have little to add to this discussion. I remain of the view that if determinism is consistent with responsibility then it is also consistent with some actions being ensured by what is called in the literature a "controller," with the qualifications shortly to be introduced. If we are free and responsible under the first, we may be free and responsible under the second.

It is widely assumed by indeterminists that God's ensuring that an action A occurs necessarily removes the human agent of A from moral responsibility. Katherin Rogers repeatedly presses the point, in various different verbal forms, that if God causally necessitates a choice then the human chooser is not responsible for it. Rogers thinks that the argument in favor of indeterminism from the incompatibility of God the all-controller and human responsibility can strengthen the intuitions on which the indeterminist rests. "The concept of God is systematic and complex, so intuitions on His regard will not be based solely on a narrow role in the controller argument."[19] God is not of questionable character as is a mad neuroscientist or a deranged behavioral engineer,[20] he is perfectly just[21] and necessarily good.[22] So if our intuitions suggest that such a God's all-control of an action would be inconsistent with the ascription of responsibility to an agent for

---

16. "Ensurance"—"The action or a means of ensuring or making certain" (*Oxford Shorter Dictionary*, "Insurance"). I dust off this archaic word to use it to make the point that God's controlling an outcome, making the occurrence of an action certain, may take various forms, not only that of efficient causality.

17. Helm, *Eternal God*, 144–70.

18. See Rogers, "Divine Controller Argument," 275–94, and the literature she cites. I am indebted to Rogers' article for stimulus in writing much of what follows in this section.

19. Ibid., 277.

20. Ibid.

21. Ibid., 278.

22. Ibid., 280.

that action (as Rogers thinks they do) this should strengthen the intuition that a secular determinism would also be inconsistent.

What I shall briefly argue is that Rogers' idea of divine control lacks nuance, a nuance that is necessary if we are to maintain other aspects of the activity of God who is perfectly just and necessarily good in a way that she regards as essential. I shall argue that in Christian theism, at least in its Augustinian and Calvinist versions, it has to be the case that God has the power or know-how to ensure that particular human actions occur without it being the case that he causally necessitates those actions. Causal necessitation, the expression uniformly used by Rogers, is no doubt sufficient for ensuring the occurrence of some human actions, but for the Augustinian it cannot be necessary for a divine controller's control of all human actions.

In addition, Rogers' argumentative strategy has one obvious weakness. Her strategy is to show that the intuitions that support the claim that it is unfair of an agent whose actions are controlled by a mad neuroscientist or a megalomaniac behavioral engineer to be blamed for what he does, are strengthened by supposing that God is the controller. She begins her intuition-strengthening strategy by developing the divine controller argument, as follows:

(1) If God causally necessitates your choice, then you are not morally responsible for it.[23]

(2) Causal necessitation of your choice due to natural causes in a deterministic universe is relevantly similar to divine causal necessitation.

Therefore:

(3) If natural causes in a deterministic universe causally necessitate your choice, you are not morally responsible for that choice.

It seems to follow from (1) that if the all-controlling God holds you responsible for your choice then, being perfectly good, he must have a good, justifying reason for holding you responsible. The all-good, perfectly just divine controller must have a way of ensuring that this is fair. In a footnote Rogers says that she is not saying the divine causation is like natural causation, but only that both can causally necessitate an effect.[24] Indeed. But she has also to allow, in consistency with her assumption that the goodness and justice of God are a necessary part of (1), that if God is a controller then he must be able to ensure that an act takes place in a way that is not relevantly

---

23. But why should a Calvinist accept (1)? It is from his standpoint an obvious *petitio*.

24. Rogers, "Divine Controller Argument," 277, no. 7.

different from those caused by malevolent neuroscientists or hypnotizers. It is natural for Rogers, with her particular interests in the role that she sees divine controller arguments playing, to concentrate on the inference: if God is an all-controller, perfectly good and just, then he cannot hold people responsible for actions he causally necessitates. But it equally follows from her argument that if such an all-controlling God does hold people responsible for their actions this is because it is just to do so.

It is the need to flag up the point about the unsatisfactoriness of the bare "causal necessitates" when ascribed to God that has led theologians and others to use language about God's ensuring capabilities besides that of causal necessitation.[25] Consider the variety of language used of God's ensurance in Scripture So, for example, God is said to decree all that comes to pass, to ordain all that happens, to bring to pass what happens, to will it with the will of his good pleasure, to appoint an end for a person, to ensure that a person does a particular action by inciting him, to permit an action in such a way that the occurrence of the action is ensured (the permission is not a "general permission," but permission that ensures that this action occurs and not that action), and so on. Besides this he leads, guarantees, covenants, promises, opens, works according to his good pleasure, chooses, and brings to pass, withholds, forsakes, and so on. These various expressions allow for God's ensuring capabilities to include ways other than causal necessitation that requires efficient causation in the sense used by Rogers.

When you think about it, this is an entirely reasonable qualification, given the myriad different circumstances in which creatures are placed, and the natures they possess, and the moral and spiritual qualities that, at any time, the creatures who are each moment held in being by their Creator, possess. The idea that the divine control that God exercises must be of the one size that fits all variety is not what one should expect. Rather the reverse. And the fact that we may not be able to imagine how some of these kinds of control may work is also to be expected, frustrating though it is to our project of having one tightly-drawn, univocal account of such control.[26] Of course if someone has problems with God's control of all things then the fact that he may have many ways of effecting his control is neither here nor

---

25. This is why I believe it is important to distinguish between God's decree being a case of determinism, and it being consistent with the determinism of one creature by another.

26. The seventeenth-century Reformed theologian Francis Turretin, a man not given to hyperbole, writes of the harmony of the providence of God and second causes, that God "has a thousand ways (to us incomprehensible) of concurring with our will, insinuating himself in us and turning our hearts, so that by acting freely as we will, we still do nothing besides the will and determination of God" (*Institutes*, 511).

there. Nevertheless, such a matter may free us from thinking that our understanding of God's control is relevantly similar to that of neuro-scientists and hypnotizers.

There are other ways of making this point. In the Westminster Confession of Faith, for example, in the chapter on the divine decree, it is stated that

> God from all eternity did, by the most wise and holy counsel of his own will, freely and unchangeably ordain whatsoever comes to pass, yet so as thereby neither is God the author of sin, nor is violence offered to the will of the creature, nor is liberty or contingency of second causes taken away, but rather established.[27]

The structure of these assertions is to assert the decree in an unqualified way and then to append negative clauses to ward off the drawing of inferences which are, in the eyes of the Westminster divines, not warranted to anyone who wishes to adopt the Scriptural view of God's decree.[28]

Of course from a philosophical point of view this is an irritating procedure. We should love to know *how* God ensures the occurrence of an action without causally necessitating it, to be able to articulate a theory which explains it. But as Alvin Plantinga has said on a number of occasions, why should we be the first to know what this account is? A touch of apophaticism seems entirely in place when considering the nature of the eternal Creator's action upon his creation, even though this may not do anything to refine our intuitions. Are we in fact in a position to know how God exercises any aspect of his control? It can be safely predicted that such an approach will not be welcomed by hard determinists or by indeterminists, but nevertheless it has the makings of a consistent account of theological control, the compatibility between God's all-control, his ensurance, and human responsibility.

---

27. Leith, *Westminster Confession of Faith*, 198.

28. This strategy of denying a series of inferences that we might think it natural to draw from a particular dogmatic statement has a considerable history. Consider these words from the Definition of Chalcedon (451 CE): "[We also teach] that we apprehend this one and only Christ—Son, Lord, only-begotten—in two natures [and we do this] *without* confusing the two natures, *without* transmuting one nature into the other, *without* dividing them into two separate categories, *without* contrasting them according to area or function." Ibid., 36 (emphases added).

EFFECTUAL GRACE

This discussion of divine control, together with the covenant-making example that we introduced earlier, takes us to the heart of our final question, namely the character of divine grace. I am aware that the positive references to God's discriminating as being (for various reasons) necessarily included in the distribution of his benevolence, do not figure in much modern philosophical discussion, and where they figure, they usually do not distinguish Pelagians from Augustinians, or Calvinists from Arminians. Both are left, for example, with the problem of how those who are chosen receive God's benevolence.

What distinguishes these positions from each other in fact is not the recognition of divine choice but its character, and particularly the ground of the choice.[29] For the Pelagian or Arminian the choice of God is grounded in what he foresees, for the Augustinian or Calvinist, it is grounded in his own will in an unconditional or absolute way. So the difference in the understanding of the character of God's goodness here expressed as grace has a factual basis. For the Arminian, people have an inalienable capacity to accept or reject God's overtures of grace, whereas for the Augustinian there is no such power, but instead human beings are in servitude, or in a state of spiritual death. Their need is not to be persuaded, but to be awakened, revived, or re-born—all these changes, when successful, entail a point of passivity in the one undergoing such a change.

What I do in the remainder of this final section of the paper is to develop some of the sentiments expressed earlier in order to defend the Augustinian sense of "call."

First we shall consider how Augustine develops this concept and how he understands it. Then I shall offer an argument to undercut the conventional objection to such a call, namely that it is impersonal, mechanical or coercive, and therefore cannot be a proper expression of God's goodness. I shall discuss the question of the alleged impersonality of the "call," not the question of whether a benevolent God is ever justified in treating people impersonally.

In an early letter, before he became engaged in controversy with the Pelagians, Augustine wrote

---

29. Note that in what follows that I shall be exclusively concerned with God's choices that are portrayed as being efficaciously gracious. Wider questions, such as the strong cultural tide against the social exclusion of any group, and the almost axiomatic place that human libertarian freedom has in current philosophical theology, are not my concern here.

If God wills to have mercy on men, he can call them in a way that is suited to them, so that they will be moved to understand and to follow. It is true, therefore, that many are called but few chosen. These are those that are effectually [*congruenter*] called. Those who are not effectually called and do not obey their calling are not chosen, for although they were called they did not follow.[30]

Augustine here distinguished between a call of God to understand and to follow him, which is an expression of the good will of God, that does not move the one called "to understand and to follow." No doubt Augustine puts such a failure down to human sin and recalcitrance. But in the other cases, God's call, the kind of call which unfailingly brings about the intended response of the one called, is accompanied by a choice, because the call of God is given in a way that is suited to them, in such a way that the one called understands and which is brought about effectually by the action of God. That is, the change is due solely to God's resolve to make the change. Sometimes Augustine uses the term "call" to denote this, and sometimes "chosen." (Jesus referred to many who are called, and to the comparative few of those who are called as "chosen," and Augustine appropriates this usage). And he also qualifies the word "call" in order to make clear that the call is effective or effectual, as in Augustine's and of course Paul's expression "called according to the purpose of grace."[31] Sometimes he uses other terms. God is said to work in men and women "to will and to do of his good pleasure." But care is needed, because sometimes the same term, "call," is used to refer to an ineffectual call, one which falls short of producing the spiritual change. So, on the one hand, as Augustine shows, "For whoever are elected are without doubt also called; but not whosoever are called are as a consequence elected."[32] "There is a certain sure calling of those who are called according to God's purpose . . .Therefore he said 'But of him that calleth'—not with any sort of calling whatever but that calling wherewith a man is made a believer."[33] Paul refers to God having called him [Paul] by his grace, and refers to the Corinthian Christians who were called even though there were not many who were wise etc. Augustine thinks that these are references to those who are called effectually.

So

---

30. Augustine, "To Simplician," 395. This letter was written in 397 CE.
31. Augustine, *On Rebuke and Grace*, 477.
32. Ibid.
33. Augustine, *Predestination of the Saints*, 513. Cf.: "They are acted upon that they may act." Augustine, *On Rebuke and Grace*, 473.

> Necessarily, if God effectually calls B, B is thereby effectually called

And

> Necessarily, if God calls B, B may or may not be thereby effectually called

The Reformed understanding of the first kind of call came to be referred to as "effectual call" (*vocatio efficax*) or "internal call" (*vocatio interna*) "which is the inward calling of the Spirit which creates the communion between man and God necessary for the *vocatio externa* also to be the *vocatio efficax*."[34] The soul is, at the first, spiritually passive, because spiritually dead. A person may be active in all sorts of other ways, but in regeneration, at the onset of effectual calling, he or she is acted upon.

> This effectual call is of God's free and special grace alone, not from anything at all foreseen in man, who is altogether passive therein, until, being quickened and renewed by the Holy Spirit, he is thereby enabled to answer this call, and to embrace the grace offered and conveyed in it.[35]

In the first paragraph of the chapter on effectual calling in the *Westminster Confession*, the Divines use a variety of strong expressions to characterize the call. The Spirit (with and through the word) *enlightens the mind* to give understanding; *takes away the heart of stone* and gives a heart of flesh, *renews their wills*, and *determines them to that which is good*. (Does the Westminster Confession explicitly teach divine determinism? Occasionally it does, as here.) Note the varied elements on this divine control. The action is unilateral, Monergistic.

These emphases are subject to now standard charges that in an effectual call the recipient is manipulated, and comparisons are drawn with brainwashing, or the application of mechanical force, being a puppet,[36] or (more recently) with being "programmed," or undergoing other types of coercion. Those who think of divine-human relations in the exclusively "conversational" pattern typical of much modern theology seem to think

---

34. "*Vocatio*," in Muller, *Dictionary of Latin and Greek Theological Terms*, 329.
35. *Westminster Confession of Faith* (1647), 10.2.
36. "If God causes the agent to will some moral good, then we might attribute some moral goodness to God in consequence, but why would we attribute moral goodness to the agent, who is nothing but a puppet of God's will?" Stump, "Sanctification," 412. For other similar references, see Alston, *Divine Nature*, 148; and Gale, *Nature and Existence of God*, 121.

they cannot consistently find a place for effectual calling in this Augustinian sense.[37]

Besides laboring the point that God is not a programmer or a puppet-master, to this sort of objection to effectual call the following reply can be made. Think of Augustine's and Calvin's "effectual call" as a successful "kiss of life," as akin to mouth-to-mouth resuscitation, or heart massage, though unlike the human cases, every such case of divine resuscitation succeeds. It is the kiss or massage that brings a response. True, the one resuscitated was not physically dead, but nevertheless he couldn't help himself. He is a "patient" in the full etymological sense of the word. It is surely a plausible principle of the human cases that "Attempted resuscitations are often in the patients' best interests." There are occasionally cases where resuscitation takes place despite the patient's previously-expressed wish not to be resuscitated, perhaps because that wish is not known to the resuscitator. So what about "Resuscitations undertaken by someone who is all knowing, wise and loving are always in the patients' best interests." This seems plausible, and if so then "God's effectual call is always in the patients' best interests" is equally plausible.

Those who respond to God's effectual call "come most freely, being made willing by his grace." How is this to be understood? It is plausible to give an account of the freedom in causally deterministic terms. We may think of the divine activity as tailored to fit the uniqueness of the total life-situation of each recipient. There may be a tension here between congruence, the matching of ways in which grace is conveyed with the traits and circumstances of character on the one hand, and the direct "supernatural" nature of the divine calling and regeneration on the other. One theological danger lies in "naturalising" effectual calling, thinking of it as the mere rearrangement or reordering or strengthening of the patient's already-present powers. But this is not an insuperable difficulty.

So in the case of effectual grace, we may think (along with Augustine) that there is a meshing of the endowments and character of an unregenerate person with the exact divine operations bringing new birth, new life, illumination to this darkened mind, and so on. Not the one without the other.

So it is best not to think of the Spirit's work in regeneration as an operation of a general kind working in a blanket fashion in all those who receive it. It need not be thought of as "one size fits all" but as the one work of regeneration, essentially the same, operating as it is "tailored" to the personality and history and prospects of each particular recipient of the call by grace. Whether or not such a relation is "personal," in the sense employed

---

37. See, for example, the remarks of Vanhoozer, *Remythologizing Theology*, 370–75.

in modern theology, we cannot imagine that the relation of the benevolent God to his human "patient" is less personal than are relations between one human person and another, but (if anything) more so. So the supernatural work of God in grace may (for all we know) be congruent with the personalities, circumstances and the particular needs of the recipient. It touches the springs of the personality as the manifold wisdom of God is seen in the gathering in of his elect.

Undoubtedly there is a one-sidedness to the divine effectual call. But this is entirely consistent with God acting benevolently, as one person to another, in accordance with what he judges to be the best interests of the one who is loved. We might reasonably suppose that there are times when a human being does not know what is in his own best interests, but that God does. So God's omnibenevolence is consistent with, and may be expressed as, an unconditional effectual call that is personal and kindly and gentle and winsome, yet firm and resolute.

The objection may be put rather differently not as against the unilateralism of the call, but as against what may be regarded as its coerciveness. It is not clear that Augustine allows that the effectual call is coercive in the sense that it overcomes felt resistance, but let us suppose that it is. Saul of Tarsus's conversion, which involved him being thrown to the ground and temporarily blinded, seems to be a case in point. It might be replied that in human father-child relations, a father may manhandle his child out of sudden danger, or permit anaesthetic to be administered for an invasive operation, or insist, against the grain of the child's wishes, that he learns the rudiments of arithmetic, and attends to the painful business of reading from a page. So objections to such an effectual call, for example, that it overcomes felt resistance, and therefore unacceptably coercive, are unconvincing.

These features of an effectual call that we have been identifying in Augustine, have been recognized by Reformed theologians, as is seen in the language that they characteristically use. So Francis Turretin. "[T]he omnipotent and efficacious operation of the Spirit is not opposed to that sweet method by which God acts through precepts, exhortations and other things of the same kind, by which God speaks after our mode, although with all these he acts after his own."[38] The outward call meshes with the inward call. Again,

> The Spirit does not force the will and carry it on unwillingly to conversion, but glides most sweetly into the soul (although in a wonderful and ineffable manner, still most suitably to the will) and operates by an infusion of supernatural habits by which

---

38. Turretin, *Institutes*, 526.

it is freed little by little from its innate depravity, so as to become willing from unwilling and living from dead. The will so renewed and acted upon immediately acts, converting itself to God and believing.[39]

Incidentally, we should not conclude that the work of effectual calling need be free from force. Yet often it is more gentle (as, perhaps, in the case of Nathanael, and Lydia of Thyatira). The change may even, in its beginnings, be unnoticed.

Behind the answers to these objections lies the belief that the call is the first step in a person's life in which he is being returned to his true self. The effectual call is not a secular change, but the first stage in the return of the one made in the image of God to his Lord and Father. Part of this consists in the removal of the mists of self-deception. Is the change a good thing? What will the one called say to the question, "Would you rather not have been changed?" The answer is obvious, the "old man" was in a course that is objectively abnormal, a deviation, a rebellion, and his return through the effectual call is the return to his true self, and to his first destiny.

The passivity of the soul in regeneration is not like that induced by anaesthetic. Regeneration is the imparting of life, the onset of gestation, the first shining of a beam. Inseparable in fact—though separable in thought—from the ensuing process of sanctification, it is not an event that is temporally distinct from it. Here the one favored is necessarily passive. The divine action leads at once to a human reaction, though even here God is at work in such a person, "to will and to work for his good pleasure" (Phil 2:13).

To any state of affairs that is due to the exercise of a choice the following question springs to mind; Why this choice? Why is A effectually called, and not B? The question presses, because according to Augustinianism the effectual call is neither given universally nor indiscriminately, nor given according to the merits of the one who receives it. But as we noted at the beginning of this piece such a "Why?" question can be also asked of the character of God's creation of something rather than nothing, and all the way down. For,

> such things are not conferred on the merits of will, as bodily strength, good health, and beauty of body, marvellous intellects and mental natures capable of many arts, or such as fall to man's lot from without, such as are wealth, nobility, honours, and other things of this kind, which it is in the power of God alone that a man should have . . . let them condescend with us to

---

39. Ibid., 524.

be ignorant, without a murmur against God, why it is given to some and not others.[40]

This response is continuously given by Augustine. "[I]f I am asked why God should not have given them perseverance to whom he gave that love by which they might live Christianly, I answer that I do not know."[41]

CONCLUSION

In this paper I have attempted to argue two or three different yet connected matters, connected by the theme of divine discrimination and ways in which this is carried out, according too the Calvinist. The first, to show that being a Perfect Being who is also a benevolent Creator involves that Being in making choices. Perfect benevolence cannot be wide and continuously flat. The second, to make some remarks about the nature of God's control of his creatures, what I have called "ensurance." Finally, to show that divine benevolence can include the merciful choice to effectually call a human being. We should resist the temptation of modifying the theological facts in the interests of obtaining a smoother philosophical theory of the divine operations, and if necessary be prepared to say, in answer to the unsuccessful search for answers to obvious questions, "I do not know."[42]

---

40. Augustine, *On Rebuke*, 479.
41. Ibid., 478 (see also Augustine, *Gift of Perseverance*, 531).
42. Thanks to James Anderson for helpful remarks on an earlier draft of this paper.

BIBLIOGRAPHY

Alston, William. *Divine Nature and Human Language*. Ithaca, NY: Cornell University Press, 1989.
Augustine, *On Rebuke and Grace*. In *Saint Augustine: Anti-Pelagian Writings*, edited by Philip Schaff. Select Library of the Nicene and Post-Nicene Fathers 5. Grand Rapids, MI: Eerdmans, 1971.
———. *On the Predestination of the Saints*. In *Saint Augustine: Anti-Pelagian Writings*, edited by Philip Schaff. Select Library of the Nicene and Post-Nicene Fathers 5. Grand Rapids, MI: Eerdmans, 1971.
———. *On the Gift of Perseverance*. In *Saint Augustine: Anti-Pelagian Writings*, edited by Philip Schaff. Select Library of the Nicene and Post-Nicene Fathers 5. Grand Rapids, MI: Eerdmans, 1971.
———. "To Simplician—On Various Questions. Book I (*De Diversis Quaestionibus*)." In *Augustine: Earlier Writings*, edited by John H. S. Burleigh, 376–406. London: SCM, 1953.
Calvin, John. *The Secret Providence of God*, edited by Paul Helm, translated by Keith Goad. Wheaton, IL: Crossway, 2010.
Gale, Richard. *On the Nature and Existence of God*. Cambridge: Cambridge University Press, 1991.
Helm, Paul. "Can God Love the World?" In *Nothing Greater, Nothing Better: Theological Essays on the Love of God*, edited by Kevin J. Vanhoozer, 168–185. Grand Rapids, MI: Eerdmans, 2001.
———. *Eternal God: A Study of God without Time*. Oxford: Oxford University Press, 2010.
Hill, Daniel J., ed. *Divinity and Maximal Greatness*. London: Routledge, 2005.
Jordan, Jeff. "The Topography of Divine Love." *Faith and Philosophy* 29, no. 1 (2012) 53–69.
Leith, John H., ed. *Westminster Confession of Faith*. In *Creeds of the Churches*, 193–230. Garden City, NY: Anchor, 1963.
MacDonald, Scott, ed. *Being and Goodness*. Ithaca, NY: Cornell University Press, 1991.
Mackie, J. L. "Evil and Omnipotence." In *The Philosophy of Religion*, edited by Basil Mitchell, 92–104. Oxford: Oxford University Press, 1971.
Muller, Richard A. *Dictionary of Latin and Greek Theological Terms: Drawn Principally from Protestant Scholastic Theology*. Grand Rapids, MI: Baker, 1985.
Plantinga, Alvin. *God, Freedom, and Evil*. London: Allen & Unwin, 1974.
———. *Warrant and Proper Function*. New York: Oxford University Press, 1993.
Rogers, Katherin A. "The Divine Controller Argument for Incompatibilism." *Faith and Philosophy* 29, no. 3 (2012) 275–94.
Rowe, William. "Friendly Atheism, Skeptical Theism, and the Problem of Evil." *International Journal for Philosophy of Religion* 59, no. 2 (2006) 79–92.
Stump, Eleonore. "Sanctification, Hardening of the Heart, and Frankfurt's Concept of Free Will." *Journal of Philosophy* 85, no. 8 (1988) 395–420.
Turretin, Francis. *Institutes of Elenctic Theology*, edited by James T. Dennison, translated by G. M. Giger. 3 vols. Phillipsburg, NJ: P & R, 1992–97.
Vanhoozer, Kevin. *Remythologizing Theology*. Cambridge: Cambridge University Press, 2010.

7

On Grace and Free Will

—Hugh J. McCann

> For it is by grace you have been saved, through faith—and this is not from yourselves, it is the gift of God—not by works, so that no one can boast. (Eph 2:8)

READERS FAMILIAR WITH THE subject will recognize that my title is stolen from Augustine, who toward the end of his life wrote a treatise that goes by the same name. Augustine's treatise was aimed at calming a small furor that had arisen over the perceived implications of his earlier arguments against pelagianism; it represents one of Augustine's last sustained attempts to come to grips with a problem that for him would not go away, and that I think has still not gone away. It is the problem of how to reconcile two doctrines, one of Christianity and the other of common sense. The first is that at least in their postlapsarian condition, men cannot by their own endeavors either earn or enter into Christian salvation; rather, salvation is to be gotten only by God's grace, which at least on one understanding is only selectively bestowed. The common sense view, also endorsed by many philosophers and theologians, is that rational creatures are possessed of free will, the exercise of which is required for us justly to be held responsible for what we do. This problem of grace versus works is a particular version of a more general problem—that of how to reconcile human freedom and divine sovereignty. What differentiates it is the idea that the achievement of salvation requires, in addition to the operation of the human will, something called "grace," the role of which seems to be to assure that those destined to be saved will do whatever it is that needs to be done in order to reach a standing of acceptability before God. The more general problem is, no doubt, the more purely philosophical as well. I have addressed the general problem of sovereignty elsewhere.[1] Here I wish to explore the implications of that general position for theological disputes about grace and works.

I. A BIT OF HISTORY

The general problem may be seen to arise in connection with the doctrine that God not only creates the world "in the beginning," but sustains it throughout its existence. That this is so implies that God's activity as first cause extends to every aspect of the universe. Augustine agrees, holding that all things owe their being to God,[2] and that the only thing not owing to his action is the movement of finite wills away from him and toward lesser goods.[3] Aquinas seems to go further, arguing that the causality of God extends to anything that exists in whatever manner,[4] and that this applies even to those acts in which we sin.[5] If this is so then God's action as First Cause is present in any movement of creaturely will, whether toward God or away. This alone is enough to raise significant difficulties, both about human freedom and about God's role in the occurrence of evil. In the Christian setting, however, the difficulty is compounded.

The compounding factor is the doctrine of election, according to which the question who is to enjoy God's friendship for eternity is settled entirely by his decision. This decision, we are told, does not await our deeds, nor does it depend on what they are; rather, the elect are chosen from the foundation of the world, according solely to the pleasure of God's will.[6] Election seems, moreover, to involve not only God's will but also his knowledge. "For those God foreknew he also predestined to be conformed to the likeness of his Son . . . And those he predestined, he also called; and those he called, he also justified" (Rom 8:29-30). By this account, the division between sheep and goats is entirely subject to God's sovereignty, exercised through his knowing will. That this is so seems evident from Scripture, and

---

1. McCann, "Divine Sovereignty and the Freedom of the Will," 582–98; McCann, "Author of Sin," 144–59. See also McCann, "Free Will and Divine Sovereignty," 92–112.
2. Augustine, *Confessions*, 7.15.
3. Ibid., 12.11.
4. Aquinas, *Summa Theologica* I, q. 22, a. 2.
5. Ibid., I–II, q. 79, a. 2.
6. Eph 1:4–5.

the doctrine is ratified all through the mainstream of Western theology. Augustine's antipelagian writings are founded upon the theme of election, as is part 2 of Calvin's *Institutes*. The doctrine is clearly subscribed to by Aquinas, who gives a detailed treatment of it in *Summa Theologica* (I, q. 23), and endorsements of the doctrine can be found in the writings of virtually every prominent figure from the Middle Ages through the Reformation and beyond.

In principle, God's choice of the elect could be on any basis, or for that matter on no basis at all, but instead a point of strict arbitrariness—a situation that has troubled many. In his letter to the Romans, Paul suggests it is fitting that some creatures be destined to manifest God's wrath and others his mercy (9:12–13). That this should be so is welcomed by, for example, Augustine,[7] who reminds us that there can be no accusation here that anyone is wronged, since both the saved and the lost are deserving of reprobation in light of their sinfulness; the same sentiments are echoed by Calvin.[8] But as to why particular individuals are found in one category or the other Augustine is forced to confess that he can find no answer;[9] on this point both he and Calvin can only have recourse to God's unsearchable wisdom and judgments. Furthermore, all of the authors cited agree on the import of our opening passage from Ephesians. Salvation is not by works but by grace. And this means more than that the forgiveness of sins is accomplished only through the redemptive suffering of Christ, so that the opportunity for friendship with God once lost by original sin is now newly available to us. It means that we as individuals cannot take advantage of that availability, that we cannot move to a stance of personal reconciliation with God—indeed, that we cannot even prepare ourselves to take such a step—without his grace.

Romans 8:29–30, cited above, says in effect that the election of the saints is brought to realization in their justification by the power of God. Individual justification may be taken to occur in the sinner's conversion, the event wherein rebellion against God is relinquished, and the task of managing the individual's destiny is left in God's hands.[10] Now relinquishing rebellion implies some action on the part of the individual, some sort of at least momentary surrender. And one might think that this act of submission

---

7. Augustine, *Gift of Perseverance*, chapter 12.
8. Calvin, *Institutes*, 2.23.11.
9. Op cit., chapter 18.
10. In classic cases—e.g., Paul on the way to Damascus (Acts 9:36), or Augustine in the garden in Milan (*Confessions*, 8.12)—conversion is momentary. This does not rule out its being at times a more extended process, but I think the essential features remain the same even when the process is drawn out.

is the foundation for the penitent's justification. There is, however a tension here, for the passage from Romans seems to belie this; it says those who are foreknown and chosen by God are also called and justified *by him*. This fits perfectly with our passage from Ephesians, according to which salvation is a gift of God, not accomplished by any doing on the part of those who are saved. That this is so is the guiding principle of Augustine's antipelagian writings, where he is careful to insist that even the beginning of faith is a gift of God,[11] and this is again ratified by Aquinas, who reiterates the point that the sinner cannot even prepare himself to receive "the light of grace" except by the help of God,[12] and by Calvin.[13] Finally, we should note that the grace of conversion is to be understood as *efficacious*: that is, once bestowed it guarantees not only the sinner's liberation from the bondage of sin, but also his perseverance to eternal life.[14]

But now we have a problem. It seems that in mainstream theology, our salvation is not up to us. If the grace of God is both required for our justification, and by its efficacy sufficient for it, then it seems certain that God is able to guarantee a sinner's justification simply by bestowing grace on that individual. Equally, he is able to guarantee the sinner's damnation simply by withholding his grace. But then what about the testimony of common sense that seems to contradict all of this—namely, that we rational creatures possess of free will, and can deserve no blame or punishment without its exercise? Is this simply to be denied? This is the problem Augustine set out to address in his *On Grace and Free Will*, and to which we now turn.

II. IDENTIFYING THE ANTAGONISTS

A good way to begin is by asking exactly what is meant in these disputes by the term "grace." And it is important to realize first that in one meaning of the term, grace is simply a disposition of mind. One is gracious toward another if one exhibits an attitude of favor or good will toward them—in particular, as concerns the present discussion, an attitude of pardon or forgiveness, should the other be guilty of some offense. Consider, then, the passage from Ephesians cited above. Read in accordance with this first definition it says only that it is out of God's kindness toward them that his creatures (or some of them, anyway) are saved, and that they come to participate in this salvation not through deeds but through faith, through trust

---

11. Augustine, *Predestination of the Saints*, chapters 3–4.
12. Aquinas, *Summa Theologica* I–II, q. 109, a. 6.
13. Calvin, *Institutes*, 2.3.5.
14. Cf. Augustine, *Rebuke and Grace*, chapter 14.

in God. Nothing is said about the exact process by which the newly formed believer reaches a stance of faith. In particular it is not, on this understanding, asserted that grace constitutes some sort of force or power that works in certain agents—a force that influences them to place their trust in God, or is causally efficacious in that project.

One need not, however, think and speak of grace merely as an attitude of indulgence on God's part. Often, indeed most of the time, it is spoken of as something more, as some sort of aid or assistance provided by God to the individual in need of salvation, or on the pathway to it. Usually, this kind of aid is treated as necessary for salvation to be achieved; indeed, some have held that in the fallen state of humanity the assistance of grace is required if they are to accomplish any good actions at all. It will simplify things, however, if we concentrate as much as possible on assistance that is directed specifically toward the individual's adopting a stance of religious faith. And we should note that apart, perhaps, from its origin, there need be nothing especially supernatural about such help; it could consist simply in everyday sorts of occurrences. One might, for example, pick up a Bible or a hagiography out of curiosity and find it interesting reading. One might be drawn by chance into some sort of charity work that brings one into contact with religious people; or be nagged by one's spouse into attending church, where one hears a persuasive sermon. Perhaps the "assistance" would take a more negative form: serious business reverses, or grave danger to oneself or one's family that motivates one to try to enlist whatever help may be available, divine or otherwise. Such occurrences as these—we might call them "ordinary assistance"—need not arise miraculously in order to be considered a form of grace. Like all events they fall under God's meticulous providence. This being the case they can be ordered by him toward a sinner's salvation, or at least toward enabling it, while remaining entirely a part of the natural order.

I think, however, that grace considered as positive aid is often thought of as more than ordinary assistance. It tends to be treated as a sort of spiritual energy or empowerment whose source is external to the individual's ordinary experience or resources—an energy that encourages and perhaps even impels the person toward adopting a stance of faith. There are, however, two ways to understand such energy. On the first it has a kind of phenomenal footprint. It is not unusual even in nonreligious contexts for people in crisis situations to discover in themselves some sort of power or resolve that they would not have expected to find, and that assists them in addressing whatever difficulty they face. A similar phenomenon often attends religious conversion: thus, beset with a sense of spiritual crisis a person hitherto given entirely to self-reliance might unexpectedly find himself with a readiness to place reliance upon God. And although at least in the religious context it may be natural to do so, neither there nor in the secular setting are we necessarily driven to postulate an extraordinary or miraculous intervention of divine agency to explain the empowerment. If all that occurs in the world is subject to God's providential will, the grace of conversion could in principle turn out to have a natural accounting, while at the same time retaining all of its spiritual significance. But of course it does not have to be that way, and persons of faith are prone to hold that in the crisis that leads to faith, and perhaps in more ordinary crises as well, there is direct heavenly involvement.

The other way to think of grace understood as internal empowerment calls for no phenomenal footprint at all. We may not notice its presence, yet believe that grace is operative throughout our lives, and that without it all our efforts to do good would come to nothing. If so we may begin to see grace as a strictly spiritual kind of empowerment, entirely supernatural in its nature and operation, and having no experiential manifestation, internal or external, other than the effects to which it leads. If this were to occur in a case of conversion, the sole manifestation of the working of grace would lie in the individual's act of placing trust in God, of accepting what Christians call the free gift of salvation.

The competitor of grace in the disputes we are considering is "works." What are we to understand by this term? For the most part, just the normal sorts of doings for which one would usually be accorded moral credit. Some of these are actually refrainings: resisting the temptation to lie on a tax return, for example, or refusing to engage in gustatory overindulgence. But mostly, works are positive. They include carrying out the duties of one's station in life: being a good employee, partner and parent. But there are also positive deeds that are not, or at least not specifically, obligatory: contributing to charity, helping others in need, advising friends who seek counsel, consoling the bereaved and lonely, and so forth. Works can also include actions that express an interest in religion: reading on spiritual subjects, for example, or heeding the spouse's urging to attend church. But the most important work we need to consider here is the one mentioned above: the act associated with religious conversion, of abandoning ultimate reliance upon oneself and instead placing one's trust in God. This is not, I think, an act for which the agent who succeeds at it would wish to claim moral credit. For many believers, however, it is the central event of their religious experience, the step that moves them from a position of alienation from God to a position of acceptance. The question of the relation of this act to divine grace is therefore of crucial importance.

III. THE CONFLICT

How, then, is the pathway to salvation to be understood? If we are imbued with a strong sense that rational creatures are ultimately responsible for their own destiny, we might suppose that whether or not a person comes to salvation must in the end be a question of how they exercise their moral autonomy. Moreover, it seems that autonomy should be understood here—and I think believers usually do understand it this way—in a libertarian sense.[15] For, they would argue, it is only under this understanding that the agent is finally and truly accountable for what he does. The question of salvation, then, must be a question of how one employs libertarian free will. But—and this is the crucial point—this at least suggests that if creatures are in the end responsible for their own fate, then it must be possible to achieve salvation essentially on one's own hook—that is, by employing the natural powers of deliberation and choice with which God has endowed every rational individual. By such means it should be possible to put aside habits of wrongdoing, attend to one's duties in life, take up activities of religious observance, and perform whatever other positive deeds might be necessary to achieve a stance of acceptability before God. And once that standing is achieved, a just God would not withhold his favor and friendship; rather, he would number the individual in question in the company of the elect, granting him the salvation that, by his own endeavors, he had earned or merited.

Now it should be apparent that, at least from the point of view of orthodox theology, this simply will not do. It is in fact the very pelagianism to which Augustine was so resolutely opposed, and that has been condemned by any number of church synods and councils down through the centuries. As mentioned above, some would argue that it is impossible to engage in any meritorious act without the aid of some kind of grace. But even if we reject this idea, we certainly should wonder whether anyone could by normal means come to a position so far removed from any previous moral corruption that God would be required as a matter of equity to bestow his friendship on that person. Even if God is subject to the demands of equity—itself a debatable point—this would seem to belittle the redemptive sacrifice of Christ, which orthodoxy holds indispensable to salvation.[16] But

---

15. Some caution is called for here since there is more than one version of libertarian causation. Virtually all libertarians require that a free action be exempt at least from natural causation—what theologians usually refer to as *secondary causation*. In most philosophical discussions the question of divine or *primary* causation does not arise. However, when it does most writers seem inclined to assume that it too is ruled out—especially if they hold, as many libertarians do, that the agent of any free action must be its sole or ultimate source.

16. Gal 2:21. Cited by Augustine, *Grace and Free Will*, chapter 25; also Calvin, *Institutes*, 2.17.5.

the most important point can be gotten simply by recurring to our text from Ephesians. According to that passage, when it comes to basic salvation none of the things our do-gooder might accomplish even matter. Works may be important as a sign that someone has reached a position of good standing with God; and if, as is usually claimed, the individual's attaining to that status normally results in a gradual increase in saintliness, then regardless of what may occur on the pathway to acceptability, we should anticipate that good works will ensue after it is achieved. But as far as one's coming to salvation is concerned such deeds are entirely beside the point. Those who reach salvation do so not by justifying themselves to God, but by taking exactly the opposite course: by abandoning their own efforts, by giving up the enterprise of proving themselves to God and placing their trust in him.

But what about this act—that is, the very act of entrusting one's destiny to God rather than trying to forge it on one's own? As was said above, this is not the kind of act for which it would be reasonable for a newly converted soul to claim any kind of moral credit. Just the opposite: it would be the essence of bad faith to claim credit for an act a part of whose very content is to lay aside completely the business of seeking to justify oneself before God. Rather, it seems, the agent should be thankful for having been led to perform such an act. But what exactly does the phrase "being led to" mean in this context? It would be disturbing to take it as implying an absence of freedom. After all, if the contrast between the destiny of the saved and that of the lost is anything like tradition portrays it to be, one should wish that even in surrendering his fate to God the believer exercises free will. It is, after all, a decision in which everything hangs in the balance, and even if the good deeds of the repentant sinner can exert no claim on God's justice, it seems surely that the penitent's autonomy in selecting his destiny must be left intact. Perhaps, then, the correct position is that while the sinner is unable to win his way to salvation, it is at least up to him whether he chooses it or not once it is made available.

But in this view too there are problems. The Ephesians passage speaks of salvation as God's free gift, and it suggests that the gift is free not just in its availability but in its actual bestowal upon and acceptance by the individual. Moreover, to speak of the question of salvation as entirely a matter of the individual's decision is to suggest that God exercises no sovereignty on the point, and there are many other Biblical texts that seem to belie that. In Exodus, God repeatedly hardens Pharaoh's heart, so that he refuses the Israelites' demands to be let go.[17] In Ezekiel, on the other hand, he promises exiled Israel, "I will put my Spirit within you and cause you to walk in my

17. Exod 4:21, 10:20, 14:4.

statutes" (Ezek 36:27). In the New Testament the entire issue of salvation tends to be portrayed as a matter of election or predestination, concerning which the individual appears to have little if any say.[18] Indeed, even the fate of Judas the betrayer is portrayed, in Christ's own words, as having come about "that the scripture might be fulfilled" (John 17:12). The idea that those who reach a stance of faith settle by their own decision whether they are to be numbered among the saved or not, seems, then, to have a lot of textual evidence going against it. What is especially important for our purposes however is that, at least as so far described, this view seems entirely to overlook the question of grace. How can it be "by grace" that one is saved if it is one's own *fiat*, and not God's empowerment, that finally settles the matter?

Grace can be brought into the picture if we adopt a doctrine of *prevenient* grace—that is, an empowerment divine in origin, whose infusion prior to conversion enables the sinner to surrender his life to God. Perhaps, then, we should opt for a view according to which it is only through the empowerment of what is known as "prevenient" grace that the sinner is able to surrender his life to God. If we do, however, it looks like we are in danger of having to adopt a deterministic account, according to which what at first purported to be an aid or empowerment actually necessitates the individual's accepting the salvation proffered by God. How else are we to guarantee that it is God's election that settles the question who—and indeed whether *anyone*—will be saved, rather than the autonomous choice of individual agents? It looks as though this point of orthodoxy cannot be sustained unless God's grace is understood not only as empowering but also as *efficacious*, in the sense of being causally sufficient to bring about the individual's decision. And then of course we will be back in the position of wondering how it is that creatures, who now seem helpless to settle their eternal destiny, could possibly be deemed responsible for accepting or refusing God's offer of friendship, and to deserve whatever punishment or reward their fate may involve.

IV. HUMAN FREEDOM AND DIVINE SOVEREIGNTY

We saw earlier that the dilemma of grace versus works seems to have troubled Augustine for most of his life as a Christian. It is clear, however, that by the end he had settled in favor of grace, at least to the point of insisting that it is divine election, not creaturely decision or deeds, that settles the matter of who is to be saved. Moreover, he is ready in his later writings to renounce

---

18. Eph 1:4; Rom 8:29–30.

earlier efforts to give free will priority in the matter.[19] Yet he seems still to want to insist that freedom is at work here also. In *On Grace and Free Will*, for example, he cites with approval Philippians 2:13: "For it is God who works in you both to will and to do of his own good pleasure." But then he hastens to add:

> It is not, however, to be for a moment supposed, because he [i.e., Paul] said, "It is God that works in you both to will and to do of his good pleasure," that free will is taken away. If this, indeed, had been his meaning, he would not have said just before, "Work out your own salvation with fear and trembling" [Phil 2:12]. For when the command is given "to work," their free will is addressed; and when it is added, "with fear and trembling," they are warned against boasting of their good deeds as if they were their own, by attributing to themselves the performance of anything good.[20]

At this point, then, it looks as though Augustine wanted to have things both ways. One means of reconciling this apparent conflict is to understand Augustine as having, by the end of his life, abandoned libertarian freedom in favor of a version of compatibilism.[21] That is, those who reach salvation do so freely, in that it is by an exercise of their wills that they place their trust in God; yet it is God who causes their willing by the influence of causally efficacious grace—so that their freedom consists only in acting in accordance with God's influence. Now there is certainly textual evidence that Augustine came to view grace as a causal force of this kind.[22] But if this was Augustine's final position, then I think he gave up too soon. It is possible to hold to a far more robust conception of freedom, while at the same time according God complete sovereignty over creaturely willing.

To see how, we need to understand what it is about our decisions that leads us to say that they are a matter of our own responsibility, that they are "up to us." So consider my decision to write this paper. I certainly think of

---

19. "In the solution of this question I labored indeed on behalf of the free choice of the human will, but God's grace overcame . . ." Augustine, *Predestination of the Saints*, chapter 8.

20. Augustine, *Grace and Free Will*, chapter 21.

21. More than one author has made this suggestion. For a recent discussion see Couenhoven, "Augustine's Rejection of the Free-Will Defense," 279–98,

22. For example, "It is certain that it is we that will when we will, but it is He who makes us will what is good, of whom it is said . . . , 'The will is prepared by the Lord' (Prov 8:35). Of the same Lord . . . it is said, 'It is God who works in you, even to will'! (Phil 2:13). It is certain that it is we that act when we act; but it is He who makes us act, by applying efficacious powers to our will." Augustine, *Grace and Free Will*, chapter 32.

that decision as having been up to me, but what is required for this to be so? Someone might suggest that what is required is that I have *caused* the decision—that I, as agent, have produced the decision or, as we might say, have conferred existence on it.[23] But I think this is wrong. I am aware of no doing by which I produce or give rise to my decisions. I simply decide. I form an intention; and as far as I know, that was all I did in making up my mind to write this paper. Furthermore, there is good reason to think that notions like producing and existence conferral *cannot* shed light on what it was for my decision to have been free. For either I produced the decision by some other, perhaps prior act, or else I did so as part of the deciding itself. Now if my decision was produced by some other act of mine, then that act, not my decision, will become the focus of our concerns over freedom. It in turn will have to have been "up to me," and then we are headed for a vicious regress. On the other hand, it is hopeless to claim that I produced my act of deciding as part of that very act. For until the act was on hand there was nothing to do the producing, and once it *was* on hand there was nothing left to produce. It has to be concluded, I think, that whatever causes our decisions—whatever their existence is owing to—it is not us.[24]

But a defender of libertarian freedom need not be committed to the notion of agent causation. Indeed, most if not all that is crucial to libertarian freedom has little to do with causation. There is, of course, the negative point that a free decision or action cannot be the product of *event* causation: that is, it cannot be the brought about by forces that operate upon the agent in such a way that he is passively compelled to act. An exercise of will is not free if it is merely the product of the agent's strongest motive, or of deterministic brain processes, or the operation of another agent upon him. But that only tells us what free will is not; and the positive features that characterize free willing have nothing at all to do with causing. There are, I think, two of these. First, free decisions and actions have what Carl Ginet calls the "actish phenomenal quality": there is a felt spontaneity about them, so that when we engage in them we know that we are *acting*, rather than having something done to us.[25] And second, free exercises of will are intrinsically

---

23. For defenses of the concept of agent causation, see Chisholm, "Human Freedom," 24–35; Rowe, "Two Concepts of Freedom," 43–64; and O'Connor, *Persons and Causes*. Agent causal accounts receive an extensive discussion in Clarke, *Libertarian Accounts of Free Will*.

24. The reader will notice that this argument is perfectly general, so that the same dilemma would apply to any act of will on God's part, including his action as primary cause of the world and all that it contains. For the beginnings of an attempt at a solution see McCann, "Divine Will and Divine Simplicity," 213–36.

25. Ginet, *On Action*, 13.

intentional: that is, it is impossible to engage in them without intending to do precisely what one is doing. It would be a self-contradiction to say that I unintentionally or inadvertently decided to write this paper, because it is of the very nature of deciding that when one decides one *means* to decide, and to decide exactly as one does. And although there are many overt actions that I might perform unintentionally (e.g., knocking over a cup of coffee), the volitional activity that lies at the bottom of such actions (say, willing the exertional movement required for me to reach the book that lies just beyond the cup of coffee) can only be intentional.[26]

It is possible, then, to offer a positive account of freedom that rejects agent causation, and is libertarian at least to this point: that it also rejects the idea that our decisions and actions are products of event causation—that is, of any worldly influence that might be held to compel us to behave as we do. If, moreover, this account holds true of my decision to write this paper, there is every reason to hold me responsible for that decision. For while it was not determined by any natural cause, neither did my decision occur in a vacuum. It was made for the sake of the ends I thought I might achieve by writing this paper: learning more about the subjects to be discussed, engaging in eventual dialog with fellow scholars, and so forth. And by the account just given my decision was made spontaneously and with the intention of deciding precisely as I did. As far as I can see it is perfectly just to treat me as responsible for a decision made in this way. Presumably, moreover, doing so would provide me with motives that could influence similar decisions I might make in the future. So you could encourage me if you think this paper is any good, or discourage me if it's bad.

But now suppose we add one more thing to the mix. Suppose that God, as creator, counts as the "first cause," as is usually said, of my action. That is, in creating the world he creates me and all that pertains to me, and in so doing he provides for the existence of my decision to write for this volume. One's first inclination might be to think that this added circumstance changes everything as far as my responsibility for my decision is concerned. In fact, however, it changes nothing. My decision is still mine: it is predicated of me, not God. Furthermore, it still has all the characteristics of freedom just described. That God should be its creator does not turn my act of deciding into something that befalls me, or is in any way passive. It still has the phenomenal quality of action; it is still intrinsically an act that I meant

---

26. It helpful here to keep in mind the contrast between events of passive willing, such as the onset of a desire, with the active use of the will that occurs in decision and volition. The onset of a desire is always in itself passive and never intentional. Active willing, by contrast, cannot fail to be intentional. It cannot fail to be something we mean to do, in the very doing of it.

to be performing. Furthermore, it is still an act in whose performance I was not acted *upon* by any force that overwhelmed my will, or compelled me to do what I did. It might be protested that this last claim cannot be true, that if my decision to write this paper owes its existence to God's activity as creator then I must be driven to act in that way. But that is not so, at least on the account of creation to which I subscribe. God does not create the world "in the beginning," after which it persists on his own. Rather, he sustains it throughout its existence, so that his relation to each phase of its history is precisely the same. He does not, therefore, create my decision by entering into the world and acting upon me or my will. Neither does he do so by infusing me with some invisible spiritual energy that in turn overtakes my will, compelling me by event causation to decide as I do. If this were the correct way to model the efficacy of grace, its operation would indeed undo my freedom. But the model is wrong, because God need not employ any means, spiritual or otherwise, to have me decide anything. Rather, God creates me *in* my act of deciding, and indeed in all of my exercises of agency, which leaves all of the features that I have argued characterize free decisions and actions intact. Even if we count God as its primary cause, then, we still have plenty of reason to think of my decision to write this paper as an exercise of genuine free will, and of me as responsible for it.

There is, however, an aspect of this picture that may be found unsettling. If it is correct, then while my decision to write this paper may have been up to me as far as event causation is concerned, there is still a sense in which I am not ultimately responsible for it. God is. He chooses me for the person I am: complete not only in my powers as an agent and the circumstances in which I find myself, but in the exercise of those powers as well. And while it may be true that none of the aspects of freedom described above are violated in God's creating that person, it is also true that nothing I might do can ever thwart God's will for me. Rather, whatever I might do simply *is* his will. In light of this, someone might want to argue that while the sort of freedom I have described is indeed pretty robust, it does not deserve the adjective "libertarian." For, the argument would run, libertarian freedom requires that *I*, not God, be ultimately responsible for the things I do.

Natural as this sentiment may seem, I think it is misguided. Part of what leads to it is a mistaken view of creation, according to which God's activity as creator is preceded by a kind of deliberational activity, in which he examines different potential realities or "possible worlds" and selects one as the world he prefers to create.[27] Only then does he proceed to the activity

---

27. If, as Leibniz claimed, God creates the best possible world, then that is the

of creation proper, which consists in actualizing or lending existence to the world chosen. If this is the way things go, and if part of the endeavor of creation is for God to provide for the existence of our decisions and actions, it becomes reasonable to think that prior to creation there are on offer numerous versions of each rational being who might be created, reflecting the various careers that that being might pursue—that is, the various sequences of action in which he or she might engage. And then it is sure to appear that prior to creating us God actually decides *for* us which decisions and actions we will undertake in our lifetime. This picture is in my view completely wrong. God does not deliberate prior to creation. What would his purpose be, to insure against error? Only an inferior God would have to do that. A perfect God creates what he does as part of his very nature, immediately and spontaneously, with no prior consideration whatever.[28] And he gets it right the first (and only) time. We as agents consider various futures for ourselves, and select among them. God does not. He sees our lives in their entirety from beginning to end, and he sees them from the foundation of the world. In that foundation, moreover, he sees them as good, and his seeing them that way is in itself his willing our existence. In that willing we are known and predestined, called and justified;[29] and in that willing we live, and move, and have our being[30] with untrammeled freedom. As creator God does not, then, select among possible potential versions of you and me. He entertains no "possible persons," and he does not settle our actions for us in advance any more than, subsequent to our creation, he determines our wills by inducements or impulsions from without. Rather, there is a perfect division of labor. It is only we who decide our actions, and it is only God who lends existence to them, as the foundational manifestation of his love for each of us.

There is a lot more that can be said in response to the objection we are considering, but for now three points will have to do. First, "libertarian freedom" is a term of art, that we may define as we wish. Not all definitions of it call for us to be ultimately responsible for our decisions and actions in any sense stronger than the one I endorse, which rejects only the claim that our decisions and actions are subject to worldly or secondary causation. I have no objection if someone chooses to use the term in a stronger sense, one

---

world he selects. Some have argued, however, that there may be no best possible world. See or example Adams, "Must God Create the Best," 317–32. I adhere to the Leibnizian position. McCann, "Divine Freedom," 155–75.

28. This is not meant to imply that the created world counts in any way as a part of God, only that his act of creating it is essential to him.

29. Rom 8:29–30.

30. Acts 17:28.

that would reject God's action as First Cause also. I would caution, however, that if we take "ultimate responsibility" to imply a doctrine according to which we confer existence on our own doings, then unless the idea of agent causation can be resuscitated, libertarian freedom will turn out very quickly to be something we not only do not but also cannot have. Second, even if we decline to call the type of freedom I have outlined "libertarian," that kind of freedom is certainly robust enough to justify attributions of moral responsibility. Indeed, a moment ago this kind of freedom seemed to justify treating me as responsible for my decision to write this paper, even though we had at that point discerned no cause of any kind for my so deciding. If that stance was correct, then we should not cease to hold me responsible if my decision turns out to owe its existence to God's activity as creator—provided, of course, that I am correct in claiming that the nature of primary causation is such as to leave the crucial features of free agency intact. Finally—and most important from the point of view of faith—no matter what we choose to call libertarian freedom, the relationship I have defined between human agency and God's activity as creator has the advantage of being precisely what is needed to resolve the age-old controversy over grace and works. Let me therefore turn, in the little space that remains, to a brief description of how I see the two as related.

V. GRACE AND WORKS

It should be plain that if there is a God whose relation to the world has the character just described, then what holds of my decision to write this paper holds of all my decisions, and of every decision ever made by any rational agent. Consider, then, the decision of the sinner to place his trust in God. Obviously, that decision owes its existence to God, not because of any prior force or energy that impels the agent to decide as he does, but simply because God creates him the person he is to be, and thereby exercises direct sovereignty over every exercise of his will. This fits perfectly with the scriptural language of predestination, according to which the saved are foreknown and foreordained for justification.[31] But it also allows for the agent to choose his destiny in an act characterized by all that is essential to responsible freedom. As for how "grace" is involved in the transaction, it turns out that the most relevant sense of that term is actually the first of those delineated earlier. There may of course be helpful occurrences of the sort I have called ordinary assistance; indeed, in the usual case there probably will be. And there may be a felt sense of empowerment, though

---

31. Rom 8:29–30.

not a determining one. But these things are not vital, and there is never an operation in which the agent's will is rendered passive, so that salvation is thrust upon him rather than being freely chosen by him. Just the opposite: in the end the grace by which the elect come to salvation is not some spiritual energy that drives them there, but simply God's favor—the very same favor, in fact, through which their existence is provided for in the first place. And although coming to a stance of faith is effected through one's own decision, the decision is nothing to boast about, for its existence is finally owing solely to an act of divine election—an act that is from the foundation of the world, and is in fact part of the act that is the penitent's very creation. No one would want to take credit for that.

Substantially the same account applies to the various sorts of good deeds that belong to the category of "works." These belong of course to the agent, in the sense that they are predicated of him and are effected through the operation of his will. Yet at the same time they are manifestations of grace, in that they owe their existence to the favor displayed simply in God's activity as creator. Further, our text from Ephesians tells us that they do not earn salvation for the agent, nor in themselves can they guarantee that he will ever humble himself to accept God's gift of salvation. We should not, however, conclude that grace in the sense of inner empowerment, or in the sense of ordinary assistance, has no role to play in one's coming to a stance of faith, or in the performance of meritorious acts. It would, I think, be a serious mistake to view either sort of grace as deterministically efficacious. But no act of will can be considered responsible or even rational if it is not made in awareness of the alternatives, and in appreciation of the value those alternatives have. Properly appreciated, the role of these other forms of grace is just to produce this kind of appreciation and awareness.[32] Neither should it be thought that if God plays the role I have described in creaturely willing, then the decisions and actions of rational agents must regularly appear as radical breaks from the past, discontinuous with the deliberational setting in which they occur, and representing no coherent evolution of character. If anything, we should expect the opposite: that if God as creator exercises sovereignty even over creaturely willing, the beings that result will display far greater unity and coherence of character than could ever be achieved by the operation of the *utterly* causeless will some libertarians imagine. The natural way to achieve that coherence is by ordinary means; and as I tried

---

32. A caveat is in order here. If there is a suspect notion of grace it is the one that makes grace wholly invisible, make it an entirely spiritual impulsion with no phenomenal footprint at all. If as creator god is himself the First Cause of our actions, then this sort of mediating but invisible "energy" is either an unnecessary go-between, or is simply to be identified with the creative will of God.

to intimate earlier on, most of what is called grace is in my view probably pretty ordinary stuff. It is easier to think of it that way once we realize that creaturely wills don't have to be pushed around in order that God's purposes for them be achieved.

A final word may be in order on the role of original sin in all of this. It was Augustine's view that although prior to their fall Adam and Eve were able to sin or not to sin, postlapsarian humans are unable to avoid sin without the aid of grace. Now of course not all follow Augustine in taking the Eden story literally. But even so it is important to consider how both the redemption of fallen humans and their ability to do good might represent greater manifestations of grace than would otherwise be the case. I think it can be seen that is so in two senses. First, that the saved are brought to a position of friendship with God—a position, in fact, of sharing in his very life—is in itself a greater manifestation of God's favor than would be achieved if such intimacy were granted only to beings who had never sinned. So our first sense of grace is satisfied here. This sense is satisfied also in the fact that humans at times do good in spite of being sinful, since their actions of well-doing are manifestations of God's will as well as of theirs. Furthermore, it is pretty obvious that if sinful humans are to have coherent moral lives, grace in the further senses of assistance and empowerment is much more necessary for them to act well than would be the case if they were free of sin. It is fair, I think, to say that as rational beings we humans have a native ability to appreciate the good. But we are also prone to place our own good above all else in our decisions and actions, which is all that sin requires. Whether we could ever, through rational deliberation, come to set this tendency aside with no help whatever from God may well be doubted—especially when we remember that all of the good we see around us is to be counted as grace, and is from him.

VI. CONCLUSION

I think, then, that it is possible to develop an account of free will and of God's role as creator that makes it possible to resolve the apparent conflict between grace and free will that so troubled Augustine and many others, and the attendant theological conflict over grace and works. There is, of course, an aspect of the view I have proposed that promises trouble. If God creates us deciding the things we do, then he is as much responsible for creaturely decisions in which salvation is rejected, or at least turned away from, as for those in which it is accepted. Assuming, then, that not all are to be numbered among the elect, the fate of the lost is as much a matter of

God's will as that of the saved. And some may wonder how such a thing can be squared with God's supposed goodness. In essence, however, this is not a new problem. It will arise in some form or other on any account according to which, in creating the world, God knows exactly which world he is creating. And in any case, it is a problem I shall have to leave for another time.[33]

---

33. An earlier version of this paper was read at a meeting of the American Philosophical Association Pacific Division in 2008, and at the University of Texas at San Antonio in 2009. I am grateful for the comments received on those occasions, as well as for comments from the editors of this volume.

BIBLIOGRAPHY

Adams, Robert M. "Must God Create the Best?" *The Philosophical Review* 81 (1972) 317–32.

Augustine. *Confessions*. In *Nicene and Post-Nicene Fathers: First Series*, vol. 1: *Confessions and Letters of Augustin: With a Sketch of His Life and Work*, edited by Philip Schaff et al. 2nd ed. Peabody, MA: Hendrickson, 1966.

———. *On the Gift of Perseverance*. In *Nicene and Post-Nicene Fathers: First Series*, vol. 5: *Saint Augustin: Anti-Pelagian Writings*, edited by Philip Schaff et al., 521–552. 2nd ed. Peabody, MA: Hendrickson, 1966.

———. *On Grace and Free Will*. In *Nicene and Post-Nicene Fathers: First Series*, vol. 5: *Saint Augustin: Anti-Pelagian Writings*, edited by Philip Schaff et al., 436–467. 2nd ed. Peabody, MA: Hendrickson, 1966.

———. *On the Predestination of the Saints*. In *Nicene and Post-Nicene Fathers: First Series*, vol. 5: *Saint Augustin: Anti-Pelagian Writings*, edited by Philip Schaff et al., 493–520. 2nd ed. Peabody, MA: Hendrickson, 1966.

———. *On Rebuke and Grace*. In *Nicene and Post-Nicene Fathers: First Series*, vol. 5: *Saint Augustin: Anti-Pelagian Writings*, edited by Philip Schaff et al., 468–492. 2nd ed. Peabody, MA: Hendrickson, 1966.

Chisholm, Roderick. "Human Freedom and the Self." In *Free Will*, edited by Gary Watson, 24–35. New York: Oxford University Press, 1982.

Clarke, Randolph. *Libertarian Accounts of Free Will*. New York: Oxford University Press, 2003.

Couenhoven, Jesse. "Augustine's Rejection of the Free-Will Defense: An Overview of the Late Augustine's Theodicy." *Religious Studies* 43 (2007) 279–98.

Ginet, Carl. *On Action*. New York: Cambridge University Press, 1990.

McCann, Hugh. "Divine Freedom." In *Creation and the Sovereignty of God*, 155–75. Bloomington, IN: Indiana University Press, 2012.

———. "Divine Sovereignty and the Freedom of the Will." *Faith and Philosophy* 12 (1995) 582–98.

———. "Divine Will and Divine Simplicity." In *Creation and the Sovereignty of God*, 213–36. Bloomington, IN: Indiana University Press, 2012.

———. "Free Will and Divine Sovereignty." In *Creation and the Sovereignty of God*, 92–112. Bloomington, IN: Indiana University Press, 2012.

———. "The Author of Sin?" *Faith and Philosophy* 22 (2005) 144–59.

O'Connor, Timothy. *Persons and Causes: The Metaphysics of Free Will*. New York: Oxford University Press, 1995.

Rowe, William. "Two Concepts of Freedom." *Proceedings and Addresses of the American Philosophical Association* 61 (1987) 43–64.

8

The First Sin
A Dilemma for Christian Determinists

—ALEXANDER R. PRUSS

1. INTRODUCTION

CHRISTIANS WHO HOLD A deterministic view of creaturely freedom face a particular problem with explaining the first sin. The goodness of creation is a basic Christian doctrine, and evil enters the world through sin. But if determinism holds, then how could a sin arise from a good world?

I shall make this precise as an argument against Christian determinism by organizing my argument around a dilemma for Christian determinists. Creaturely free action either is determined only by God or also by explanatorily prior finite causes. The view on which it is determined only by God is associated with a theologically deterministic reading of Thomas Aquinas—I shall not decide whether the reading is right or not. According to this Thomist view, freedom is incompatible with determination by laws of nature, and hence deterministic Thomism is a species of incompatibilism in the contemporary sense. The second view is that of Jonathan Edwards according to which creaturely[1] action is determined by a combination of inner state and circumstances, much as standard contemporary compatibil-

---

1. Jonathan Edwards also applies this to divine action, but I shall consider the view only as restricted to creaturely action.

ists say it is. I shall run an argument against each variant of the Christian deterministic dilemma.

According to Christian orthodoxy, the first sin is the sin of an angel, presumably Lucifer. However, I shall not assume this except in the case of one variant of my argument, and the main arguments shall apply equally well whether the first sin is that of Eve or that of Lucifer. Moreover, I shall sometimes use Eve's sin purely for illustrative purposes, because we have a very unclear picture of what Lucifer's sin actually consisted in.

2. DETERMINISTIC THOMISM

2.1. The Argument

According to (theologically) deterministic Thomism, creaturely free actions are determined by God's causality and not by any finite causes. The difficulty with this in the case of the first sin—and, in fact, all sin—is simple. As we shall see, it is very hard to avoid saying that God intentionally causes the person to sin,[2] even if only as a means to some great good, like the goods of Christ's redemptive work.

Now, St Paul rhetorically asks whether we should do evil that good may come of it,[3] and the Christian tradition has taken it as a basic ethical principle that one may not do evil that good may come of it. This deontological principle (DP) is intuitively quite plausible: one should not do evil as a means to the good. Application of the deontological principle tends to be bound up with the principle of double effect (PDE), which provides a partial converse. A standard formulation of the PDE is that it can be permissible to act in ways that result in an intrinsic evil, when (a) that evil is not intended either as an end or as a means, (b) the action in itself is not morally wrong, and (c) there is an intended good to which the unintended evil is not disproportionate.[4]

The DP is violated by God's intentionally producing a sin, whether God intends it as a means or as an end. Insofar as the Christian tradition

---

2. I say that "x intentionally φed" providing that x φed in fulfillment of an intention to φ. Both Anscombe, *Intention*, 1; and Bratman, *Intentions, Plans, and Practical Reason*, 377, will dispute this as an analysis of "intentionally φed." Those who dispute this analysis should take my use of "intentionally" as stipulated in order to avoid the awkwardness of the redoubled locution "φed in fulfillment of an intention to φ."

3. Rom 3:8.

4. In the end, I do not think the standard formulation is correct, but it is close enough for the purposes of this paper. For a better version, see Pruss, "Accomplishment of Plans."

accepts the DP, the question we need to ask, thus, is whether the deterministic Thomist can avoid saying that the first sin is intended by God, or caused in some other morally impermissible way.

If God *directly* causes the first sin, then one cannot say that the first sin is an unintended causal side-effect of an action, in the way civilian deaths might be an unintended causal side-effect of the bombing of a military installation in a justly conducted war. But perhaps there are other kinds of side-effects possible, besides causal ones. For instance, actions are always intended under a description, and so it may be that God does not intend the first sin under a description that includes the first sin's sinfulness. In the Eve case, maybe God intends that she eat the yummy fruit, and not the *forbidden* fruit, even though God knows that the coarsely-individuated events *eating the yummy fruit* and *eating the forbidden fruit* are identical. A similar story can, perhaps, be told about Satan's first sin, except that we have a much less clear picture of what that sin might be.

But this still raises the question of theodicy. If God intentionally causes Eve to eat the yummy fruit, while knowing that it is forbidden, he must have a good reason for this, a reason proportionate to the sinfulness of the action. One might make that reason be the great goods of Christ's work of redemption and/or the exercises of virtue that sin makes possible (forgiveness, repentance, etc.). But Christ's work of redemption is a work of redeeming us from *sin* as such, and the best of the exercises of virtue that sin makes possible, such as forgiveness and repentance, depend on sin as such. Thus then the sin is an intended means to these goods,[5] and DP is violated.

2.2. Objections

Objection 1: DP applies to creatures but not to God. It is plausible that there are many moral rules that do not apply to God. For instance, it would be wrong for a human being to command Abraham to sacrifice his son, but it does not appear to be wrong for God to do so.

Response: Some substantive moral rules that apply to us do not literally apply to God simply because they make no sense in the case of God. For instance, a duty to seek forgiveness for wrongdoing makes no sense in the

---

5. Perhaps it is a constitutive rather than causal means. However, Double Effect when rightly read should prohibit intending evils as constitutive means just as it prohibits intending evils as causal means. For instance, committing a murder is a constitutive means to *being justly punished for a murder*. Someone who committed a theft in order to be justly punished for it in order to better understand the phenomenology of punishment would still be impermissibly intending the theft, even if the goods achieved were proportionate to the evils.

case of a sinless being. Other substantive moral rules would make sense in the case of God, but nonetheless do not apply. The prohibition against killing the innocent is an example. God is the owner of our lives, and has no duty to continue sustaining us in existence. However, DP is not a substantive but *structural* moral rule, and it is very plausible that if we are created in the image and likeness of God, and if we are exhorted in Scripture to imitate God, then at least our *structural* moral rules should apply in the case of God.

Moreover, it seems obvious that it would be wrong for God to intentionally cause an innocent person to suffer for eternity. That this idea is plausible even to determinists such as Calvinists is clear from their emphasis on the compatibilistic claim that when God causes someone to sin and then damns the person, he causes the sin in a way that makes the person *responsible* for the sin and hence makes the damnation a just punishment.

But what would be wrong with God intentionally causing an innocent person to suffer for eternity? The obvious answer is that it is unjust intentionally to cause a harm of at least that order of magnitude to an innocent person. Call a harm of that order of magnitude a "grand harm."

Now, I claim, that sin is also a grand harm. We learn from Socrates that it is worse to do wrong than to suffer wrong. To be a murderer is worse than to be murdered. Sin is *in itself* a harm to the sinner, apart from any punishment for it, in proportion to how grave the sin is. At the same time, the punishment deserved for a wrongdoing is also proportionate to the gravity of the sin. Any wrongdoing that deserves eternal suffering is very grave indeed. (This point is unaffected by the view of many Protestant Christians that *all* sin deserves eternal damnation; for on that view, *all* wrongdoing is very grave indeed.) In particular, the following thesis is now very plausible in light of the proportionalities between deserved punishment and the gravity of the offense, and between the gravity of the offense and the harm to the wrongdoer: a wrongdoing that deserves eternal suffering is a *grand harm* to the wrongdoer, a harm of at least the order of magnitude of eternal suffering.

But if what would be wrong with God intentionally causing an innocent person to suffer for eternity is that this would impose a grand harm on an innocent, then by the same token to impose sin on an innocent should be wrong for the same reason.

Objection 2: It does not appear that *any* Christian—deterministic Thomist, Edwardsian, or theological incompatibilist—can avoid the problem that a plausible theodicy makes God be an intender of sin. For all Christians hold that God at least *permits* sin to happen. A theodicy for that permission is needed, and it seems that the theodicy will need to make reference to the goods to which the sin will be a means.

Response: The Edwardsian, Molinist, simple-foreknowledge theorist and open theist can each give a story on which God intends a set of initial conditions that in fact lead to sin, but God has a reason for intending these initial conditions that is independent of the fact that they lead to sin.

It is not my purpose here to develop theodicies for God's allowing the first sin, so I will give a mere sketch of what can be said. The open theist can say that God simply did not know that the initial conditions would lead to sin, and that the possibility of freely choosing to obey God was worth trying for. The value of this possibility is not dependent on the unfortunate resulting sin. The simple foreknowledge theorist can give a similar story, since on simple foreknowledge God's decision as to which conditions to actualize cannot depend on what free choices will result from that decision, on pain of explanatory circularity (God's deciding which conditions to actualize in part because of what choice is made under the conditions and the choice being made in part because of the conditions).[6] Thus, God's decision might be made on the basis of the value of the possibility of the agent's freely obeying God rather than the value of the results of sin. Note that in these two stories, it is the great good of significantly freely *acting well* that is involved in the theodicy, rather than just the good of significant freedom.

The Edwardsian compatibilist can say that God might have a reason to produce a set of initial conditions that are valuable in ways independent of the fact that they necessitate sin. Thus, these initial conditions might be particularly simple and hence intrinsically valuable, or they might give rise to a particularly elegant set of evolutionary developments. The Molinist can give a similar story, except that now the initial conditions do not necessitate sin, but they counterfactually imply sin.

There is, nonetheless, a problem with these responses when made by the Christian. The Christian tradition places an emphasis on Adam's sin as a *felix culpa*, a sin that happily leads to the great goods of the redemption. It seems plausible that any theodicy faithful to the Christian tradition will have to make use of the valuable consequences of sin, while the above sketches do not. This highlights an apparent tension in the Christian tradition between DP and standard Christian theodicies.

The tension can, however, be resolved, by incorporating the *felix culpa* into the sketches above. Each sketch offered a possible divine reason R for producing a particular set of initial conditions, a reason independent of the valuable consequences of sin. However, there is a defeater S for these reasons: the fact that sin might (open theism, simple foreknowledge), would (Molinism) or must (Edwards) result. The *felix culpa* account then acts as a

---

6. Cf. Adams "Middle knowledge," 113.

defeater for S. God does not, then, produce the initial conditions in order to produce the great goods of redemption. To do that would be to intend sin as a constitutive means to these great goods. Rather, God recognizes these great goods as a defeater to a defeater to R, and what God intends are the goods in R such as orderly initial conditions, freedom, etc. The felicity of the *culpa* is then important to God's decision to permit the *culpa*, but is nonetheless not intended.

This defeater-defeater story is structurally like Frances Kamm's[7] "triple effect" story of the party. You want to hold a party. But you have a defeater for it—the party will generate a mess needing cleanup. You also have a defeater for the defeater, however: the guests are the sorts of people who are going to help you clean up. Now, it would be absurd to say that you hold the party with the intention that the guests help you clean up. After all, if you don't hold the party, no cleanup will be needed. But the availability of the cleanup acts as a defeater to a defeater.

Perhaps, though, the deterministic Thomist can avail herself of a defeater-defeater story as well. Maybe God intends Eve to eat a yummy fruit, for the sake of the good R of eating a yummy fruit, or maybe for the sake of the good of being motivated by a natural gustatory inclination. The fact that the yummy fruit is forbidden is a defeater D for R. And then the great goods of redemption defeat D.

This, however, stretches triple effect too far. Consider the following paradigmatic illustration of DP.[8] A terrorist has twenty innocent captives. He offers you a gun and tells you that if you don't kill one of them, he'll kill all of them himself; but if you kill one, he'll let the others go. One can also vary the story as follows: if you don't kill a particular one, he'll kill the others and let that one go; if you do kill that one, he'll let the others go. Choose whichever version you find gives you the more plausible argument below. Now, the paradigmatic claim of DP is that you shouldn't take up the offer.

However, unrestricted defeater-defeater reasoning would allow it. Suppose you intend the cognitive good of learning what it feels like to pull a trigger while a loaded and primed gun is pointing at a mammalian heart. You have a defeater for this good—the captive will almost surely die if you gain the good. You then have a defeater for the defeater: on balance nine or eight (depending on the variant) lives will be saved. So you can pull the trigger, without intending the death of the captive.

This sort of reasoning would trivialize DP. There is, however, a reasonable response that can be made. The defeater-defeater reasoning depends

---

7. Kamm, *Intricate Ethics*, 103.
8. Cf. Williams, "Critique of Utilitarianism."

on Double Effect. However, Double Effect has a proportionality condition. This condition should not simply be that the action is consequentialistically right. Plausibly, a necessary condition for proportionality is that the intended good non-intended evil not be *completely out of proportion* to the intended good. In particular, if the non-intended evil is grave, the intended good cannot be something trivial. Further goods arising out of the non-intended evil can count as defeater-defeaters, but the intended good must do a significant amount of the moral pulling in itself. And the evil of the death of an innocent person is completely out of proportion to the trivial cognitive good of learning what it is like to pull the trigger of a loaded and primed gun pointing at a mammalian heart.

Likewise, the evil of the first sin is clearly completely out of proportion to the minor good of enjoying a yummy fruit or of being moved by a natural gustatory inclination. On the other hand, on the open theist, simple foreknowledge, Molinist and Edwardsian stories, God's reason for causing conditions that might or would or must lead to sin could be grounded in a non-trivial good of freedom or the orderly arrangement of the universe.

The Thomist may respond[9] that God does not perform discrete actions, such as causing Eve to sin. Rather, God creates the cosmos in all its spatiotemporal extent as a whole, and hence the means-end analysis is inapplicable. However, the inapplicability of means-end analysis does not follow. For even an agent who produces a sophisticated work as a whole "all at once" would be apt to engage in means-end reasoning such as: "This part of the work (e.g., Eve's sin) is to exist *to make fitting that part* (e.g., the work of redemption)." The means here may not be *causal* means, but they are nonetheless intended for the sake of other aspects of the work.

I do not have an argument that the deterministic theist cannot come up with *some* great good that God is intending, a good to which sin is not a means. However, because the deterministic Thomist cannot advert to the good of particular initial conditions or to an attempt to have the agent freely obey God, the task is much more difficult for the deterministic Thomist.

2. EDWARDS-STYLE DETERMINISM

2.1. The Argument

The argument is based on this principle (where the "if...then..." is a material conditional):

---

9. I am grateful to David Alexander for this response.

1. If *x*'s internal state and circumstances necessitate *x*'s wrongdoing, and the wrongdoing is culpable, then *x*'s internal state was in some way vicious prior to the choice.

Without the culpability clause in (1), the principle might not be true. One might reasonably think that a person who is innocently ignorant that *A* is wrong could be necessitated by an entirely virtuous character to do *A*.

Principle (1) is neutral between compatibilists and libertarians. For instance, those compatibilists like Hume who hold that actions are culpable only to the extent that they reflect a wicked character will certainly accept (1). Libertarians who think that necessitation is incompatible with responsibility will accept (1) as trivially true, because its antecedent is necessarily false. Other libertarians will allow that a person could be necessitated into culpable wrongdoing, but only if the necessitating inner state is a vicious state produced by earlier non-necessitated free actions.

Here is one way to think about (1). Any character that has a tendency to act wrongly in normal circumstances possesses a vice. Vices may be more or less specific. Thus, someone who has a tendency to cheat on exams has a less specific vice than someone who has a tendency to cheat on chemistry exams administered at noon by short professors with German accents. Whenever *C* is a set of normal circumstances, if *C* together with one's inner state necessitated a wrongdoing *A*, then one had a tendency to do *A* in *C*, and that, surely, was a vice. The relevant kind of "normalcy" for circumstances here is that the circumstances are not responsibility-canceling, in the way that extreme circumstances or circumstances where one does not know what the right thing to do is are. In responsibility-canceling circumstances, however, the wrongdoing is not culpable. Therefore, any tendency to *culpable* wrongdoing constitutes a vice, and any case of necessitation of an action by the inner state and circumstances constitutes a tendency to do wrong in precisely these circumstances. And so (1) is true.

Now, let us add to (1) the following two premises:

2. Nobody was in any way vicious prior to the first sin.

3. The first sin was culpable.

Premise (2) expresses the Christian idea that creation was originally good and evil entered the world through sin. Premise (3) also appears quite plausible, whether the first sin is taken to be that of Eve or that of Lucifer.

But now the rest of the argument is easy:

4. The first sinner's internal state was in no way vicious prior to the first sin. (By 2)

5. The first sinner's internal state and circumstances did not necessitate the first sin. (By 1, 3 and 4)

Hence, Edwards-style compatibilism does not hold of the first sin.

Let me illustrate (1) in the case of a first sin. Suppose, for simplicity, the first sin was that of Eve and that it was literally as described in the Book of Genesis. Eve, thus, disobeyed God out of a desire to gain a forbidden knowledge and eat a yummy-looking fruit. If her action was necessitated by her inner state and circumstances, then she had a tendency to disobey God when she could gain such-and-such forbidden knowledge and eat such-and-such yummy-looking fruit. But such a tendency, surely, implies a vice.

2.2. Objections

Objection 1: Principle (1) sets too high a bar for being free of vice. A person whose internal state under extreme circumstances necessitated a yielding to temptation would not count as having had a vice in her internal state.

Response: Insofar as we find it plausible that the person would not count as having had a vice in her internal state, we also find it plausible that she was not responsible for her wrongdoing. But (1) only applies to culpable wrongdoing.

One might, however, try to walk a fine line and insist that a non-vicious person who was necessitated to sin in extreme circumstances could still have *a little bit* of culpability. I think this is not plausible—precisely to the extent that she was necessitated to sin *little bit culpably*, she was also *a little bit vicious*. However, if we do accept the suggestion, then (1) and (3) in my argument will need "culpably" to be replaced with "significantly culpably." With that modification, (1) and (3) remain plausible.

Objection 2: The argument highlights the very difficult problem of how someone without vice could sin. This problem is just as difficult for the libertarian as for the determinist.

Response: The argument I gave works only against the determinist, since principle (1) only applies to actions that are necessitated. Now, one might wonder whether some parallel argument might not apply against a libertarian. To do that, the antecedent of the conditional in (1) would need to be modified to be relevant to the libertarian. Probably the way to do that would be:

1*. If x's internal state and circumstances make x's wrongdoing possible, and that wrongdoing is culpable, then x's internal state was in some way vicious prior to the choice.

But (1*) is quite implausible. That someone is *capable* of sin does not imply that her character is in any way vicious. It is plausible to say that a non-vicious character makes it possible to avoid culpable wrongdoing—and that is what (1) says. But it is not plausible to say that a non-vicious character makes culpable wrongdoing impossible.

Objection 3: Suppose that out of greed, Sarah formed the false belief that underreporting one's income to tax authorities is permissible. Sarah has since repented of her greed. She realizes that she has some beliefs about financial behavior that were formed under the influence of the greed, and is sincerely striving to figure out which of them are false. She has not yet managed to figure out that her belief about the permissibility of underreporting income is false. This belief, together with circumstances, then necessitates her to underreport her income. In so doing, she is acting culpably, because her ignorance is her own fault—it came from her earlier greed. Yet she lacks any vice, at least as far as the story goes.

Response: This is the closest to a counterexample to (1) that I have been able to find, but I doubt it is a counterexample to it, because I doubt that Sarah is culpable. It seems that she was culpable for having formed the belief, but having repented of her earlier greed, and having sought to eliminate its ill cognitive effects, she is no longer culpable for the *continuation* of the belief.

If one is not convinced by this, I will need to modify (1) as follows:

1**. If x's internal state and circumstances necessitate x's wrongdoing, and that wrongdoing is culpable, then at some time prior to the choice, either x's internal state was in some way vicious or x did something wrong.

The rest of the argument adapts to work with (1**), since by definition nothing wrong was done before the first sin, and (4) applies to all times prior to the first sin.

Objection 4: The first sin was not culpable. Instead, the first sinner bootstrapped himself into culpability by a two-step process. First, he sinned non-culpably, necessitated by his circumstances and entirely non-vicious inner state. This caused him to acquire a vicious character. This vicious character then necessitated a second, this time culpable, sin.

Response: It is tempting for those with libertarian sympathies to respond that the second sin wasn't culpable as it was necessitated by a character feature F such that the sinner was not responsible for the acquisition of F. But that would beg the question against the compatibilist.

A non-question-begging response is to note that the two-step story does not appear plausible in the story of Eve as described in the Book of

Genesis. Her first sin seems to be the eating of the forbidden fruit, and God holds her responsible for it. And even though in Christian orthodoxy it isn't the case that Eve is the first sinner, my argument with (1), (3) and (4) as premises appears to be sound if we replace "first sin" with "Eve's first sin" and "first sinner" with "Eve," even if Eve isn't the first sinner. So the bootstrapping argument might be thought to work for Lucifer—though probably only because we don't have a good picture of his sin (and that may be a good thing!)—but it doesn't seem to work for Eve.

One might, however, try to add another level of bootstrapping to solve the problem with Eve. Perhaps Lucifer, after having committed his second, culpable sin (or maybe *as* his second, culpable sin) corrupted Eve's character, causing her to become vicious through no fault of her own. And then Eve sinned culpably, out of that vicious character. I feel the pull of the rejoinder that if one's character was corrupted by another through no fault of one's own, then one is not responsible, but I suspect that this rejoinder will be rejected by some compatibilists. A better rejoinder is that it appears to be a standard Christian doctrine that moral corruption entered the human world through human sin. The snake tempted Eve, but the corruption of humanity was her and Adam's work.

Moreover, the bootstrapping itself can be questioned in the case of Lucifer. How exactly is Lucifer supposed to have non-culpably sinned the first time around? Was he ignorant of the moral law? He is supposed to have been a great and intelligent angel. Perhaps his first failing was in some very abstruse moral matter, beyond Lucifer's intelligence. But is it plausible that such an abstruse failing would have corrupted his angelic character sufficiently to necessitate the subsequent culpable sin? Or was Lucifer forced or mindwashed into sin? But by whom? Surely not by God. The bootstrapping story does not, thus, appear very plausible even in Lucifer's case.

4. CONCLUSIONS

The Christian determinist faces a particularly thorny problem of explaining how the first sin was possible. In the case of the deterministic Thomist, that problem to some extent generalizes to subsequent sins. In the case of the Edwardsian, that problem is particularly pressing in the case of the first sin. For the Edwardsian has the resources to explain subsequent sins in terms of God's simply allowing the causal consequences of the first sin and by making use of the good of natural causality.

The best moves for the Christian determinist would be either (1) to go for the Thomistic version of the view and then give a sophisticated defeater-defeater account of the first sin[10] or (2) to go Edwardsian but make an exemption for the first sin, which is libertarian-free.

It is interesting, however, that neither option would allow the Christian determinist to make use of standard arguments against libertarianism based on the idea that undetermined action is incompatible with agency. For on the Thomistic story, a free action is not determined by the agent's character and circumstances (though it is in some sense determined by God's primary causality), while on the modified Edwardsian story, it is *possible* for a free action not to be determined by the agent's character and circumstances. Nor can the modified Edwardsian run any argument against libertarianism based on God's foreknowledge or sovereignty, since such an argument either applies to all creaturely choices or to none. Therefore, both of the possible moves help the Christian libertarian.[11]

---

10. See the response to Objection 2.2.2.

11. I am very grateful to David Alexander for many very helpful and incisive comments and to Daniel Johnson for deep conversations on these topics.

BIBLIOGRAPHY

Adams, Robert M. "Middle Knowledge and the Problem of Evil." *American Philosophical Quarterly* 14 (1977) 109–17.

Anscombe, G. E. M. *Intention*. Cambridge, MA: Harvard University Press, 2000.

Bratman, Michael. *Intentions, Plans, and Practical Reason*. Cambridge, MA: Harvard University Press, 1987.

Kamm, Frances M. *Intricate Ethics: Rights, Responsibilities and Permissible Harm*. New York: Oxford University Press, 2007.

Pruss, Alexander R. "The Accomplishment of Plans: A New Version of the Principle of Double Effect." *Philosophical Studies* (forthcoming).

Williams, Bernard. "A Critique of Utilitarianism." In *Utilitarianism: For and Against*, edited by J. J. C. Smart and Bernard Williams. Cambridge: Cambridge University Press, 1973.

9

Calvinism and the First Sin

—James N. Anderson

> *Adam lay ybounden,*
> *Bounden in a bond;*
> *Four thousand winter,*
> *Thought he not too long.*
> *And all was for an apple,*
> *An apple that he took.*
> *As clerkes finden,*
> *Written in their book.*
> *Ne had the apple taken been,*
> *The apple taken been,*
> *Ne had never our ladie,*
> *Abeen heav'ne queen.*
> *Blessed be the time*
> *That apple taken was,*
> *Therefore we moun singen.*
> *Deo gracias!*[1]

According to orthodox Christian teaching, the entire human race is fallen in sin and subject to death because of the first transgression of the first member of that race. As the apostle Paul wrote to the church in Rome, "sin came into the world through one man, and death through sin, and so death

---

1. "Adam Lay Ybounden," late-medieval English carol. The version quoted here is from Rickert, "Adam Lay Ybounden."

spread to all men because all sinned."[2] The Second Council of Orange (529 AD) in its anathemas against Pelagianism and semi-Pelagianism took for granted the historical existence of a first man, Adam, whose first sin brought corruption and death upon the whole human race.[3]

Historically the notion of a first human sin has proven important in the services of Christian theodicy.[4] Skeptics naturally ask: If God created the universe, and humans in his own image, why is the human race in such a sorry state? Why do we treat each other so abominably? Why do we suffer sickness and death? Why do so many of us experience such misery, not least at each other's hands? The idea of an Adamic fall, centered on a first sin, offers a (relatively) straightforward answer. Adam was the fountainhead and representative of the human race. He was created good, and free to choose between good and evil, to obey or to disobey God's commandments. At some point in time, for reasons we may never understand, Adam chose evil over good—he rebelled against his Creator—and in so doing he corrupted human nature and brought the penalty of death upon himself and his progeny.

Despite its potential for theodicy, the notion of an Adamic fall raises some difficult questions. Some of these concern the relationship between Adam and his progeny. How did his sin corrupt not only Adam but *mankind*? Why should you and I suffer today because of the single transgression of a distant ancestor? Perhaps the most perplexing question of all is simply this: If Adam was created good, why did he commit evil?

The mystery of the first sin is one that must be faced by Christians of all theological traditions.[5] It is commonly thought, however, that of all

---

2. Rom 5:12 (English Standard Version). Cf. 1 Cor 15:21–22.

3. "CANON 1. If anyone denies that it is the whole man, that is, both body and soul, that was 'changed for the worse' through the offense of Adam's sin, but believes that the freedom of the soul remains unimpaired and that only the body is subject to corruption, he is deceived by the error of Pelagius and contradicts the scripture which says, 'The soul that sins shall die' (Ezek 18:20); and, 'Do you not know that if you yield yourselves to anyone as obedient slaves, you are the slaves of the one whom you obey?' (Rom 6:16); and, 'For whatever overcomes a man, to that he is enslaved' (2 Pet 2:19). CANON 2. If anyone asserts that Adam's sin affected him alone and not his descendants also, or at least if he declares that it is only the death of the body which is the punishment for sin, and not also that sin, which is the death of the soul, passed through one man to the whole human race, he does injustice to God and contradicts the Apostle, who says, 'Therefore as sin came into the world through one man and death through sin, and so death spread to all men because all men sinned' (Rom 5:12)."

4. For the record, I agree with the traditional Christian view that the very first sin was angelic rather than human (2 Pet 2:4; Jude 6). In this essay I use "first sin" simply as shorthand for "first human sin."

5. It has become *de rigueur* among modern theologians to deny the historicity

Christians Calvinists face the most intractable problems in accounting for the first sin. These problems, it is supposed, derive from Calvinism's commitment to *divine determinism*, the view that everything that takes place in the creation is ultimately determined solely by the decree of God. From the premise of divine determinism, at least three major objections arise:

(1) *God the author of sin.* If God determines all things by his eternal decree, it follows that God determined the first human sin. God didn't merely *foreknow* that Adam would sin. He didn't merely *allow* that Adam would sin. No, God *deliberately determined* that Adam would sin. That is to say, God decided in advance that Adam would sin and then somehow *caused* Adam to sin. On this view God intentionally caused the first sin, which thus makes God the *author of sin* (or at least the author of *human* sin). But this conclusion is incompatible with God's moral perfection, which is an essential tenet of Christian theism.[6]

(2) *The challenges of compatibilism.* In keeping with Christian orthodoxy, Calvinists want to insist that Adam freely sinned and was held morally responsible for his sin.[7] Calvinists must therefore be committed to *compatibilism*: the thesis that human freedom and moral responsibility are compatible with determinism.[8] However, there are some formidable philosophical arguments against compatibilism, such as the Consequence Argument and the Manipulation Argument.[9] If Calvinism is committed to compatibilism, the argument runs, then so much the worse for Calvinism.

---

of Adam, mainly due to perceived pressure from scientific reconstructions of human evolutionary history. Here I take for granted the historicity of Adam and an Adamic fall. It should be noted that denying the historicity of Adam does not make the problem of the first human sin go away, for it remains the case that (i) at some time t1 there were no humans and (ii) at some time t2 > t1 there was a human who sinned. For theological and scientific defenses of the historicity of Adam, see Collins, *Did Adam and Eve Really Exist*; Rana and Ross, *Who Was Adam*; Gauger et al., *Science and Human Origins*.

6. For variations on this criticism, see Walls and Dongell, *Not a Calvinist*; Olson, *Arminian Theology*; Olson, *Against Calvinism*.

7. See, for example, chapters 6 and 9 of the *Westminster Confession of Faith*.

8. Some philosophers have argued that determinism may not be compatible with *freedom* (at least, the kind of freedom that allows for choosing otherwise in exactly the same circumstances) but is nonetheless compatible with *moral responsibility* (provided that certain other conditions are met). This position has been dubbed "semi-compatibilism." See Fischer and Ravizza, *Responsibility and Control*; Fischer, "Compatibilism," 44–84. For simplicity's sake, I will gloss over the distinction between compatibilism and semi-compatibilism, since nothing in my argument turns on it. I will use the label "compatibilism" for the view that determinism is compatible with moral responsibility and thus with whatever kinds of freedom are necessary for moral responsibility. I take it that worries about the implications of divine determinism for human freedom are fueled primarily by concerns about moral responsibility.

9. For influential formulations of the Consequence Argument and Manipulation

(3) *No causal explanation for the first sin.* As noted in the previous point, Calvinists appear to be committed to a compatibilist account of human freedom. Typically for such accounts a person S's choice at some time t is sufficiently explained by S's internal state at t (S's character, beliefs, desires, dispositions, etc.) and S's external circumstances at t. (The compatibilist doesn't claim that *every* such choice is free, only that *some* such choices are free.) In the case of Adam's first sin, while the external circumstances included a diabolical tempting agent, that outside influence cannot be considered a *sufficient* explanation for Adam's sin, otherwise he could not be held morally responsible, even on compatibilist grounds. Yet Adam's internal state, prior to the first sin, was wholly good. He had no evil desires or dispositions. On the contrary, he was by nature wholly disposed toward good. On compatibilist grounds, then, it seems that Adam *should not* have sinned.[10] There is no sufficient causal explanation for Adam's sin.

The first and second of these problems, it may be noted, are not unique to the first sin. They apply to *all* human sins. So why address those problems in an essay devoted to the first sin? One reason for doing so is that Adam's sin, as a primal act of rebellious disobedience toward God, is paradigmatic of human sin. Another reason is that the first sin was foundational to all human sin, because (according to orthodox Christian doctrine) Adam's sin brought corruption on the whole human race, such that we are all born into a fallen state and inevitably sin. All sins therefore trace back to that first sin. Furthermore, the first sin presents a special challenge because it was the sin of an *unfallen* human. So to the extent that Calvinists can account for the divine determination of the first sin, they will have resources to account for the divine determination of human sin in general.

On the face of it, the three problems summarized above appear daunting for Calvinists. While the entrance of sin may prove to be an inexplicable mystery for any Christian theologian, non-Calvinists contend that a commitment to divine determinism makes the problem of the first sin far harder than it needs to be, and this amounts to a significant strike against Calvinism. Indeed, the three problems above may count as three distinct strikes—and we all know what *three* strikes means.

It is precisely this assessment of Calvinism that I wish to challenge in this essay. My argument will proceed in three stages. First, I will argue that divine determinism *per se* doesn't give rise to the three problems described

---

Argument, see van Inwagen, *Essay on Free Will*; Pereboom, *Living without Free Will*. For an overview of arguments against compatibilism, see Vihvelin, "Arguments for Incompatibilism."

10. Note that the "should" here carries an explanatory rather than moral sense, as in "The bridge *should not* have collapsed under that weight of traffic."

above—or at least, not to such a degree as to justify eliminating Calvinism as a serious theological candidate. Secondly, while conceding that Calvinism still faces some difficult questions, I will argue that the major alternatives to Calvinism face problems of their own that are no less perplexing. If the Calvinist must appeal to mystery at some points, non-Calvinists must also appeal to mystery at key junctures, and there's nothing uniquely distasteful about the Calvinist's appeal. Finally, I will contend that when the Calvinist account of the first sin is compared with competing accounts, and the virtues and vices of each position are considered on a level playing field, the Calvinist account is on balance more appealing than the alternatives. My overall goal is relatively modest: I do not argue that Calvinism faces no real problems or perplexities when it comes to the first sin, but only that it faces no *greater* problems or perplexities than its competitors.

DIVINE CAUSAL DETERMINISM

It should be conceded at the outset, and without any embarrassment, that Calvinism is indeed committed to divine determinism: the view that everything is ultimately determined by God. I will not argue this point—it can be amply documented from representative Calvinist sources—but will simply take it for granted as something on which the vast majority of Calvinists and their critics agree. To be more precise, I will assume that Calvinism is committed to divine determinism in the following sense:

> (DD) For every event E, God decided that E should happen and that decision was the ultimate sufficient cause of E.[11]

In other words, every event that occurs is willed by God, God's willing an event is a sufficient cause of that event, and the divine will has no prior cause.[12]

Having established this baseline, it is important to recognize that there are several kinds of determinism to which Calvinists need *not* be committed. In the first place, Calvinists need not be committed to *material* or *physical*

---

11. A recent edited volume purports to cast doubt on the notion that the early Reformed theologians held to divine determinism. van Asselt et al., *Reformed Thought on Freedom*. I cannot engage with such historical arguments here, but will simply state my conviction that John Calvin and the Westminster Divines—to name no others—held to divine determinism as I've defined it. Readers who doubt that judgment can take this essay as addressing the following hypothetical: "Suppose, as many do, that Calvinism is committed to divine determinism. How bad would that really be?"

12. This is not to say that God's will is the *efficient* or *immediate* cause of every event, a claim which most Calvinists have been careful to deny.

determinism: the thesis that every event, including human decisions and actions, is determined entirely by prior physical events in conjunction with physical laws. This observation is significant not least because physical determinism is often believed to be incompatible with human free will and moral responsibility. To what extent this belief is justified is an interesting and important question, but largely irrelevant to the debate over Calvinism.

Secondly, we should note that Calvinism doesn't entail *causal determinism* in the sense most often in view in discussions about free will. Causal determinism, in this technical sense, is the idea that events subsequent to t are necessitated by (and thus in principle could be logically deduced from) the entire state of the world at t and those causal laws that govern the world.[13] On this view, every event in the world has prior sufficient causes within the world and events are determined by their causes in strict law-like fashion (thus some philosophers prefer the term *nomological determinism* for this species of determinism). Calvinists, however, have invariably held that God can direct events both *through* second causes and *apart from* second causes.[14] For example, God could act directly to raise Jesus from the dead in such a way as to overrule the natural course of events (i.e., whatever subsequent events would be entailed by the laws of nature alone). Such direct divine action in the world is consistent with Calvinism but inconsistent with causal determinism.

So Calvinism is committed to divine determinism, but not to physical determinism or to causal determinism in the narrow sense (i.e., nomological determinism). This fact will become important when we later come to consider the relationship between Calvinism and compatibilist accounts of freedom. Nevertheless, there is still *some* sense in which Calvinism posits a kind of causal determinism. For every event E, God *determines* that E will take place and the decree of God is the ultimate sufficient *cause* of E. How then should we understand this divine causation? What exactly are Calvinists committed to here?[15]

---

13. Hoefer, "Causal Determinism." Cf. van Inwagen, *Essay on Free Will*, 65; Mele, *Free Will and Luck*, 3; Timpe, "Free Will"; Timpe, *Free Will*, 12. Note that causal determinism in this sense is not equivalent to physical determinism, since it might be granted that not all events are physical events and not all natural laws are physical laws (e.g., there could be psychological laws that are distinct from physical laws).

14. See, e.g., *Westminster Confession of Faith*, 3.1 and 5.3.

15. I should note that some Calvinists have shied away from the language of causation with regard to divine foreordination. It seems to me that this reticence to speak about divine causation, at least with respect to creaturely sins, owes more to semantic qualms than to sober metaphysics: it is thought that the very term "causation" carries undesirable entailments. At any rate, I hope to show that even if one grants (as I do) that Calvinism is committed to divine *causal* determinism, this doesn't introduce

It is well known that the philosophical analysis of the notion of causality is fraught with difficulties.[16] There are competing accounts and analyses of the cause-effect relation, each with its own virtues and vices. For this very reason it's important to recognize that Calvinism *as such* isn't committed to any *particular* theory or account of causality. It is one thing to affirm that God's will is the ultimate sufficient cause of every event; it is quite another to give a philosophical account of divine causation. In what follows, I will not defend or assume any particular theory of causality. I will simply use the term *cause* in the generally understood sense of *bringing about*: for God to *cause* E is for God to *bring about* E. (Since Calvinists have been concerned to affirm that God does not bring about events by a passive "bare permission," we might add that God *deliberately* and *actively* brings about E—but we need be no more specific than that to maintain our Calvinist credentials.)[17]

The Calvinist notion of divine foreordination must thus be seen as *some* kind of causation. In ordaining whatsoever comes to pass, God is the *first cause* of every event and God's decree is the *ultimate sufficient cause* of every event. Nevertheless, we must be careful not to assume that divine causation is similar in every way, or even in most ways, to those kinds of causation that we routinely experience in the world. Divine causation is not on a par with *intramundane* causation.[18] As any orthodox Christian theist ought to recognize, divine causation is unique in a number of respects. For example, as causal agents we can bring about changes in existent things, but unlike God we do not have at our disposal the kind of causation that can bring things into existence *ex nihilo*, sustain them in existence, or annihilate them. Intramundane causes have a spatial location; God does not. Moreover, the majority view in the Christian tradition is that God isn't bound by time in the way that we are: God is either absolutely timeless or exists in a transcendent eternal moment. However one understands God's eternality,

---

insuperable problems for Calvinists. For a defense of the view that Reformed theology affirms "divine omnicausality," see Helseth, "God Causes All Things," 25–52.

16. For an overview of the bewildering variety of analyses that have been offered, see Schaffer, "Metaphysics of Causation." John Earman has lamented that to try to define determinism in terms of cause-and-effect is to "seek to explain a vague concept—determinism—in terms of a truly obscure one—causation." Earman, *Primer on Determinism*, 5. Van Inwagen shares the same aversion, confessing that the notion of causation "is a morass into which I for one refuse to set foot." Van Inwagen, *Essay on Free Will*, 65.

17. See, e.g., Calvin, *Institutes*, 1.16.8 and 1.18.1. Cf. *Westminster Confession of Faith*, 5.4.

18. The term "intramundane causation" is borrowed from Helm, "God Does Not Take Risks," 228–37.

divine causation isn't temporal in the way that intramundane causation is temporal.[19]

In light of the Creator-creature distinction, then, we should recognize that divine causation is of a wholly different order than creaturely causation. It operates on a level of its own. Divine causation is *sui generis* and is thus related only *analogically* to creaturely causation.[20] For this reason, the use of phrases such as "first cause" and "sufficient cause" shouldn't mislead us into thinking that Calvinism is committed to what we might call the *Domino Model of Providence*. Readers will no doubt be familiar with the elaborate domino-toppling feats that break world records from time to time. In such displays, tens of thousands of domino pieces are meticulously arranged such that each will be caused to fall in its proper sequence by the toppling of a preceding domino. Invariably these schemes are initiated by the fall of a single first domino, which is pushed over by a human agent (once it has been confirmed that the cameras are rolling).[21] If all goes to plan, the human agent only needs to *directly* cause the first domino to fall. But if the chain of dominos fails at some point, the human agent may choose to intervene by directly causing another domino to fall, thus enabling the chain to continue as planned. In such a scheme it makes good sense to say that the human agent is the both *first* cause and the *sufficient* cause (either directly or indirectly) of every domino fall.

It would be tempting to think of divine providence in such terms. God creates and arranges a complex system of "dominos"—the universe of second causes in its original state—and initiates his providential plan with a flick of the divine finger, so to speak. Furthermore, in keeping with the view that God isn't obliged always to work through second causes, God may choose to directly start some chains of dominos at later times or even to directly interrupt some chains.[22] The Domino Model of Providence may be represented as in Figure 1. While this model might well be *consistent* with the Calvinist view of providence, on a superficial level at least, it is badly

---

19. Another possible difference: exercising intramundane causal powers may come at some *cost* to creaturely agents, whereas it costs God nothing to exercise his causal powers.

20. I note in passing that non-Calvinists have to say something similar about their notion of divine *permission* (vis-à-vis creaturely permission). For one, God's permission of creaturely sins entails that God actively sustains the existence and causal powers of the sinning creature. I'm grateful to Paul Manata for drawing this point to my attention.

21. For an entertaining example, see: https://www.youtube.com/watch?v=_1x99bOX7Yo

22. This direct divine action, apart from means or second causes, need not imply some failure or imperfection on the part of God. The domino analogy should not be pressed too far here.

flawed insofar as it fails to reflect the reality that divine causation operates at a fundamentally different level than intramundane causation. In the Domino Model, the lines of causation are entirely "horizontal." They all operate on the same ontological plane. On this view, God and the universe amount to an arrangement of univocal causal chains. Not only are Calvinists not committed to anything like such a model, they ought to firmly repudiate it in light of their high doctrine of God.

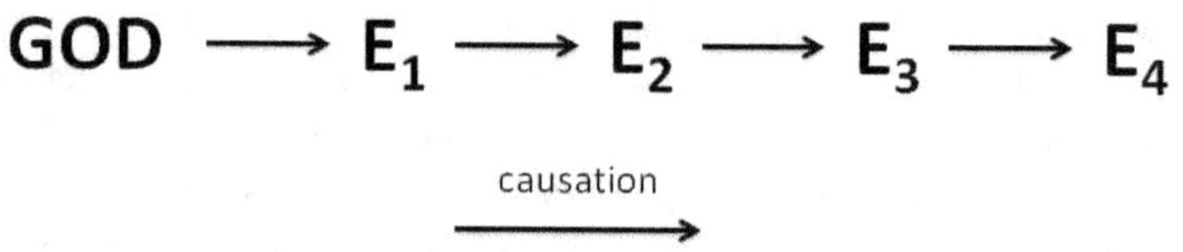

$$\text{GOD} \longrightarrow E_1 \longrightarrow E_2 \longrightarrow E_3 \longrightarrow E_4$$

$$\xrightarrow{\text{causation}}$$

Figure 1: The Domino Model of Providence

A far more fitting model would be what we might call the *Authorial Model of Providence*.[23] On this way of thinking God's acts of creation and providence are analogized to the human authoring of a novel. At the ultimate level, the author *determines* everything that takes place in his novel. He creates a world and he populates it with characters. Indeed, he *creates* the characters—in a relative sense, he brings them into existence. He bestows them with certain personalities and causal powers (which need not correspond to the causal powers in his own world—think fantasy and sci-fi genres). The author sets up the circumstances in which the characters live and play out their roles in the overarching storyline. Some of the characters may commit morally objectionable, even wicked actions—actions which the author himself disapproves, but which are necessary for the sake of the story and its outcome. Tolkien presumably did not morally approve of Gollum's actions in *The Lord of the Rings*, but the novels would hardly have been the same without Gollum and his schemes. As we all recognize, a good story can contain bad characters who commit wicked acts; indeed, one could argue that a *truly* good story would *have* to contain such elements.[24] We might say then that the author of the novel has *ordained* that sinful actions take place *within* the world he has created, but the author himself does not thereby commit any sinful actions or imply his approval of them. In a broad

---

23. For variations on this model, see Crabtree, *Most Real Being*; McCann, *Creation and the Sovereignty of God*.

24. Even the most benign of children's fairy tales involve *some* bad characters and actions.

sense, the novelist is the first and ultimate sufficient cause of everything that takes place in his creation. Yet at the same time, this authorial causation operates on a very different level than the *intranarrative* causes. An Oxford don does not appear in Middle Earth and place the One Ring on Sméagol's finger.

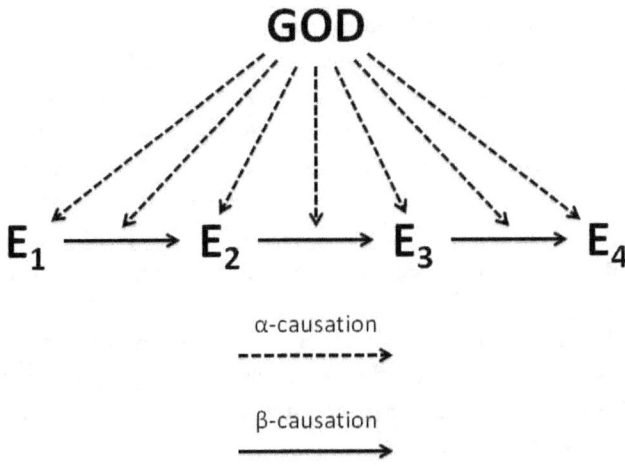

Figure 2: The Authorial Model of Providence

If the Domino Model can be represented as in Figure 1, the Authorial Model can be represented as in Figure 2. In the latter model, God isn't merely one cause in a chain of horizontal causes. On the contrary, divine causation is of a fundamentally different order than intramundane causation; indeed, it is foundational to it in every respect. With this model in mind, we may thus draw a fundamental distinction between α-causation (divine causation) and β-causation (intramundane causation). For every creature C: (1) God α-causes C to exist in the first place; (2) God α-causes C to *continue* to exist (i.e., α-causally sustains C's existence); and (3) God α-causes C to have the β-causal powers that it has. Furthermore, as I think Calvinists should also affirm: (4) God α-causes C to exercise its β-causal powers in precisely the way that it does. Given that α-causation and β-causation operate on different levels, we should avoid saying "God caused C to cause E," which suggests a univocal, horizontal causal chain (as in "Dieter caused the first domino to cause the second domino to fall"). Instead, we do better to say "God caused C's causing of E"—or more precisely, "God α-caused C's β-causing of E."

It should be evident that the Authorial Model of Providence captures the fundamental Creator-creation distinction in a way that the Domino

Model of Providence does not. However, the Authorial Model doesn't rule out the possibility of God acting on the horizontal level, so to speak, as an agent alongside creaturely agents. Just as an author can write himself into his own novel, appearing as one character among the others, so God can write himself into the creational storyline.[25]

Of course, an obvious point of disanalogy in the Authorial Model is that the world created by God "really exists" whereas the world created by the human novelist doesn't.[26] God's creation isn't a divine fiction, an imaginary universe. But we shouldn't consider the Authorial Model inapt for that reason. I have already noted the *sui generis* character of divine causation. God has the power to create *ex nihilo*; we do not. Is it unreasonable to suppose that the Divine Author has the power to *realize* his novel in a way that human authors do not? Indeed, perhaps God's authoring a creational story *just is* what it means for the creation to be realized.[27] Given the *sui generis* nature of divine causation, it would be presumptuous to rule out this scenario altogether.

No doubt the Authorial Model has its limitations and invites some objections. I suggest nonetheless that it is an appealing and potentially fruitful way for Calvinists to model their commitment to divine determinism and what it entails regarding divine causation.

THREE SUPPOSED PROBLEMS FOR CALVINISM

With this brief exploration of divine causal determinism behind us, we're now in a stronger position to evaluate the three supposedly crippling problems faced by Calvinism with regard to the first sin. Once the metaphysical commitments of Calvinism are more carefully delineated, it becomes less clear that the aforementioned problems present sufficient grounds for dismissing it. Let's consider each problem in turn.

(1) *God the author of sin*. At first glance it might seem that the Authorial Model confirms the worst fears of Calvinism's critics. If God is the author of the entire creation and its storyline, it follows that God is the author of the sinful actions that take place within that creation. Doesn't the Authorial

---

25. The literary technique is known as "self-insertion."

26. It would be too strong to say that that the world created by the author doesn't exist in *any* sense. It exists, at least, in a relative sense: it exists in the mind of the author (and perhaps too in the mind of the readers).

27. Although it hasn't caught on among his fellow Calvinists, Jonathan Edwards' theistic idealism may offer some underappreciated advantages at this point. For a critical assessment of Edwardsian idealism, see Crisp, *Jonathan Edwards*.

Model *entail* that God is the author of sin? Well, yes—in *some* sense. But as we've seen, there are morally unobjectionable senses in which someone can be "the author of sin," viz., by authoring a novel in which sinful acts are committed, even though morally disapproved by the author.[28]

The real question is whether Calvinism implies that God is "the author of sin" in any *morally objectionable* sense. (Recall that the objection in view here is that Calvinism is inconsistent with God's moral perfection.) The Westminster Divines—good Calvinists all—explicitly denied that God is "the author or approver of sin," yet they also explicitly affirmed that God foreordains all events, including sinful human acts.[29] So at a minimum they would have granted that God is "the author of sin" in the relatively thin sense entailed by divine determinism; that is, God determines, by some causal means, that in the course of history certain sins will be committed by his creatures. Their insistence that God is not the *approver* of sin is clear enough: God, being pure and holy, does not take pleasure in or approve of sin *qua* sin. When one of his creatures sins, God does not think, "Good for you!"

But what about the Divines' insistence that God is not the *author* of sin? Here we should note the immediately preceding statement in the Westminster Confession: "the sinfulness thereof proceedeth only from the creature, and not from God." The core notion here, I take it, is that sin is always a *creaturely* action and never a *divine* action. Creatures commit evil acts, but God never commits evil acts, even though he *foreordains* the evil acts of creatures—which is not the same thing at all. In terms of our earlier distinctions, Calvinists may say that creatures β-cause evil, but God never β-causes evil. God does, however, α-cause the creatures' β-causing of evil.[30]

At this point the objector may complain that the original problem remains. Wouldn't it be morally objectionable for God to α-cause a creature's β-causing of evil? Wouldn't that make God *culpable* for the evil? There are two ways in which this problem could be pressed. The first is to argue that God would be culpable on account of some culpability-transfer principle. It's commonly supposed that culpability is transferred across causes.[31] If I

---

28. Cf. Edwards, *Freedom of the Will*, section IV, part 9.

29. *Westminster Confession of Faith*, 3.1 and 5.4.

30. Should Calvinists who adopt this model also say that God α-causes evil? I don't consider it an essential tenet of the Authorial Model that God α-causes evil. After all, if God α-causes S's β-causing A, that is sufficient for the occurrence of A; there is no need to add the claim that God α-causes A. Furthermore, it is open to the Calvinist to say that S's β-causing A is a simple event (i.e., A is not a distinct event). In any case, my arguments in this section do not turn on whether or not God α-causes evil.

31. The transfer in view here is analogous to the transfer of debt from A to B,

cause you—by hypnosis, say, or some other manipulative means—to shoot Smith in cold blood, I will be morally culpable for Smith's death. You may have been the *proximate* cause of Smith's death, but because I caused you to cause his death, the culpability for his death is transferred from you to me. In the same way, the objector might argue, if God α-causes your β-causing of evil then culpability is transferred from you to God—and that is theologically intolerable.

It is very questionable, however, that such a culpability-transfer principle holds in general. Consider, for example, a police sting operation in which a dangerous criminal is lured into committing a felony so that he can be arrested and prosecuted, thus preventing further (perhaps more serious) crimes. Suppose that in such a scenario the police indirectly cause the criminal to break the law. Should we infer that culpability for the crime is transferred to the police, such that the police become guilty of the crime? That seems very implausible. Part of the problem here is that culpability depends not merely on whether there is a certain kind of causal connection but also on the *intentions* of the agents involved and whether the agents have *morally justifying grounds* for their actions. Causation alone is not sufficient to transfer culpability.

A second way of pressing the culpability problem is to argue not that culpability *transfers* via causation but that culpability *arises directly* from a causal connection to evil. The idea here is that any sinful action is an evil, thus if God causes (either directly or indirectly) one of his creatures to sin then God must be culpable for evil. But this rests on another dubious inference. If S causes some evil E it may well follow that S is *responsible* for E (at least in part) but it doesn't necessarily follow that S is *culpable* for E. To repeat the earlier point: culpability depends not only on whether there is a certain kind of causal connection between S and E, but also on S's intentions in bringing about E and whether S has morally justifying grounds for bringing about E.[32] In fact, not only is causation not *sufficient* for culpability, it isn't strictly *necessary* either—a point too often neglected by those who assume that attenuating or denying the causal connection between God and the evil actions of his creatures will get God "off the hook" for evil.[33]

In any case, even if we were to grant that these kinds of culpability principles apply to *intramundane* causation, it would be hasty to assume

---

where A becomes the "owner" of the debt instead of B. I'm grateful to Paul Helm for prompting me to clarify this point.

32. The biblical story of Joseph is instructive here; note especially Joseph's interpretation of events in Gen 45:8 and 50:20.

33. For various illustrations showing that causation is neither necessary nor sufficient for culpability, see Rosen, "Causation," 405–434.

that such principles also apply to *divine* causation. As I've emphasized, α-causation is *sui generis*. It operates at a different level than β-causation—one might even say it operates *orthogonally*—and it differs from β-causation in significant respects. Couldn't this be one more point of difference? If the Authorial Model of Providence is close to the mark, why think that the Divine Author must be culpable for realizing a novel in which the characters commit sins?[34]

As best I can tell, divine causal determinism *as such* doesn't obviously entail that God is the author of sin in any morally objectionable sense. The first sin is no different than any other sin in this regard. The burden of proof thus lies with the critics of Calvinism to show that divine causation *must* transfer or generate moral culpability, at least in some instances, or that even with the best intentions God could not have morally justifying reasons for α-causing his creatures' β-causing of evil.

In sum, what is widely regarded as a grave problem for Calvinism—that it makes God the author of sin—only appears so while the term "author" is left ambiguous and unanalyzed. The critics have much more work to do if this commonplace objection is to have any real bite.

(2) *The challenges of compatibilism.* The second complaint, to recap, is that Calvinism is committed to a compatibilist account of human freedom but such accounts are susceptible to serious objections. Several things may be said in response. In the first place, compatibilism is not nearly as beleaguered as is often made out. Indeed, compatibilists are more than holding their own in the contemporary debates over free will. A 2009 poll of professional philosophers found that 59.1 percent favored compatibilism (compared with 13.7 percent favoring libertarianism) and 53.5 percent of those who *specialize in the philosophy of action* favored compatibilism (compared with 18.6 percent favoring libertarianism).[35] It's true that compatibilism has its challenges—what serious philosophical theory doesn't?—but it should

---

34. *Objection*: In a novel, we "abstract" the author away from the world he has created. For example, it's no part of the story that Tolkien caused Gollum to deceive Frodo. But it is part of *our* story (according to the Calvinist) that God caused Judas to betray Jesus. *Reply*: The objection commits a confusion of scope with respect to the Authorial Model. In the model, the scope of the "story" is restricted to *intramundane* events. We may wish to speak also of a higher-level "story" that covers *all* events (including God's creating, sustaining, and directing the universe) but that is not the "story" primarily in view in the Authorial Model. It is important in the Authorial Model to distinguish between God's role as *author* and God's role as *character* in the story he authors.

35. Full details of the survey can be found online: http://philpapers.org/surveys/ To be clear: my point is not that philosophical debates can be settled by head counts, only that a significant proportion of trained philosophers believe that compatibilism is credible and defensible.

also be acknowledged that the major alternative among Christian theists, libertarianism, faces some daunting challenges of its own. (More on this point shortly.)

Secondly, we must be clear about what *kind* of compatibilism Calvinists are committed to. If compatibilism is defined simply as the thesis that moral responsibility is compatible with determinism, then Calvinists must endorse *some* form of compatibilism if they hold to divine determinism. However, in the contemporary debates over compatibilism, the kind of determinism in view is typically *causal* determinism (in the narrow sense) and the main arguments against compatibilism target that specific form of determinism. For example, Peter van Inwagen's celebrated Consequence Argument trades on the observation that we do not have control over the past or the causal laws of the universe.[36] But as I noted earlier, divine determinism doesn't entail causal determinism in *that* sense (i.e., nomological determinism). Calvinists don't have to be *that* kind of compatibilist.

Still, one might reply, can't the standard incompatibilist arguments be adapted so as to target the divine determinism affirmed by Calvinists? Perhaps so; but this needs to be spelled out in more detail by those who raise this problem for Calvinists. In any event, Calvinists have at least two lines of defense available to them. The first is this: if the standard incompatibilist arguments can be adapted and deployed against Calvinism, then the compatibilist responses to those arguments can also be adapted and deployed in its defense—and there are sophisticated responses to all of the standard incompatibilist arguments.[37] Furthermore, there are a number of sophisticated compatibilist accounts of moral responsibility, many of which

---

36. Inwagen, "Three Arguments for Incompatibilism," 55–105. The argument aims to show that if determinism is true then we cannot do otherwise than we actually do. Van Inwagen also gives a "Direct Argument" to the effect that if determinism is true then we cannot be held morally responsible for our actions. Inwagen, *Essay on Free Will*, 182–88. In both cases, however, the determinism in question is *nomological* determinism.

37. In my view, the most formidable arguments for incompatibilism today are versions of the Manipulation Argument, such as the much-discussed "four-case argument" developed in Pereboom, *Living without Free Will*. See also Pereboom, "Hard Incompatibilism," 85–125. Compatibilists have developed some impressive responses to the Manipulation Argument, and the debate seems to hang—as such debates often do—on conflicting intuitions. McKenna, "Responsibility," 169–92; Haji and Cuypers, "Hard- and Soft-Line Responses"; McKenna, "A Hard-Line Reply," 142–59; Demetriou, "The Soft-Line Solution," 595–617; Haas, "In Defense of Hard-Line Replies," 797–811; McKenna, "Resisting the Manipulation Argument." It's worth noting that the papers by McKenna ("A Hard-Line Reply") and Haas consider the case of theological determinism, arguing (in effect) that such determinism would no more undermine moral responsibility than "ordinary" determinism.

posit conditions for moral responsibility that are consistent with divine determinism.[38] There's little reason to think that merely adding God to a compatibilist account will thereby derail it.[39]

The second line of defense is to appeal again to the Authorial Model and the distinction between α-causation and β-causation. Certain types of incompatibilist arguments invite us to reflect on a scenario in which a person's choices have been causally determined and our intuitions tell us that the person cannot be held morally responsible for those choices. It is then argued, in various ways, that those same intuitions ought to hold sway in *other* scenarios in which a person's choices have been causally determined— indeed, in *any* such scenario. The aim of such arguments is to persuade us that it is the common factor of causal determination and not some feature unique to the first scenario (such as the involvement of manipulating agents) which undermines moral responsibility.

The immediate problem with adapting such arguments to target Calvinism is this: the intuitions they depend upon are elicited entirely by reflection on cases of *intramundane* causal determination. It's all too easy for the adapted argument to run roughshod over the crucial differences between divine causation and intramundane causation. The Calvinist says that God α-caused Adam's sinning, but he did not β-cause it. We cannot simply *assume* that our natural intuitions about β-causation can be transferred without qualification to α-causation. Thus to deploy standard incompatibilist arguments against Calvinism without any sensitivity to the Creator-creature distinction is to commit the fallacy of equivocation.

For obvious reasons, I cannot examine all the major incompatibilist arguments here. But consider the Manipulation Argument by way of illustration.[40] This argument (or family of arguments) depends on the intuition that the presence of *human* manipulators typically undermines moral responsibility.[41] My point here is simply that we shouldn't apply those intu-

---

38. McKenna, "Compatibilism"; McKenna, "Contemporary Compatibilism," 175–98.

39. Fischer makes this very point in regard to his own (semi-)compatibilist account. "Even if God causes all human activity, the crucial issue is the *way* He causes it. If God causes human actions via a process analogous to causal determinism, simply *qua* causal determinism (and not *special* causation), then arguably the process itself can be weakly reasons-responsive. And if so, I do not see why human agents cannot be morally responsible for their behavior, even if it is caused this way by God." Fischer, *Metaphysics of Free Will*, 181.

40. See footnote 37.

41. In Alfred Mele's much-discussed "zygote argument," a version of the Manipulation Argument, the manipulator is a goddess ("Diana") rather than a human. But this goddess is more like the deities of Greco-Roman polytheism than the transcendent

itions without qualification to the case of a "divine manipulator," given the significance of the Creator-creature distinction. God has causal powers at his disposal which his creatures do not, and we shouldn't assume that the exercise of those causal powers has the same entailments as that of human causal powers. (I would also suggest that the word "manipulator" unfairly prejudices the issue to a degree.)

(3) *No causal explanation for the first sin.* Recall that the third problem for Calvinists also concerns their supposed commitment to compatibilism. According to compatibilist accounts of freedom, so it is claimed, S's choice at some time *t* must be sufficiently explained by the conjunction of S's internal state at *t* and S's external circumstances at *t*. If Adam's internal state prior to the first sin was wholly good, what could possibly explain his sin—or at least explain it in such a way as to accommodate his moral culpability?

I've already observed that Calvinism *as such* is only committed to compatibilism in the broad sense noted above: human moral responsibility is compatible with *divine* determinism. Calvinists aren't *necessarily* committed to the variety of compatibilist account from which this particular perplexity about the first sin arises. Indeed, so far as I can see, it is entirely consistent with the Calvinist view of divine providence to maintain that Adam was an *intramundane* first cause when he first sinned, i.e., that there were no prior sufficient β-causes of Adam's sin (whether internal or external or both). Regardless, Calvinists *can* affirm that there is a sufficient *ultimate* explanation for Adam's sin: God decreed it. Indeed, there is a sufficient *causal* explanation: God α-caused Adam's sinning.

No doubt some will view this response as a dodge. Doesn't it commit the very kind of level confusion I've been at pains to expose? Surely to say that God foreordained the fall goes no way toward explaining why unfallen Adam would freely choose to sin, any more than God foreordaining the outcome of the 2012 presidential election would explain why more Americans voted for Barack Obama than for Mitt Romney.

At this point I must confess that further answers are not readily forthcoming. It is true that some Calvinists, such as Jonathan Edwards, have defended compatibilist accounts according to which a person's choices have sufficient *intramundane* causal explanations. On such accounts, it proves very difficult to explain the first human sin. How could unfallen Adam's internal states (beliefs, desires, dispositions, motivations, etc.) have given rise to a sinful choice? On the other hand, it's no easy task to show that

---

God of Christian theism. She is, in effect, a *superhuman* agent, and the force of Mele's thought experiment still relies on our intuitions about human manipulators. For a non-theological critique of Mele's argument, see Kearns, "Aborting the Zygote Argument," 379–89.

these accounts *couldn't in principle* explain the first sin. One would have to argue, presumably, that on any such account a sinful act *must* arise from some prior *sinful* state. No doubt it would be extraordinarily unlikely, on any compatibilist account, for unfallen Adam to freely sin. But while God cannot foreordain *impossible* events, surely God is entirely at liberty to foreordain *improbable* events.

I do not wish to suggest that the pantry is bare, so let me propose at least one possible way forward here, an avenue offered by contemporary discussions of the phenomenon of *akrasia*: weakness of will.[42] It is widely acknowledged that people often perform weak-willed actions, that is, they freely choose to act against their own better judgments. (Think, for instance, of the person—purely hypothetical, of course—who cannot resist visiting a social media website even though he knows it will almost certainly prove to be an unedifying waste of his time.) In his insightful discussion of akrasia, Alfred Mele notes that our better judgments are based, at least in part, on our evaluations of the objects of our desires, and he suggests that weak-willed actions arise from a misalignment between those evaluations and the motivational strengths of our desires.[43] Mele argues that weak-willed actions can be *free* (uncompelled) actions on either a compatibilist or a libertarian account of freedom.[44] He also distinguishes between an akratic *action* and an akratic *character trait*, and observes that there is no reason to think the former is necessarily due to the latter: it is possible for a weak-willed free action to be committed by a person without a weak-willed character. As he explains:

> What Aristotle called akrasia is, very roughly, a trait of character exhibited in uncompelled intentional behavior that is contrary to the agent's better judgment. What he called enkrateia (self-control, continence, strength of will) is, again roughly, a trait of character exhibited in behavior that conforms with the agent's better judgment in the face of temptation to act to the contrary. . . . There is a middle ground between akrasia and enkrateia—the character traits—and there is no requirement that all akratic actions manifest akrasia. Suppose that Ann, who is more self-controlled than most people in general and regarding alcohol consumption in particular, freely succumbs to temptation in that sphere contrary to her better judgment in a particularly trying situation. Even though she does not exhibit akrasia, as

---

42. I'm indebted to Paul Manata for drawing this possibility to my attention.
43. Mele, *Backsliding*, 73–77.
44. Ibid., 33–55.

Aristotle represents that trait, she may exhibit an associated imperfection—imperfect self-control—in an akratic action.[45]

If Mele is correct on these points, it seems open to Calvinists to argue that Adam's first sin was a compatibilist-free akratic action, which would be consistent with all of the following: (1) divine foreordination; (2) intramundane causal determinism; (3) Adam's prior sinlessness (i.e., his lacking any vicious character traits); (4) Adam acting freely; and (5) Adam being held morally responsible for his action. That a misalignment of evaluations and motivational strengths should arise in the normal course of events (albeit exacerbated by a diabolical temptation) need not be regarded as a design flaw, as though God were guilty of suboptimal engineering; if not quite a design feature, it could at least be explained in terms of a justified trade-off necessitated by design constraints.[46] In any case, this proposal is no more problematic than the standard Christian claim that Adam was created sinless but not impeccable, uncorrupted but not incorruptible.

The phenomenon of akrasia is certainly a mysterious one—hence the lively philosophical debate over it from Aristotle to the present-day. That being the case, however, perhaps the mysteriousness of the first sin can be largely accounted to the mysteriousness of akratic action.

But suppose for the sake of argument that this avenue turns out to be a dead end. Indeed, suppose the worst: that the Calvinist cannot begin to explain how a sinless man could have freely chosen to sin. Suppose we end up conceding, with certain Reformed theologians, that sin is intrinsically irrational and inexplicable, and the entrance of human sin into the world is simply shrouded in mystery.[47] Still, I cannot see how such a concession would be a strike against Calvinism over against any other theological tra-

---

45. Ibid., 3–4. Note that what Mele calls "imperfection" should not be understood in terms of prior moral deficiency (e.g., sinful character traits). The point is that Ann lacked *perfect* self-control: the kind of self-control that would result in her *never* succumbing to temptation in that sphere. Both Calvinists and non-Calvinists ought to agree that Adam lacked perfect self-control in *that* sense, despite being created "very good" (Gen 1:31); for if Adam had been created with perfect self-control he *could not* have succumbed to temptation. Yet he did succumb; ergo, he exhibited imperfect self-control.

46. For a discussion of design trade-offs, see Plantinga, *Warrant and Proper Function*, 38–40. Plantinga's argument regarding human *cognitive* faculties could also be applied to human *volitional* faculties.

47. See, e.g., Bavinck, *Reformed Dogmatics*, 69–70; Shedd, *Dogmatic Theology*, 540. This is not to concede, of course, that the *doctrine* of sin is irrational. One can be rational in believing that something is irrational or inexplicable. Similarly, it should not be thought that appeals to mystery or paradox are inherently irrational. For an extended argument on this point, see Anderson, *Paradox in Christian Theology*.

dition within Christianity. As Jonathan Edwards aptly observed, even if a deterministic causal account of human free will faces difficulties explaining the first sin, it's far from clear that an indeterministic account is in any stronger position.[48]

This point can be illustrated by highlighting one difficulty faced by libertarian accounts of free will. It has been objected that libertarian free choices would involve an element of chance or luck that would serve to undermine rather than underwrite moral responsibility. Since our focus here is on Adam's first sin, consider that particular instance of free choice. Let α be the actual world and *t*o the moment at which Adam chose to sin. If Adam had libertarian freedom, there is a possible world β with a history exactly identical to this world prior to *t*o but in which Adam chooses *not* to sin at *t*o.[49] What then explains why α is the actual world rather than β? Surely a consistent libertarian has to say: ultimately nothing at all. Most pertinently, nothing *in Adam* explains that fact. But in that case how could it be fair to hold Adam morally responsible for the entrance of sin into the world? If libertarianism is true, it's ultimately a matter of luck—extraordinarily *bad* luck—that Adam chose to sin.[50]

If the entrance of sin into the world is a fundamental mystery, it is one that Calvinism's competitors seem no better placed to resolve. I therefore conclude that none of the three objections I have discussed here should be regarded as decisive against Calvinism. Calvinists may be committed to divine causal determinism, but divine causal determinism *as such* isn't obviously incompatible with either divine moral perfection or human moral responsibility with respect to the first sin. It may not explain all we would like to have explained about Adam's sin, but its failure to answer every

48. Edwards, *Freedom of the Will*, section IV, part 10. One might argue that an indeterministic account, by reducing the causal contributions to the event of Adam's sin, is even *less* equipped to explain why that event occurred.

49. Strictly speaking we should say *intramundane* history, so as to exclude God's foreknowledge of Adam's choice.

50. Some libertarians may be tempted to respond that the explanation for Adam's choice lies in Adam's *reasons* for so choosing: his desires, intentions, motivations, etc. What this response overlooks is that Adam's reasons are included in the (identical) world-history of α and β at *t*o. So they cannot account for why α is actualized rather than β. To suggest that Adam's choice is explained by his reasons is (ironically) to move in a compatibilist direction. For extended discussions of the luck objection to libertarianism, see Mele, *Free Will and Luck*; Levy, *Hard Luck*. I should acknowledge that Levy directs his version of the luck objection at both compatibilism and libertarianism. However, my point here is not that compatibilism is unproblematic but rather that libertarianism isn't clearly *less* problematic than compatibilism. For a recent refinement of the luck objection to libertarianism, see Tognazzini, "Grounding the Luck Objection," 127–38.

explanatory question shouldn't be counted against it unless competing accounts *can* offer such answers.

WEIGHING THE ALTERNATIVES

I've argued that the common objections to the Calvinist account of the origin of human sin are far from decisive, even if they leave some pressing questions unanswered. When assessing the merits of Calvinism, however, it is important not to evaluate it in isolation from the leading alternatives but alongside them. Calvinism must be judged on a level playing field. It's fair to say that Calvinists have to appeal to mystery at some points. But do Calvinists have to make such appeals to any greater degree than non-Calvinists?

Quantifying appeals to mystery is no easy feat, and I will not attempt to do so here. Instead, I will briefly survey three major alternatives to Calvinism and summarize the main challenges faced by their own accounts of the first human sin.[51] All three positions, as species of theological libertarianism, differ from Calvinism on two closely related points: first, they reject divine causal determinism; and second, they affirm human libertarian freedom. With respect to the first sin, the second point entails that there was no *sufficient* prior causal explanation of Adam's sin. In other words, the causal history of the universe up to that point did not *entail* that Adam would sin; it was consistent both with Adam sinning and with Adam not sinning.[52] Beyond these two shared disagreements with Calvinism, the three accounts take different positions on the first sin as follows (see summary in Table 1).[53]

---

51. In what follows I have avoided using the label "Arminianism" for any or all of the three alternatives to Calvinism. There is ongoing debate over whether Jacob Arminius advocated Molinism (or something close to it) and whether Arminians ought to embrace Molinism. If my own observations are reliable, most self-described Arminians today favor the Simple Foreknowledge view. Some, such as Roger Olson and Jerry Walls, contend that Molinism's commitment to meticulous divine providence places it too close to Calvinism to be endorsed by an Arminian. Others have argued that Open Theism is the most consistent form of Arminianism. For the purposes of this discussion, I wish to side-step these historical and theological debates.

52. Some may be tempted to reply that Adam's *decision* to sin was a sufficient prior causal explanation of his sin. If the distinction between Adam's sin and Adam's decision to sin is pressed, the point can be readily reformulated in terms of Adam's decision.

53. In what follows I make a distinction between "world" and "universe": the former refers to a maximal state of affairs (as in "possible world" and "actual world") whereas the latter refers to the created cosmos.

	Calvinism Account	Molinist Account	Simple Foreknowledge Account	Open Theist Account
Divine Causal Determinism	Yes	No	No	No
Human Libertarian Freedom	No	Yes	Yes	Yes
Pre-Creation Foreknowledge of Adam's Sin	Yes	Yes	No	No
Post-Creation Foreknowledge of Adam's Sin	Yes	Yes	Yes	No

Table 1: Four Competing Accounts of Adam's Sin

The Molinist Account

According to the Molinist account, God possesses *middle knowledge*, that is, knowledge of the counterfactuals of libertarian freedom. These counterfactuals take the following form:

If S were in circumstances C, S would freely do A.

Although God cannot *causally determine* free human actions, God can *weakly actualize* some possible worlds by creating certain individuals and determining the precise circumstances in which those people will make their free choices. Since God possesses middle knowledge, he knows precisely how those people will freely act in those possible worlds. Thus, logically prior to his decision to create, God is presented with a set of *feasible* worlds (i.e., *weakly actualizable* worlds, a subset of all possible worlds) and he chooses to weakly actualize a world in which Adam is created and subsequently freely chooses to sin. God presumably chooses this feasible world over other candidates because this world is overall more valuable—or at least no less valuable—than the alternatives available to him.

The Simple Foreknowledge Account

According to the Simple Foreknowledge account, God lacks the middle knowledge posited in the Molinist account.[54] God therefore does not know, in advance of his decision to create, what Adam would do if he were placed in different circumstances. However, God does possess exhaustive infallible foreknowledge of the actual world, and this foreknowledge is compatible (so it is argued) with human libertarian freedom. Once God has decided to create a particular universe, and to populate it with particular humans, God knows precisely and infallibly how those humans will act at every point in time. Thus, *having decided* to create Adam and to expose him to temptation, God acquired the knowledge that Adam would sin. But contrary to the Molinist account, God did not create the universe *knowing in advance* that Adam would sin. Nevertheless, God knew that Adam *might* sin and God knew in advance (one assumes) exactly how he would respond to that eventuality.

The Open Theist Account

According to the Open Theist account, God possesses neither middle knowledge (as in the Molinist account) nor exhaustive infallible foreknowledge (as in the Simple Foreknowledge account). God decided to create a universe and to populate it with humans possessing libertarian freedom. Since human free choices are indeterministic, the Open Theist argues, the future is as indeterminate (open) for God as it is for humans. God knew in advance that Adam *might* sin, of course, but could not know that he *would* sin. Indeed, God did not know that the actual world would contain sin until such time as the first sin actually occurred. God was willing to take the risk of creating such a universe because of the high value of libertarian freedom (or more precisely, the high value of genuine Creator-creature love relationships, of which libertarian freedom is taken to be a precondition).

With these three alternatives before us, let us now consider some of the problems they face that Calvinism does not. We should first note that since all three affirm human libertarian freedom, all three have to wrestle with the philosophical objections to libertarian accounts. It is routinely taken for granted, particularly by modern theologians, that libertarianism is the

---

54. There can be different motivations for rejecting middle knowledge, but perhaps the most common motivation is the conviction that the very nature of libertarian freedom rules out there being true counterfactuals of freedom, at least prior to God's decision to create.

'commonsense' view and that, unlike compatibilism, it isn't troubled by any serious philosophical problems. On both counts, this is far from the truth. Early results from the emerging field of experimental philosophy are challenging the widespread assumption that incompatibilism is favored by pre-philosophical intuitions.[55] Moreover, even if incompatibilism were true, it wouldn't follow that *libertarianism* is true; for it could be that freedom is undermined by *both* determinism *and* indeterminism (albeit in different ways). Indeed, as a number of philosophers have observed, if determinism threatens our freedom and moral responsibility, it's hard to see how introducing indeterminism into human decision-making would improve matters.[56] So we can immediately see that these alternatives to Calvinism face some difficulties arising from their common commitments. We can go further, however, and observe that each one faces some distinctive problems of its own when it comes to the entrance of human sin.

Problems for the Molinist Account

Arguably the greatest difficulty faced by the Molinist account is making sense of the notion of divine middle knowledge in the first place. The problem is brought into clearest focus by the so-called Grounding Objection.[57] Molinism presupposes that there are counterfactuals of human libertarian freedom that are true prior to God's decision to create. Such counterfactuals would include something like the following:

(C) If Adam were placed in the Garden of Eden and tempted by Satan, he would sin.[58]

According to Molinism, C must be a *contingent* truth and independent of God's will (i.e., not entailed by some free decision of God). But in virtue of what, exactly, would C be true? Its truth cannot be grounded in God's nature

---

55. Nahmias et al., "Surveying Freedom," 561–84; Nahmias et al., "Is Incompatibilism Intuitive," 28–53; Nahmias et al., "Free Will, Moral Responsibility, and Mechanism," 214–42; Feltz et al., "Natural Compatibilism versus Natural Incompatibilism," 1–23; Nahmias and Murray, "Experimental Philosophy on Free Will," 189–216; Sripada, "What Makes a Manipulated Agent Unfree?," 563–93.

56. Double, *Non-Reality of Free Will*; Pereboom, *Living without Free Will*; Inwagen, "A Promising Argument," 475–83; Levy, *Hard Luck*; Campbell, *Free Will*. Campbell refers to this as the "indeterminism-can't-help argument."

57. The literature on the Grounding Objection is considerable and continues to grow. For an overview, see Laing, "Middle Knowledge." For some of the latest salvos in the ongoing debate, see Perszyk, *Molinism*.

58. In reality, the circumstances in each counterfactual would be fully specified, down to the last detail.

or God's will, for then it wouldn't fall under God's *middle* knowledge. But neither can it be grounded in Adam himself or in any other creature, since C must be true *prior* to God's decree to create. (God's decision to create is based in part on his middle knowledge.) Molinists have offered different responses to the grounding objection.[59] Some have tried to explain how the counterfactuals could be grounded in something within God (e.g., God's pre-creational idea of Adam). But perhaps the most common response has been to argue that the counterfactuals *don't need* to be grounded in anything actual. They're sheer brute facts that God eternally knows—somehow, we know not how. But one has to ask: Is this account of divine knowledge any less mysterious than the Calvinist's account of divine causation?[60]

A second (and quite distinct) objection to the Molinist account is that it seems to offer no *moral* advantage over the Calvinist account. While Molinism rejects divine *causal* determinism, it nonetheless holds to a weaker form of divine determinism:

(DD') For every event E, God decided that E should happen and that decision was a sufficient condition for E's occurrence.

Clearly this includes Adam's sin. According to the Molinist account, God surveyed all the feasible worlds and decided to weakly actualize a world in which Adam would (freely) choose to sin. Given the truths of the counterfactuals, this divine decision *entailed* that Adam would be created, be tempted, and sin. On both the Calvinist and the Molinist accounts, then, God *decreed* that Adam would sin and that decree *infallibly determined* that Adam would sin.[61] So the pertinent question is this: If God is culpable for Adam's sin on the Calvinist account, why wouldn't God also be culpable on the Molinist account? Both accounts are deterministic in the sense speci-

---

59. See the summary in Laing, "Middle Knowledge."

60. *Objection*: The Molinist's mystery is less severe than the Calvinist's mystery, for the former represents merely a lack of understanding ("God knows the counterfactuals of freedom but we have no idea how!") whereas the latter represents a full-blown paradox ("Our choices are both determined and free!"). *Reply*: Whether determinism really is incompatible with freedom depends on precisely what kind of freedom is in view. It's widely conceded that determinism is incompatible with the freedom to choose otherwise in exactly the same circumstances. But why think the Calvinist needs to affirm *that* kind of freedom? As I observed earlier (footnote 8) the real concern here is with moral responsibility, and it's a disputed question among philosophers (and even among libertarians) whether the freedom to choose otherwise is necessary for moral responsibility. In the end, Calvinists and Molinists face the same *kind* of mystery: a conflict between one of their key tenets and some metaphysical principle that enjoys strong intuitive support.

61. I assume that the Molinist affirms the following principle of divine infallibility: necessarily, if God decrees that event E will occur then E will occur.

fied above. Both affirm meticulous divine providence. Both imply that God acted in such a way as to ensure Adam's sin. So what *moral* difference would *causal* determinism make? It's far from clear that Molinism actually offers any real advantage over Calvinism at this point.[62]

Problems for the Simple Foreknowledge Account

The Simple Foreknowledge account avoids the two problems faced by the Molinist account because (i) it rejects divine middle knowledge and (ii) on this account God's decree to create this world (including Adam, the Garden of Eden, Satan, etc.) does not *entail* Adam's sin. However, those who favor the Simple Foreknowledge account face two different problems. First, it remains questionable whether exhaustive divine foreknowledge can be reconciled with human libertarian freedom. If God infallibly knows yesterday what I will choose tomorrow, how could I choose otherwise? The past possesses a certain kind of fixity: we cannot act in the present so as to influence the past. The past is "over and done with," as we say. But if certain future events are logically entailed by the past (as my choice tomorrow is logically entailed by God's knowledge yesterday) how could they be any less "fixed"?

One popular response to this problem is the so-called Ockhamist solution, which turns on a distinction between "hard" and "soft" facts about the past.[63] A hard fact is one entirely about the past, whereas a soft fact is one that is ostensibly about the past but whose truth-value depends (at least in part) on future events (e.g., "It was true last year that England will win the next World Cup"). Only hard facts, it is claimed, are fixed in the past. However, facts about God's foreknowledge are *soft* facts; thus God's knowledge in the past isn't fixed in any way that would threaten our future free choices.

One prominent objection to this solution is that it smacks of special pleading since it exempts God's beliefs about future events (and no one else's) from the fixity of the past solely on the grounds that God's beliefs about future events (and no one else's) *entail* the occurrence of those events. What *independent* reason is there to think that divine beliefs are 'softer' than human beliefs? Linda Zagzebski puts the point well:

> It seems to me that it is very difficult to give an account of the necessity of the past that preserves the intuition that the past has a special kind of necessity in virtue of being past, but which has

---

62. For a more detailed argument that Molinism offers no theodical advantages over Calvinism, see the essay by Greg Welty in this volume.

63. Adams, "Existence of God," 492–503; Plantinga, "On Ockham's Way Out," 235–69.

the consequence that God's past beliefs do not have that kind of necessity. The problem is that God's past beliefs seem to be as good a candidate for something that is strictly past as almost anything we can think of, such as an explosion last week. If we have counterfactual power over God's past beliefs, but not the past explosion, that must be because of something special about God's past beliefs that is intuitively plausible apart from the attempt to avoid theological fatalism. If it is not independently plausible, it is hard to avoid the conclusion that the Ockhamist solution is *ad hoc*.[64]

A second problem for the Simple Foreknowledge account is the familiar objection that God's foreknowledge is acquired "too late" to be providentially useful. Since the actual history of the world is contingent on God's decision to create it (and to create it a certain way, e.g., to populate it with libertarian free humans) God's foreknowledge of the course of human history, including the first sin, must be *subsequent* to his settled decision to create. In large measure, God's decree to create is *blind*. If humans have libertarian freedom, God cannot foresee how things *will* turn out prior to creation; he can only foresee how things *might* turn out. (To put the point differently: if God had foreknowledge of the actual history of the world *prior* to his decision to create then that decision couldn't be free; it would be already fixed by that foreknowledge.) Furthermore, once God foreknows the entire history of his creation, the future is essentially settled and cannot be changed even by God. The upshot is this: even though on the Simple Foreknowledge account God possesses comprehensive foreknowledge of his creation, God has no more control over the course of history—including the first sin—than he does on the Open Theist account.[65] Consequently, if God's lack of foreknowledge and control prior to creation is morally problematic on the Open Theist account, the same must be true on the Simple Foreknowledge account. Let us therefore turn to consider the third alternative to Calvinism.

---

64. Zagzebski, "Foreknowledge and Free Will."

65. David Hunt has vigorously challenged the claim that simple divine foreknowledge is providentially useless. See, e.g., Hunt, "Providential Advantages," 374–85; Hunt, "Contra Hasker," 545–550. In a recent penetrating analysis Dean Zimmerman has argued that Hunt's Simple Foreknowledge account offers *some* providential advantages over the Open Theist account. It seems to me, however, that these advantages are relatively marginal (and Zimmerman notes that the Open Theist may be able to "mimic" some of them). The fact remains that both accounts involve God taking significant risks with his creation. Zimmerman, "Providential Usefulness of 'Simple Foreknowledge,'" 174–96.

Problems for the Open Theist Account

One major problem for the Open Theist account can be succinctly stated: it portrays the Creator of the universe as a cosmic gambler. According to this view, God created humans with libertarian freedom so that he and they could enjoy genuinely reciprocal love-relationships. However, since God couldn't know in advance whether humans would freely choose good or evil, God couldn't know in advance whether, over the long run, the actual world would be overall more good than evil. God thus engaged in a high-risk, high-stakes gamble. And if the gamble didn't play out well, the main victims would be the creatures rather than the Creator, because their capacity to suffer pain and loss is so much greater than his. On the face of it, this doesn't seem consonant with divine goodness and wisdom. In the field of human affairs, we think poorly of those who take high risks not only at their own expense but at the expense of others who never consented to those risks. Why should we think well of a God who plays a cosmic-scale game of roulette with the lives of his creatures?

One of the common motivations for embracing Open Theism is to get God "off the hook" for the moral evil in his creation. God cannot be held responsible, so it is argued, for the sinful libertarian-free choices of his creatures. But isn't a divine dice-thrower the epitome of irresponsibility? In short, it's far from obvious that the Open Theist account of the first sin offers any *moral* advantage over Calvinism or any other alternative, once the dire consequences of that first sin are taken into account. Open Theism suffers from a *prima facie* conflict with divine goodness no less than Calvinism and Molinism. Furthermore, as I've already noted, this problem applies equally to the Simple Foreknowledge account, because God's foreknowledge cannot be factored in to his decision to create and once attained that foreknowledge rules out any "course correction" as events unfold.

THE WORST ACCOUNT...

The problem of evil is widely regarded as the most serious philosophical challenge to Christian theism. Yet it is often thought that Calvinism, with its commitment to divine determinism, makes that problem even more intractable, not least with regard to the initial entrance of sin into the world. I suggest that this common opinion does not reflect a sober-minded and fair-handed assessment of Calvinism over against competing positions.

Admittedly the Calvinist account of the first sin leaves some matters shrouded in mystery. Nevertheless, I've argued that once the essential commitments of Calvinism are clarified it is far from clear that Calvinism is vulnerable to any decisive objections on that front. It must also be recognized that each of the alternatives to Calvinism has its own problems; the puzzles presented by Calvinism are no more perplexing than the puzzles presented by its competitors. There may be metaphysical mystery involved in Calvinist claims about divine causation, but surely there is no *greater* metaphysical mystery here than one finds in Molinist claims about the grounding for true counterfactuals of freedom or in Ockhamist claims about the 'softness' of divine beliefs. Likewise, the moral questions raised by meticulous divine providence shouldn't be thought any more disturbing than those raised by risky divine providence.

Each position must be fairly weighed not only in terms of the philosophical perplexities it raises but also in terms of the theological advantages it offers. It therefore seems appropriate to finish by summarizing five significant virtues of the Calvinist account:

1. Unlike its competitors, the Calvinist account does full justice to the divine perfection of *aseity* (God's self-existence and absolute independence). There are no events in the creation that take place apart from God's will, and God's knowledge isn't dependent on brute facts or on anything in the creation.

2. Unlike its competitors, the Calvinist account doesn't require God to take chances or to rely on "good fortune." (Even the Molinist account subjects God to some degree of chance insofar as God has to play the hand of feasible worlds that is dealt to him, so to speak, by the counterfactuals of freedom.)[66]

3. Calvinism affirms the doctrine of meticulous providence, which receives strong support in both the Christian scriptures and the Christian tradition.

4. On the Calvinist account there is an ultimate sufficient explanation for the first sin, namely, the good and wise decree of God. God has authored a creational story in which human sin plays an integral role. While the first sin may have been irrational in terms of Adam's nature, character, and circumstances, it was not irrational in terms of God's decree. The first sin was not ultimately an irrational brute event in God's universe. God worked out his sovereign plan *through* Adam's sin rather than *around* it.

---

66. Cowan, "Molinism," 156–69.

5. Calvinists can affirm that the first sin *considered in itself* was a supremely evil act while at the same time affirming that God decreed Adam's sin for his good and wise purposes—ultimately, for his own glory manifested in his mercy and his justice—as part of the overall storyline of the history of creation.[67]

Winston Churchill famously quipped that democracy is "the worst form of government, except all those other forms that have been tried from time to time." Like democracy, Calvinist theology has its problems and does not satisfy at every point. Nevertheless, after fairly evaluating it alongside the alternatives, perhaps we should come to this conclusion: Calvinism offers the worst account of the first sin, except all those other accounts that have been tried from time to time.[68]

---

67. Cf. Paul's argument in defense of divine election in Rom 9:1–24.

68. I am indebted to David Alexander, Oliver Crisp, Steve Hays, Paul Helm, Daniel Johnson, Greg Welty, and especially Paul Manata for helpful comments on earlier versions of this essay.

BIBLIOGRAPHY

"Adam Lay Ybounden," *Ancient English Christmas Carols: 1400–1700*, edited by Edith Rickert. London: Chatto & Windus, 1914.

Adams, Marilyn. "Is the Existence of God a 'Hard' Fact?" *The Philosophical Review* 76, no. 4 (1967) 492–503.

Anderson, James N. *Paradox in Christian Theology: An Analysis of Its Presence, Character, and Epistemic Status*. Paternoster Theological Monographs. Eugene, OR: Wipf & Stock, 2007.

Asselt, Willem J. van, et al., eds. *Reformed Thought on Freedom: The Concept of Free Choice in Early Modern Reformed Theology*. Baker Academic, 2010.

Bavinck, Herman. *Reformed Dogmatics: Sin and Salvation in Christ*, vol. 3, edited by John Bolt, translated by John Vriend. Grand Rapids, MI: Baker Academic, 2006.

Campbell, Joseph Keim. *Free Will*. Cambridge: Polity, 2011.

Collins, C. John. *Did Adam and Eve Really Exist?: Who They Were and Why You Should Care*. Wheaton, IL: Crossway, 2011.

Cowan, Steven B. "Molinism, Meticulous Providence, and Luck." *Philosophia Christi* 11, no. 1 (2009) 156–69.

Crabtree, J. A. *The Most Real Being: A Biblical and Philosophical Defense of Divine Determinism*. Eugene, OR: Gutenberg College Press, 2004.

Crisp, Oliver D. *Jonathan Edwards on God and Creation*. Oxford: Oxford University Press, 2012.

Demetriou, Kristin. "The Soft-Line Solution to Pereboom's Four-Case Argument." *Australasian Journal of Philosophy* 88, no. 4 (2010) 595–617.

Double, Richard. *The Non-Reality of Free Will*. Oxford University Press, 1990.

Earman, John. *A Primer on Determinism*. Dordrecht, The Netherlands: Kluwer Academic, 1986.

Edwards, Jonathan. *The Freedom of the Will*. In *Works of Jonathan Edwards*, vol. 1, edited by Paul Ramsey. New Haven, CT: Yale University Press, 2009.

Feltz, Adam, et al. "Natural Compatibilism versus Natural Incompatibilism: Back to the Drawing Board." *Mind & Language* 24, no. 1 (2009) 1–23.

Fischer, John Martin. "Compatibilism." In *Four Views on Free Will*, 44–84. Oxford: Blackwell, 2007.

———. *The Metaphysics of Free Will: An Essay on Control*. Aristotelian Society Monographs. Oxford: Wiley-Blackwell, 1995.

Fischer, John Martin, and Mark Ravizza. *Responsibility and Control: A Theory of Moral Responsibility*. Cambridge: Cambridge University Press, 1999.

Gauger, Ann, et al. *Science and Human Origins*. Seattle: Discovery Institute, 2012.

Haas, Daniel. "In Defense of Hard-Line Replies to the Multiple-Case Manipulation Argument." *Philosophical Studies* 163, no. 3 (April 2013) 797–811.

Haji, Ishtiyaque and Stefaan E. Cuypers. "Hard- and Soft-Line Responses to Pereboom's Four-Case Manipulation Argument." *Acta Analytica* 21, no. 4 (2006) 19–35.

Helm, Paul. "God Does Not Take Risks." Edited by Michael L. Peterson and Raymond J. Van Arragon. Oxford: Blackwell, 2003.

Helseth, Paul Kjoss. "God Causes All Things." In *Four Views on Divine Providence*, edited by Dennis W. Jowers, 25–52. Grand Rapids, MI: Zondervan, 2011.

Hoefer, Carl. "Causal Determinism." In *Stanford Encyclopedia of Philosophy*, edited by Edward N. Zalta. Last updated January 21, 2010. http://plato.stanford.edu/archives/spr2010/entries/determinism-causal/.

Hunt, David P. "Contra Hasker: Why Simple Foreknowledge Is Still Useful." *Journal of the Evangelical Theological Society* 52, no. 3 (September 2009) 545–50.

———. "The Providential Advantages of Divine Foreknowledge." In *Arguing About Religion*, edited by Kevin Timpe, 374–85. New York: Routledge, 2009.

Kearns, Stephen. "Aborting the Zygote Argument." *Philosophical Studies* 160, no. 3 (2012) 379–89.

Laing, John D. "Middle Knowledge." *Internet Encyclopedia of Philosophy*, ISSN 2161-0002. 2005. http://www.iep.utm.edu/middlekn/.

Levy, Neil. *Hard Luck Undermines Free Will and Moral Responsibility*. Oxford: Oxford University Press, 2011.

McCann, Hugh J. *Creation and the Sovereignty of God*. Indiana Series in the Philosophy of Religion. Bloomington, IN: Indiana University Press, 2012.

McKenna, Michael. "Compatibilism." *Stanford Encyclopedia of Philosophy*, edited by Edward N. Zalta. Last updated October 5, 2009. http://plato.stanford.edu/archives/win2009/entries/compatibilism/.

———. "Contemporary Compatibilism: Mesh Theories and Reasons-Responsive Theories." In *The Oxford Handbook of Free Will*, edited by Robert Kane. 2nd ed. Oxford: Oxford University Press, 2011.

———. "A Hard-Line Reply to Pereboom's Four-Case Manipulation Argument." *Philosophy and Phenomenological Research* 77, no. 1 (2008) 142–59.

———. "Resisting the Manipulation Argument: A Hard-Liner Takes It on the Chin." *Philosophy and Phenomenological Research* (forthcoming).

———. "Responsibility and Globally Manipulated Agents." *Philosophical Topics* 32 nos. 1/2 (2004) 169–92.

Mele, Alfred R. *Backsliding: Understanding Weakness of Will*. Oxford: Oxford University Press, 2012.

———. *Free Will and Luck*. Oxford: Oxford University Press, 2006.

Nahmias, Eddy, and Dylan Murray. "Experimental Philosophy on Free Will: An Error Theory for Incompatibilist Intuitions." In *New Waves in Philosophy of Action*, edited by Jess Aquilar, et al., 189–216. New York: Palgrave Macmillan, 2011.

Nahmias, Eddy, et al. "Free Will, Moral Responsibility, and Mechanism: Experiments on Folk Intuitions." *Midwest Studies in Philosophy* 31 (2007) 214–42.

———. "Is Incompatibilism Intuitive?" *Philosophy and Phenomenological Research* 73, no. 1 (July 2006) 28–53.

———. "Surveying Freedom: Folk Intuitions about Free Will and Moral Responsibility." *Philosophical Psychology* 18, no. 5 (October 2005) 561–84.

Olson, Roger E. *Against Calvinism*. Grand Rapids, MI: Zondervan, 2011.

———. *Arminian Theology: Myths and Realities*. Downers Grove, IL: InterVarsity, 2006.

Pereboom, Derk. "Hard Incompatibilism." In *Four Views on Free Will*, 85–125. Oxford: Oxford University Press, 2007.

———. *Living without Free Will*. Cambridge: Cambridge University Press, 2001.

Perszyk, Ken, ed. *Molinism: The Contemporary Debate*. Oxford: Oxford University Press, 2011.

Plantinga, Alvin. "On Ockham's Way Out." *Faith and Philosophy* 3, no. 3 (1986) 235–69.

———. *Warrant and Proper Function.* Oxford: Oxford University Press, 1993.
Rana, Fazale, and Hugh Ross. *Who Was Adam?: A Creation Model Approach to the Origin of Man.* NavPress, 2005.
Rosen, Gideon. "Causation, Counterfactual Dependence and Culpability: Moral Philosophy in Michael Moore's *Causation and Responsibility*." *Rutgers Law Journal* 42, no. 2 (2011) 405–34.
Schaffer, Jonathan. "The Metaphysics of Causation." In *Stanford Encyclopedia of Philosophy*, edited by Edward N. Zalta. Last updated August 13, 2007. http://plato.stanford.edu/archives/fall2008/entries/causation-metaphysics/.
Shedd, William G. T. *Dogmatic Theology.* Edited by Alan W. Gomes. 3rd ed. Phillipsburg, NJ: P & R, 2003.
Sripada, Chandra Sekhar. "What Makes a Manipulated Agent Unfree?" *Philosophy and Phenomenological Research* 85, no. 3 (2012) 563–93.
Timpe, Kevin. "Free Will." *Internet Encyclopedia of Philosophy*, 2006. ISSN 2161-0002. http://www.iep.utm.edu/freewill/.
———. *Free Will: Sourcehood and Its Alternatives.* 1st ed. Continuum Studies in Philosophy. Continuum, 2008.
Tognazzini, Neal A. "Grounding the Luck Objection." *Australasian Journal of Philosophy* 93, no. 1 (2015) 127–38.
Van Inwagen, Peter. *An Essay on Free Will.* Oxford: Clarendon, 1983.
———. "A Promising Argument." In *The Oxford Handbook of Free Will*, edited by Robert Kane, 475–83. 2nd ed. Oxford: Oxford University Press, 2011.
———. "Three Arguments for Incompatibilism." In *An Essay on Free Will*, 55–105. Oxford: Clarendon, 1983.
Vihvelin, Kadri. "Arguments for Incompatibilism." In *Stanford Encyclopedia of Philosophy*, edited by Edward N. Zalta. Last updated March 1, 2001. http://plato.stanford.edu/archives/spr2011/entries/incompatibilism-arguments/.
Walls, Jerry L., and Joseph R. Dongell. *Why I Am Not a Calvinist.* Downers Grove, IL: InterVarsity, 2004.
Zagzebski, Linda. "Foreknowledge and Free Will." In *Stanford Encyclopedia of Philosophy*, edited by Edward N. Zalta. Last updated August 25, 2011. http://plato.stanford.edu/archives/fall2011/entries/free-will-foreknowledge/.
Zimmerman, Dean W. "The Providential Usefulness of 'Simple Foreknowledge.'" In *Reason, Metaphysics, and Mind: New Essays on the Philosophy of Alvin Plantinga*, edited by Kelly James Clark and Michael C. Rea, 174–96. Oxford: Oxford University Press, 2012.

10

A Compatibicalvinist Demonstrative-Goods Defense

—Christopher R. Green

SOME LIBERTARIAN THEISTS—THOSE WHO think that God exists and that freedom is incompatible with determinism—argue that many bad things about the world can be reconciled with the existence of an all-knowing, all-powerful, all-good God through a proper appreciation of the value of freedom and the obstacles freedom might pose for God's desire to create a world without such bad things. For all we know, such thinkers contend, God *cannot* create a world with free creatures but without evil. God cannot freely foreordain free actions, where such foreordination entails designing creatures and setting, without any prior constraint, the truth values of "counterfactuals of freedom," *i.e.*, what free creatures would do if placed in certain circumstances. Other thinkers go further and contend that God cannot even *foreknow* free choices and their results.

However, many theists within the Calvinist tradition (and elsewhere) think that human freedom and responsibility are compatible with God's foreordination of whatsoever comes to pass and his fully sovereign design of his creatures. Because theological foreordination poses virtually all of the same problems for free will and responsibility as does physical determinism, such Calvinists have reason to be compatibilists: compatibicalvinists, for short. I here aim to show how such theists might fill in the gaps left by the removal of a libertarian free will defense from their repertoire. My chief replacement will be *demonstrative goods of uncertain size*. Evil provides the occasion for new modes of presentation of what God is like, such as his justice, power, and grace. Without begging theologically-controversial questions, we cannot know the size of such demonstrative goods, and so cannot know that they do not justify any particular evil. The problem of evil is thus defanged as a reason to shift theological views away from theism, or away from compatibicalvinism.

I will appropriate, for my purpose here, the progress that the literature on the free will defense has made regarding what standard must be met for a *defense* (as opposed to a *theodicy*): "a story that includes both God and evil and, given that there is a God, is true for all anyone knows."[1] The compatibicalvinist who thinks that it is *not* true that, for all anyone knows, freedom is incompatible with divine pre-determination of action will want to tell such a story, but a different one than do many theists.

I will make three main points in telling an alternative story.

My first point is perhaps the least important, but lays important groundwork: even on a compatibicalvinist view of the world, the existence of human agents still makes a difference for the nature of God's responsibility for the results of free actions. Certain objections to utilitarianism make clear that an actor might be the *one who decides* whether an evil result will take place, but still avoid immediate responsibility for the evil result if he is not the one *who performs* the relevant evil actions.

Second, I will stress the importance of *demonstrative goods*: the goodness of the existence of particular modes of presentation of facts. It is good for certain facts to be demonstrated, and good for those facts to be demonstrated in various ways. Those who complain that God is hidden, for instance, understand that, if God existed, it would be important for God to demonstrate certain facts about himself in various ways. Likewise, if some evil makes possible some particular mode of presentation of an important fact—for instance, God's justice, or God's power—then the evil makes possible some demonstrative good.

Third, I will stress the *theologically controversial nature of our access to the future*. Unless we have reliable access to the means by which order is preserved in the universe and the reason *why* the future generally resembles the past, we can say very little about the future and the respects in which the future *will* resemble the past. That is, contentions that the future will be a certain way inevitably presuppose views about the governing powers of the universe. So any argument that aims to be able to affect our base-level

---

1. Inwagen, *The Problem of Evil*, 70. Plantinga's definition of a defense is a bit different.

beliefs about whether there is a God who is the governing power of the universe ought not to depend very strongly on claims about the future. If the goodness of God entails that the future will be in some way different from the past, such reasoning will provide the theist equally good reason to believe that God *will* make the future so to differ as to believe that God does not exist.

COMPATIBICALVINISM

Let me first summarize elements of compatibilist Calvinism as expressed in the Westminster Shorter Catechism. Foreordination of all things is stated in question 7: "What are the decrees of God? The decrees of God are his eternal purpose, according to the counsel of his will, whereby, for his own glory, he has foreordained whatsoever comes to pass." Detailed providence of human actions is affirmed in question 11: "What are God's works of providence? God's works of providence are his most holy, wise and powerful preserving and governing all his creatures, and all their actions." The Kantian doctrine that ought implies can, friendly to incompatibilism, is implicitly contradicted in Questions 39 and 82. Question 39 tells us we *ought* to obey—"What is the duty which God requires of man? The duty which God requires of man is obedience to his revealed will."—but Question 82 tells us we *can't*—"Is any man able perfectly to keep the commandments of God? No mere man since the fall is able in this life perfectly to keep the commandments of God, but daily breaks them in thought, word and deed." I will not attempt any full exposition or interpretation of the Calvinist system beyond noting the idea that God designs every detail of his creation for some purpose. Contingent facts are true because God has decreed them to be true, and God takes ownership of them all; God's making them true must be consistent with his being all-good. "Whatsoever comes to pass"—by which I understand, any contingent fact—has some particular purpose, to wit, God's glory.[2]

It is within this context that I will consider the problem of evil. In particular, I will consider what particular good God might, for all we know, have in mind in foreordaining particular bad things we see in our world. Put another way, the value of demonstration is one way of understanding what God's glory amounts to.

---

2. I should say that I am not attempting to show in this paragraph that the Calvinistic system follows from the statements in the Catechism, but merely quoting them to illustrate the view. Non-calvinists might agree with some of these statements, depending on how they understand such terms as "foreordain." But the controversial claim, which free-will defenses deny, is that God determines the truth values of all contingent facts.

FREEDOM AND THE CALVINIST DEFENSE

It might be thought that the compatibicalvinist might find no use of human freedom or responsibility in explaining the existence of evil. Yet Calvinists have historically laid stress on human freedom in the origin of evil. For instance, consider Shorter Catechism question 13: "Did our first parents continue in the estate wherein they were created? Our first parents, being left to the *freedom of their own will*, fell from the estate wherein they were created, by sinning against God." Freedom is plainly important to the explanation of evil on the standard Calvinist account.

Libertarians who use the free-will defense argue that free human actions cannot be determined: God cannot foreordain the results of free human acts, and so a fog of freedom stands between the good God and the bad result. Some such libertarians deny God's foreknowledge, so that he cannot even *see* through the fog of freedom; others deny God's foreordination, so that God merely cannot *act* as he might like through the fog of freedom.

The compatibicalvinist's argument would rely, not on the *fog* which free human actions create for foreordination, but rather on the *different intentional arrangement* that exists whenever God foreordains free human actions. The results of those actions are properly attributable to the free human actors and to God in different ways. The basic idea is summarized in Genesis 50:20, where Joseph tells his brothers after the death of their father, referring to his sale into slavery, that "you meant evil against me, but God meant it for good." If an event E is a free human action, God is morally responsible or blameworthy in an entirely different way for the results of E than he would be were the event not a free human act.

This difference in responsibility is familiar from examples used to criticize utilitarianism.[3] Suppose a mob says credibly that it will kill 20 innocent people if the good sheriff does not execute one innocent person. Is the failure of the sheriff to execute the innocent significant reason to think that the sheriff is not good? No, because the sheriff is blameworthy for consequences that result from others' reliably-forecast free actions, if at all, in an entirely different way than he is blameworthy for his own direct and unmediated actions that are no one else's free actions. The blood of the 20 innocents is on the mob's hands, and not the sheriff's, because they performed the action, even though the sheriff's choice not to execute the one innocent causally contributed—we can even say, was causally sufficient given the mob's character—to their murders.

---

3. See, for instance, the sorts of examples considered in Williams, *A Critique of Utilitarianism*.

Jonathan Edwards is one prominent exponent of the importance of human agency in rebutting the charge that, because God is the "author of [humans'] being," he is therefore "the author of their depravity."[4] Edwards argues that, before the fall, God supplied mankind with a supernatural principle which prevented mankind's natural self-seeking tendency from operating. God's actions in withdrawing the supernatural principle, while sufficient to produce the fall, do not make him the author of sin. "[F]or God so far to have the disposal of this affair, as to *withhold* those influences, without which, *nature* will be *corrupt*, is not to be the *author of sin*."[5] Edwards here cites his earlier work in *The Freedom of the Will*: "There is no inconsistenc[y] in supposing, that God may hate a thing as it is in itself, and considered simply as evil, and yet that it may be his will it should come to pass, considering all consequences. . . . Men do *will* sin as sin, and so are the authors and actors of it: they love it as sin, and for evil ends and purposes. God does not will sin as sin, or for the sake of any things evil; though it be his pleasure so to order things, that, he permitting, sin will come to pass. . . . His willing to order things so that evil should come to pass, for the sake of the contrary good, is no argument that he does not hate evil: and if so, then it is no reason why he may not reasonably forbid evil as evil, and punish it as such."[6] God, on Edwards's account, is akin to the sheriff who refuses to execute the innocent. The sheriff thereby *causes* the mob to kill the 20—by depriving the mob of the means necessary to quench its anger—but because the sheriff's intentions were different, he is not directly accountable for those results as if he performed them personally. Similarly, God's depriving human beings of the necessary means (or environment) to prevent their

4. See Edwards, *Original Sin*, 217.

5. Ibid., 219. Edwards's views here about the extent of man's *natural* self-seeking tendencies, which inevitably produce sin when additional supernatural influences are withdrawn, do not seem essential to his basic argument. Some readers have suggested that Edwards's speculations are in tension with Genesis 1:31's statement that God created all things good and smacks of the Catholic doctrine of *donum superadditum*. One might replace the idea that man is *naturally* or *essentially* self-seeking, however, with a story about man's environment. Under this sort of story, man was created physically able to do either good or evil, and before he had done evil, he was properly described as righteous. God's additional decree that men would later be in an environment in which they would sin—for instance, because of evil temptations—would still be distinct from God's performing the action *as sin*. In short, from the perspective of rebutting the charge that God was the "author" of sin, it is only critical for Edwards that God not perform the act as sin. It does not seem critical philosophically whether the fall happened (a) because of a withdrawal of supernatural influences or (b) because of a change in environment; the issue can thus be resolved on exegetical or other theological grounds.

6. Edwards, *The Freedom of the Will* section IV, part 9.

self-caused fall does not, in itself, mean that God is accountable for the fall as if he performed it personally.[7]

This limited sort of free will defense can only go so far, however. Even if God is not *automatically* responsible for every action that is performed merely because he ultimately determines the truth value of all contingent propositions—that is, there is a critical distinction between *making it the case that A happens*, on the one hand, and *performing action A*, on the other—God is still responsible for his making those determinations. Even if God cannot be charged with evil person E's evil actions as such, he might still be charged with (a) making it the case that E has E's character, and (b) making it the case that E's evil actions affect others the way they do. Because libertarians use freedom to answer *these* sorts of questions, their defense of God's existence in the face of evil can be rooted in freedom in a further way the compatibicalvinists' cannot. As stated, I aim to show how God's actions of type (a) and (b) make possible the existence of modes of presentation of truths about himself that could exist in no other way. The existence of particular sorts of evil character (type (a)) makes possible either, on the one hand, God's expression of justice in condemning the possessor of that character, or, on the other, God's expression of mercy and grace in forgiving the possessor of that character. The existence of particular effects on others (type (b)) makes possible a greater and more vivid expression of the wrongfulness of the actions, which heightens the expression of either God's justice or grace.

---

7. Edwards's approach is very like that of Bishop Berkeley, who insists in his Hylas and Philonous dialogue that it is the intention that chiefly determines responsibility. Berkeley uses this principle to rebut the charge that "in making God the immediate author of all the motions in Nature, you make him the author of murder, sacrelige, adultery, and the like heinous sins." Berkeley's response is to focus on intention:

> [S]in or moral turpitude doth not consist in the outward physical action or motion, but in the internal deviation of the will from the laws of reason and religion. This is plain, in that the killing of an enemy in battle, or putting a criminal legally to death, is not thought sinful, though an outward act be the very same with that in the case of murder. Since therefore sin doth not consist in the physical action, the making God an immediate cause of all such actions, is not making him the author of sin. . . . [Also,] thinking rational beings [have] the use of limited powers, ultimately derived from God, but immediately under the direction of their own wills, which is sufficient to entitle them to all the guilt of their actions.

Berkeley, "Third Dialogue," 237.

DEMONSTRATIVE GOODS AND SCRIPTURE

The Scriptures speak repeatedly of God's using particular bad things as means for demonstrating, or showing, things about himself. Take seven examples of bad events described in the Scriptures:

a. a man born blind,

b. the destruction of the southern kingdom by Babylon,

c. Pharaoh's mistreatment of the Israelites,

d. Paul's continued persecution of the early church, including assistance in the killing of Stephen,

e. the death of Lazarus,

f. the killing of Jesus,

g. the rebellious life, prior to their repentance, of those brought to salvation.

The Scriptures say that all of these evils provide occasions for God to show what he is like.

> John 9:1–3: As he passed by, he saw a man blind from birth. And his disciples asked him, "Rabbi, who sinned, this man or his parents, that he was born blind?" Jesus answered, "It was not that this man sinned, or his parents, but *that the works of God might be displayed in him.*
>
> Exodus 9:16: But for this purpose I have raised you up, to *show you my power*, so that my name may be proclaimed in all the earth.
>
> Ezekiel 37:11–14: Then he said to me, "Son of man, these bones are the whole house of Israel. Behold, they say, 'Our bones are dried up, and sour hope is lost; we are indeed cut off.' Therefore prophesy, and say to them, Thus says the Lord God: Behold, I will open your graves and raise you from your graves, O my people. And I will bring you into the land of Israel. And *you shall know that I am the Lord*, when I open your graves, and raise you from your graves, O my people. And I will put my Spirit within you, and you shall live, and I will place you in your own land. *Then you shall know that I am the Lord*; I have spoken, and I will do it, declares the Lord."
>
> 1 Timothy 1:15–16: The saying is trustworthy and deserving of full acceptance, that Christ Jesus came into the world to save sinners, of whom I am the foremost. But I received mercy for

this reason, that in me, as the foremost, Jesus Christ might *display his perfect patience* as an example to those who were to believe in him for eternal life.

John 11:14–15: Then Jesus told them plainly, "Lazarus has died, and for your sake I am glad that I was not there, *so that you may believe*. But let us go to him."

Romans 3:24b–26: [All] are justified by his grace as a gift, through the redemption that is in Christ Jesus, whom God put forward as a propitiation by his blood, to be received by faith. This was to *show God's righteousness*, because in his divine forbearance he had passed over former sins. It was to *show his righteousness* at the present time, so that he might be just and the justifier of the one who has faith in Jesus.

Ephesians 2:1–7, 3:8–10: And you were dead in the trespasses and sins in which you once walked, following the course of this world, following the prince of the power of the air, the spirit that is now at work in the sons of disobedience—among whom we all once lived in the passions of our flesh, carrying out the desires of the body and the mind, and were by nature children of wrath, like the rest of mankind. But God, being rich in mercy, because of the great love with which he loved us, even when we were dead in our trespasses, made us alive together with Christ—by grace you have been saved—and raised us up with him and seated us with him in the heavenly places in Christ Jesus, *so that in the coming ages he might show the immeasurable riches of his grace in kindness toward us in Christ Jesus*. . . . To me, though I am the very least of all the saints, this grace was given, to preach to the Gentiles the unsearchable riches of Christ, and to bring to light for everyone what is the plan of the mystery hidden for ages in God who created all things, *so that through the church the manifold wisdom of God might now be made known to the rulers and authorities in the heavenly places.*

So, to take one example: God creates Hitler with his wicked character, Hitler commits his evil actions, and then God punishes Hitler in order to demonstrate his hatred of Hitler's character. God's demonstration of his righteous hatred of Hitler's character, expressed in his wrath on Hitler, can only be presented if Hitler exists with his evil character. Hitler's existence makes possible this mode of presentation of God's glory. This particular good cannot be achieved in any other way. Is such a presentation worth the candle? Those who think not depend, I think, on a different moral stance toward the value of God's demonstration of himself than that taken by at least some theists. As I will argue below, we lack good reason to think such theists' moral position is wrong.

EFFECTS ON OTHERS

Perhaps I have shown that the *existence* of Hitler makes possible a particular demonstrative good not otherwise available. But why does God allow Hitler to affect others—in David Lewis's expression, why not put evildoers in a sandbox? One reason is that our grasp of the existence of evil is far different if we can grasp its effects. Evil that victimizes others allows a far different mode of presentation of evil character, and so a far different mode of presentation of the justice in condemning those with such character, than would exist otherwise. Several of the scriptural evils listed above involve harm to others. The harm to Stephen, for instance, allowed a fuller presentation of Paul's wickedness before he repented, in turn allowing a fuller presentation of God's patience.

God, we may suppose, wants to demonstrate the effects and seriousness of rebellion. If God allows innocents to feel the effects of rebellion, he can more fully demonstrate the wickedness of sin—given which demonstration, of course, God can more fully demonstrate his justice in condemning it, or his grace in forgiving it. We can more fully understand the justice in Hitler's condemnation if we understand it through an understanding of Hitler's effects on innocents. In his free will defense, Peter van Inwagen notes such a demonstrative good as a means of showing rebellious humanity that they need to be rescued: "For human beings to cooperate with God in this rescue operation, they must know that they need to be rescued. They must know what it means to be separated from him. And what it means to be separated from God is to live in a world of horrors."[8] The compatibicalvinist can appeal to same epistemic good of knowledge, but suggest that it is useful both in its own right, and as a means to other goods: in particular, the understanding and demonstration of God's justice and grace.

THE VARIETY OF DEMONSTRATIVE GOODS

Now, it is true that God's righteousness, patience, and power *might* all be displayed in different, easier ways: God might just *tell* someone about these attributes, for instance. But the argument from hiddenness recognizes that the value in presenting some divine character quality is not exhausted

---

8. Inwagen, *The Problem of Evil*, 88 no. 1.

merely in *one* presentation. Rather, those who think God is too hidden demand evidence for *themselves*—that is, in the place and time they find themselves. They demand an additional mode of presentation. But if they recognize the value of an additional mode of presentation in the context of the argument from hiddenness, they should also recognize it in the context of the argument from evil. Additional modes of presentation of the same truth have additional value. How much value? As I will argue below, I do not think we have any reason to think it is less than the disutility of the evil at stake.

Consider the various modes of presentation of something that we can see, taste, or smell. These are *different* demonstrative goods that do not duplicate each other, even when they present the same fact. Hearing a sound in stereo, through the dual modes of presentation of our two ears, is a far different, and more valuable, epistemic good than hearing it in only one ear. Our grasp of a fact can be stronger and fuller if it comes to us through a variety of means. Consider also the value that presumably exists in the *persistence* of belief. It is not enough that a person be presented *once* with a belief that could not be stored: there is an additional important good to be found in the fact that the belief presents itself again and again to a person in memory. Memory beliefs produce additional modes of presentation of the same fact, and these additional modes have value as such.

One might object that, past a certain point, additional modes of presentation add nothing. The analogy with additional faculties of sense perception, for instance, reaches a limit: when all of our faculties are engaged, there are no additional modes of presentation of the same fact the value of which we can grasp simultaneously. However, I doubt that we can have reliable knowledge about the value of a given number of modes of presentation of a given fact unless we can have reliable knowledge about the future progress of our cognitive faculties, or the current cognitive capacities of anyone else who may be observing the history of our world. And as explained below, assessing either the future development of our cognitive capacities or the existence of other observers of our world is fraught with theological controversy: knowledge about either must presuppose too much to be useful to an argument that aims to alter our view about whether God exists.

WHY NOT NIGHTMARES?

Why couldn't God achieve the same demonstrative good by allowing us to know the same thing through, say, nightmares? He surely could allow the same *type* of demonstrative good—that is, a demonstration of the same *fact*—through nightmares, or through a simple text message explaining the same point: for instance, "I *would* punish Hitler in thus-and-so a manner if he *were* to exist." But that would not be the same *demonstrative good*. It would be a different mode of presentation. And additional modes of presentation have additional value.

THE SIZE OF DEMONSTRATIVE GOODS

Now, what is the value of a demonstrative good? How big is it? Is it worth the cost? Absent theologically-controversial assumptions—that is, assumptions of the sort that an atheist cannot either make or deny without begging the question against a theistic critic of his argument from evil—we cannot say.

One reason we cannot properly assess the magnitude of demonstrative or epistemic goods is that we do not know how many people may be watching. This, for instance, is one of the lessons of the beginning parts of the book of Job. Job's life, with all of its suffering, has an audience of which Job is not aware: Satan, who has disparaged Job's devotion to God. God brags about Job to Satan, telling him at 1:8, "Have you considered my servant Job, that there is none like him on the earth, a blameless and upright man, who fears God and turns away from evil?" Later, after Job's first round of suffering, God adds at 2:3, "Have you considered my servant Job, that there is none like him on the earth, a blameless and upright man, who fears God and turns away from evil? He still holds fast his integrity, although you incited me against him to destroy him without reason." At least on a naïve reading, the evils of Job's first round of suffering made possible this mode of presentation of Job's qualities: God allows the evils in Job's life in part to *demonstrate* to Satan Job's devotion to God.[9]

Another element of our near-complete ignorance regarding the magnitude of demonstrative goods—an element that may be appreciated even by those who want to eschew reference to fallen angels—is that we have little or no idea how many (ordinary) people God may choose to tell about some particular mode of presentation of some fact. Consider God's display of his power over Pharaoh described in Exodus 9:16: "But for this purpose I have

---

9. The same idea appears regarding what Jesus tells Peter in Luke 22:31–32: "Simon, Simon, behold, Satan demanded to have you, that he might sift you like wheat, but I have prayed for you that your faith may not fail. And when you have turned again, strengthen your brothers." In this picture, Satan is viewing the progress of human history, which plays out partly for his benefit—that is, for the good of demonstrating certain things to him, not for the purpose of serving Satan's interests. See also the reference in Ephesians 3, quoted above, to the "rulers and authorities in the heavenly places" to whom the salvation of the church is displayed.

raised you up, to show you my power, so that my name may be proclaimed in all the earth." We do not know how many people will learn of this display, because we do not know how many (more) billions of people will learn about this history by reading the book of Exodus. And if we do not know how many people will be exposed to a particular demonstrative good, we cannot know its size.

For all we know, then, any particular demonstrative good might be appreciated an indefinitely large number of times over because of contemporaneous viewers like Satan, and might *also* be appreciated an indefinitely large number of times over because of future viewers like you and me. If there is *any* demonstrative value to some particular mode of presentation of some fact, then we lack any convincing basis on which to assess its size as small.[10]

OUR KNOWLEDGE OF THE FUTURE AND THEOLOGICAL CONTROVERSY

Several aspects of the evil in this world depend on the future. For instance, worries about whether God is fair in failing to compensate particular individuals who suffer, such as Job, depend on assumptions about what God will, in fact, do in the future. Absent presuppositions about the fundamental processes at work in our world, however, we have poor basis for saying anything about what will happen to any particular person who has lived in history. For instance, examples in which individual people cease existing, forever, cannot be examples we have conclusive reason to think occur in our history. Absent theologically controversial assumptions, I do not think we can say of any particular person who has lived that he or she will not have a future experience X. God might, after all, still do it.[11] As I said before: if God's goodness requires that person P have future experience X, then such an argument is just as good a reason for the theist committed to God's goodness to think that God will give person P future experience X as for the theist to think that God does not exist. Any defeater for that belief would,

---

10. If demonstrative goods are *incommensurable with* the evils that make them possible, we likewise lack convincing reason to think they are *smaller than* those evils.

11. For instance, William Rowe's example of a burning fawn in "some distant forest"—i.e., a forest beyond human knowledge—depends on God failing to inform people later about the fawn. See Rowe, "The Problem of Evil," 337. The example also seems to assume that the fawn is not itself later resurrected and allowed compensating pleasures. Ivan Karamazov likewise complains about a suffering child's "unrequited tears." Dostoevsky, *Brothers Karamazov*, 245.

at best, presuppose theologically controversial inference from past performance to future results.

That our beliefs about the future presuppose our fundamental beliefs about the governing processes of the universe seems to be at least one lesson to draw from the seemingly endless literature on the justification of induction. Unless we think that we have made a reliable assessment of the nature of the most fundamental processes governing of the world, we cannot think we have reliable access to the inference from what *has* happened to what *will* happen: from past performance to future results, in the language of stock prospectuses.

Now, someone who already *is* an atheist, making an argument from evil that depends on an example of evil that requires the world to have some feature ~F, may well think it ridiculous that the future will have feature F. For the purpose of the argument from evil, I will not insist that the atheist accept my view of whether F will happen—I only insist that his atheism is influencing that belief. That is, someone doxastically open to the view that there is a perfectly good governor of the world, confronted with the view that the goodness of that governor requires the future to be F, will also be doxastically open to the idea that the future will be F.

One part of this view that we cannot yet tell the whole story about any particular person may be *metaphysically* controversial: the idea that God may yet continue the existence of any particular person from the past. I depend here on my metaphysical views of the *possibility* of resurrection and continued life. If, pursuant to the decree of the God in charge of the laws of nature, someone otherwise like me rises from the ground thousands of years after my death, has my memories, identifies with my projects and actions, and thinks of himself as having lived my life, and God agrees with this assessment of identity, holding that person responsible for my actions, I see no reason to think that this is not a case of intermittent existence. The same, I think, could be said for any being at all. It is *possible* for any object to be brought back together, were the God in charge of the laws of nature to want it to be so. Absent, then, *theologically* controversial assumptions, we are not in a position to know whether any particular person P will or will not have future F.

ANIMALS

What about animal suffering? My chief aim here is to show that the compatibicalvinist can do with demonstrative goods whatever the libertarian can do with the free will defense. And the free will defense needs modification, or elaboration, if it is to deal with animal suffering. Perhaps the libertarian says that animal suffering is necessary in order to prevent the world from being "massively irregular." But he does not do so as a libertarian, and so the compatibicalvinist can say the same thing. Indeed, the value of regular laws might felicitously be seen as a demonstrative good: the demonstration, for instance, of God's regularity, faithfulness, and stable nature. Jeremiah 33:20, for instance, appeals to "my [God's] covenant with the day and my covenant with the night" as showing the likelihood that God will be faithful to his covenant with Israel and particularly with David. There are also some special demonstrative goods to be gained through animal suffering. Hebrews 10:3 describes the Israelite animal sacrifices as "a reminder of sins every year." Reminders, of course, are demonstrative goods.

THE DISTRIBUTION OF EVIL?

I have said little about the *distribution* of evil. Here, I again think our ignorance of the future is important. Unless we know what the future will bring to the individuals involved, we have no basis for saying anything about the ultimate distribution of evils over the entire course of history. We can have no assurance, for instance, that anyone's suffering will be uncompensated.

CONCLUSION

In sum, an appreciation of demonstrative-epistemic goods can undermine one of the big motivations for open theism, Molinism, or other non-compatibicalvinist theology, as well as provide a defense appropriate to answering proponents of the argument from evil to whom libertarianism is implausible. Theists need not explain particular evils in light of the more general good of freedom. If we are convinced that, for all we know, God will use particular evils to perform some sufficiently-valuable demonstration in the future, then theists can avoid difficult territory pertaining to the value or preconditions of freedom.[12]

---

12. Thanks to Robert Audi, Gatlin Bredeson, Oliver Crisp, Taylor Cyr, Trent Dougherty, Chris Eberle, Tom Flint, Aaron Hoak, Jon Hueni, Peter van Inwagen, Jeff Jordan, John Keller, Hugh McCann, Michael Pace, Myron Penner, Brian Pitts, and Mike Rea, and to participants in discussions at the Society of Christian Philosophers and the Notre Dame Center for the Philosophy of Religion.

BIBLIOGRAPHY

Berkeley, George. "Third Dialogue." In *Philosophical Works: Including the Works on Vision*, edited by Michael R. Ayers, 217–252. London: Everyman, 1975.

Dostoevsky, Fyodor. *The Brothers Karamazov*. Translated by Richard Pevear and Larissa Volokhonsky. New York: Farrar, Straus & Giroux, 1990.

Edwards, Jonathan. *The Great Christian Doctrine of Original Sin Defended: Evidence of Its Truth Produced, and Arguments to the Contrary Answered*. In *The Works of Jonathan Edwards, A.M.*, vol. 1, edited by Edward Hickman, 143–233. London: Ball, Arnold & Co., 1840.

———. *A Strict and Careful Inquiry into the Modern Prevailing Notions of that Freedom of Will, Which Is Supposed to Be Essential to Moral Agency, Virtue and Vice, Reward and Punishment, Praise and Blame*. In *The Works of Jonathan Edwards, A.M.*, vol. 1, edited by Edward Hickman, 1–93. London: Ball, Arnold & Co., 1840.

Rowe, William. "The Problem of Evil and Some Varieties of Atheism." *American Philosophical Quarterly* 16 (1978) 335–41.

Van Inwagen, Peter. *The Problem of Evil*. Oxford: Oxford University Press, 2006.

Williams, Bernard. "A Critique of Utilitarianism." In *Utilitarianism: For and Against*, edited by J. J. C. Smart and Bernard Williams. Cambridge: Cambridge University Press, 1973.

11

Calvinism and the Problem of Hell

—Matthew J. Hart

1. INTRODUCTION

Calvinists, I shall assume, are theological determinists.[1] They hold that God causes every contingent event, either directly (without the use of secondary causes) or indirectly (via secondary causes).[2] Arminians, however, are libertarians; they think that there is an important class of event that God does not cause: freely willed decisions. They are incompatibilists: they think it is necessary for moral responsibility for a decision that that decision be uncaused, or at least that there is some sort of indeterminacy somewhere in the process. Calvinists on the other hand, not wishing to deny the moral responsibility of human beings, are usually compatibilists, holding that uncaused actions (or whatever indeterminacies the libertarian demands) are

---

1. Some may wish to style themselves as Calvinists while denying theological determinism—perhaps claiming that the good and true message of Calvin and Luther was corrupted by the later Synods and Jonathan Edwards. At any rate, the most prominent *qua* Calvinist philosopher active today, Paul Helm, is a theological determinist. See Helm, *Eternal God*, ch. 9 and "God, Compatibilism and the Authorship of Sin." See also his treatment of Calvin's view of the freedom of the will in *John Calvin's Ideas*, ch. 6.

2. Those sympathetic to agent-causation might contend that an agent-causing is not an event and therefore that this definition of determinism is too weak: it is compatible with an agent-causal libertarianism. Then let us add that if there are any agent-causings, then all such agent-causings are caused by God, either directly or indirectly.

not necessary for moral responsibility, and therefore that moral responsibility is compatible with determinism.[3]

What I intend to do in this paper is to sketch a theodicy of hell that is consistent with theological determinism and compatibilism about moral responsibility. I think many are skeptical of the plausibility of such a theodicy. Consider Pereboom's remarks:

> Historically, perhaps the most effective reason for rejecting any sort of divine determinism, and endorsing instead libertarian free will is the unconscionability of God's damning people to hell after determining them to sin.[4]

I believe this feeling of unconscionability persists and is widely shared. Here are Baggett and Walls on the matter:

> [D]amnation involves infinite, eternal misery. For God to choose to consign persons to such a fate when he could have just as easily determined them to joy and happiness [in heaven] is . . . morally obnoxious . . . [It] strikes us as a paradigmatic example of hateful behaviour, not loving behaviour.[5]

Of course Arminians, being libertarians, deny both that God determines anyone to sin and that it is a straightforward matter for God to ensure people's entrance into heaven: the free decisions of humanity, and in particular the decision to accept or reject God's offer of salvation, upon which entrance to heaven is contingent, are, at least in some sense, beyond God's complete control. This belief permits the deployment of various free-will theodicies of hell: God greatly desires to save us all from hell, but it would be wrong for him not to respect our free choice to form, if we wish, a character that is implacably opposed to him, as Swinburne proposes;[6] or Craig's suggestion[7] that although God dearly wishes to save everyone from hell, when God consults his middle knowledge it so turns out that in all those worlds in which a significant number freely choose to go to heaven a significant

---

3. Flint in "Two Accounts of Providence" thinks that this Protestant distinction between Calvinism and Arminianism corresponds well to the division in Catholic doctrine between the Thomist (which tends to compatibilism) and Molinist accounts of divine providence. I shall let Catholics judge for themselves.

4. Pereboom, "Free Will, Evil and Divine Providence," 82.

5. Baggett and Walls, *Good God*, 74.

6. Swinburne, "A Theodicy of Heaven and Hell."

7. Craig, "'No Other Name.'" For criticism of Craig see Seymour, "A Craigian Theodicy of Hell."

number go to hell, and God isn't going to let the fact that many will go to hell prevent him creating one of those worlds.

But no such defense is available to the theological determinist, for on his view God has complete control over what human beings will choose, because he is the ultimate cause of all human choices. In short, if Calvinism is true, it seems perfectly easy for God to create a world in which universalism is true—a world in which everyone accepts God's offer of salvation and goes to heaven. Why wouldn't God do this? What could stop him? "Surely nothing," says the Arminian, "and so Calvinism is false."

In this paper I offer what I hope are plausible reasons why God wouldn't, despite a comprehensive control over what his creatures choose, make it the case that all accept the offer of salvation. The reasons I offer are not that novel. They can be found in Jonathan Edwards, John Calvin and across the Reformed tradition in Christian thought. Here is Calvin on the reprobate (that is, those predestined to damnation):

> they were raised up by the just but inscrutable judgment of God, to show forth his glory by their condemnation.[8]

Here is the *Westminster Confession*, ch. 3, "Of God's Eternal Decree":

> VII. The rest of mankind [that is, the non-elect] God was pleased, according to the unsearchable counsel of His own will, whereby He extends or withholds mercy, as He pleases, for the glory of His sovereign power over His creatures, to pass by; and to ordain them to dishonour and wrath for their sin, to the praise of His glorious justice.[9]

Here is one way of reading these two quotations: important aspects of the divine majesty are not displayed if everyone is saved, so God decrees that many shall refuse his offer of salvation in order that, as the Westminster Confession mentions, the glories of his sovereign power and justice might be displayed in their eternal destruction.

But note that displaying is a triadic relation, and we need to ask to whom God is displaying his glories. A traditional assumption is that it is the elect in heaven, those whom God predestined to salvation. The theodicy I will propose here aligns with this suggestion. I suggest it is for the sake of the occupants of heaven that God creates people to occupy hell. It is good to understand God's character and our relation to him, and the occupation of hell enables both an understanding of God's nature and good attitudes towards God on the part of the elect that wouldn't be possible otherwise.

8. Calvin, *Institutes*, 3.24.14.
9. Schaff, *Creeds of Christendom*, 610.

This paper will list these benefits. Although my chief aim is to give a Calvinist theodicy of hell, what I say will have repercussions for the problem of evil more generally, and I shall close with some remarks to that effect.

2. THE PROBLEM OF HELL

But let us first state the problem of hell more carefully. What is hell? Following Kvanvig,[10] I define hell as follows: it is (or will be) an inhabited place, from which there is no escape, of unending conscious torment, whose function is to mete out retributive punishment on its occupants. What is the problem of hell? As I see it, the problem of hell is a special case of the problem of evil. Rowe's formulations of the argument from evil have been influential. Let us take the version from his well-known "The Problem of Evil and Some Varieties of Atheism" paper:

1. There exist instances of intense suffering which an omnipotent, omniscient being could have prevented without thereby losing some greater good or permitting some evil equally bad or worse.

2. An omniscient, wholly good being would prevent the occurrence of any intense suffering it could, unless it could not do so without thereby losing some greater good or permitting some evil equally bad or worse.

3. There does not exist an omnipotent, omniscient, wholly good being.[11]

The problem of hell can be cast in the same mould. Let us put it like this:

4. If hell exists, then hell is an instance of intense suffering which an omnipotent, omniscient being could prevent without thereby losing some greater good or permitting some evil equally bad or worse.

5. An omniscient, wholly good being would prevent the occurrence of any intense suffering it could, unless it could not do so without thereby losing some greater good or permitting some evil equally bad or worse.

6. If hell exists, then there does not exist an omnipotent, omniscient, wholly good being.

---

10. Kvanvig, *The Problem of Hell*, 25.

11. I am aware of Rowe's later formulations of the argument which Rowe judges to be superior (viz. his "Ruminations about Evil" and "The Evidential Argument from Evil: A Second Look"). However, I use this presentation of the argument since it better facilitates an exposure of a mistake I take to be commonplace in discussion of the argument from evil: the idea that the justifying good must be greater.

The Arminian free-will theodicies mentioned before can be construed as a denial of (4). The greater good God would lose by ensuring there is no hell is the freely chosen fellowship of his creatures, something over which God has no direct control. Again, the theological determinist cannot make any such move: he believes it is within God's power to bring it about that all creatures freely choose him. The Calvinist could however make some of the standard moves the theist makes in response to the problem of evil: he could appeal to skeptical theism and claim that the odds of us knowing God's justifying goods are small, so the fact that we are unable to think of what the goods might be is of little surprise. Wykstra[12] and Alston[13] are prominent examples of this strategy. I see no reason for this sort of response to be any less successful here.[14]

But I intend to give a theodicy. What is a theodicy? Plantinga distinguishes between a theodicy and a defense:[15] the latter simply suggests broadly logically possible reasons God might have for permitting evil, to show that there is no broadly logical inconsistency between the existence of God and the existence of evil; but to give a theodicy, on Plantinga's rather strict account, is to give the actual reasons God has for permitting evil. I demur; I think only *plausibly actual* reasons are needed. David Lewis agrees with me, saying: "Defense is too easy; knowing God's mind is too hard. I think the topic worth pursuing falls in between . . . [The Christian] can hope to advance from a predicament of not having a clue to a predicament of indecision between several not too-unbelievable hypotheses."[16] And that is the task I set myself here: to offer a plausible explanation of why God would predestine anyone to hell. I shall adopt the following account of a plausible actuality:

> Some state of affairs S is plausibly actual (PA) =df there is no clearly probative argument against us supposing S to be the case.

---

12. Wykstra, "The Humean Obstacle."
13. Alston, "The Inductive Argument from Evil."
14. Though I happen to think the Calvinist should not stop here. I read Paul in Romans 9:22–23 as proposing a theodicy of the same kind I defend in this paper. Admittedly, Paul's remarks are preceded by a "what if," so he who takes the inspiration of Scripture seriously (as the Calvinist surely will) is arguably not committed to the *truth* of Paul's proposal, but surely neither is what Paul says to be ignored as worthless. It seems that the happy *via media* is therefore to take Paul's theodicy as adequate, or true for all we know. So if the Calvinist reads Paul as I do, then he is committed to the *adequacy* of the theodicy I give here, if not its truth.
15. Plantinga, *The Nature of Necessity*, 192.
16. Lewis, "Evil for Freedom's Sake?" 105–6.

My task is therefore to provide plausibly actual reasons that God might have, if he exists, for decreeing that some people shall occupy hell, and I shall use PA to denote the property of plausible actuality as defined above. Note that I am not, therefore, concerned to prove that the reasons I propose will do the job; rather, I rest content just so long as no-one can prove they cannot do the job.[17]

There are other distinctions we must be cognizant of. We need to realize that the decree of *reprobation* must be distinguished from the decree of *damnation*: the former takes place before the creation of the world, while the latter occurs at the Day of Judgement. We can think of the decree of reprobation as representing God's decision to create, from all possible persons, some he intends to occupy hell for all eternity. The decree of damnation only concerns itself with created persons: at the Second Coming the quick and the dead are all summoned before God for judgement, and of these God damns to hell those whose sins remain unforgiven. It is clear that the motivation for the decree of damnation is to see justice done, but it seems no such motivation can lie behind the decree of reprobation, for when God is reprobating there are not yet any guilty people in existence.

Finally, the decree of reprobation stands opposed to the decree of *election*, the decree of election being God's decision to create certain persons (the elect) intended to occupy heaven with him forever. An issue on which Calvinists and Arminians are divided is the explanatory place of the decree of election: Arminians generally hold that it took place after God consulted his foreknowledge of free creaturely decisions; Calvinists say that it did not; on the contrary, they say it was God's decree that determined what God foreknew. My belief is that Arminians generally do not believe in a decree of reprobation (at least on the way I understand the decrees here); even if God is creating with the foreknowledge that some will be damned, their damnation is always a foreseen but unintended consequence of creating.

The issue therefore centers around this great and terrible decree of reprobation. Let it be clear: I am not going to deal with question of the permissibility or justice of the decree of *damnation*—Adams attacks it in her "Hell and the God of Justice" for instance, and defenses of the idea that one can justly merit the punishment of hell are available elsewhere[18]—I am instead defending here the righteousness of God's decree of reprobation, that is to say, his intentionally causing many to merit a decree of damnation, which is a different affair altogether. (It might therefore be said that I am not

17. Also, for the record: I myself would not like to be interpreted as claiming that the theodicy I give here is true; my claim is likewise only that I see no clear objection to its truth.

18. See Hart, "The Justice of Hell," for instance.

really offering a theodicy of hell, but a theodicy of reprobation. I am happy to accept this.) So I assume it is possible for a human being to justly merit eternal punishment; I am concerned with why God would bring it about that any human being did *in fact* merit eternal punishment.

Let it also be clear that I am precluded from giving a more thorough demonstration of the permissibility of divine reprobation. For simply having some greater good in mind isn't sufficient to exonerate one from bringing about some evil for which that good is necessary. Objections of a deontological stripe may be made: perhaps bringing about damned souls would be to do something categorically impermissible, such as intend evil, or to violate someone's rights, or to treat people as mere means rather than ends in themselves, or to exhibit a defect of character, and so on. But, for reasons of space, objections from double effect, rights, Kantian doctrine, divine benevolence and so forth must be dealt with on another occasion (though I do deal here with considerations from divine paternity and also briefly consider whether God's motive in reprobation is loving); my chief task here is only to lay out the goods God seeks.

But before I lay out the goods God seeks in reprobation, let us note that two things are required of these goods. The first is that they must be goods for which the inhabitation of hell is a necessary condition. The second is to make sure that we can believe they are worthwhile given the evil they require. So I propose that we can offer an explanation of why God would be motivated to reprobate if there is (a) some good state of affairs for which reprobation is a necessary condition, and also that (b) the degree of intensity or amount of the good state of affairs is not so low as to make it obviously not worthwhile given the evil that accompanies it. Only if the goods I propose satisfy both conditions are they goods that would provide God with plausibly actual reasons for reprobation. Also, if the good in question presupposes particular doctrinal or philosophical commitments, then it must also be the case that these doctrinal or philosophical commitments possess PA.[19] I shall first suggest the different goods and then discuss the question of their worthwhileness.

---

19. It must also be supposed, if only for the sake of argument, that theological determinism itself possesses PA—that there is no clearly probative argument against its truth either.

3. CALVINIST THEODICY

I have already given a broad outline of the goods which Calvinists have proposed historically. John Piper is a contemporary theologian who gives a more recent statement of the suggestion:

> My answer to the question about what restrains God's will to save all people is this: it is God's supreme commitment to uphold and display the full range of his glory through the sovereign demonstration of all his perfections, including his wrath and mercy, for the enjoyment of his chosen and believing people . . . This everlasting and ever-increasing joy of God's people in all of God's perfections is the shining forth of God's glory, which was his main aim in creation and redemption.[20]

Importantly, unlike Piper, I do *not* insist that the displaying of his glories is God's main aim in creation. I don't deny it either, but the point is that the theodicy I give here doesn't require this claim. It requires only the more minimal suggestion that if some state of affairs grants us a clearer or greater or better understanding of the nature of God (or some other good attitude), then God, if he seeks our good, would have reason to actualize that state of affairs (because such a mental state is a good). Whether or not he would grant it because of a more ultimate objective to display the range of his glory is a separate issue. This theodicy does not propose God's glory as the good for which God actualizes evil, rather displays of God's glory are here viewed as good because they ennoble or enhance the state of mind of the elect. It is these states of mind of the elect in heaven (and maybe Earth) which I am suggesting are the goods for which God reprobates.

Leaving that element of Piper's view aside, we can push a minimal Calvinist theodicy based on his suggestion that the good for the sake of which God reprobates is simply this: a richer sense of God's just character on the part of the elect, made possible by the display of God's wrath upon the occupants of hell. Is this an adequate Calvinist theodicy of hell?

The following suggestion from Oliver Crisp intimates that it is not adequate:

> God's grace and mercy [can be] shown to all human agents in their election (in Christ), and his wrath and justice [can be] shown in the death of Christ, which atones for the sin and guilt of all fallen human agents.[21]

---

20. Piper, *The Pleasures of God*, 339.
21. Crisp, "Augustinian Universalism," 137.

So it is suggested that God can demonstrate his wrath satisfactorily with only the death and suffering of Jesus. God is therefore free to save everyone else, and it again seems that the occupation of hell (by any non-divine being) is an unnecessary evil.

But is it true that any good acquired through the display of God's wrath in reprobation is also available in God's display of wrath directed toward Jesus in the crucifixion and in his possible descent to hell? Interestingly, Crisp himself no longer appears to think so. He writes in a more recent paper:

> Were Christ to be the only human person upon whom divine justice was visited, as a vicarious substitute for sinners . . . , this would not have the right connection to desert because Christ does not deserve to be punished—he acts vicariously (and sinlessly) on behalf of sinful human beings deserving of punishment.[22]

So one good that is lost is the good of seeing *wrath from God that has the appropriate connection with desert*, which is surely better to see than wrath which does not. Here are some other goods which would be lacking in a world in which only Christ bore the wrath attending damnation.[23]

An ongoing spectacle. Perhaps God reprobates in order to give people in heaven an ongoing spectacle of God's retributive justice being enacted in punishment, an aspect of the divine character that they otherwise would only be able to recall if Christ's atoning sacrifice on the cross was all of God's punishment, for Christ suffers and dies but once, and then is risen forevermore. Seeing something presently is better than merely being able to remember it, even perfectly remember it, and Christ's punishment is only of finite duration. So an ongoing perception of God's activity in wrath is a good that would be lost to the elect in heaven.

A better understanding of what justice demands for different sins. If Christ is the only object of God's wrath, then all the types of sin in the world are conglomerated with respect to punishment. But then in Christ's punishment we don't perceive the punishment that various sins deserve: we don't see the punishment appropriate to sins of greed, pride, lust, etc., we only see what happened to Christ. This limitation hampers an understanding of the justness of God, because we are hindered from seeing what justice demands in particular cases. This good looks like it would provide God with

---

22. Crisp, "Is Universalism a Problem?," 22.

23. I draw heavily on Jonathan Edwards in what follows. He has probably done more than anyone to provide a Calvinist theodicy of hell: in at least four places in Edwards's *corpus* do we find substantial material which we can construe as offering reasons for God's reprobative decree.

a motivation to reprobate several people with different characters all given over to different vices.

A greater perception of the majesty of God. Jonathan Edwards says that in the punishment of sinners God "vindicates and honours [his majesty], and makes it appear, as it is indeed, infinite, by showing that it is infinitely dreadful to contemn or offend it."[24] Edwards believes that the gravity of an offense should be proportional to the importance of the being against whom the offense is committed. In the eternal destruction of the wicked we discover how grave a thing it is to offend God, and by implication the majesty of his being. But if Christ alone was the object of God's wrath then, since Christ's punishment was only temporary and to our appearance finite, the elect wouldn't have as full a perception of the magnitude of God's majesty.

Gratitude through appreciation of the nature of the alternative. Edwards also writes of the elect in heaven, "When they shall see how dreadful the anger of God is, it will make them the more prize his love. They will rejoice the more, that they are not the objects of God's anger, but of his favour..."[25] This is true because of the following principle: "A sense of the opposite misery, in all cases, greatly increases the relish of any joy or pleasure."[26] He expounds on the principle and its implications more fully here: "There would be no manifestation of God's grace or true goodness, if there was no sin to be pardoned, no misery to be saved from. How much happiness soever he bestowed, his goodness would not be so much prized and admired, and the sense of it not so great, as we have elsewhere shown. We little consider how much the sense of good is heightened by the sense of evil, both moral and natural."[27] So were Christ's misery all the elect saw, they would not have as great a realization of the fate they had been saved from, and therefore all the joys attendant on being in heaven would be less appreciated.

4. CALVINIST THEODICY IMPROVED

Yet all that these various goods show is that God is permitted to create a modest number of people for hell (a few hundred perhaps), but presumably there will be many more people in hell than that. So we still face a problem: what could motivate God to reprobate such a great number? The following goods achieve this.

---

24. Edwards, "Eternity of Hell Torments," 87.
25. Edwards, "Wicked Useful in Their Destruction," 127.
26. Edwards, "Eternity of Hell Torments," 87.
27. Edwards, "Concerning the Divine Decrees," 528.

Gratitude through appreciation of the likelihood of the alternative. We have seen above that by God's displaying eternal punishment the elect would become more grateful of their place in heaven. We also saw that this idea doesn't provide reason for the reprobation of a great number. But consider this quotation from Edwards: "When [the elect] see others, who were of the same nature, and born under the same circumstances, and plunged in such misery, and they so distinguished, O it will make them sensible how happy they are."[28] The picture is this: I was just like so-and-so, yet I am exalted and they are debased, and the fact that they were just like me makes me happier than I would otherwise be at my exaltation. But why is this? One answer concerns likelihood: it is because the closer I was to them in nature and circumstances, the more likely it would be that I end up like them. So when I discover that my fate has been radically different and better than theirs, my joy over my fate acquires greater intensity.

This is because your gratitude should be proportional to, in addition to the good you are the recipient of, the closeness of the possible worlds in which you fail to have it. The idea is that the closer such worlds are (in other words, the more appropriate it becomes to say 'I might not have got it'), the greater your gratitude. Take the 2011 Tōhoku earthquake and resulting tsunami. I am (or should be) grateful that I did not die in it. But I won't be as grateful as a Japanese person who narrowly escaped the onrushing water, in part because worlds in which he dies because of the tsunami are much closer to the actual world than worlds in which that happens to me.

So if plucked from a sea of unbelievers, you would therefore have much more cause to be grateful. Now we see that God has reason to make it the case that the damned numerically far outstrip the elect, for if there were many people who were just like the elect were but who didn't have faith and were damned, then this would increase the likelihood of the elect being damned considered relative to various facts, such as their being human beings, or their being born on Earth, or in New York, and so on. The more reprobated earthly companions the elect receive, the more appropriate or 'truer' it will be for them to say, 'I could have been damned,' and their gratitude at being in heaven will increase—in proportion to both the number of these companions and the similarity of situation of these companions to themselves.

Gratitude through appreciation of the frequency of the alternative. This good is closely related to the preceding, but I believe it is distinct. Consider the following scenario: you attend a house-party to which you received an invitation. The wine flows and the heart is made glad. Now suppose you

---

28. Edwards, "Eternity of Hell Torments," 87.

discover that there are a great many people outside, all clamoring for entry, but who can't enter because they have not been invited. Your happiness at being invited is likely to increase, and this reaction is surely appropriate. The rarer a desirable commodity, the higher it is valued. Moreover, your gratitude will increase in proportion to the number of people who can't get in—the greater the number, the greater your gratitude.

One way of understanding this reasoning is according to the counterfactual likelihood interpretation we dealt with above: you are happier because you realize the possible-world odds were against you getting an invitation. But we can interpret it as concerning only the actual world, and ignoring what happens in others. You are happy simply because the of the actual rarity of your position.

I am uncertain how significant the difference is between this and the previous item, but it is nevertheless clear that between them they provide the sort of motivation the Calvinist seeks. By reprobating a greater number to hell, the elect in heaven are permitted a great gratitude not otherwise available to them: a gratitude at being part of the few that are saved.

A justification for pragmatic preoccupation with salvation. If Christianity is true, then the way we relate to God is the most important aspect of the human life, and acquiring salvation the most important objective. It is better if important things occupy your thoughts than unimportant things. But suppose you think you are very likely to secure the important things. In that case your attention will naturally move to less important things. But all things being equal, it is better for your mind to be occupied with the more important things. So one way in which God could secure that your mind is occupied by the more important things is by discouraging ease with regard to the important things. But suppose that all or most people are saved; this encourages ease with regard to one's standing before God insofar as it permits the following reasoning: I need not seek so hard for my own salvation as I otherwise would because I know that the odds of me being saved are in my favor. So when a man comes to learn that most are reprobated he acquires a justification for preoccupying himself with making his "calling and election sure" that he would otherwise lack. (So the likelihood of ending up in hell is also relevant when we consider this life.)

A justification for historical preoccupation with salvation. The good immediately above is entirely pragmatic or this-worldly. But something similar holds from the historical perspective in the afterlife. Suppose that someone is writing the history of a wood. But the thing is everyone who entered into the wood took the westerly path at the first fork in the road; no-one took an easterly path, and consequently that entire region is unexplored. Suppose if they had taken the easterly path their journey would have been dangerous and possibly fatal. Since the path to the west offers pleasant and uneventful passage, their decision to take the westerly road would have been their most important decision. But the history of the wood would not reflect this—everyone took that path and historical attention would not be drawn to that decision as much as it would have if some had taken the other path. The focus of the history would instead be given to the different things that happen on the western path—things of comparatively less importance.

Now consider elect men and angels surveying the history of mankind. They know that salvation is the hinge on which a man's destiny swings, opening to him either an eternity of anguish and terror or one of everlasting joy and fellowship with God. But if all or the vast majority of these destinies swung one way, toward fellowship with God, then, because of this, salvation would become an item less worthy of historical interest. But nothing is more important in the history of men than their salvation. The reprobation of a great number makes it more appropriate for people's reflections on history to be preoccupied with the important matter of rightly relating to God than would be the case if few were reprobated. Interestingly, this good, unlike those preceding it, does not appear to tend to the maximization of reprobation, since if either election or reprobation came to be the more common fate then interest would move away from salvation.

A greater appreciation of one's dependence upon God. Edwards suggests that, "The misery of the damned will give them a greater sense of the distinguishing grace and love of God to them, that he should from all eternity set his love on them, and make so great a difference between them and others who are of the same species, and have deserved no worse of God than they."[29] The idea here, I take it, is this: when the elect observe the suffering of the damned, they will note that it is only by virtue of the grace of God that they differ from them. "Every time they look upon the damned, it will excite in them a lively and admiring sense of the grace of God, in making them so to differ."[30] We have already noted the way reprobating would increase the gratitude of the elect, but here we are interested in something different. The elect will surely be drawn to contemplation of what it was that secured their salvation—what was it that gave them a fate separate from the reprobate? The Calvinist explanation lies in the decrees we discussed at the beginning. It was by God's sovereign decision that some were elected and others reprobated. Made aware that the most important aspect of their life lies in the hands of God, the elect are made aware of God's sovereignty over them and their dependence on him. This provides a motivation for the reprobation

---

29. Edwards, "Wicked Useful in Their Destruction," 127.
30. Edwards, "Eternity of Hell Torments," 87.

of many for the same reason that the importance of salvation does: more justified attention is drawn to important facts, in this case facts about God's sovereignty, than if God had not reprobated many.

A greater appreciation of God's prerogative in salvation. I derive this motive from the following passage from John Gill's *The Cause of God and Truth*, part 3, section 2:

> [I]f God had decreed to save all men, and had prepared saving grace for all men, here would indeed have been a display of the glory of his grace and mercy; but where would have been the declaration of his wrath and justice? Especially, the glory of God's sovereignty more appears by these distinct decrees, than if no such distinction had been made; for hence it is evident, that he will have mercy on whom he will have mercy, and whom he will he hardeneth.[31]

The suggestion expressed in the first sentence has been discussed already; it is the idea in the second sentence that I wish to discuss here. Arminians and universalists are sometimes happy to grant that God is under no obligation to save anyone and that this is something important to realize (though they typically quickly add that God's good nature or character is such that it precludes him from letting any perish if he can help it). But if it is important to know that an agent has a right to X, then one good way of gaining a better understanding of this fact is to see the agent acquiring or performing X. Suppose the government had a right to confiscate your property at a moment's notice and could exercise this right at a whim. This right of theirs would not be readily appreciated if they never exercised it either with regard to you or anyone else. It would be there 'on paper' but would little intrude upon anyone's experience, contemplation or decision-making. So now we have one way of reading Gill's suggestion: the "glory of God's sovereignty" refers to his privilege to bestow and refrain from bestowing salvation as he wishes, without obligation. If God has such a privilege, such a fact is surely worth appreciating, and it is by these "distinct decrees" of election and reprobation that a greater appreciation becomes available. This supports the reprobation of many because if God's privilege to bestow salvation was exercised too frequently then his privilege to refrain from bestowing it would be proportionately unappreciated.

A greater appreciation of God's hatred of sin. It is surely good for us to understand that God, because of his holiness, hates sin and wickedness. Moreover, the thought is, it is good for us to understand that this hatred is inexhaustible. How could we get a better appreciation of this fact? One way

---

31. Gill, *Cause of God and Truth*, 162.

is through the reprobation of many. For suppose a human judge is required to lash fifty men who had each committed a crime. He lashes, let us say, twenty of them, but after that can lash no more; not because he is physically exhausted—we can suppose that he has a very strong arm—but because his anger at their wickedness is exhausted. Absent such anger he feels only pity. But he is wrong to give into this emotion and he should continue: the remaining thirty are no less guilty. But if God reprobates many, then it will be available for all to see for all eternity that God has a hatred of sin which is not exhausted, despite both the terrible number of them and the interminable nature of their torment. Whenever the elect look upon hell they will be reminded that God's hatred of all that is wicked and vile remains implacable. Again our appreciation will be proportional to the number of those damned: we more clearly see that there is no worry of God's hatred petering out when we see it directed continually at a greater number.

A greater appreciation of God's power. A great display of God's power is also available if God reprobates many and their eternal destruction is viewed. (Cf. "The sight of the wonderful power ... of God, manifested in the eternal punishment of ungodly men.")[32] If we suppose that an emperor only ever befriended his enemies and never waged war with them, that he wined and dined them, entertained them but never threatened them, showered them with gifts but never demanded tribute, then it is not unreasonable for the suspicion to form that the emperor is weak: he lacks the power to destroy his enemies, and that is why he always befriends them. Reprobating many gives a grand testament to God's power to destroy his enemies and frustrate their plans. As before, the more damned there are being destroyed, the greater God's power is perceived to be through their destruction.

So I have specified eight goods for which the reprobation of many is necessary: gratitude from the likelihood and frequency of damnation, justification both pragmatic and historical for preoccupation with salvation, a greater sense of dependence upon God, of his prerogative in salvation, of his hatred of sin, and of his power. Now I discuss the question of their worthwhileness.

5. DIVINE PATERNITY

An opponent may complain: 'The sort of goods you suggest and the level of them just aren't worth reprobating for. Hell is a great terror, and to reprobate so many people to such a place for the sake of such comparatively small goods as a greater appreciation of God's attributes and so forth is not

---

32. Edwards, "Eternity of Hell Torments," 87.

morally acceptable: the goods fail to justify because they are outweighed by the magnitude of the evil.'

Well, the theodicy I am giving here might not look good on a utilitarian analysis, but that is of little consequence: I take it few Christian philosophers are utilitarians. It isn't clear that it fails non-consequentialist criteria for justifying goods. In this vein I shall to appeal to the view known as familial partialism, a species of what John Cottingham calls 'philophilic partialism.' Philophilic partialism is the view that it is morally correct to favor "not just one's friends, but one's children, siblings, spouse—all who are beloved or "dear" to the agent."[33] But I shall suppose here only familial partialism, the view that it is morally correct to favor members of one's own family.

What might this mean in practice? Consider the following thought experiment. A genie shows you two cages hovering above a lake of lava; one contains a family member and the other one five strangers; he tells you that you can pick one of the two cages and he will save whomever is in that cage from plunging into the fiery lake below; if you pick neither, both will fall. Are you permitted to choose the cage with the family member? A utilitarian may baulk at the suggestion, but if a partialism to family members is morally expected, then it is either permissible to choose the cage with the family member, or at worst no longer clear. In more mundane cases privileging one's family can be seen in the way you would, for example, give your child spending money rather than distributing it equally across all the children on the street, or pay special attention to your child's grievances, an attention that you wouldn't give to your neighbor's child, and so on. At any rate, given that Cottingham describes philophilic partialism as "A pillar of all, or certainly most, viable ethical systems,"[34] I shall take it that familial partialism possesses PA.

But then it is by appealing to familial partialism that the Calvinist can give a model to show how the goods can justify. To explain, we can understand Christendom as containing two views on the nature of the fatherhood of God. One view, and perhaps the more common one, is that of Universal Divine Paternity (UDP): the claim that all of humanity are God's children. But the Calvinist will probably deny UDP and hold instead to Particular Divine Paternity (PDP): the claim that it is only a significantly proper subset of humanity that are God's children, namely those that are (or will be)

---

33. Cottingham, "Partiality, Favouritism and Morality," 368.
34. Ibid.

Christians. God is not the Father of the persistent unbeliever, but only those he has elected to partake in the salvation of Jesus Christ.[35] Calvin writes,

> In calling God our Father, we certainly plead the name of Christ. For with what confidence could any man call God his Father? Who would have the presumption to arrogate to himself the honour of a son of God were we not gratuitously adopted as his sons in Christ?[36]

For Calvin and those who follow him the honor of being a son of God is acquired through adoption, not through creation—the set of human beings that can (truthfully) call God 'Father' is coextensive with the set of elect human beings. And of course, since it is only the non-elect that go to hell, God is therefore not guilty of sending any of his children to hell, and so any argument to the effect that God has violated his paternal obligation to the reprobate in reprobating him will beg the question against the Calvinist: God has no paternal obligation to the reprobate on the Calvinist view.

So here is how the Calvinist should explain why the comparatively lesser goods the elect receive are worth the comparatively greater evils involved in the damnation of a great number of reprobates: the elect are God's children, his family, while the reprobated are not and never were. And if we agree that familial relations are an appropriate source of privilege, then the Calvinist can say that from God's perspective, God's first-person valuation, the goods the elect receive, on account of his paternal relation to them, are esteemed greater than, or at least equal to, the evils which befall the reprobated, despite the intrinsic valuation going the other way. And this is no different in principle from the way familial partialism expects you to value your relatives' joy more than that of people you aren't related to.

This is why proposition (5) above is false. It was the claim that it is only greater goods that permit God to allow evil, but we should not be interested in whether the suggested justifying goods are *intrinsically* greater, but whether God, given the value of these things *for him*, is justified in permitting the named evils. The value of something for an agent can be much greater than its impersonal value.[37]

---

35. Cf. *The Westminster Confession*, chapter 12, "Of Adoption," in Schaff, *Creeds of Christendom*, 628.

36. Calvin, *Institutes*, 3.20.36.

37. Familial relations are one putative source of this sort of agent-relative value. By Nagel's reckoning there are three categories of value for an agent that appear irreducibly agent-relative: (i) autonomy, which includes one's own desires, projects, commitments, and personal ties; (ii) deontology, which includes respecting rights—in general the idea that one must not be a doer of certain things; (iii) obligation, which includes special obligation one owes to spouses, children and other family members. See Nagel, *The View from Nowhere*, 165.

Can my opponent persist and claim that, even granted what I have said above, the goods still do not justify and this should be evident? I concede that I cannot *prove* that the goods of the elect outweigh the evils of the reprobated from God's position, but I fail to see how my opponent can prove that they do not outweigh them. I can see how he can see their comparative intrinsic value, but not how he can see that the disparity of intrinsic value is more than the paternal tie can justify. I certainly do not see this—I can't tell how much the paternal bond is capable of justifying. And I am content to leave things there; as I stated in section 2, plausible actuality only requires one to give an account of God's reasons against which no clearly probative objection can be made, and this objection does not meet that requirement.

Some may protest the idea that God is only the father of the elect. So how plausible is PDP? Does it possess PA? Issues surrounding the fatherhood of God were recently broached by Jeff Jordan.[38] He argues that we are mistaken to think that God is required to love all of his (human) creatures equally because such a 'flatness' requirement would be seen as a defect in any human being: "a human who loved all other humans equally and impartially would have a life significantly impoverished,"[39] citing friendships, marriage and family as features that would be lacking in such a life. He infers that, since UPD implies a flatness in love and therefore an impoverished divine life, we have good reason to reject UPD and endorse PDP.[40]

Some might object, as Talbott does in his response to Jordan, on biblical grounds.[41] Talbott pushes Acts 17:28–29, Eph 3:14–15 and 4:6 as Scriptural evidence for UPD. I'm not convinced of this; "*genos*" (offspring), like '*sperma*' (seed), is a less personal term than '*teknon*' (child) or '*huios*' (son)—its connotation is primarily biological in sense and so the description of the relation in Acts 17:28–29 lacks connotation of parental intimacy;[42] Eph 3:14–15 could simply refer to the patterning of all families after the fatherhood of God; and paying careful attention to the context of Eph 4:6 makes it permissible to restrict the 'of all' to mean 'of all of us'—in v. 3 Paul's concern is with the unity of believers, and it is to this end that he emphasizes the oneness of their calling in vv. 4–6.[43]

38. Jordan, "The Topology of Divine Love."

39. Ibid., 60.

40. Ibid., 68.

41. Talbott, "A Response to Jeff Jordan," 305.

42. Rom 9:7 is a good example of a place where this difference in connotation is exploited: "neither because they are Abraham's seed are they all children [of Abraham]" (translation mine).

43. A reader has insisted I deal with Mal 2:10. This can be done with the following interpretation of the verse: "Have we, the Israelites, not one Father? Has not one

But even if the above interpretations are misguided there remains another response. The Reformed theologian John Murray claims that there is more than one sense in which we can refer to God as 'Father.' He draws a distinction between the creative and adoptive senses of God as 'Father.' Of the former sense he says, "Creatively and providentially he gives to all men life and breath and all things . . . [I]t may be scriptural to speak of this relation which God sustains to all men in creation and providence as one of fatherhood and therefore of universal fatherhood."[44] But the adoptive sense describes "that most specific and intimate relationship which God constitutes with those who believe in Jesus' name" and to conflate this sense with the former one "means the degradation of this highest and richest of relationships to the level of that relationship which all men sustain to God by creation."[45] And it is this adoptive conception which carries prominence of place in the New Testament, and is found in passages such as John 1:12–13, Rom 8:14–17, Gal 3:26—4:7 and 1 John 3:1-2, where it is clear that becoming a child of God is something which attends conversion. So Murray could respond to Talbott by granting universal divine creative paternity, but denying universal divine adoptive paternity.

For my part, if I were to believe there is a sense in which God is the father of the reprobate, I think I would see this sense as *analogous* to the true sense of fatherhood which God has only to the elect, rather than parcel fatherhood into discrete senses as Murray appears to do. But, however the distinction is explicated, the point is this: this sense in which the unbeliever has God as a father is too weak a sense to offer clear support to the claim that God has violated paternal obligation in the reprobation of the unbeliever.[46]

But Talbott has more to say. He points us to a salient difference between earthly parents and God: while we only freely choose to bring into being a few, not all, human beings, every non-divine human being that has ever existed has been brought into being as a result of God's free choice. But to fail to have paternal love for a human being you have brought into existence is an imperfection. But no imperfection is to be found in God, so

---

God created us *qua* nation-state?" This national reading is supported by the fact that Malachi is attempting to extend the rebuking directed at the tribe of Levi in 1:6—2:9 to Judah and Israel more generally in 2:10–16.

44. Murray, *Redemption*, 127–8.

45. Ibid., 128.

46. See also Kelly James Clark's "I Believe in God the Father," which accepts that God is the father of all, but contends that the great differences between God the Father and earthly fathers means that God does not enter into the network of human obligations in any simple way, such that there is no easy inference from the permissions and obligations of earthly fathers to the permissions and obligations of God the Father.

God's paternal love must extend to all and PDP is false. To put it in Murray's terms, Talbott thinks that creative paternity entails adoptive paternity; he concludes that "a morally perfect God would, of necessity, love (or will the best for) each of those persons whom he freely chooses to create."[47]

But is it true that creating a human being is sufficient for one to fall under paternal obligations towards it? Intuitions to this effect are weak in cases where the offspring are created fully grown.[48] Suppose that God presented you with a futuristic six-foot capsule that had a button on the side. If you press the button, a fully grown adult male will be formed in the capsule and emerge from it. You would have created this being, but would you be its father? Suppose it emerges needing no help and wishing to be on its way. I'm inclined to think there is no paternity here. But what if the principle is restricted to creating human *babies*? Even then there are counterexamples. Suppose the futuristic capsule creates day-old babies, and that a caretaker is assigned the task of creating them and giving them to people who then become the child's parents. Are we forced to view the creator, the caretaker, as the father of all the children he creates? I don't feel any pressure to say that.

But suppose despite this that it were true that

7. For any human being A created by another human being B, A is the child of B.

Would this show that PDP were implausible? No, for the difference between man and God is great, and it would be to go beyond our epistemic bounds to insist that there were no feature of the divine situation which could make a difference in preventing paternity arising from creation. To move from (7) to (8) is quite a step.

8. For any human being A created by another (sufficiently intelligent, etc.) being B, A is the child of B.

6. TWO OBJECTIONS

So I conclude that PDP possesses PA, and I deal now with two remaining objections.

Objection from awareness by other means: All of the goods I propose involve an item of appreciation possessed by the elect as the end which God seeks. It was suggested that God reprobates in order to give the elect an awareness of his hatred of sin, for instance. But why does God have to show

---

47. Talbott, "Response to Jeff Jordan," 304.

48. I think it is significant to note in this connection that in the Genesis narrative Adam is created fully grown.

us his wrath before we realize that his hatred of iniquity is inexhaustible? Why can't he, by exercising his omnipotent powers, place such an awareness in our minds directly? Or perhaps he could fill our minds with imagery that demonstrates these things? Why not, instead of actually creating people for hell, doesn't he show the elect what it would be like if there were?

Response: Note first that the first four goods I listed are immune to this criticism. You can't have a (non-misguided) gratitude at being one of the few elect if everyone is elected. Neither can the great amount of lost souls (truly) justify your preoccupation with salvation if there are no lost souls.

But this objection raises issues for the remaining four. Let us work with an analogy. Suppose I know that Bruce is a very strong man. I have it on good authority that he can lift trucks with his bare hands. I have never seen this for myself, but nevertheless have a justified belief to this effect. However, one day I encounter Bruce at a show and there I do see him lift a truck with his bare hands. Insofar as my appreciation of Bruce's strength goes, I judge it much enhanced by witnessing this exhibition. What I gained there was not knowledge—I already had a true, justified belief that Bruce was a very strong man who could lift trucks—what I acquired was something like a feeling of awe at Bruce's strength.

Could God provide this without Bruce lifting anything? I agree that God could do this, but then the awe would be irrational—it would lack justification (or whatever the analogous relation is that governs emotions). To return to the example of the Japanese man who narrowly escapes the 2011 tsunami, God could make me feel, as I sit at my desk, as relieved and euphoric as he did, but it would be irrational because there is nothing in my environment to prompt it.[49]

So perhaps God could provide a mental cinematic showcasing Bruce's strength. But this is inadequate for the sort of reason Nozick gave with his 'experience machine' thought experiment.[50] Climbing a mountain in real life is a better thing to desire than climbing it in an experience machine, even if the experience is identical. Perceptive experience plus reality is greater than merely the experience, and therefore it is better for the elect that they receive the former. Also, once you realize that the display is not of reality a great deal of the sting is appropriately lost: a man who reacts emotionally to everything he sees in a film as if it were real is dysfunctional. I conclude that

---

49. I think this is a neglected evil in the use of drugs. They make you happy, but they mostly make you happy without justification.

50. Nozick, *Anarchy, State, and Utopia*, 42–45.

this irreducible advantage of a real display provides God with significant motivation to give real demonstrations of his attributes.[51]

Objection from God's love: It might be thought that the theodicy I give here fails to do justice in some way to God's love. Recall Baggett and Walls's complaint that reprobation was a "paradigmatic example of hateful behaviour, not loving behaviour."[52]

Response: Hateful behavior is behavior that is motivated by hate. So if we can consistently suppose that God in reprobating is doing so from a loving motive, then this objection will lose its force. But I think it is clear that on the theodicy I have sketched here God's motive is a loving motive, for he reprobates out of a desire for his creatures' good, albeit the good of the elect. Here is the explanatory order of God's decisions on the account I have given: God first sets his love on a particular set of possible creatures; these are his elect, and he loves them as a father and desires what is good for them. To bring this love to consummation he decides to create them. But what is good, indeed best, for the elect is that they love God and understand his nature and relation to them. Now God can partially achieve these objectives by displaying his power, his hatred of sin, his sovereignty in salvation, and all the other items I listed previously. But God cannot use the elect for these displays because that would be inconsistent with his paternal love for them. So God also forms the intention to create other human beings (the reprobates) for whom he does not have a paternal love in order to manifest these displays. But it is God's *love* for certain of his creatures that is the overarching motive here, illustrated by the fact that the decree of reprobation is explanatorily posterior to the decree of election—the reprobate is useful instrumentally, for the goods which God, from a loving motive, desires to bestow on the elect.[53]

Now this is sufficient to answer the charge of hateful behavior, but it leaves open the question of the nature of God's affective relation to the reprobate. Does God love them at all? For more developed discussion of this question see section 2.3 of Dan Johnson's essay and section 2.3 of David Alexander's essay, chapters 1 and 5 of this volume respectively. For my part I am happy to ascribe to God a non-paternal love for the reprobate (and therefore a desire for the reprobate's good) just so long as it is remembered

---

51. Kyle Scott drew my attention to the helpful case of couples in love: they, despite knowing that they love each other, often buy their partner gifts as a means of demonstrating that love. This helps illustrate the general principle that it is better to see that *p* rather than to merely know that *p*. Also, imagine that the suitor, instead of buying a ring, bought a picture of him doing so! I do not think that would go down well.

52. Baggett and Walls, *Good God*, 74.

53. This also makes it clear that the theodicy I am offering is supralapsarian.

that familial partialism is going to give God a much greater desire for the elect's good. I am also happy to grant that God feels sorrow over the fact that he must reprobate to achieve his ends, just so long as it is remembered that his joy over the consequent ennobling of the elect is of greater measure than his sorrow.

7. CONCLUSION

That concludes my Calvinistic theodicy of hell. It is natural to try to extend the theodicy given here to evil more generally, and I think this appears a promising prospect, though developing it remains a task for another time. Just as God's hatred of sin is seen in the destruction of the reprobate, so it can also be seen in the natural disasters which humankind is subject to. And so on for all the other aspects of God's character that can be displayed in such things. However, there are two important differences between the afterlife and this life that would result in a slightly different treatment being required. Firstly, while in the afterlife the veil is lifted and the elect see God and understand their relation to him and can be counted on to infer correctly and prioritize righteously, in this life things are different: many spare little thought for the Lord God, and so may not perceive a divine display in some catastrophe. Secondly, while on the New Earth no evil shall ever befall a believer, evil befalls believer and unbeliever alike on this earth, so some explanation of why God is letting believers suffer is required.[54]

---

54. I would like to thank the audience at the 2011 Tyndale Philosophy of Religion Conference for their helpful comments on an earlier version of this paper, and especially Daniel Hill, who offered relentless criticism of an earlier draft.

BIBLIOGRAPHY

Adams, Marilyn McCord. "Hell and the God of Justice." *Religious Studies* 11, no. 4 (1975) 433–447.
Alston, William. "The Inductive Argument from Evil and the Human Cognitive Condition." *Philosophical Perspectives* 5 (1991) 29–67.
Baggett, David, and Jerry Walls. *Good God: The Theistic Foundations of Morality*. Oxford: Oxford University Press, 2011.
Calvin, John. *Institutes of the Christian Religion*. Translated by Henry Beveridge. Rev. ed. Peabody, Massachusetts: Hendrickson, 2008.
Clark, Kelly James. "I Believe in God the Father, Almighty." *International Philosophical Quarterly* 35, no. 1 (1995) 59–69.
Cottingham, John. "Partiality, Favouritism and Morality." *The Philosophical Quarterly* 36 (1986) 357–373.
Craig, William Lane. "'No Other Name': A Middle Knowledge Perspective on the Exclusivity of Salvation through Christ." *Faith and Philosophy* 6, no. 2 (1989) 172–188.
Crisp, Oliver. "Augustinian Universalism." *International Journal for Philosophy of Religion* 53, no. 3 (2003) 127–145.
———. "Is Universalism a Problem for Particularists?" *Scottish Journal of Theology* 63, no. 1 (2010) 1–23.
Edwards, Jonathan. "Concerning the Divine Decrees in General, and Election in Particular." In *The Works of Jonathan Edwards*, edited by Edward Hickman, 2:525–43. Edinburgh: Banner of Truth, 1974.
———. "The Eternity of Hell Torments." In *The Works of Jonathan Edwards*, edited by Edward Hickman, 2:83–89. Edinburgh: Banner of Truth, 1974.
———. "The Wicked Useful in Their Destruction Only." In *The Works of Jonathan Edwards*, edited by Edward Hickman, 2:125–29. Edinburgh: Banner of Truth, 1974.
———. *The Works of Jonathan Edwards*. 2 vols. Edited by Edward Hickman. Edinburgh: Banner of Truth, 1974.
Flint, Thomas. "Two Accounts of Providence." In *Divine and Human Action*, edited by Thomas Morris, 147–81. Ithaca, NY: Cornell University Press, 1988.
Gill, John. *The Cause of God and Truth*. London: Collinridge, 1855.
Hart, Matthew. "The Justice of Hell." Unpublished manuscript.
Helm, Paul. *Eternal God: A Study of God without Time*. 2nd ed. Oxford: Oxford University Press, 2010.
———. "God, Compatibilism, and the Authorship of Sin." *Religious Studies* 46 (2010) 115–24.
———. *John Calvin's Ideas*. Oxford: Oxford University Press, 2004.
Jordan, Jeff. "The Topography of Divine Love." *Faith and Philosophy* 29, no. 1 (2012) 53–69.
Kvanvig, Jonathan. *The Problem of Hell*. Oxford: Oxford University Press, 1993.
Lewis, David. "Evil for Freedom's Sake?" *Philosophical Papers* 22 (1993) 149–172.
Murray, John. *Redemption, Accomplished and Applied*. Edinburgh: Banner of Truth, 2009.
Nagel, Thomas. *The View from Nowhere*. Oxford: Oxford University Press, 1986.
Nozick, Robert. *Anarchy, State, and Utopia*. New York: Basic, 1974.

Pereboom, Derk. "Free Will, Evil, and Divine Providence." In *God and the Ethics of Belief*, edited by Andrew Chignell and Andrew Dole, 77–98. Cambridge: Cambridge University Press, 2005.

Piper, John. *The Pleasures of God*. Rev. ed. New York: Multnomah, 2000.

Plantinga, Alvin. *The Nature of Necessity*. Oxford: Oxford University Press, 1974.

Rowe, William. "Ruminations about Evil." *Philosophical Perspectives* 5 (1991) 69–88.

———. "The Evidential Argument from Evil: A Second Look." In *The Evidential Argument from Evil*, edited by Daniel Howard-Snyder, 262–285. Bloomington, IN: Indiana University Press, 1996.

———. "The Problem of Evil and Some Varieties of Atheism." *American Philosophical Quarterly* 16, no. 4 (1979) 335–341.

Schaff, Philip. *The Creeds of Christendom*. Vol. 3. 3rd ed. New York: Harper & Brothers, 1882.

Seymour, Charles. "A Craigian Theodicy of Hell." *Faith and Philosophy* 17, no. 1 (2000) 103–115.

Swinburne, Richard. "A Theodicy of Heaven and Hell." In *The Existence and Nature of God*, edited by Alfred J. Freddoso, 37–54. Notre Dame, IN: University of Notre Dame Press, 1983.

Talbott, Thomas. "The Topography of Divine Love: A Response to Jeff Jordan." *Faith and Philosophy* 30, no. 3 (2013) 302–16.

Wykstra, Stephen. "The Humean Obstacle to Evidential Arguments from Suffering: On Avoiding the Evils of 'Appearance.'" *International Journal for Philosophy of Religion* 16, no. 2 (1984) 73–93.

12

Calvinism, Self-Attestation, and Apathy toward Arguments from Evil

—Anthony Bryson

1. INTRODUCTION

HISTORICALLY, REFORMED THINKERS HAVE supplied philosophers with a unique set of replies to arguments from evil. But sometimes the reformed community does not develop these replies because of their indifference to the philosophical problems evil poses. I speak here from my own experience and what I have observed as a member of the reformed faith. We don't take arguments from evil seriously enough, and consequently, don't appreciate the seemingly intractable difficulties lodged in our worldview. We brush the issue aside all too quickly. Here is what I mean. Some argue that if God is sovereign, he has the right to create any world he chooses. So we have no right to complain about the extent, variety, and distribution of evil.[1] Not only this, but we don't deserve any better because of our proclivity for sin. In fact, because of God's grace, we possess many good things we don't deserve. And finally, because God has no obligation to create us, he has no obligation to place us in circumstances we find agreeable.

---

1. Does not the potter have a right over the clay? (Rom 9:21).

Although these replies may have merit when fully developed,[2] in their contracted form they don't fully appreciate the difficulty posed by arguments from evil. They take God's existence for granted as if that matter has already been settled, when that is really the bone of contention. The problem is not how to decide which explanation of evil among Christians is the best, as if the debate were in-house. The argument from evil penetrates to the most basic level of all: God's very existence.

Why think the quick reformed reply takes God's existence for granted? For one, these swift replies have little plausibility in isolation. Specifically, their plausibility hangs on the strength of our justification for belief in God and the belief that we know what God has taught about this confounded issue. To see what I mean, suppose we use a strong form of theological voluntarism to repel an argument from evil. We argue that God's will, and God's will alone, determines what is right or wrong. Anything he does is right by definition. Therefore, he can't possibly be evil for creating and minutely directing the present world.

Because this answer is prima facie so counterintuitive, our prior justification for belief in God must be high enough to evidentially overwhelm the answer's implausibility and economy. Imagine that God's existence is too obvious to ignore and he undeniably teaches an unqualified theological voluntarism. Then our justification for those two truths may swamp the initial implausibility of the above reply to arguments from evil.[3]

The free-will defense, on the other hand, is more plausible in isolation apart from any assumption that God exists and that he is sovereign in the reformed sense of the word (which may be why many Christian philosophers drift in that direction). Because it is prima facie more plausible, it depends less on a particular conception of God or our confidence that we know God's mind. It is otherwise for the quick reformed reply. If we doubt that we know what God teaches about this issue, we should probably doubt that the suggested solution is on the right track, at least in the absence of further philosophical argument.

Thus our justification for belief in God and what he has taught must be strong enough to buttress the quick reformed solution. Yet the argument from evil is designed to attack just this: our justification for belief in God. So when we assume that our justification is unaffected, as if arguments from evil only raise problems for certain theological systems but don't strike at

---

2. Hence, one reason for the present volume.

3. Bear in mind that because the solution is so counterintuitive, most Christians are unlikely to reach it unassisted. A recognized authority must suggest it to them, whether it be the church or Scripture.

their core, we are insensitive to the instinctive problems that evil poses for belief in God.

In other words, some reformed Christians treat arguments from evil as though God's existence has already been settled without remainder. We already have indefeasibly strong justification for believing that God exists and is sovereign. Arguments from evil can't do anything to affect this justification.

In my experience, one prominent source for this attitude is the reformed Christian's unflagging trust in Scripture. We clearly know that God exists because of what the Bible says. Since God is its author, it is infallible. And we know its author is God because of its own self-testimony. In short, the Bible is self-attesting.[4]

In what follows, I argue that this way of handling arguments from evil is a variation of the Moore switch and thus inherits its strengths and infirmities. Implicit appeal to the Bible is not irrational *per se*, but only if we have strong prior justification for trusting Scripture. In this instance, that justification is supposed to come from Scripture's self-attestation. I argue that self-attestation imparts very little justification to the reformed Christian's trust in Scripture and consequently the quick reformed reply is much weaker than many realize.[5]

Toward the end I argue that self-attestation not only has little epistemic value but, what is more, is epistemically otiose. The self-attestation view flows, in part, from the desire to satisfy the demands of epistemic internalism. But self-attestation, as a form of justified belief, is quite at home within the framework of epistemic externalism. This explains why the self-attestation approach to Scripture looks so unsatisfying: It tries to satisfy the demands of internalism with the apparatus of externalism. Advocates of self-attestation arguments would do better to accept either internalism alone or externalism alone. Whichever route they choose, neither epistemic theory deems self-attestation necessary for, nor conducive to, justified belief that God exists, even in the company of arguments from evil.

---

4. This sort of reformed reply comes in degrees. There is the terse, dismissive reply in which one is astonished that others would even think that evil poses any difficulty for Christian belief. And there is another that is more humble and less impetuous. It admits that evil is a genuine puzzle, but still depends a great deal on the self-attestation of Scripture.

5. In my experience, members of the Dutch reformed tradition (specifically presuppositionalists) use this style of reasoning most often. Thus some of the quotations I use will be drawn from representatives of this tradition though I am interested in the broader self-attestation tradition (which seems to extend beyond the borders of presuppositionalism).

2. THE MOORE-REFORMED SWITCH

I mentioned in the introduction that quick reformed replies to arguments from evil bear a strong resemblance to G.E. Moore's strategy for handling skepticism about our knowledge of the external world. At first sight, Moore's anti-skeptical argument looks underdeveloped and question begging. He doesn't seem to fully appreciate the worries that prompt doubt about our knowledge of the external world. As we'll see, quick reformed replies to arguments from evil engender the same reservations.

2.1 What is the Moore switch?

In the first half of the 20th century, G. E. Moore developed what is now a famous reply to arguments for skepticism (sometimes dubbed "the Moore switch").[6] Suppose you're presented with a set of inconsistent claims. How do you decide which members of the set to believe? Common sense instructs us to believe the most obvious claims that form a consistent subset. Now suppose you look at a set of claims that includes a) epistemic principles that seemingly lead to skeptical conclusions and b) a claim that we know truths about the external world. Supposing you recognize their logical incompatibility, you should, Moore tells us, cling to the more obvious of the two—that we know truths about the external world—and reject those obscure epistemic principles that beckon us, like a Siren, toward skepticism. The idea is that external world knowledge claims will always (or nearly always) have greater intuitive plausibility than the epistemic principles that indirectly challenge them.

As Moore says,

> It seems to me a sufficient refutation of such views as these, simply to point to cases in which we do know such things. This, after all, you know, really is a finger: there is no doubt about it: I know it and you all know it. And I think we may safely challenge any philosopher to bring forward any argument in favour either of the proposition that we do not know it, or of the proposition that it is not true, which does not at some point, rest upon some premiss which it is, beyond comparison, less certain than is the proposition which it is designed to attack.[7]

---

6. I speak here of one kind of local skepticism, viz. skepticism that our beliefs about the external world are justified.

7. Moore, *Philosophical Studies*, 228.

Even if Moore does not refute the skeptic's argument (as I believe), his method still gives philosophers a lot to mull over. He manages to place the parties to the debate on equal footing. Whether one side gives a better philosophical argument should not depend on who gets to go first. If skeptics present their argument first, non-skeptics must show where the premises go wrong. They're unlikely to succeed at this. On the other hand, if non-skeptics go first, skeptics must demonstrate what is wrong with the premises, and they are likely to attack the premises by advancing those infernal worries that favor a skeptical judgment. Moore recommends instead that we take in both arguments at the same time (so to speak). We shouldn't waste our time proving the skeptical premises false, as if trying to move piecemeal, link-by-link through a chain of reasoning. That way lies defeat. We should instead juxtapose the premises of the two arguments and compare their credibility.

2.2 The reformed switch

We have some sense of how the Moore switch works, but to see exactly how the quick reformed reply is a variation on this Moorean theme, we need to sketch in one or two more details.

In his well-known piece "The Problem of Evil and Some Varieties of Atheism,"[8] William Rowe suggests that theists can use a Moore switch to answer arguments from evil. According to Rowe's description, Moore doesn't attack the premises of an argument for skepticism; he observes instead that the premises imply an obvious falsehood—e.g., "I don't know this pencil exists." Next, Moore turns the valid skeptical argument on its head. He swipes out a premise and the conclusion, negates both, and finally juxtaposes the skeptical argument with its inverted cousin. Here is an example:

Skeptical argument

1) If the skeptic's epistemic principles are correct, then I cannot know that this pencil exists.

2) The skeptic's epistemic principles are correct.

3) Thus, I don't know that this pencil exists.

The Moore switch

1) Same as 1) above.

2) I do know this pencil exists.

---

8. Rowe, "Problem of Evil," 6–7.

3) Thus, the skeptic's epistemic principles are incorrect.

Theists can use the same maneuver when faced with an argument from evil. They can switch out a premise and the conclusion, negate both, and voilà—the conclusion "God does not exist" becomes the premise "God does exist."

Theistic/Moore switch

1) An omniscient, wholly good being would prevent the occurrence of any intense suffering it could, unless it could not do so without thereby losing some greater good or permitting some evil equally bad or worse.

2) There exists an omnipotent, omniscient, wholly good being.

3) Therefore it is not the case that there exists instances of intense suffering which an omnipotent, omniscient, wholly good being could have prevented without thereby losing some greater good or permitting some evil equally bad or worse.[9]

The quick reformed reply to the argument from evil resembles this version of the Moore switch. Specifically, because God undeniably exists (premise 2), we should deny that God is blameworthy for instances of intense suffering or deny that the world contain evils that would render God less than perfectly good. Whichever sorts of evils premise 1 stipulates God would not allow, the reformed thinker is bound to conclude that either there are no such evils, or if there are, they neither speak against God's existence nor his moral perfection. Knowing that God exists secures this result.

Rowe correctly observes that the Christian can reply to the argument from evil with a Moore switch. But he seems to have something else in mind when he explains how this might go. He mentions as grounds for belief in God arguments for the existence of God, religious experience, or the theist's ability to explain certain phenomena. This looks less like the Moore switch and more like the total evidence requirement for justified belief.[10] The Moore switch proper relies on specifically perceptual evidence in order to turn the tables on the skeptic, and so too does the quick reformed reply.

2.3 Several other similarities

There are several more reasons to think that the quick reformed reply is a type of Moore switch. First, to take advantage of a Moore switch, we need

---

9. Ibid., 7.

10. Religious experience does more closely resemble the role of perception in the Moore switch, but arguments for God's existence have no analogue in the Moore switch.

not know how perception works or how to argue on the basis of perception that we know truths about the physical world. Because we clearly know external world truths, we can take the reliability of perception for granted. This places a refutation of philosophical skepticism within reach of the philosophical novice. We need not be seasoned epistemologists to refute the skeptic.

The same can be said of the reformed switch. Christians supposedly know that something is amiss with arguments from evil, but they need not be able to identify what it is, and even if they could, they need not be able to give a direct and cogent reply to the offending premise. It is clear to them that something is wrong with the argument because they are assured that God exists. While perception is the foundation of certainty for the Moore switch, the reformed switch grounds its certainty on the testimony of Scripture.

Second, the Moore switch forces us into an epistemic standoff early on in the dialectic. Some common sense epistemologists/dogmatists are confident that they will never find any skeptical argument plausible (even those that may someday come to light). Skeptics can't say anything that would compel them to question their knowledge of the external world. As a result, any give-and-take between the skeptic and dogmatist is illusory.

Much of this is true as well for the reformed switch. Some reformed Christians immediately announce that arguments from evil are benign. Because God so clearly exists, the argument from evil must have very little plausibility. It is not that the evidence in favor of Christian belief vastly outweighs the evidence from instances of evil. We don't know with absolute certainty that God exists because cosmological, ontological, and teleological arguments supply an indefeasible amount of evidence. Rather it is undeniably clear that God exists just as it is obvious that I am now typing on a computer and sitting in my favorite chair. The latter are obvious because of the testimony of perception; the former, because of the testimony of Scripture.

Because the reformed switch leans so heavily on Scripture to ground our assurance that there must be something wrong with arguments from evil, a natural question arises: Why is it so clear from Scripture that God exists? It is clear that Scripture claims that God exists (and much more besides). But why is it so obvious that Scripture is right? It is here that the self-attestation argument in support of the Bible's trustworthiness appears.

3. THE SELF-ATTESTATION VIEW OF THE BIBLE

There are several different views on how Christians can rationally believe that the Bible is trustworthy. One view is more inductive in spirit. Our justification for trusting Scripture can include general historical evidence, evidence of the reliability of those who witnessed the resurrection, fulfilled prophecy and miracles, among other things.[11] Basically it demands that we have non-question begging reasons for accepting the trustworthiness of Scripture and claims to divine authorship.[12] It counsels us not to expect epistemic certainty that the Bible is the word of God and inerrant. As with most things in life, the best we can hope for is high probability.[13]

The self-attestation (SA) model is another view of how we can rationally trust Scripture. It is the preferred model of many biblical inerrantists.[14] The central idea is this: If we have justification to believe that the Bible is inspired, we immediately have justification to completely trust it; the trustworthiness of the Bible follows by definition from divine authorship. Not only is God morally perfect and so would not lie or deceive us, he is infallible—he doesn't have, nor can he have, any false beliefs.

For the sake of argument, I will assume that this inference holds.[15] If a piece of writing is divinely inspired, it is completely reliable in all that it asserts. But how can we know that the Bible is inspired?

---

11. For an illustration of inductive and deductive approaches, see Davis, *Debate about the Bible*, 40–41.

12. Kruger, *Canon Revisited*, 88 describes the view as follows: "They all ground the authority of the canon in something outside the canon itself. It is this appeal to an external authority that unites all of these positions . . . Richard Gaffin notes that such an approach is in danger of 'subjecting the canon to the relativist of historical study and our fallible human insight . . . it would destroy the New Testament as canon, as absolute authority.'"

13. Once we learn that epistemic certainty is indeed a rare thing, it is not that troubling. Even when doing long division, most of us can't aspire to epistemic certainty. Sometimes I get the impression that SA theorists think that if we have access to an infallible source of belief, the epistemic certainty of those beliefs necessarily follows. But that is not true. Much more is involved in epistemic certainty than managing somehow to alight on an infallible source of belief.

14. See Abraham, *Divine Inspiration*, chapter 1 for one thorough characterization of this deductive approach to Scripture.

15. Many have challenged the inference from divine inspiration to Biblical inerrantism. They argue that the most cited proof texts don't actually speak to inerrancy, and that inerrancy follows only if we know that God's plan for the Bible is that it be free from error in everything it asserts. See Abraham, *Divine Inspiration*; and Achtemeier, *Inspiration and Authority*, 9, 40. Some question whether God is truly interested in giving us a science of nature, a philosophy of time and omnipotence, or a theory of knowledge.

3.1 Knowing that the Bible is inspired

The most common answer from SA theorists is that Jesus and the rest of the Scriptures teach that it is.[16] Yet clearly, just because a book claims to be the word of God, it doesn't necessarily follow that it is, nor do we immediately acquire a reason to believe that it is. Why believe the Bible's claim to divine inspiration rather than some other religious text? The answer is quite simple: because God claims to have written the Bible; he does not claim to have authored those other sacred texts.[17]

As a first pass, we can sketch the trajectory of the argument as follows: We know that the Bible is trustworthy because it is inspired. We know that it is inspired because it was written by God. And we know that it was written by God because God, in the Bible, has written that it was written by him.

If you feel that the argument doesn't do much to advance its conclusion, that by knowing the premises we do little to improve our epistemic position, you aren't alone. To many, it looks like this sort of reasoning simply begs the question or, at the very least, brushes aside a nest of tough epistemic questions.[18] And this feeling that something is not right with the argument is harder to ignore when we apply self-attestation reasoning to the issue of biblical inerrancy.

---

16. For the Biblical evidence, see Grudem, "Scripture's Self-Attestation."

17. See Davis, *Debate about the Bible*, 49, 62, for other renditions of the argument. Other times, what Jesus taught is the crux of the argument but the problems that emerge are very similar. See Helm, *Divine Revelation*, 82; Abraham, *Divine Inspiration*, 26–27; and Achtemeier, *Inspiration and Authority*, 41.

18. After claiming that, "The Bible is the Word of God because it says it is," Frame goes on to say that, "There is a profound truth vividly displayed in this narrow argument, namely, that there is no authority higher than Scripture by which Scripture may be judged, and that in the final analysis we must believe Scripture on its own say-so" (*Apologetics to the Glory of God*, 14). Grudem, *Systematic Theology*, 78, who has no qualms with SA arguments, gives this summary of the argument: "We believe that Scripture is God's word because it claims to be. And we believe what it claims to be because it is God's word." Hesselink notes that "the argument is obviously circular: Why do we believe that Bible is the Word of God? Because God by his Spirit assures us of this truth. How does God do this? Through the Bible." He adds that circularity is not a problem because the only other alternative is an appeal to an external authority; and the latter is anathema (*Calvin's First Catechism*, 59). According to Kruger, this is just how foundational authorities are authenticated (*Canon Revisited*, 92). And even though Frame recognizes that this argument is unlikely to convince the non-Christian, he believes it should convince him: "But this brings us back to the narrowly circular proof we originally considered. The unbeliever ought to accept that proof together with the scriptural authority which it presupposes" (*Apologetics to the Glory of God*, 63).

3.2 Inoculation against disconfirmation

SA arguments fence off inerrancy claims so that we cannot possibly acquire good reasons for thinking that the Bible, or just a part, is uninspired.[19] God's self-authentication is the most fundamental and important piece of evidence for the inspiration/inerrancy of Scripture. All other evidence depends on it and must be interpreted in light of this epistemic base.[20] The self-attestation of Scripture is not one piece of evidence among others that happens to weigh more. It determines what else can count as evidence, including how or whether we even ought to search for evidence.[21] Put another way, for the SA theorist belief in biblical inerrancy resembles the sort of belief lodged in the middle of a Quinean doxastic web. The belief will (and ought to) be held, come what may.

Thus nothing can give us a good reason to doubt the Bible; nothing can override the evidence of God's own self-attestation.[22] Inductive evidence, like the evidence of historical investigation or the search for logical consistency, cannot, in principle, give us a reason to think the Bible contains errors.[23] So what role can historical evidence play? Historians can help us

---

19. See Abraham, *Divine Inspiration*, 20–27; Helm, "Faith, Evidence, and the Scriptures," 83; Achtemeier, *Inspiration and Authority*, 37, 39, 44, 47, 48, 59; and Davis, *Debate about the Bible*, 25–27, 36. In addressing this, my aim is not to look at what role self-attestation should play in apologetics. I'm interested in how the Christian can know that the Bible is the word of God. In the SA literature, these sometimes get confused.

20. Members of the Dutch reformed tradition are apt to be the most explicit about this: "We should make plain that even our methods of knowledge, our standards of truth and falsity, our views of logic, and our scientific methods must be reconciled first of all with God's revelation" Frame, *Apologetics to the Glory of God*, 220. Achtemeier, *Inspiration and Authority*, 46, argues that a presupposition that Scripture is inerrant is fed into the interpretive process so that their hermeneutical principles guarantee a certain outcome. Abraham agrees (*Divine Inspiration*, ch. 1).

21. Kruger writes, "the Scriptures themselves provide the grounds for considering the external data: the apostolicity of books, the testimony of the church, and so forth. Of course, this external evidence is not to be used as an independent and neutral 'test' to determine what counts as canonical; rather it should always be seen as something warranted by Scripture and interpreted by Scripture" Kruger, *Canon Revisited*, 90. Also "the use of such evidence is not inconsistent with the self-authenticating model because it does not stand alone but is interpreted and understood by the norm of Scripture" Ibid., 111.

22. See Davis, *Debate about the Bible*, 27–28. He points out that SA theorists propose implausibly high criteria for showing that the Bible makes a false claim. Because these criteria are so demanding, no evidence could indicate that the Scriptures have erred.

23. See in particular, Abraham, *Divine Inspiration*, 24. According to J. I. Packer, "Present-Day Views of Scripture," 77, if we think the Bible is inerrant, then we should not "cut the knot of any problem of Bible harmony, factual or theological, by allowing

learn, through the use of historical evidence (like the circumstances and date of the writings), what the authors meant by the words they used. But they shouldn't use their knowledge of history to check on a biblical author's reliability. This does not mean historical evidence is ignored entirely. SA theorists welcome historical findings that lend credence to the accuracy of Scripture.[24] But since their method guarantees beforehand that the evidential chips will fall in their favor, it's unclear how this is any sort of evidence at all.[25]

SA theorists go on to say that we must not permit reason or science to pass judgment on God's word. God must be our ultimate authority. Science and reason should only inquire, not judge; they should only receive evidence, not adjudicate; they should not pronounce but comprehend.[26] God's word should guide us so that we recognize the true conclusions of reason and science; not the other way around.[27]

---

ourselves to assume that the inspired authors were not necessarily consistent with themselves or with each other. It is because the word *inerrant* makes these methodological points about handling the Bible, ruling out in advance the use of mental procedures that can only lead to reduced and distorted version of Christianity, that it is so valuable and, I think, so much valued by those who embrace it."

24. Frame on the use of historical evidence: "The primary sources are the Scriptures themselves. Extrabiblical sources confirm what the early Christians believed, but they do not add much to the biblical testimony concerning the events themselves." Frame, *Apologetics to the Glory of God*, 119.

25. Such evidence might give us reason to believe a biblical passage has been interpolated, or that we may have been wrong in elevating a certain book to the canon. Further, to say that historical evidence could help disconfirm the accuracy of Scripture does not mean that whenever any evidence from history goes against Scripture, we must side with the historical evidence. The Christian might reasonably think that even though historical evidence could disconfirm the truth of a passage, that evidence would need to be quite strong, especially since the Bible is one source of our historical evidence. So we must guard against viewing this matter in extremes: that if we think historical evidence could show that a passage of Scripture errs, we must also think that it is quite easy for historical evidence to trump the historical witness of Scripture.

26. Archer, "Witness of the Bible," 94, says that Christ doesn't require the Old Testament to be validated by critical scholarship. "He clearly presupposes that whatever the Old Testament taught was true because it was the infallible Word of God. It needed no further screening process by human wisdom in order to be verified." He goes on to say that "We find the attitude of Christ and the apostolic authors of the New Testament was one of unqualified acceptance" (Ibid.). Kruger quotes Turretin to this effect: "Thus Scripture which is the first principle in the supernatural order, is known by itself and has no need of arguments derived from without to prove and make itself known to us." Kruger, *Canon Revisited*, 89–90. And Frame gives an argument that uses the truth of Scripture as an axiom (*Apologetics to the Glory of God*, 61).

27. This is the point made by Louis Gaussen in his *Theopnustia: The Plenary Inspiration of the Holy Scriptures*, cited in Abraham, *Divine Inspiration*, 23.

Even though all of this looks like a case of cooking the books so that the desired result is secured from the start,[28] SA theorists have several replies. First, they argue that there is no other choice. We can either presuppose the divine authorship and inerrancy of Scripture or human authorship and fallibility.[29] As they say, historical investigation is not conducted from a neutral standpoint; our presuppositions color our findings. A God honoring historical investigation begins with a commitment to inerrancy on the basis of God's own testimony and interprets historical findings in the light of that commitment.[30] And even if this does make disconfirmation of biblical inerrancy impossible, such is life as a human being. There is no neutral standpoint. Any method guarantees a certain result from the start (assuming we reason consistently).[31]

Second, if we say that historical evidence, or evidence of any kind, can disconfirm the accuracy and divine authorship of Scripture, we stumble headlong into what may be the most egregious epistemic sin of them all. We trust fallible beings and their fallible methods for ferreting out the relevant evidence over the testimony of the infallible word of God. We stand in epistemic judgment of God and his word, which now brings the moral dimension into play.[32] This isn't just about using the most reliable method

---

28. Packer, "Present-Day Views of Scripture," 79, is an example: "Though the confession of inerrancy does not help us to make the literary judgments that interpretation involves, it commits us in advance to harmonize and integrate all that we find Scripture teaching, without remainder, and so makes possible a theological grasp of Christianity that is altogether believing and obedient."

29. Archer, "Witness of the Bible," 93, hints at this: "We are faced with a basic choice in the matter of biblical authority. Either we receive the Scripture as completely reliable and trustworthy in every matter it records, affirms, or teaches, or else it comes to us as a collection of religious writings containing both truth and error." And Ibid., 98: "No reasonable alternative is left but to reduce the Bible to the status of a mixture of truth and error requiring the validation of its truth by human reason or else take our stand with Jesus Christ and the apostles in a full acceptance of the infallible, inerrant authority of the original autographs."

30. According to Achtemeier, "Much of what raises the ire of conservative scholars is identified under the rubric of putting some other authority over Scripture by using it to judge whether or not Scripture may be understood as being inerrant. Whether such other authority be a bias against the supernatural or some kind of philosophical presupposition that would question inerrancy, conservatives are quick to point out that such an act not only questions inerrancy but denies the Bible its entire authority." Achtemeier, *Inspiration and Authority*, 42.

31. I note, in passing, that quite a lot could be said and needs to be said about the concepts used in this reasoning and whether the reasoning itself is sound. But we must press onward.

32. As Archer writes, "Such judgment presupposes a superior wisdom and spiritual insight competent to correct the errors of the Bible, and if those who would judge the

to form true beliefs about Scripture. Our loyalty should be to God alone; we should have complete and unwavering trust in him.

Here is how the SA method operates when used in the trenches. Some scholars argue that Joshua is not a historical book because God certainly would not have commanded Israel to slaughter its enemies. That jars with God's moral perfection. SA theorists reply that this inference has managed to get things turned around. We're using reason and its supposed moral insights as our ultimate standard. We are trusting above all else our moral intuitions. Instead of adjusting our view of Joshua and the truth of its claims, we should adjust our moral beliefs.[33] God's acts and commands must guide our moral judgments. Hence, we shouldn't doubt Joshua's historicity but should recognize that we came to the Bible with two false assumptions: 1) It would be necessarily wrong for Israel to slaughter its enemies and thus 2) it is necessarily true that God would never issue that shocking command.

SA theorists also aver that without their method, we can't have full assurance or certainty that the Bible is inerrant (or even very trustworthy).[34] This is probably their strongest argument. They claim that our only other option is to build up our trust in Scripture piecemeal, as the evidence comes in, or as we recognize the evidence already there (like the internal coherence of Scripture). This, they say, would significantly weaken the importance of Scripture, for we wouldn't have anything close to the kind of assurance that would justify organizing our lives around its teachings. For all we know, some new evidence might come to light tomorrow that would destroy our

---

veracity of the Bible lack the necessary ingredient of person inerrancy in judgment, they may come to a false and mistaken judgment—endorsing as true what is actually false, or else condemning as erroneous what is actually correct in Scripture." Archer, "Witness of the Bible," 93–94.

33. Frame, *Apologetics to the Glory of God*, 174. On p. 178 he argues that God has the sovereign right to do what he wishes, and on p. 57 he says that God defines rationality and morality for us so he can't say what is immoral or irrational.

34. See Helm, *Divine Revelation*, 102; and Cowan, *Five Views on Apologetics*, 254. Hesselink, *Calvin's First Catechism*, 57, maintains that self-attestation is the only objective basis for the certainty of Scripture. We can affirm with unqualified certainty that the Bible flows to us from the very mouth of God (Ibid., 58). And Frame claims that we know Jesus died for us because of Scripture and that there is no greater ground for certainty Frame, *Apologetics to the Glory of God*, 127. See also Achtemeier, *Inspiration and Authority*, 23, 34.

Of course, we must address the question of what kind of assurance/certainty is spoken of. There are at the very least psychological certainty and epistemic certainty. Which does the Bible claim we should have? The distinction is an important one. Too often writers just assume the Bible is speaking about epistemic certainty. Lest I be the first to break with tradition, I will assume that SA theorists have something akin to epistemic certainty in mind.

justification for trusting Scripture.[35] We need not comb through the journals of philosophy and archeology to justifiably maintain our commitment to inerrancy. Only one piece of evidence matters: the evidence furnished by God himself in his word. When we have access to the mind of God, why trust anything else?

4. SOME PROBLEMS WITH SA[36]

Even though SA is supposed to be incompatible with an evidentialist conception of justified belief in Scripture's reliability, when pressed on why we should trust the Bible rather than some other competing sacred text, SA theorists occasionally morph into quasi-evidentialists.[37] For instance,

---

35. Davis, *Debate about the Bible*, 76, speaking for the inerrantist, says, "But if your policy is to accept whatever the Bible says unless there is convincing evidence not to do so, you can never know that what you *accept* from the Bible is true." In other words, if we ground our trust in Scripture on the evidence, we must always be on the lookout for potential defeating evidence so that we can never have full assurance of Christianity's truth. Since there could quite possibly be good objections that either we'll never come across or never think of on our own, Christian belief must be qualified: I believe in God, but for all I know tomorrow I could come across an argument that will completely undermine my justification for theistic belief. Our confidence in the truth of Christianity would need to reflect this qualification that there should always be, however slight, a hesitance to speak or believe with certainty. And probably God expects nothing less than complete and unflinching certainty that he exists. Davis goes on to argue that this sort of objection suggests that inerrantists are searching for Cartesian certainty that Scripture is trustworthy (ibid., 77).

36. A few warnings to the reader before going further: First, much of the SA literature has been written by theologians who do not, nor need not, have the same cognitive aims as the analytic philosopher. Consequently, trying to make their claims more precise and clear is difficult. The analytic philosopher has to fill in quite a few gaps and some of that is educated guesswork. As we already noted, there is a further problem with their use of "certainty" and "assurance." Sometimes they seem to have psychological certainty in mind, and at others, epistemic certainty. I assume for the most part that they're arguing for some kind of epistemic certainty on behalf of Christian belief or belief in the divine authorship of Scripture. Finally, it is not easy to see where their arguments fit into their general epistemic framework. Are they foundationalists or coherentists? (I doubt they are infinitists.) If foundationalists, what constitutes non-inferential justification? How broad can the foundations be? If coherentists, why speak of circular reasoning instead of rejecting the linear conception of reasoning common to foundationalists?

37. I am using the term "evidentialist" in a technical sense. An evidentialist is not simply someone who thinks our judgments of Scripture should be rooted in the evidence; for even SA theorists sometimes say that self-attestation is 'evidence' for biblical inspiration. For us, an evidentialist is a person who doesn't think we have non-inferentially justified belief that Scripture is divinely authored and that the evidence of self-attestation is only a small chunk of a larger network of evidences that support divine authorship.

Wayne Grudem argues that the Bible is more persuasive than other books because all others are inconsistent with the experiences of life, or have other shortcomings.[38]

But as I will presently argue, SA has an odd account of how we could learn that some competing religious text is not inspired: We don't learn much if anything at all. And whatever the process may involve, at the end when we have formed the belief that some competing text is not inspired, our epistemic position doesn't improve at all either with regard to our belief in Scripture's reliability or the belief that there are fewer possible contenders for the appellation of being divinely inspired. I contend that this is an implausible implication of SA and that the problem stems from a more basic difficulty, i.e. SA's troubled account of how we acquire justification to believe that certain books belong in the canon.

4.1 The no-increase-in-justification implication

Initially, we might think that a standard route for increasing our justification for trusting Scripture, if only by a small degree, is to learn that Scripture is completely self-consistent and coherent. This epistemic state is preferable to, say, not knowing much of the Bible's content and thus not knowing how all the parts hang together and mutually reinforce each other.

For the purposes of our argument, we need not say that this new epistemic position would always be a vast improvement over any possible prior epistemic position (i.e. prior to acquiring knowledge of the Bible's internal virtues). We need only say that intuitively there is at least a marginal epistemic improvement from being ignorant of the Bible's internal virtues (consistency, coherence, beauty, etc.) to learning about them.

The reason this is a difficulty for SA theorists is that they can't even admit this much. Once we have God's self-attestation, we occupy the best epistemic position possible and so know that the Bible is perfectly coherent and consistent, even before becoming familiar with the Bible's content and the manifold cases of consistency and mutual reinforcement.[39] Against the

---

38. Grudem, *Systematic Theology*, 79.

39. Helm raises a worry in the same neighborhood: "It would appear then that those who appeal to the candidate special revelation as its own evidence are faced with a straight choice. They might mean by this that the candidate-revelation has the status of an axiom. If so, then for them the revelation will be certainly true . . . they commit themselves to the truth of the candidate special revelation as *basically* true. If they do this, it would seem that the special revelation must be the *sole* source of truth 'in the doctrine of religion,' for they could not combine their internalism with an appeal to external sources (since internal might conflict with external), nor does there seem to be any need to contemplate such a combination." Helm *Divine Revelation*, 111.

backdrop of SA, the claim that the Bible has the internal virtues and, what is more, is perfectly accurate, is secured from the start.[40]

Not only this, but if SA is true, we should never search for the internal virtues, as if trying to discern or verify that some Biblical text bears the marks of inspiration. For one, we would subject God to our fallible human judgment. And two, we're likely to bungle the job and judge that two consistent texts are inconsistent. Better to believe that the Bible has all the internal virtues (marks of divine inspiration) on the basis of its self-attestation alone.[41]

So by learning that the Bible does evince the internal virtues or even that it has been shown historically accurate, we don't improve our epistemic position, even marginally, for believing that the Bible is inspired and thus completely trustworthy. There is no epistemic reason to learn about these things. Consequently, by extension, there isn't any epistemic reason to search for and learn about the infirmities in competing religious texts. Upon reading a text that attests to the Bible's divine inspiration, we already know with ideal justification that any competing religious text must harbor some cursed errors or logical improprieties, even before we know anything about its content. And we can know the Bible is innocent of these defects before knowing anything about its content beyond that it testifies to being inspired.[42]

---

40. With regard to using evidence to support the trustworthiness of Scripture, Frame writes, "Now the argument is still circular in a sense, because the apologist chooses, evaluates, and formulates these evidences in ways controlled by Scripture. But this argument tends to hold the unbelievers attention longer and to be more persuasive" (*Apologetics to the Glory of God*, 14). Note how his appeal to evidence is more pragmatic in nature—not epistemic. For charges that Frame and others like him are inconsistent or unclear when they talk of using evidence, see the replies to Frame's entry in Cowan, *Five Views on Apologetics*.

41. Some think that if we only focus on the internal evidence of Scripture (e.g. internal coherence) and not the external evidence (e.g. historicity) that we're using the SA methodology and allowing a book to authenticate itself. But given what some SA theorists say (especially members of the Dutch reformed tradition), the explanation of what occurs when using internal coherence shouldn't be classified as self-authentication. For instance, imagine that you occupy the best epistemic position possible with respect to God; you are directly aware of God himself and so see him face-to-face. God says to you "X." Obviously you shouldn't check to see if X is an internally coherent claim, or perhaps less obviously, you shouldn't check to see if X is consistent with other claims God has made. If you think you remember a past claim Y made by God which is inconsistent with X, then most likely 1) you misremembered and God did not say "Y" or 2) you have mistakenly judged that X and Y are inconsistent. (I agree with this assessment as well.) Thus, to use SA's language, God should be the ultimate standard, even the standard for recognizing genuine inconsistencies and not just recognizing true historical claims or true a priori judgments (at least when the Bible is applicable).

42. I am not saying that any person who learns about these things will come to

Imagine someone who is not a Christian, nor an adherent of any other religion, desiring to inspect different religious texts to see which have the most going for them. We place a Bible in front of him along with other competing religious texts (e.g., the Koran, Book of Mormon, etc.). This person, let's call him John, opens up the Bible and manages to land on one of the few self-attestation texts, which he then reads. At this point, SA theorists should probably say that there is no epistemic reason for him to learn anything more about the content of the Bible *relative* to knowing that the Bible is divinely inspired and completely trustworthy. God has just told him, in the Bible, that the Bible indeed is inspired.

Not only does John not have an epistemic reason to search for whether Scripture can boast of the internal virtues, he shouldn't even try, for as we've seen he would be putting God to the test and he might bungle the job. So learning about the internal virtues of the Bible, or even of the external evidences, would do nothing to improve his epistemic position.[43] To my mind, this is very unintuitive. But we can say more.

He already knows with epistemic certainty that the other religious texts we placed before him are uninspired, and this before knowing anything whatsoever about their content (or whether they contain any claims of self-authentication). In fact, to examine other texts to see if they do have significant defects, as if trying to learn and make a judgment about whether they do, is wrong and even sinful. He would implicitly deny that he already occupies an ideal epistemic position; he would not trust God alone.

So SA theorists must say two things here: John's epistemic position vis-à-vis knowing that the Bible is inspired doesn't improve the more he learns about the content of Scripture and recognizes its internal virtues. Nor can he assess other candidate texts, note their infelicities, and thus earn better justification for eliminating them as possible divinely inspired texts.

Apply this result to the average Christian. SA must say that when your average Christian learns about the Bible's internal virtues or the Bible's

---

believe that Bible is inspired or believe with more confidence that it is. My claim only pertains to what justification they have for believing. In other words, I am speaking about that sort of justification called "propositional justification."

43. Another reason SA theorists won't (or shouldn't) think internal virtues like coherence are a kind of self-attestation is because we're unlikely to get the kind of assurance and certainty many SA theorists think is available to us. A property like internal coherence will, even when combined with other evidences, always fall below the threshold of epistemic certainty and assurance. Thus Paul Helm writes, "And so it does not follow from the fact that the only acceptable evidence is internal evidence that it is unchallengeable, for there may be internal evidence *against*, evidence of self-contradiction, moral turpitude and the like" (*Divine Revelation*, 111). For SA theorists then, it is not ultimately internal evidence that is important but one specific type of that evidence.

reliability via historical evidence, and adds to that a thorough knowledge that competing texts have intractable difficulties, he doesn't acquire better epistemic reasons for trusting that Scripture is truly God-breathed. He doesn't have an epistemic right to be more confident since he already occupies an ideal epistemic position—being confronted with God's own self-testimony.

Note once again that to raise this concern against SA, we need not say that prior to learning these things, a Christian's epistemic position for knowing that the Bible alone is the inspired word of God is abominably deficient. His epistemic position could already be good enough to give him justification to trust the Bible. But even here, SA theorists can't say that this person's epistemic position for believing that the Bible is inspired improves one iota. A child who believes the Bible because his parents do and because the Bible claims to be from God is in an equally good epistemic position as his father, a Christian theologian, who is an expert in the problems that hound competing religious texts and in the internal virtues and accuracy of the Bible.

To my mind, what SA theorists must say about John or your average Christian is implausible. But if you're attracted to SA, I doubt these cases will move you much, if at all. And that's probably because we're thinking about this problem from a post-canonization point of view. There is, according SA theorists, no epistemic worry that the books included in the New Testament canon are the books that actually belong there. There isn't any chance that the church excluded a divinely inspired book or included an uninspired one. What is more, there doesn't seem to be much of a chance, at least prima facie, that individual passages of certain books are uninspired, perhaps because they were interpolated.[44]

To make the above arguments more acute then, we can look at whether those worries have any traction when applied to the canonization of Scripture—specifically the New Testament. The present epistemic problem is really an offshoot of the more basic problem of identifying divinely inspired books. Given the method that SA theorists must use to evaluate competing religious texts today, I don't see how that same method is epistemically viable for determining (or for having determined in the early church) which books belong in the canon.

---

44. I think this is what follows from the SA view. I'm not sure that SA theorists are always willing to make such strong claims.

4.2 The problem of canonization

What criteria should have been used for deciding which books to include in the New Testament canon?[45] According to our SA strictures, we must not permit reason and science to pass judgment on God's word. They should play the role of inquirer, not judge; they should receive evidence rather than adjudicate.[46] So prima facie, SA stipulates that we add a book (book X) to the New Testament canon only if a previously canonized book (book Y) mentions in some way that book X is divinely inspired. SA theorists cannot and could not have relied on internal virtues like consistency, coherence, or beauty because that would subject God to human reason, and again, we might judge two consistent claims inconsistent. Nor could they site historical trustworthiness as if this latter property could help us figure out which books to include in the canon and which to leave out. Instead, they must bootstrap their way up to the book of Revelation with each previous book authenticating some other book. Of course, they need not follow this formula exactly. This is just a simplified application of SA. Still, whatever they do, it should be a variation on this theme. The other option is to save SA until the canon has been compiled, but that would be a little too late in the epistemic game.

What criteria were actually used to compile the New Testament canon? In the *Canon of the New Testament*, Bruce Metzger lists the following: conformity with Christian tradition, apostolicity (i.e. written by an apostle or someone closely connected to an apostle), and widespread acceptance by

---

45. In what follows I give the impression that canonization was a self-conscious process which led finally to a public declaration that a certain set of books, and only that set, should be read as coming from God. I don't think that is how things came about. But my cleaning up and simplifying the process is only a means of expediency and clarity. None of my critique hinges on describing the canonization process in this way.

46. Recall an earlier quote from Kruger describing non-SA approaches to canonization: "They all ground the authority of the canon in something outside the canon itself. It is this appeal to an external authority that unites all of these positions . . . Richard Gaffin notes that such an approach is in danger of 'subjecting the canon to the relativist of historical study and our fallible human insight . . . it would destroy the New Testament as canon, as absolute authority" (*Canon Revisited*, 88). One would think the following from Frame applies to canonization as well: "[God's] word has supreme authority. And just as it cannot be disproved by something else of greater authority, so it cannot be proved in such a way" (*Apologetics to the Glory of God*, 135); or, "We should make plain that even our methods of knowledge, our standards of truth and falsity, our views of logic, and our scientific methods must be reconciled first of all with God's revelation" (ibid., 220). And lastly, "Since we believe [God] more certainly than we believe anything else, he (and his Word) is the very *criterion*, the ultimate *standard* of truth. . . What higher standard could be more authoritative" (ibid., 7).

the church at large.[47] SA fits awkwardly into this picture which reveals one horn of an emerging epistemic dilemma. If SA is what gives us epistemic assurance and certainty that the Bible is from God, by relying on something else to compile the canon, we inherit any of its epistemic defects and pass those on to SA's use after the canon's completion. However, if SA theorists admit that other types of evidence could rationally be used during the process, then why not allow that kind of evidence to play a *legitimate* epistemic role afterwards? For instance, new historical evidence could reveal to us, or could have to those in the early church, that someone made a mistake—if not in canonizing a book, at least with regard to including various passages. But as we've seen, SA restricts our historical evidence to whatever favors inerrancy. This excludes any evidence, either acquired now or back then, that questions whether every book included in the New Testament ought to be, whether some have been left out, or whether certain passages were erroneously judged inspired in the first place.[48]

In brief, SA can only recommend that the church include in the canon those books that the canonized books testify belong there. More nuance is needed, and Michael J. Kruger in his book *Canon Revisited* may deliver just that. Kruger is a self-conscious adherent of the SA epistemology and does think about how SA fits into the canonization process. Like other SA advocates, he believes the process of choosing which books to include in the New Testament canon should not be grounded in some external authority, but in its own. For example, the final decision for inclusion in the canon doesn't lie in the epistemic authority of the church, but in the canon itself. And even though the Bible didn't come with a table of contents already filled out, we have the next best thing—the books themselves.[49] The books set the terms for their own validation; they define what counts as evidence for canonicity. So Kruger is laudably consistent when he says that the New Testament

---

47. Cited in Swinburne, "Authority of Scripture, Tradition, and the Church," 12.

48. Why think that because we use non-SA evidence to form the canon that SA theorists must allow that this kind of evidence could undermine self-attestation afterwards? I think SA theorists should worry that at some point we subjected God to human reason. Even if, through reasoning, we get to the point that we trust God alone, that for them is unacceptable. That is a part of their "ultimate standard" argument. If we use a priori reasoning to arrive at the conclusion that God exists and continue onward through a variety of inferential processes to the claim that the Bible is trustworthy, then reason somehow becomes the final court of appeal. If we use scientific evidence to show that God exists, then we are beholden to the direction the scientific winds happen to be blowing. Although I don't buy this reasoning myself, this is part of their view that the Bible must be the ultimate standard, and why some get the impression that their view implies we can't reason at all.

49. Kruger, *Canon Revisited*, chapter 3.

canon cannot be authenticated without relying on those books that actually belong in the New Testament canon.

Kruger believes that SA sanctions the use of other kinds of evidence, like the internal virtues of a book, to pick out the divinely inspired books. Yet, despite this broadening of potential evidence, his view collapses into the strict self-attestation view. He requires that we beg the question and assume which books belong in the cannon to figure out which books should be included in the canon. Unless God, via some other form of communication, enlightens us as to the list of canon making attributes, we must rely on God's word. Consequently, we must have already isolated the right books so that we can extract from them the criteria for canon inclusion.

For instance, Kruger believes that the beauty of the Bible, along with its efficacy and harmony, is evidence of inspiration. But how does he know to search for these attributes? Primarily because of what he knows about God and his character. And he acquired this knowledge, I believe he would say, from Scripture.

At this point, we've hit up the second horn of our dilemma: We must already know some of the books that belong in the New Testament canon apart from this method. For if we know that book X belongs in the canon and then learn that according to that book, properties a, b, and c are indicative of divine inspiration, those properties must not initially explain how we first learned that book X is inspired. This makes it especially difficult to explain how we can rationally trust the criteria implicitly recognized in book S rather those implicit to book Q when both can't find a place in the canon because of conflicts between them.

We can now see in whole the epistemic dilemma that faces the SA epistemology. If SA applies only to Scripture canonized, then there is the untoward result that the kind of reasoning denounced by SA theorists constitutes our evidential base for thinking our canon is the right one. If the evidence of historical investigation is epistemically flawed apart from the presupposition that certain books are divinely authored, then the justification we have for trusting Scripture via SA ultimately inherits those flaws. On the other horn of the dilemma, if SA reasoning applies even to the canonization process, we must already know the truths we are trying to learn in order to acquire the evidence that is supposed to reveal the truths we are trying to learn. What looks like an appeal to some sort of evidence on SA is ultimately based on our prior knowledge of the truth that evidence is supposed to help us know. That is like having to know the actual outcome of a decision before you can rationally make that decision.

Kruger and other SA theorists can argue that the church (or someone in particular) is guided by the Holy Spirit, at least in their choice of which books to canonize. So the canon is immune to mistakes, and we can have present-day epistemic certainty that the Bible is inspired and fully trustworthy. This is the position they often fall back to. It is something in the neighborhood of Alvin Plantinga's epistemology.[50] The Holy Spirit caused the early church, and causes us as well, to infallibly recognize which books to include in the canon, or that the right books have been included in the canon.[51] But then SA, contrary to what we've been led to believe, is not epistemically vital. God simply chooses different occasions to bring about the right belief in us, and reading a claim to self-attestation may be one of those occasions when God causes us to believe via the Holy Spirit that 1) Scripture is God breathed and 2) that it is inerrant. But this is not what goes on when using circular reasoning or a question begging argument. In Plantinga's epistemology, God's self-attestation would function primarily as the occasion for our trusting Scripture; it is not essential to our belief's positive epistemic standing.

As Kruger says, "In order for believers to rightly recognize these attributes of canonicity, the Holy Spirit works to overcome the noetic effects of sin and produces belief that these books are from God." Nevertheless, those attributes don't serve to evidentially indicate or differentiate the inspired and uninspired books. They are just one of many prompts God could have used as the occasion for the Holy Spirit's operation. This is where we get our first hint that SA is epistemically otiose, a point I argue for in section 5.

4.3 The SA epistemology is underdeveloped

The above problems point to another question that SA theorists seem inattentive to. For the above scenarios should help make clear that saying God can self-authenticate his word doesn't dissolve the epistemic conundrum. There is still a pressing question: "Is this claim of self-attestation in this text the self-attestation of the one true God?" It is not a necessary truth that any claim to divine self-authentication is true. We need some reason to think the text we believe to be self-authenticating is in fact a genuine case of self-authentication from the Divine. We need some way to differentiate the genuine God-produced self-authenticating claims from the bogus ones. Otherwise we may need to rely on the naïve epistemic principle that we should trust anything that claims to be the word of God.

---

50. Plantinga, *Warranted Christian Belief*.

51. Whether the Holy Spirit is operating on Protestants or Catholics causes some trouble for this view's explanation of how we know that the right books, and only the right books, constitute the present canon.

Put another way, SA does not tackle the question, "How do we know some text is God breathed?" but pushes it back another step. We must now figure out how we know that a claim to be God's word is truly God-breathed.

5. SELF-ATTESTATION IS EPISTEMICALLY OTIOSE

There is another reason to think that the epistemic significance of self-attestation is much weaker than SA theorists may realize. When we attend to the debate between internalists and externalists, the lessons that have emerged from that discussion instruct SA theorists to choose one of two options. One option is to grab hold of an unabashed externalism that authorizes them to set aside those objections that tempt them into begging the question. However, they may have the internalist intuition that we need epistemic reasons for trusting the Bible. If so, they should acknowledge that question begging reasons don't improve our epistemic position nor do they impart the assurance we seek when we ask about the inspiration of Scripture. Whichever option SA theorists choose, there is no reason to use SA to ground our justification for trusting Scripture. SA is epistemically otiose.

5.1 A brief glance at the epistemic landscape

Epistemologists disagree over how best to define "internalism" and "externalism." For our purposes, we'll use internal state internalism as our exemplar of an internalist. According to the internal state internalist, the justification that we have at t for belief B supervenes on our occurrent mental states at t (our internal states). "If two believers are in identical internal states at t and there is justification for one to believe that P at t, then there is that same justification for the other to believe p at t."[52] Externalists, on the other hand, typically believe that factors outside an agent's mental states are crucial to justified belief. For instance, if our beliefs are produced by reliable belief forming mechanisms, they could be justified, even if we have no clue what mechanism we used or whether it is even reliable.

This contrast between the internalist and externalist is perhaps most perceptible for justified belief via testimony. Oversimplifying a bit, many externalists believe that we can justifiably believe that P because someone else, who justifiably believes that P, testifies to P, even when we don't have a reason to believe that person is trustworthy or justifiably believes that P. Internalists are likely to disagree. We need some reason to trust another's

---

52. Fumerton, "Epistemic Conservatism," 64.

testimony, and that can't be obtained by asking that same person if he is trustworthy.

If epistemic externalists mostly care that epistemic agents bear the right sort of causal relation to the world even if they are unaware that they do, they must remain steadfast and not be tempted by internalists into something more, namely meta-justification that the conditions for justified belief obtain. For example, if they succumb to pressure from internalists and move up a level to locate reasons to believe that their first level beliefs proceed from reliable belief forming mechanisms, their arguments won't placate internalists since they can acquire their evidence all too easily.[53] If sense experience is in fact reliable, they can consistently use sense experience to show that it is. If memory is reliable, they can remember remembering event E and remember event E to secure evidence favoring the reliability of memory. If what matters most for epistemic justification is, at least, true belief achieved via a reliable method of some sort, then as long as we have a reliable method for forming beliefs, we can use it anytime and anywhere we can reliably do so, including to verify its own reliability.[54]

In other words, externalism sanctions the use of track record arguments to justify relying on a particular source of belief, which is a style of argument internalists typically find odious. These track record arguments lead to the problem of easy knowledge or bootstrapping.[55] Suppose that sense experience is indeed reliable. We can acquire justification to believe that sense experience is reliable by using sense experience to supply the premises of a track record argument:

> Premise 1: I am having the visual sensation A and A is the case.
>
> Premise 2: I am having the visual sensation B and B is the case.
>
> Premise 3: I am having the visual sensation C and C is the case.
>
> Premise 4: I am having the visual sensation D and D is the case.
>
> Conclusion: Thus, my visual experience is reliable.

---

53. See Fumerton, *Metaepistemology and Skepticism*, chapter 6.

54. McGrew and McGrew, "Level Connections in Epistemology," argue that this leads to some very unsatisfying results. See Reed, "Epistemic Circularity Squared," as well. For a paper that tries to blunt the blow of this worry, see Sosa, "Reflective Knowledge," 187–203.

55. See Cohen, "Basic Knowledge"; and Vogel, "Reliabilism Leveled," for this type of objection. An earlier version can be found in Fumerton, *Metaepistemology and Skepticism*, chapter 6.

In each instance, we rely on visual sensation to know the right conjunct, even though the reliability of visual sensation is the very thing we're trying to prove.[56]

Alston dubs this style of argument an "epistemically circular argument."[57] For an epistemically circular argument, the conclusion doesn't explicitly appear in the premises. Rather, to justifiably believe the premises, we must assume the conclusion is true. In the above argument, I have a justified belief that A, a justified belief that B, etc. only if vision is a reliable guide to the external world. My justification for believing the premises depends on the truth of the conclusion—the very claim I wish to know. So I must assume that visual experience is a reliable guide to the physical world to construct premises I am justified in believing, which premises are designed to support the conclusion that my visual experience is a reliable guide to the world.

Put another way, when we use an epistemically circular argument, we use a source of belief formation to verify the trustworthiness of that source. But if we must already assume the truth of what we are trying to prove, what good is secured by the question begging argument? At most, we show that a source of belief formation doesn't yield inconsistent results; but our epistemic position improves marginally since completely unreliable sources can produce consistent outcomes. We might as well, when wondering whether to trust a person, repeatedly ask that very person whether he is trustworthy.[58]

Some externalists realize that it is best to deny any need to move up levels and show that a source of belief formation is trustworthy. We don't need a justified belief that a belief source is trustworthy for us to acquire justified beliefs through the use of that source. When confronted with externalist conditions, internalists will demand that we internalize them and that means justifiably believing that those external conditions obtain. This is why internalists demand that externalists have a non-question begging reason for thinking their beliefs are produced by the right sort of process. But if we aren't internalists, there is no need to internalize those external

---

56. See Lemos, "Sosa on Epistemic Circularity," 188.

57. Alston, "Epistemic Circularity."

58. There are, unfortunately, a host of issues that go along with this that I don't have space to address. Some argue that if we don't accept epistemically circular arguments, we will be lead into an infinite regress to verify that some source is trustworthy. Reed, "Epistemic Circularity Squared," 186. According to another potential problem, if we think beliefs can enjoy non-inferential justification, there's no reason why we can't use those beliefs in an epistemically circular track record argument. Brown, "Non-Inferential Justification," 343.

conditions. What matters is that those conditions are satisfied, not that we know they are.

We can now better appreciate the epistemic options that face SA theorists. They can think like internalists and be tempted to obtain an epistemic reason for believing the Bible is the word of God. But they shouldn't then argue that we know the Bible is written by God because God has told us, in the Bible, that he wrote it. This will hardly pacify internalists and one intuition motivating internalism—that we should achieve something more than a causally reliable relation to truth. On the other hand, if they adopt the externalist mindset, they don't need to ascend a level and obtain justification to believe the Bible is God-breathed since there is no need for meta-level justification that the Bible is trustworthy. It does little to improve our epistemic position, and externalists insist that, in general, there is no epistemic requirement that we have justification for trusting our sources of belief.

SA theorists are pulled in both directions by their internalist and externalist intuitions. Their internalist intuitions emerge when they acknowledge that we need a good reason for trusting the Bible. But then their externalist intuitions take over when they think that self-attestation can actually supply that reason. If SA theorists are torn between irreconcilable intuitions, what would incline them one way rather than another? What follows is a brief sketch of why they might hoist the flag of externalism or the flag of internalism.

5.2 A predilection for externalism

One reason SA theorists might favor externalism is that if externalism is true, the class of non-inferentially justified beliefs can be much larger than what is available to most internalist foundationalists.[59] Any type of belief, whatsoever, can be non-inferentially justified as long as we bear the right sort of relation to the world. For instance, suppose Plantinga is right and warrant is the product of properly functioning faculties that operate in the right environment according to a segment of the design plan successfully aimed at truth.[60] God has many options for how to outfit our cognitive equipment for true beliefs. We can imagine a possible world in which a person, by design, accepts propositions only at the instigation of the Holy

---

59. This would apply, of course, only to those who accept some form of foundationalism. Foundationalism is the idea that the justification for some beliefs need not even be constituted in part by their relation to other beliefs.

60. See Plantinga, *Warrant and Proper Function*, chapter 1.

Spirit, and the Holy Spirit causes him, for any belief that he has, to form that belief non-inferentially.[61] All his beliefs would be warranted and all would amount to knowledge.

Consequently, if they do embrace externalism, SA theorists can say that we know the Bible is God's word—period. We don't know this on the basis of evidence, not even the evidence of self-attestation. The belief need not be inferred from anything else we believe. Rather, if God exists, we can acquire properly basic belief that Scripture is the word of God when, upon reading some biblical text (even a non-self-attestation text), we find ourselves with the belief. Even a sunset could occasion this properly basic belief if that is how God designed our cognitive equipment to work.[62] Yet all this may be superfluous since from an externalist point of view, we don't even need to know that the Bible is the word of God to justifiably base our beliefs on it. What matters is that it is the word of God, not that we're aware it is.

If SA theorists take the bait dangled by internalists and use a circular argument, there is no reason why they shouldn't feel tempted to ascend another level, and another, *ad infinitum*. Whatever reason they had for ascending a level at the start will reappear at the second level.[63] Consequently, there will be little if any improvement in their epistemic predicament.

One reason they don't continuously ascend levels is that the Bible doesn't present the option. If it did, they would probably need to. For instance, imagine that the Bible not only testified to being God-breathed, but testified to the fact that it claimed to be God breathed, with increasingly complicated iterations. So in one part of Scripture we would read, "I the Lord declare that I said Scripture is inspired." In another part we would find, "I the Lord declare that I said that I said that Scripture is inspired." And to drive the point home, in another part of Scripture we would read, "I the Lord declare that I said that I said that I said that Scripture is inspired." If knowing that the Bible is authored by God requires his attestation of authorship, then God must attest to the fact that he said that he wrote it, and must attest to the fact that he said that he said that he wrote it. In short, if God's

---

61. Both Fumerton, "Plantinga, Warrant and Christian Belief"; and Fales, "Proper Basicality," 37,5 stress this feature of externalist theories of justification.

62. There is still the issue of dealing with possible defeaters to non-inferentially justified beliefs. I don't think if they accept Plantinga's epistemology (which will seem the most appealing to many SA theorists who decide to go the externalist route) they should allow that properly basic belief in God can be defeated. The reason is that if God designs us in part to acquire true beliefs, and of these the most important is true belief in him, he wouldn't insert a defeater system into that segment of the design plan.

63. For a similar complaint, see the McGrew and McGrew, "Level Connections in Epistemology," 85–94.

authorship is not epistemically sufficient for trusting Scripture, the same applies to his assertion of attestation.

Of course, SA theorists don't launch into an endless regress of self-attestations; they prefer circles. But isn't that because there is no endless regress for them to set off on? God doesn't attest to the fact that he attests to the fact that the Bible is inspired. At some level, they may recognize that the absence of any epistemic reason for trusting Scripture isn't a great epistemic position to be working from, so they move, not along a regress, but in a circle. But whether it be a circle or an endless regress, it is all the same at the end of the day. In both, we start off with a conditional that is never discharged. As the McGrews explain

> the subject bases his belief that P on the ground that Q—an adequate ground on the assumption that Q is true. But is it? Certainly—*if* it is the case that R, the premise on which Q itself is grounded. But what about R?...There is no escaping the conditional clause. Similarly in the case of circular reasoning, the conditional is reiterated *ad infinitum*; P if Q, Q if R, R if S, S if P. And what about P? Oh, P if Q...[64]

In other words, the transparency and assurance of truth we're searching for is always pushed one step further away.

Further, appeal to Scripture's self-attestation may, ironically, violate an SA maxim giving SA theorists another reason to embrace externalism. They claim that we shouldn't question God or put him to the test by subjecting his word to human autonomous reasoning. Doesn't it then follow that even to demand or rely on God's own self-authentication implies that God's initial word is not epistemically sufficient? If God speaks to me in the night and tells me to do X and I refuse to until he tells me that he told me to do X, I require more from God than he epistemically must provide. The same could be said about the use of self-authentication. SA theorists should think "God said it. So that settles it," not "God says that he said it. So that settles it."

SA theorists set up the epistemic situation so that we're completely dependent on God for our knowledge of the truths contained in Scripture. If we know any of those truths, it must be because they proceed from the mouth of God—the testifier than which none greater can be thought. But if we're completely dependent on the testimony of another, then it doesn't make much sense to trust what the person says even more because, when queried, he said he could be trusted. If we're right to trust his claim about whether we should trust him, it's because we are already right to trust him.

---

64. McGrew and McGrew, "What's Wrong with Epistemic Circularity," 221–22

If we already need something more to rationally trust some person, we need something more to rationally trust that person's claim to be trustworthy.[65]

5.3 A predilection for internalism

I have given a brief and incomplete sketch of why SA theorists might be attracted to the externalist option for justified belief in Scripture's reliability. As an internalist, I think they should honor their internalist intuitions and accept some form of epistemic internalism. What follows is once again a very quick, incomplete sketch of why they might want instead to hoist the flag of internalism.[66]

5.3.1 Scripture interprets scripture

If we aren't satisfied with being caused by the Holy Spirit, in accordance with our design plan, to believe that the Bible is trustworthy, we want more epistemic assurance than an unknown causal connection can provide. Perhaps this partially explains why most SA theorists endorse the plausible principle that Scripture should interpret Scripture. We doubt it is epistemically sufficient that even though we interpret some Old Testament text as saying P while another professing Christian thinks it says Q, that as long as our interpretation was caused by the Holy Spirit and aimed at truth, all is well. We look for more than this. We look for reasons to prefer our interpretation. We want some confirmation of who in fact was caused by the Holy Spirit to form their interpretation.

It's telling that many reformed Christians don't settle debates over what a particular text means by claiming that the Holy Spirit caused them to form the interpretation they did. Nor do they say that they know this because the Holy Spirit has caused them to believe that the Holy Spirit caused them to form their interpretation of the text. But if we can know that the Bible is

---

65. One thing that doesn't get parsed out well enough when discussing whether we should trust Scripture is that the epistemic conundrum is different than the standard predicament in which we find ourselves. Usually, we have no doubt that a person is there to trust. What we doubt is whether they are trustworthy. But in the case of God, it would be foolish to doubt whether he is trustworthy. What is at stake is whether God is there for us to trust.

66. My discussion is taking place within the context of foundationalism. I can't tell whether SA theorists want to accept foundationalism or coherentism. They may be trying to accept both, which is a problem. If they want to be coherentists however, then my conclusion still holds: they should be internalists. A coherentist externalism is not very plausible which is perhaps why so many externalists are foundationalists.

inspired because caused by the Holy Spirit to form the belief, why should that be insufficient for knowing which interpretation is the right one? The answer can't be because quite possibly that is not the way God designed us to operate; for even if he had designed us to reason in that way, most would still worry about their interpretive predicament and would search for more verses to support their interpretation rather than relying exclusively on the alleged fact that God caused them to interpret the text in the way that they did.

5.3.2 Internalism and inerrancy

Some SA theorists give the following as part of their argument for Scripture's inerrancy: If the Bible contains one mistake, then, for all we know, it may contain many others. I think there is a tacit internalism in this. If we're stuck having to rely entirely on the testimony of another, then this worry makes some sense from an internalist point of view.

Recall that SA theorists paint our epistemic predicament as complete dependence on the testimony of God. We don't confirm or lend greater credence to certain Scriptural truths because of what we learn through philosophy, history, science, or archeology. We already have God's sure and certain testimony. Now, if we are entirely dependent on the testimony of another, namely Scripture, then internalists will worry about the possibility of finding even just a few mistakes because those mistakes won't be offset by the positive evidence that helps to confirm other Biblical truths. We would simply have evidence to think the Bible mistaken on occasion but no non-question begging evidence to think the Bible gets many things right. Thus the need for Biblical inerrancy.

In brief, since we can't cull positive non-question begging evidence that favors the trustworthiness of scripture, any negative evidence, such as internal Scriptural conflicts, leaves us in the evidential "red." This is one reason why some think all is lost if we admit even one error in Scripture. Either we have justified belief in the inerrancy of Scripture, or we have no reason to trust Scripture at all.

If we're externalists, I don't see why discovering several errors would be so unnerving. God has options for how he designs us to secure knowledge and that could include using a text that has several errors. As noted before, we would not need to know that the Bible is reliable before justifiably relying on it. What matters is that it is indeed reliable, and it still could be, even if it contains some errors. Apparently God didn't think this an insurmountable epistemic obstacle when he designed our vision and hearing. As long as these are objectively reliable sources of belief, that should be good enough.

5.3.3 Getting in touch with our inner internalist

To further advance my claims that SA theorists have a penchant for internalism, I wish to look at things from a more basic intuitive level which, I hope, may resonate more with some readers. Speaking in my own case, when I look for reasons for what I believe, I do so because the truth of my belief is in some sense "hidden" from me. I can't just tell what the fact of the matter is to which my belief is supposed to correspond. So I look for something truth indicative, something that sheds light on what is actually the case. I doubt my case is peculiar. Others also look for reasons to support their beliefs because the truth of their beliefs is "hidden" from them. They want access to something they know to be the case and they know makes their beliefs probably true. And as we all know, offering some other alleged truth Q as a reason to believe our original claim P doesn't do us much good unless we have justification to think this other claim Q is true.

Suppose that Q's truth is not transparent to us and we require something that indicates the truth of Q, something that tells us that in our search for truth we're getting warmer. Well then, we look for something else that we justifiably believe to be true, which would then justify us in believing Q, which would then justify belief in P thus helping us to a better position vis-à-vis P's truth.

If we're on a search for the truth of P because that truth is hidden from our cognitive gaze and thus look for some truth not hidden from us that also makes P probably true, it doesn't make much sense to eventually appeal to P in this process of reasoning. The hidden truth value of P is why we set off down this trail of reasoning. If we must appeal to P to help show that P is true when the truth of P is what we're after, then the use of P does us little if any good. Either we already have justification to believe P, in which case we need not use P, or we don't, in which case using P will not illuminate the truth of the claims intended to support P. If they must be supported by P, that is like the blind leading the blind.

Put another way, when we search for epistemic reasons for our beliefs, we want something truth indicative, something that reveals the truth of the matter to us. We want some fact that we already have access to which will permit us to reasonably judge that our target belief is probably true. Think of the difference between witnessing a crime and seeing the crime scene only after the fact. If you are a crime scene investigator and you witness a crime, you don't need the crime scene evidence for *you* to justifiably believe that John committed the crime. Since you had epistemic access to the fact itself, you don't require something truth indicative, something that reveals to you what was previously hidden from your cognitive gaze. But if you didn't see the crime, you must rely on crime scene evidence. This evidence helps to bring the culprit into the epistemic light of day. But if to know that certain kinds of evidence pointed toward John as the guilty party we had to know ahead of time that John committed the crime, we would be in serious trouble. There wouldn't be much point in looking at the evidence. And if we're tempted to search for evidence, that suggests we need something truth indicative, i.e. something that points us toward the person guilty of the crime.

In light of the above reflections, SA theorists should ask themselves how good they think their current epistemic position is for knowing God. Sometimes they speak as if we occupy the best epistemic position possible; that because we have God's word, things can't get any better. But if things can't get any better, that is a forlorn truth since Christians rightly long for much more in knowing God. What they long for is not just more true information about him, but to stand in a closer epistemic relation to him—to see him "face-to-face."

To bring out the difference, consider Charles Taliaferro's thought experiment from his[67] paper on divine omniscience. In that paper, he argues that omniscience must include more than knowledge of all truths. To show this, he uses the example of two omniscient beings—Christopher and Dennis. Christopher's knowledge is not mediated through anything. He doesn't depend on anyone but knows all truths immediately and directly. We might say he is acquainted with or directly aware of all truths. Dennis, on the other hand, knows all truths, but is at the mercy of Christopher in so knowing. He knows the truth values of propositions because Christopher informs him. "Were Christopher to be less courteous or well disposed, Dennis would be completely ignorant of the world."[68]

What should we say about these two omniscient beings? Clearly, Christopher's epistemic position is preferable. His knowledge is not mediated though the testimony of Dennis so there is no epistemic distance separating him from the facts. Since he is directly acquainted with all truths, he can't occupy a better epistemic position from the standpoint of achieving assurance that what he believes is true. His relation to truth is the most intimate kind extending well beyond reliably produced belief. The superiority

---

67. Taliaferro, "Divine Cognitive Power," 133–140.
68. Ibid., 134.

of his relationship to truth is similar to a case where human John is able to see and talk to the one he loves whereas human Sam can only exchange letters with the one he loves. They may have many of the same true beliefs about their respective loved ones, but John's epistemic situation is more desirable. Externalists, on the other hand, struggle to explain the superiority of Christopher's epistemic position, especially those externalists who think of the cognitive good as true belief. Both Christopher and Dennis have all and only true beliefs which result from perfectly reliable processes. Still Christopher's position is nevertheless better from the epistemic point of view.

Because SA theorists look for God's own self-attestation to warrant their trust in Scripture, part of me thinks they don't really believe their epistemic position is ideal. They don't seem satisfied with just trusting the Bible full-stop. If that's true, they probably think Christopher's epistemic position is much better than Dennis's. If SA theorists think that one day they can expect something more epistemically, something better than just written communication from God (as if God were the supreme pen pal), they have some reason to lean toward internalist epistemic theories. According to internalists we should not be completely confident that what we believe on religious matters is true. Why? Because there is a big epistemic difference between believing that something was written by God on the evidence we now have and seeing God face-to-face when he confirms that he wrote the Bible and explains what we could not understand.

So if SA theorists look for a reason to trust Scripture, even if it be the reason of self-attestation, they don't find their prior epistemic predicament completely satisfying. As I have argued, there is an internalist lurking inside them. If they let that internalist out, they can explain why they seem to look for something more than belief caused by the instigation of the Holy Spirit. But they won't get what they want from self-attestation. They must search for other kinds of evidence to support the trustworthiness of Scripture. On the other hand, there is an externalist lurking inside them as well. If they set free their inner externalist, there is no need for the evidence of self-attestation. Whichever they let out, self-attestation is ultimately epistemically otiose.

In summary, I think the quick reformed reply doesn't take arguments from evil seriously enough and is wrongly indifferent to the difficulties that they pose. I've argued that the quick reformed move is a version of the Moore Switch and that the confidence of those who wield this dismissive reply is grounded in the self-attestation of Scripture. Thus, if their reason for being confident that the Bible is the word of God is undermined or shown to be irrelevant, they have a reason to treat the problem of evil more seriously and a reason to take philosophical developments of reformed solutions more seriously. However, if they jettison SA for an unabashed epistemic externalism by eschewing their internalist intuitions, they might have just as good a reason to rely on the quick reformed reply to arguments from evil. As an internalist, I am hoping they will let the internalist inside them drive their epistemic judgments.[69]

---

69. Thanks to Luke Westman for reading and providing excellent comments on a potentially infinite number of drafts, and to the editors for their inexhaustible patience and discriminating advice.

BIBLIOGRAPHY

Abraham, William. *The Divine Inspiration of Holy Scripture*. Oxford: Oxford University Press, 1981.

Achtemeier, Paul J. *Inspiration and Authority: Nature and Function of Christian Scripture*. Grand Rapids, MI: Baker Academic, 1999.

Alston, William. "Epistemic Circularity." In *Epistemic Justification: Essays in the Theory of Knowledge*. Ithaca, NY: Cornell University Press, 1989.

Archer, Gleason L. "The Witness of the Bible to Its Own Inerrancy." In *The Foundation of Biblical Authority*, edited by James Montgomery Boice. Grand Rapids, MI: Zondervan.

Brown, Jessica. "Non-Inferential Justification and Epistemic Circularity." *Analysis* 64, no. 4 (2004) 339–48.

Cohen, Stewart. "Basic Knowledge and the Problem of Easy Knowledge." *Philosophy and Phenomenological Research* 65, no. 2 (2002) 309–29.

Cowan, Steven B. *Five Views on Apologetics*. Grand Rapids, MI: Zondervan, 2000.

Davis, Stephen. *Debate about the Bible: Inerrancy versus Infallibility*. Lousville, KY: Westminster John Knox, 1984.

Fales, Evan. "Proper Basicality." *Philosophy and Phenomenological Research* 68, no. 2 (2004) 373–83.

Frame, John. *Apologetics to the Glory of God*. Phillipsburg, NJ: Presbyterian and Reformed, 1994.

Fumerton, Richard. "Epistemic Conservatism: Theft or Honest Toil." In *Oxford Studies in Epistemology*, vol. 2, edited by Tamar Gendler and John Hawthorne, 63–86. Oxford: Oxford University Press, 2007.

———. "Plantinga, Warrant and Christian Belief." (Unpublished draft).

———. *Metaepistemology and Skepticism*. Lanham, MD: Rowman & Littlefield, 1995.

Grudem, Wayne. "Scripture's Self-Attestation and the Problem of Formulating a Doctrine of Scripture." In *Scripture and Truth*, edited by D. A. Carson and John Woodbridge. Grand Rapids, MI: Zondervan, 1983.

———. *Systematic Theology*. Grand Rapids, MI: Zondervan, 1994.

Helm, Paul. *The Divine Revelation: The Basic Issues*. Vancouver, BC: Regent College Publishing, 1982.

———. "Faith, Evidence, and the Scriptures." In *Scripture and Truth*, edited by D. A. Carson and John Woodbridge. Grand Rapids, MI: Zondervan, 1983.

Hesselink, I. John. *Calvin's First Catechism: A Commentary*. Lousville, KY: Westminster John Knox, 1997.

Kruger, Michael J. *Canon Revisited: Establishing the Origins and Authority of the New Testament Books*. Wheaton, IL: Crossway, 2012.

Lemos, Noah. "Sosa on Epistemic Circularity and Reflective Knowledge." *Metaphilosophy* 40, no. 2 (2009) 187–94.

McGrew, Lydia, and Timothy McGrew. "Level Connections in Epistemology." *American Philosophical Quarterly* 34, no. 1 (1997) 85–94.

McGrew, Timothy, and Lydia McGrew. "What's Wrong with Epistemic Circularity." *Dialogue* 39, no. 2 (2000) 219–40.

Moore, G. E. *Philosophical Studies*. London: Routledge & Kegan Paul, 1965.

Packer, J. I. "Encountering Present-Day Views of Scripture." In *The Foundation of Biblical Authority*, edited by James Montgomery Boice, 3–18. Grand Rapids, MI: Zondervan, 1978.

Plantinga, Alvin. *Warrant and Proper Function*. Oxford: Oxford University Press, 1993.

———. *Warranted Christian Belief*. Oxford: Oxford University Press, 2000.

Reed, Baron. "Epistemic Circularity Squared? Skepticism about Common Sense." *Philosophy and Phenomenological Research* 73, no. 1 (2006) 186–97.

Rowe, William. "The Problem of Evil and Some Varieties of Atheism." In *The Evidential Argument from Evil*, edited by Daniel Howard-Snyder, 1–11. Bloomington, IN: Indiana University Press, 1996.

Sosa, Ernest. "Reflective Knowledge in the Best Circles." In *Knowledge, Truth, and Duty*, edited by Matthias Steup, 187–203. Oxford: Oxford University Press, 2001.

Swinburne, Richard. "Authority of Scripture, Tradition, and the Church." In *The Oxford Handbook of Philosophical Theology*, edited by Michael Rea and Thomas Flint, 11–29. Oxford: Oxford University Press, 2009.

Taliaferro, Charles. "Divine Cognitive Power." *International Journal for Philosophy of Religion* 18 (1985) 133–40.

Vogel, Jonathan. "Reliabilism Leveled." *Journal of Philosophy* 97 (2000) 602–23.

www.ingramcontent.com/pod-product-compliance
Lightning Source LLC
Chambersburg PA
CBHW050622300426
44112CB00012B/1613